# One heart and one soul

John Sutcliff

# *One heart*

*and*

# *one soul*

**John Sutcliff of Olney, his friends and his times**

Michael A. G. Haykin

EVANGELICAL PRESS

EVANGELICAL PRESS
12 Wooler Street, Darlington, Co. Durham, DL1 1RQ, England


First published 1994

**British Library Cataloguing in Publication Data available**

ISBN 0 85234 326 4

Printed and bound in Great Britain at the Bath Press, Avon.

To the memory of Kenneth W. H. Howard (1921-1992), a fellow historian, whose life and ministry were dedicated to the sole and eternal glory of the God of John Sutcliff.

# Acknowledgements

I am especially thankful to the late Kenneth W. H. Howard for manuscript material, advice and direction during the early stages of this book. He had long wanted to write a biography of Sutcliff and to that end had accumulated a considerable amount of knowledge regarding the sources that needed to be mined for such a biography. I am also very grateful to the Board of Directors of what was Central Baptist Seminary, Toronto, for their financing of a study leave in Great Britain during the summer of 1992. For help provided during this time I particularly wish to thank Rita Butterworth of Wainsgate Baptist Church, Yorkshire; Roger Hayden and Stella Read at Bristol Baptist College; Duncan Keys, pastor of Sutcliff Baptist Church, Olney; Elizabeth Knight of the Cowper and Newton Museum, Olney; and Donald M. MacKenzie, then pastor of Fuller Baptist Church, Kettering. Above all, I am deeply indebted to the tremendous help that I received from Susan J. Mills and Elizabeth Douill at Regent's Park College, Oxford, during the time that I was in England and after I had returned to Canada. On this side of the Atlantic I am also thankful for help received from James Lynch and the staff of the American Baptist - Samuel Colgate Historical Library, Rochester, New York; and Judith Colwell of the Canadian Baptist Archives, McMaster University, Hamilton, Ontario. Then, I am indebted to the following friends who read the whole or part of my manuscript, and gave invaluable feedback, criticism and encouragement: Stanley K. Fowler, David W. Bebbington, Robert W. Oliver, Donald E. Meek, Geoffrey Thomas and Bruce Hindmarsh. David R. Bartlett was also a great help, as was Marina Coldwell, who typed out *Jealousy for the Lord of Hosts illustrated.* Graham D. Lowe, my brother-in-law, was a sure guide in the marvellous world of word-processing. And Jamie Good is richly thanked for his superb map-making. For permission to reproduce manuscript material, I wish to thank Regent's Park College, Oxford; the Baptist Missionary Society, Didcot; the John Rylands University Library of Manchester; the National Library of Wales, Aberystwyth; the Norfolk Record Office, Norwich; and the American Baptist - Samuel Colgate Historical Library, Rochester, New York. For permission to reproduce material that has appeared already in article form, I would like to thank *The Baptist Quarterly*, the *Churchman* and the *Reformation & Revival Journal.* Finally, I am most grateful to the editorial staff of Evangelical Press for having transformed my typescript into a book.

Let it never be forgotten of the Particular Baptists of England, that they form the denomination of Fuller and Carey and Ryland and Hall and Foster; that they have originated among the greatest of all missionary enterprises; that they have enriched the Christian literature of our country with authorship of the most exalted piety, as well as of the first talent and the first eloquence … that perhaps there is not a more intellectual community of ministers in our island, or who have put forth for their number a greater amount of mental power and mental activity in the defence and illustration of our common faith; and — which is far better than all the triumphs of genius or understanding — who, by their zeal and fidelity and pastoral labour among the congregations they have reared, have done more to swell the lists of genuine discipleship in the walks of private society — and thus both to uphold and to extend the living Christianity of our nation.

Thomas Chalmers

When I was nearly grown I asked my mother, 'How was it when you and father left England in 1856 to come to America you did not locate in Massachusetts or New Jersey, where father's brothers were living, but pushed on to Iowa and located at Cascade?' Her reply was: 'When I was a girl in England I had an uncle called Rev. John Sutcliff of Olney. He was one of the founders of the Baptist Missionary Society. He told me so much about missionary work in the world, and the need of its being done, that I became enthusiastic and took a Baptist magazine published in England. In this magazine appeared letters and articles from a Rev. John Bates, missionary to Ireland and afterwards at Cascade, Iowa. So I told your father that if we were really going to emigrate to America I wanted to go to this place, Cascade, where he was pastor because I knew he had a missionary interest in the Lord's work.'

John Firth

# Contents

| | Page |
|---|---|
| Introduction | 11 |
| 1. God's preparation for a great work: The Calvinistic Baptists in the eighteenth century | 15 |
| 2. Early years in West Yorkshire | 34 |
| 3. Bristol, 'the metropolis of the West' | 48 |
| 4. Sutcliff's friends: John Ryland, Jr | 69 |
| 5. Shrewsbury and Birmingham | 85 |
| 6. Olney | 99 |
| 7. Sutcliff's friends: Andrew Fuller | 133 |
| 8. The Prayer Call of 1784 | 153 |
| 9. Sutcliff's friends: William Carey | 172 |
| 10. The Baptist Missionary Society | 198 |
| 11. 'He gave some to be pastors and teachers' | 236 |
| 12. Other friends, other ministries | 269 |
| 13. Final years | 309 |
| 14. 'The fathers are dying' | 334 |
| Appendix I: The published works of John Sutcliff | 353 |
| Appendix II: 'Jealousy for the Lord of hosts illustrated' | 355 |
| Notes | 366 |
| Index | 421 |

# List of illustrations and maps


| | Page |
|---|---|
| Frontispiece: John Sutcliff | |
| Strait Hey, the early home of John Sutcliff | 37 |
| Wainsgate Baptist Church | 43 |
| Silhouette of John Sutcliff | 52 |
| John Ryland, Jr | 68 |
| An Olney lacemaker from Sutcliff's day | 101 |
| Interior of the Baptist meeting-house, Olney | 109 |
| Chair used by Sutcliff | 109 |
| Westlands, former home of John Sutcliff | 116 |
| Andrew Fuller | 132 |
| William Carey | 177 |
| Portraits of distinguished Baptist ministers | 215 |
| Thomas, Fuller, Carey, Marshman and Ward | 229 |
| An example of Sutcliff's handwriting | 239 |
| Memorial tablet to John Sutcliff and his wife | 250 |
| Opening page of Fuller's funeral sermon for Sutcliff | 340 |
| Sutcliff's tomb and the inscription | 343 |
| Sutcliff Baptist Church, Olney, as it appeared in the nineteenth century and as it appears today | 347 |

**Maps**

| | |
|---|---|
| Eighteenth-century England with parts of Scotland | 16 |
| The environs of Olney | 103 |
| The Northamptonshire Baptist Association | 112 |

# Introduction

A besetting sin of many modern, English-speaking evangelicals is their slender sense of history. For some, it is as if nothing worthy of remembrance has occurred between their times and those of the apostles. The desire to 'belong in history' is completely foreign to them. For others, their knowledge of the vast period between the New Testament era and that of the modern day is a highly selective one. Certain individuals and certain events are regularly recalled with vividness and fondness, while others, equally important, are all but consigned to oblivion.

The memory of William Carey (1761-1834) is a good case in point. The story of his life and his epochal mission to India in the late eighteenth and early nineteenth centuries has been told and retold numerous times. Since his death Carey has been the subject of some fifty published biographies and studies, not to mention the hundreds of articles and papers.[1] His ministry in the Indian sub-continent captured the imagination of untold numbers of evangelicals in the nineteenth century, sparked the formation of a host of missionary societies and generally initiated what has been termed the modern missionary movement. Consequently, it is not surprising that later writers and historians have been so bedazzled by the historic nature of his missionary endeavour that they have unwittingly minimized or overlooked the indispensable role played by his co-workers, both at home in England and on the field in India.

When his contemporaries, though, spoke the name of William Carey, it was inseparable from five or six others: Joshua Marshman (1768-1837) and William Ward (1769-1823)—Carey's colleagues in India, who with Carey formed what has come to be known as the

'Serampore Trio' — Andrew Fuller (1754-1815), John Sutcliff (1752-1814), John Ryland, Jr (1753-1825) and Samuel Pearce (1766-1799) — the first three of whom have sometimes been dubbed the 'Home Trio'. Christopher Anderson (1782-1852), a Scottish Baptist who knew most of these men intimately and who wrote the first biographical sketch of Carey to be printed in Great Britain, once stated that for any Christian venture to issue in 'much good being done, co-operation, the result of undissembled love, is absolutely necessary'. God has to unite the hearts of those involved in the venture as 'the heart of one man'. 'Such a union,' he continued, 'in modern times existed in Fuller, Sutcliff, Pearce, Carey and Ryland.'[2] When this circle of friends were contemplating the mission which sent Carey to India in 1793, one of the images that came to their minds was that of a gold-mine. As Andrew Fuller later recalled, 'We saw there was a gold-mine in India, but it seemed almost as deep as the centre of the earth.' Who would venture down to explore it? 'I will venture to go down,' Carey said but, he stipulated, Fuller and his two other close friends, John Sutcliff and John Ryland, 'must hold the ropes'. Their response was whole-hearted, earnest and undertaken out of a fervent passion for God's glory and a deep love for Carey. 'We solemnly engaged to him to do so,' Fuller stated, 'nor while we live shall we desert him.'[3] The commitment of these men to one another is well summed up in the words that Samuel Pearce wrote in the front of a Greek New Testament printed by the Dutch firm of the Elzevir family, which he sent to Carey in the autumn of 1797. In choosing these particular words, Pearce was obviously seeking to remind Carey what God had done for them. They were in Greek and were drawn from Acts 4:32: καρδία καὶ ψυχὴ μία — 'one heart and one soul'.[4]

Now, if such was the way in which these men saw themselves and their ministries as bound up with another, one might expect that not only Carey but also his close friends would have been the subjects of numerous biographies over the years. The contrary, however, is the case. Fuller has fared the best with a handful of biographies, but only one of any substance in this century.[5] Pearce, Ryland, Marshman and Ward have each been the subject or co-subject of at least one biographical study.[6] There has been no full-length published biography of Sutcliff.[7] There are various reasons for this neglect. Prominent among them is the way in which Carey has been credited with the wisdom of his partners and colleagues, and thus lauded as the heroic figure of his era.[8] Yet these men and their ministries — what Sutcliff aptly termed their 'generation work'[9] — ought not to be forgottten. Not only are they important for what they enabled Carey to accomplish, but they are each significant in their own right.

Take Sutcliff, for example. In the eighteenth century the cultures and lifestyles of northern and southern England frequently seemed to be so different that they were like 'two countries', as Fuller once put it.[10] Calvinistic Baptists who were seeking revival in these two areas of England were thus often hampered in their efforts to work together. Sutcliff, a Yorkshireman from the West Riding who was trained at the Bristol Baptist Academy and who exercised his entire pastoral ministry in the south, proved to be an effective 'link man', who helped to bring together renewal-minded Baptists in the north and the south. The theological mentor of these like-minded Baptists was the New England divine Jonathan Edwards (1703-1758), whom the late D. Martyn Lloyd-Jones has rightly called 'the theologian of Revival'.[11] Sutcliff 'drank deeply' from the well of Edwards' theology and subsequently played a vital role in passing on the theological riches of Edwards to Andrew Fuller, whose writings encapsulated the thinking of those Calvinistic Baptists who longed for and worked for revival at the end of the eighteenth century. It was, moreover, after being deeply affected by a treatise of Edwards on corporate praying for revival, that Sutcliff urged fellow Baptists in the Northamptonshire Baptist Association to establish monthly prayer meetings for revival. From these prayer meetings and the theological renewal that Edwards' writings had ignited came revival to the Calvinistic Baptist cause. While nowhere near as dramatic as that which issued from the ranks of the Church of England in the mid-eighteenth century, this revival was just as deep and profound. One particularly important result of this revival was the formation of the Particular Baptist Society for Propagating the Gospel among the Heathen (later known more simply as the Baptist Missionary Society) in 1792. Sutcliff played a central rôle, not only in the founding of this society, but also in its ongoing effectiveness during the first couple of decades of its existence. There is thus ample justification for an account of Sutcliff's life.

Due to the fact that Sutcliff's story is inextricably interwoven with that of Ryland, Fuller and Carey, the experiences and written works of these three men also figure largely in the biography. This is as it should be. After all, God made of them 'one heart and one soul'. Indeed, their friendship was a central factor in the revival noted above, which was a watershed in the history of their denomination. From an inward-looking body the Calvinistic Baptists were transformed into one that was outward-looking and committed to fervent evangelism. Before we concentrate on Sutcliff and his friends, therefore, we need to begin with a quick overview of the state of the Calvinistic Baptists prior to their transformation.

# 1.
# God's preparation for a great work: The Calvinistic Baptists in the eighteenth century

> *'When I first published my treatise on the nature of faith, and the duty of all men who hear the gospel to believe it, the Christian profession had sunk into contempt amongst us; inasmuch, that had matters gone on but a few years longer, the Baptists would have become a perfect dunghill in society'*
> (Andrew Fuller).

'The Most High sent the glorious King William the Third, and saved us.'[1] Such was the way that Benjamin Wallin (1711-1782), pastor of Maze Pond Baptist Church in London, gave voice to what was the almost universal view of eighteenth-century Calvinistic Baptists on the accession of William III to the English throne in 1688. Prior to William's coming to power, the Calvinistic Baptists had experienced close to thirty years of intense, though intermittent, state persecution and mob-harassment, along with others who had refused to conform to the rites and doctrine of the Church of England, such as the Presbyterians, the Independents (later known as the Congregationalists) and the Quakers. The legal justification for this persecution lay in a series of laws known as the Clarendon Code, which had been passed in the 1660s and early 1670s under Charles II. This legislation made it illegal for worship or evangelism to be carried on outside of the bounds of the Church of England. When William came to the throne, though, he had an Act of Toleration passed in 1689, which provided the Calvinistic Baptists, as well as other Protestants outside of the Church of England (collectively known as Nonconformists or Dissenters), with a real measure of

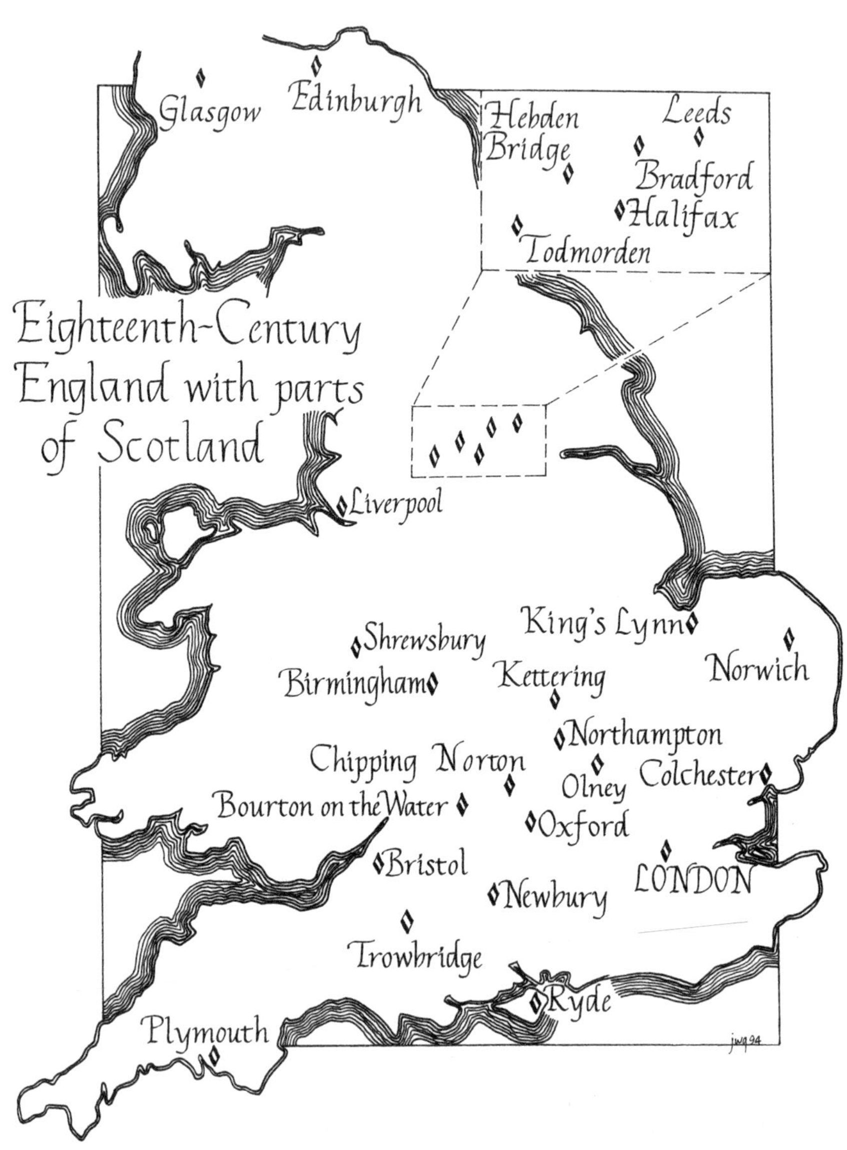


Map 1— Eighteenth-century England with parts of Scotland

religious freedom. They were now legally free to have their own distinct forms of worship, to expand their congregations, to build their chapels and even to criticize the claims made for the Church of England by Anglican preachers. At the same time, the power of the Church of England to hamper or interfere with Dissenting congregations was significantly diminished.

One would expect that given such opportunities, the Calvinistic Baptists would flourish, much as they had done during the 1650s when Oliver Cromwell, 'the father of toleration,' had ruled England. Many of the Baptists who witnessed the dawn of toleration certainly thought so. For Benjamin Keach (1640-1704), a leading figure among the London Baptists, the granting of toleration 'opened a great door for the gospel and sent us blessed harvest weather'.[2] These hopeful promises of future blessing were not to be realized, however. After a considerable degree of vitality during the reigns of William III and Anne, who was queen from 1702 to 1714, the Calvinistic Baptist cause began to decline.

## The influence of High Calvinism

Baptist writers and historians have traditionally fixed the blame for this declension on the High Calvinism, or Hyper-Calvinism, of such influential Baptist theologians as John Gill (1697-1771) and John Brine (1703-1765), both of whom pastored congregations in London.[3] For example, John Ryland, Jr, the pastor of Broadmead Church, Bristol and the principal of Bristol Baptist Academy, writing in 1816, stated that through the influence of both Gill and Brine the opinion 'spread pretty much among ministers of the Baptist denomination' that 'It is not the duty of the unregenerate to believe in Christ.' As a result Baptist preachers 'were too much restrained from imitating our Lord and his apostles, in calling on sinners to "repent and believe the gospel"'.[4] According to the Victorian Baptist historian J. M. Cramp (1796-1881), Gill was so afraid of interfering with God's work in the salvation of sinners, that he 'abstained from personal addresses to sinners, by inviting them to the Saviour, and satisfied himself with declaring their guilt and doom'. When his example and teaching were followed by many of his fellow Baptist ministers, the Baptist cause in England began to plummet.[5] The marked failure of many early eighteenth-century

Baptist churches to evangelize aggressively in the way that their seventeenth-century forebears had done was thus traced primarily to the flawed thinking of John Gill about evangelism.

Recently, however, the American historian Thomas J. Nettles has called into question the use of the term 'High Calvinism' as an accurate way of describing Gill's theology. Nettles maintains that Gill did indeed affirm that 'It was the duty of all men to repent of sin and the duty of all who heard the gospel to believe it.' Moreover, while Gill did consider the actual phrase 'to offer Christ' as having no firm biblical foundation, he had no objections to urging sinners to come to Christ. Nettles thus concludes that rather than being blamed for the spiritual leanness of the Baptist cause, Gill should be credited with having preserved the purity of the gospel, which eventually resulted in the efforts in the final two decades of the eighteenth century to evangelize the lost in Britain and overseas.[6] Especially by standing firm against heretical views of the Trinity and the nature of salvation, Gill enabled his Calvinistic Baptist contemporaries to maintain their hold on orthodoxy and so have the capacity to receive the fire of revival later in the century.

Peter Naylor, an English Baptist pastor, has argued along similar lines.[7] He admits that Gill 'frequently allowed himself to be controlled by a quasi-theological system [i.e. High Calvinism] which led him beyond New Testament boundaries'. For instance, Gill could state that God does not require saving faith of all men and women. He did allow that all human beings are obliged to exercise a faith in God as the God of nature and providence. But such a faith is obviously not saving faith: 'As for those texts of Scripture, I know of none, that exhort and command all men, all the individuals of human nature, to repent, and believe in Christ for salvation; they can only, at most, concern such persons who are under the gospel dispensation; and, in general, only regard an external repentance and reformation, and an historical faith in, or assent to, Jesus as the Messiah.'

Refusal to believe that Jesus is the Messiah is what Gill calls the 'damning sin of unbelief', not the lack of faith in Christ as Saviour and Lord. Since 'No man can believe in Christ with this [latter] sort of faith, unless it be given him of his Father,' God will not send a person to hell for failing to put their faith in Christ as the only Saviour from sin.[8] Consequently men and women outside of Christ are under no obligation to believe that Christ died for sinners. On the other hand, Naylor does point out that there are occasions when Gill can insist that saving faith is a duty incumbent upon all who hear the gospel. Thus, from time to time his writings display a commitment to evangelical Calvinism rather than High Calvinism. Yet, when Gill's thinking about faith and evangelism was pondered and acted upon by his fellow Baptist preachers, it was invariably his High Calvinism that was their lodestar. These preachers thus refrained from urging upon the lost their responsibility to embrace Christ and to trust in him alone for their salvation.

Typical of preachers of this ilk was John Eve (d.1782). Originally a sieve-maker from Chesterton, near Cambridge, Eve was set apart to preach the gospel by St Andrew's Street Baptist Church, Cambridge in 1749. In 1752 he was ordained pastor of the Baptist church in Soham, a small village about twelve miles north-east of Cambridge, where he ministered till his resignation in 1771. Andrew Fuller grew up under Eve's ministry. Of his ministry Fuller later remarked that Eve was a High Calvinist, 'or tinged with false Calvinism,' who 'had little or nothing to say to the unconverted'.[9]

Nor was High Calvinism a region solely inhabited by pastors and preachers; many in their congregations clearly shared these views to the full. Goodshaw Baptist Church in West Yorkshire had among its members in the late eighteenth century a strong High Calvinist who was not at all afraid of publicly reprimanding preachers whose sermons he found theologically disagreeable. On one occasion, the preacher had evidently pleaded with the lost in the congregation to flee to Christ for salvation. As he left the pulpit after preaching, he was accosted by the High Calvinist, who, in no uncertain terms, told him, 'Nay, nay ... this mak' o' thing will never do. Yo'n been trying all mornin' to regenerate the sinner's heart wi' human means instead o' th' sperret.'[10]

As Charles Haddon Spurgeon (1834-1892) later wrote, Gill's writings promoted a system of theology which 'chilled many churches to their very soul, for it ... led them to omit the free invitations of the gospel, and to deny that it is the duty of sinners to believe in Jesus'.[11] Nevertheless, Nettles and Naylor are right to dispute the standard view of Gill's ministry, well illustrated by Ryland and Cramp, which considers him and Brine as the leading culprits for the spiritual leanness of many of the Calvinistic Baptist churches of the time. Such a view is an oversimplification. There were other causes at work in the declension of the Calvinistic Baptists besides High Calvinism.

## Legal and social discrimination

First of all, the Act of Toleration had effectively confined Calvinistic Baptist preaching to the meeting-house, in which the congregation met to worship God. Although it gave Baptists the freedom to organize and to gather congregations, only those buildings registered as meeting-houses with the bishop of the diocese or the local Justice of the Peace could serve as places of evangelism and worship, and then only if the doors of the meeting-house were propped open during worship services.

And while the act permitted them freedom of worship, it did not give them full civil rights, which would not be granted to the Dissenters until well into the nineteenth century. Certain legal restrictions enacted during the reign of Charles II, which were designed to curtail Nonconformist participation in the mainstream of English society, remained unrescinded. Significant obstacles, for instance, continued to lie in the path of those Dissenters who sought to study at either Oxford or Cambridge University, or who wanted to pursue a career in the government at either the national or civic level. Nonconformists, Baptists included, were clearly in a position of social inferiority throughout the eighteenth century. This legal and social discrimination undoubtedly cast the Baptists in a poor light and helped to contribute to their failure to attract new members.

By and large the Baptists accepted the restrictions placed upon them and for much of the eighteenth century limited their horizons to the maintenance of congregational life. In order to preserve their distinctive Christian witness and mode of worship, they closed ranks and delighted in describing themselves as 'a garden enclosed' (Song of Solomon 4:12). As an enclosed garden, the church, in the words of John Gill, is protected and 'encompassed with the power of God, as a wall about it', and is 'so closely surrounded, that it is not to be seen nor known by the world; and indeed is not accessible to any but believers in Christ'.[12] Gill's language here well reflects the inward-looking attitudes of many Calvinistic Baptists during the early years of the eighteenth century, when they were largely content to enjoy the fruits of toleration and to rest secure behind the walls of their meeting-houses.

Baptist acquiescence in this social and legal discrimination is also seen in the following comparison which Howel Harris (1714-1773), the Welsh evangelist, made between the Nonconformist denominations and his good friend George Whitefield (1714-1770), the greatest evangelist of the eighteenth century: 'Whilst they are in their warm rooms, he ventures his life for God.'[13] As noted above, eighteenth-century Nonconformist ministers were legally required to stay within their meeting-houses to proclaim the Word of God, while the early Methodists, as members of the Church of England, had the liberty to take the gospel into the open air, the highways and the byways. This telling comparison, however, also bears witness to the way in which the spatial 'settledness' of the Nonconformists affected their spiritual health. For many Nonconformist pastors obedience to the legal restrictions regarding evangelism produced a profound spiritual 'settledness'. Far too many of the Nonconformist pastors whom Harris knew well — and this would have included Calvinistic Baptists — were content to live on their past experience of conversion and displayed little hunger for the presence and power of God in their lives.

There were, of course, exceptions 'who adapted themselves to a colder climate by hotter preaching, and deliberate evangelism'.[14] For example, between 1688 and 1705 William Mitchel (1662-1705) and David Crosley (1669-1744) evangelized towns and villages throughout east Lancashire and the West Riding of Yorkshire with unremitting ardour from their base at Bacup in the Rossendale Valley. In so doing, they laid the foundations for a large number of future Baptist churches.[15] The vigorous preaching of Robert Robinson (1735-1790), who had himself been converted through a sermon of George Whitefield, helped to transform St Andrew's Baptist Church, Cambridge, from a struggling work with only thirty-four members when he went there as pastor in 1759 to the situation in 1775, when it had 120 members and a regular attendance of 600-800. Encouraged by the example of Whitefield and acting on the advice of John Berridge (1716-1793), the evangelical vicar of the village of Everton, Robinson also became involved in itinerant preaching in neighbouring towns and villages. By the mid-1770s the Baptist preacher was regularly giving lectures on Christianity in thirteen villages within ten miles of Cambridge to around 2,300 hearers.[16] In London Andrew Gifford (1700-1784) had an extremely fruitful ministry as pastor of Eagle Street Baptist Church from 1735 till his death. A number of years prior to his death some six hundred people had been converted under his preaching and eleven men sent into the pastorate from the congregation. He was a friend of

Whitefield and Harris, and, on at least one occasion, had John Wesley (1703-1791) to dinner.[17] The evangelistic endeavours of these men, however, were the exception rather than the rule.[18]

## Doctrinal controversy

There were also internal doctrinal disputes which consumed the energy of many Baptist churches. In the 1690s, for instance, a bitter controversy developed over congregational hymn-singing. Virtually the entire leadership of the Calvinistic Baptist community in London became involved in one way or another in the controversy. It is symptomatic of the split amongst the London Baptists that the two leading figures in the denomination, William Kiffin (1616-1701) and Hanserd Knollys (*c.*1598-1691), found themselves on opposing sides.[19] It would appear that theological debate had largely been shelved during the period of persecution in the interests of survival. But once the persecution had come to an end, theological and personal differences came to the fore.

Another example comes from the experience of Baptist churches in the north of England during the mid-eighteenth century. In 1741 John Johnson (1706-1791) was called to pastor Byrom Street Baptist Church, Liverpool, and within a few years the congregation had split over his theological views. Johnson has recently been described as 'basically a prickly Hyper-Calvinist with a taste for travel, theological hair-splitting and provoking strife'; everything which he touched was 'soon seething with controversy'.[20] A variety of pamphlets and books spread far and wide his convictions about such things as the pre-existence of Christ's human soul and the fact that God has never issued a decree to permit the presence of sin in the world. Andrew Fuller testified to the force of Johnson's speculations and peculiar opinions when he stated that there was 'something imposing in his manner' of writing, 'by which a young and inexperienced reader is apt to be carried away'.[21] Johnson's teaching proved to be very divisive indeed, splitting a significant number of Baptist causes and giving birth to the Johnsonian Baptists, who stood aloof from fellowship with other Calvinistic Baptists. Among the churches influenced by 'Johnsonianism' was John Sutcliff's home church, Wainsgate, in its early years of existence.

## Isolation and lack of communication

The geographical location of most Baptist churches was a further source of weakness during this period. Many of the congregations were in small market-towns, villages and hamlets. Contact between them was especially difficult during the winter and bad weather, when poorly maintained roads became well-nigh impassable. In June 1784, for instance, Andrew Fuller was scheduled to preach at the annual meeting of the Baptist churches comprising the Northamptonshire Association. On his way from Kettering to the meeting at Nottingham, Fuller found that heavy rains had flooded a number of spots on the roads over which he had to travel. At one particular point the flooded area appeared so deep that Fuller was reluctant to continue. A resident of the area, who knew how deep the water actually was, encouraged him to urge his horse through the water. 'Go on, sir,' he said, 'you are quite safe.' As the water came up to his saddle, Fuller began to have second thoughts about continuing. 'Go on, sir,' the man said again, 'all is right.' Taking the man at his word, Fuller continued and safely traversed the flooded area of the road.[22]

Not only was communication between the churches hindered because of their rural location, but so was their working together in such joint endeavours as evangelism and church-planting. The stress in Baptist circles on the autonomy of the local church further exacerbated this problem. Each local church considered itself autonomous, recognizing no authority beyond the congregation and the Scriptures, the sole rule of its faith and practice. The *Second London Confession of Faith* (1677), reissued by a national assembly of Calvinistic Baptist churches in 1689 — the year following the accession to power of William III — expressed this conviction when it stated that Christ has vested in each individual congregation 'all that power and authority, which is in any way needful for their carrying on that order in worship and discipline, which he hath instituted for them to observe'.[23]

During the eighteenth century, moreover, there was no overarching denominational structure linking together the various Calvinistic Baptist churches. Annual national assemblies, like the first one that issued the *Second London Confession of Faith*, ceased to meet beyond the 1690s. The regional associations of churches which did exist were of varying degrees of robustness. The Western

Association, for example, which had its nerve-centre in Bristol and which comprised Gloucestershire, Wiltshire, Somerset, Devon and Cornwall, met continuously through the eighteenth century, whereas the Yorkshire and Lancashire Association, beginning in 1719, was moribund by the 1730s and would only have regular meetings again after 1786. There was no association of churches in the capital, only a board of ministers known as the London Baptist Board. Hence, there was no central leadership to the denomination. In the words of Deryck W. Lovegrove, 'The very strength of independency, the internal cohesion of the gathered church, became its weakness as geographical remoteness conspired with autonomy and lack of common purpose to foster numerical decline.'[24]

In short, the decline of the Baptists during the early and mid-eighteenth century cannot easily be attributed to simply one cause. There were a number of factors at work: political, social and geographical, as well as theological.

## Evidences of decline

Evidence for this declension can be found in a variety of sources. Calvinistic Baptist pastors who laboured in the middle of the eighteenth century were not slow to remark on the decline their denomination was experiencing.

Gill himself could state in 1750, in his funeral sermon for Samuel Wilson (1702-1750), pastor of Prescott Street Baptist Church in London: 'The harvest is great, and faithful and painful ministers are few. There are scarcely any that naturally care for the estate and souls of men, and who are heartily concerned for their spiritual welfare... And what adds to the sorrow is, that there are so few rising to fill the places of those that are removed; few that come forth with the same spirit, and are zealously attached to the truths of the everlasting gospel. Blessed be God, there is here and there one that promises usefulness, or otherwise the sorrow and grief at the loss of gospel ministers would be insupportable.'[25]

Gill's younger contemporary, Benjamin Wallin, whose own congregation at Maze Pond actually saw an increase in members during his pastorate from 1741 to 1782, frequently made mention of 'the universal complaints of the decay of practical and vital godliness'. Wallin was very conscious of living in a 'melancholy day', a day of 'present declensions' amongst Baptist churches.[26]

A somewhat less subjective indicator of decline is to be found in the statistics of Calvinistic Baptist congregations in the eighteenth century. For the first couple of decades of this era the main source of statistical evidence is a list of Nonconformist congregations largely drawn up between the years 1715 and 1718 by John Evans, the minister of Hand Alley Presbyterian Church in London. Evans was the secretary of the Committee of the Three Denominations, which had been set up in 1702 to safeguard the interests of the Presbyterians, the Independents and the Calvinistic Baptists from Anglican designs at the time of the enthronement of Queen Anne. In 1715 this committee decided to make a detailed and comprehensive survey of Nonconformist strength in England and Wales. Correspondents in each county of England and Wales were secured, and they were asked to provide the location of every Nonconformist congregation in their respective counties, along with the names of its preachers, the number of hearers and their social status, and the political strength of the congregation. While the list is reasonably accurate with regard to Presbyterian and Independent congregations, research by the English Baptist historian W. T. Whitley earlier in this century turned up a number of Calvinistic Baptist congregations not in the Evans list. On the basis of this list and his own research, Whitley estimated that there were roughly 220 Calvinistic Baptist congregations in England and Wales around the years 1715 to 1718.[27]

For the determination of Calvinistic Baptist strength at mid-century, a survey of fellow Baptist ministers in 1753 by John C. Ryland (1723-1792), at the time pastor of the Calvinistic Baptist church in Warwick, is especially helpful. Like the Evans list, Ryland's survey is somewhat incomplete. However, an analysis of this survey has provided some additions to Ryland's figures and indicates that in the early 1750s the number of Calvinistic Baptist congregations had dropped to around 150.[28] From the beginning of the century, therefore, there had been a decrease in the number of congregations by approximately one-third. While these figures are only estimates, they do reveal a pattern of decline in the Calvinistic Baptist community during the early decades of the century. Andrew Fuller summed up this situation in his own inimitable style when he declared: 'Had matters gone on but for a few years, the Baptists would have become a perfect dunghill in society.'[29]

Not reticent to speak their minds regarding this decline, pastors such as Gill and Wallin were also not hesitant to indicate how the situation should be remedied. For them the pathway to church renewal lay first and foremost in an earnest commitment to upholding the distinctives of Calvinistic Baptist church order and discipline, which had obviously played a key role in nourishing and sustaining the Calvinistic Baptist cause since its inception in the previous century.

Wallin, for instance, was insistent that as long as there was a neglect of believer's baptism and the principles of congregational church government, any attempt to revive the churches of Christ was 'essentially deficient'. As he maintained, 'They who neglect these divine institutions on a pretence that inward and spiritual devotion is all God requires, are under a plain delusion, since this is contrary to the example of the Lord, as well as to express exhortations in Scripture... More is required in gospel-worship than barely to hear the Word in the assemblies of the faithful... We learn from the New Testament that they who received the Word, were soon baptized and joined the disciples, who in every place were with one consent united in a church-state, and communed together under their several officers in the ordinances of the Lord.'[30]

## Attitudes to the revival

Genuine love to God and the desire for communion with him are inseparably linked, in Wallin's mind, to a zeal for the preservation and consolidation of proper church order, which includes submission to believer's baptism. Little wonder then that Wallin, like many of his Calvinistic Baptist contemporaries, was intensely critical of the Evangelical Revival, where the emphasis lay not so much on convictions regarding church government and the proper subjects of baptism as on the vigorous proclamation of such essential truths as salvation by grace alone and the new birth.

From the late 1730s on, Great Britain was the scene of one of the greatest demonstrations of the sovereign power of the Holy Spirit in the history of the church, namely, the Evangelical Revival. A profound spiritual revolution, the revival swept thousands into the Christian fold, gave new meaning to pastoral ministry and ultimately transformed the fabric of British society. In a letter which Howel Harris wrote to George Whitefield in 1743, Harris gave his friend what can well be regarded as a classic description of the revival: 'The outpouring of the Blessed Spirit is now so plentiful and common, that I think it was our deliberate observation that not one sent by Him opens his mouth without some remarkable showers. He comes either as a Spirit of wisdom to enlighten the soul, to teach and build up, and set out the works of light and darkness, or else a Spirit of tenderness and love, sweetly melting the souls like the dew, and watering the graces; or as the Spirit of hot burning zeal, setting their hearts in a flame, so that their eyes sparkle with fire, love, and joy; or also such a Spirit of uncommon power that the heavens seem to be rent, and hell to tremble.'[31]

Yet, up till the death of Whitefield in 1770, the majority of British Calvinistic Baptists stood aloof from this great work of God the Holy Spirit, and were largely untouched by it. The difference between those giving leadership to the revival and the Calvinistic Baptists with regard to the importance of church order, mentioned above, certainly did much to keep the two groups suspicious of, and antagonistic towards, one another.[32]

In fact, in the early years of the revival all of the key leaders — men such as Whitefield, John Wesley and his brother Charles (1708-1788), Harris, Daniel Rowland (1713-1790) and William Williams Pantycelyn (1717-1791) — were members of the Church of England, which most Baptists regarded as an apostate institution. The Church of England, John Gill wrote, giving expression to a belief common among his fellow Baptists, 'has neither the form nor matter of a true church, nor is the Word of God purely preached in it'.[33] William Herbert (1697-1745), a Welsh Baptist pastor and a friend of Howel Harris, remonstrated with the latter for staying in the Church of England. In a letter that he wrote to Harris in January of 1737, Herbert compared the Church of England to a pub 'which is open to all comers', and to a 'common field where every noisesome beast may come'. Did not Harris realize, Herbert asked his friend, that the Scripture — and he has in mind Song of Solomon 4:12 — describes the church as 'a garden inclosed, a spring shut up, a fountain sealed' — in other words, a body of believers 'separate from ye prophane world'?[34]

Arnesby Baptist Church in Leicestershire displayed similar convictions when, during the first half of the eighteenth century, it excommunicated members 'for going to Babylon to be joined together [i.e. married] according to the wicked way of the Church of England'.[35] Where such attitudes towards the established church reigned, there was a deep reluctance to regard the revival as a genuine work of the Spirit of God.

Nor did the settled aversion of both John and Charles Wesley for Dissenters in general and Baptists in particular endear either of them or their Arminian followers to the Baptists. John Wesley, for instance, was quoted as having stated publicly on one occasion: 'When a sinner is just awakened to see his state as a sinner, the people called Anabaptists [i.e. Baptists], begin to trouble him about outward forms and modes of worship, and that of baptism; but they had better cut his throat, for it is sending ... him to hell and perdition.'[36] Charles could be just as biting in his criticism. In a journal entry for 30 October 1756, he minced no words when he described the Baptists as 'a carnal cavilling, contentious sect, always watching to steal away our [i.e. Methodist] children, and make them as dead as themselves'.[37]

Calvinistic Baptist antipathy to the Wesley brothers, on the other hand, is understandable not only in the light of such remarks, but also in view of the evangelical Arminianism of the Wesleys. James Turner (d.1780), pastor of Cannon Street Baptist Church in Birmingham, expressed the opinion of most of his fellow Baptists with regard to John Wesley when he told John Sutcliff that Wesley was 'a *nothing*, both in politics and religion'.[38] Whitefield and Harris, on the other hand, were Calvinists and not averse to establishing friendships with Dissenters. However, some Calvinistic Baptists, strongly influenced by High Calvinism, complained of their 'Arminian dialect' and 'semi-Pelagian addresses', because they preached for conversions and insisted on exhorting the lost to flee to Christ for salvation.[39]

## 'Enthusiasm' associated with the revival

Another key factor which caused Calvinistic Baptists to be wary of any involvement with the revival was their deep-seated fear of enthusiasm, a widespread bugbear of the eighteenth century and something which, to many casual observers of the revival, seemed to be its leading characteristic. The mind-set of the eighteenth century, which gloried in reason, moderation, sobriety and order, regarded 'enthusiasm' in religion as particularly unsavoury. To be charged with enthusiasm in this sphere was to be accused of claiming extraordinary revelations and powers from the Holy Spirit, though the word could be used more loosely to denote any kind of religious excitement.

The English philosopher John Locke (1632-1704), who exercised a profound influence on the world-view of the eighteenth century, used the word to denote the outlook of those who have 'an opinion of a greater familiarity with God, and a nearer admittance to his favour than is afforded to others', and have thus persuaded themselves that they have an 'immediate intercourse with the Deity, and frequent communications from the divine Spirit'. Such a mind-set, Locke was convinced, arises from 'the conceits of a warmed or over-weening brain'.[40] Clearly dependent upon Locke, the lexicographer Samuel Johnson (1709-1784) defined enthusiasm in *A Dictionary of the English Language* (1755) as 'a vain belief of private revelation; a vain confidence of divine favour or communication'.[41]

To all intents and purposes the key leaders in the revival agreed. 'The quintessence of enthusiasm,' Whitefield declared in a sermon first published in 1746, was 'to pretend to be guided by the Spirit without the written word'. All inner impressions must be tried by 'the unerring rule of God's most holy Word', and if found incompatible, rejected as 'diabolical and delusive'.[42]

However, if Whitefield and other leaders in the revival were wary of falling prey to enthusiasm, their critics were certain that they had succumbed. Two early criticisms can be taken as representative of the charges levelled against the revival and its participants throughout the eighteenth century.

John Barker (1682-1762), an English Presbyterian minister and correspondent of Philip Doddridge (1702-1751), the influential Congregationalist pastor, wrote to the latter on 24 May 1739 to tell him that he had heard Whitefield preaching in London in the open air and later also at Bath. Though he thought him sincere, Barker told Doddridge, 'I still fancy that he is but a weak man — much too positive, says rash things, and is bold and enthusiastic. I am most heartily glad to hear of piety, prayer, reformation, and every thing that looks like faith and holiness, in the North or South, the East or the West, and that any real good is done anywhere to the souls of men, but whether these Methodists are in a right way, whether they are warrantable in all their conduct, whether poor people should be urged (through different persons, successively) to pray from four in the morning till eleven at night, is not clear to me; and I am less satisfied with the high pretences they make to the Divine influence. I think what Mr Whitfield says and does comes but little short of an assumption of inspiration or infallibility.'[43]

Joseph Butler (1692-1752), the Bishop of Bristol, also criticized

Whitefield and his fellow-evangelist John Wesley for what he perceived to be enthusiasm. In an interview with Wesley on 18 August 1739, Butler accused both of the evangelists of 'pretending to extraordinary revelations and gifts of the Holy Ghost', which he regarded as 'a horrid thing — a very horrid thing'. Wesley denied this charge and stated that he sought only 'what every Christian may receive and ought to expect and pray for'.[44]

If he had been present Whitefield would also have strongly disputed the accuracy of Butler's accusation, for he was adamant that the extraordinary gifts of the Spirit, such as prophecy, glossolalia and miraculous powers, had ceased with the passing of the apostles. In his sermon 'The Indwelling of the Spirit, the Common Privilege of All Believers', which Wesley helped him to edit for publication in the summer of 1739, Whitefield declared that Christ's promise of the Spirit in John 7:37-39 has nothing to do with receiving power 'to work miracles, or show outward signs and wonders'. Whitefield suggested that such signs and wonders occurred only when 'some new revelation was to be established, as at the first settling of the Mosaic or gospel dispensation'. Those who argued for a repetition of such miracles in his day Whitefield regarded with deep suspicion. Since, he continued, 'The world being now become nominally Christian ... there need not outward miracles, but only an inward co-operation of the Holy Spirit with the Word, to prove that Jesus is the Messiah which was to come into the world.'[45] Thus, both Whitefield and Wesley insisted that it was completely inappropriate to view Methodism as a species of enthusiasm. Public opinion, though, thought otherwise, and the charge of enthusiasm was regularly hurled at those involved in the revival.

One reason for this was the fact that there were some in the leadership of the revival who 'were led to expect, even lay claim to, quasi-apostolic powers: direct "impressions" from God, the power of "discerning spirits", prophesying, exorcizing, performing miraculous cures'.[46] For instance, George Bell (d.1807) claimed that he and a coterie of fellow London Methodists possessed the power to heal the sick on a regular basis. Bell himself also believed that he had broad prophetic powers, including the gift of the discernment of spirits. These he sought to exercise in 1762 when he predicted the end of the world on 28 February 1763. At this point Wesley stepped in, disowned Bell as a Methodist and denounced his prediction as fraudulent. He defended his actions with regard to Bell: 'The reproach of Christ I am willing to bear; but not the reproach of Enthusiasm if I can help it.'[47] Indeed, for many years afterwards the memory of the Bell affair continued to confirm people's suspicions that the Methodists were bona fide enthusiasts.

Nor were matters helped by the fact that those involved in the revival emphasized that the indwelling of the believer by the Holy Spirit was an experience which could be known experimentally. As Whitefield declared, to 'say we may have God's Spirit without feeling it ... is, in reality, to deny the thing itself'.[48] In Whitefield's perspective, when the Spirit of God takes up residence in a person's life, his presence has an impact on the entire person: mind, will, emotions — and even on occasion the body — are all touched and affected.

Without denying the place of experience in the Christian life, Calvinistic Baptists were none the less very critical of the 'phenomena' of the Evangelical Revival, 'phenomena' such as the following described by Howel Harris in a letter to Whitefield. Under the preaching of Daniel Rowland in March 1743, Harris noted that many were moved to 'crying out and heart-breaking groans, silent weeping and holy joy', while 'scores' fell down 'by the power of the Word, pierced and wounded or overcom'd by the love of God and sights of the beauty and excellency of Jesus'.[49] To the Baptists such manifestations of emotion seemed to be simply rank enthusiasm. The London Baptist pastor John Brine thus criticized the audiences of revival preachers, who 'love to have their passions moved'. Such individuals, he continued, 'flatter themselves that this is true edification by the Word, though it is no such thing'. They are simply 'entertained with the preacher's rhetoric'.[50]

In a similar vein, Gill stated in his magnum opus, *A Complete Body of Doctrinal and Practical Divinity* (1769-1770), that spiritual joy is 'not to be fully expressed by those who experience it; it is better experienced than expressed'.[51] Taken in its historical context, this remark is an implicit criticism of the remarkable manifestations which attended the revival and which were identical to those described by Harris.

The pastor of the Baptist church in Cardigan, South Wales, William Williams (d.1799) — not to be confused with the Calvinistic Methodist hymn-writer of the same name — maintained in 1774 that the gospel is 'most spiritual and reasonable'. It was not genuine spirituality but carnality which becomes 'excited and expanded and goes up in words, sounds, tears and agitations of the affections, which fills the mind with self-conceit, self-love, self-will, pride and contempt for others'. Williams was so opposed to the Evangelical Revival that he led his church in expelling any member who became enamoured of the revival.[52]

Williams' church was not the only British Baptist congregation during the eighteenth century which used expulsion, along with censure and the refusal of membership, as a means of keeping the revival at bay. For instance, 4 April 1759 saw the excommunication of George Death and Elizabeth Langly from Colchester Baptist Church for having 'joyned themselves with the people called Methodists, thereby wickedly endeavouring to rend and divide our Church'.[53] That same year the minute book of Tiverton Baptist Church, Devon, recorded that a Brother Carter ceased to attend the worship of the church due to the fact that the pastor, Henry Terry (d.1759), had said something which 'tended to alienate the minds of the people from the Methodists'.[54] Five years earlier, St Mary's Baptist Church, Norwich, had ruled that it was 'unlawful for any [member] ... to attend upon the meetings of the Methodists, or to join in any worship which is contrary to the doctrines and ordinances of our Lord Jesus'.[55] It is noteworthy that the previous year, 1753, Whitefield had spent a full three weeks preaching in Norwich. In a letter written with regard to these weeks, Whitefield spoke of preaching to 'thousands ... twice every day,' who 'hear with the greatest eagerness'.[56] Was the ruling of the Calvinistic Baptist church in Norwich made because some of the members of the congregation had gone to hear the well-known evangelist and become attracted to a more affective form of preaching and emotional style of worship?

## More encouraging trends

These remarks should not be taken to imply that Baptist church life and spirituality for the first two-thirds of the eighteenth century were devoid of vitality and warmth, and knew nothing of the Spirit's reviving power. Mention has already been made of the ministries of William Mitchel, David Crosley, Robert Robinson and Andrew Gifford. Others, such as those of Benjamin Beddome (1717-1795) at Bourton-on-the-Water in the Cotswolds and Hugh Evans (1713-

1781) in Bristol, will be encountered in the course of this book. However, when George Whitefield died at Newburyport, Massachusetts, in 1770, the Calvinistic Baptists were still largely dormant and unaffected by the revival. This period of declension, though, was fast drawing to a close. During the final three decades of the century the Baptists became a dynamic force in England and Wales, outward-looking and seeking to recruit new members for their congregations. In this amazing transformation of Baptist life and witness, the Yorkshireman John Sutcliff and his three friends — Andrew Fuller, John Ryland, Jr and William Carey — were to play vital and central roles. In many ways this group of friends, and others close to their circle, became the voice of the British Calvinistic Baptists. Imbued with learning and a profound spirituality, they were able to lead their fellow Baptists to the point where they could speak as one and thus become a religious force to be reckoned with in the affairs of the nation.

# 2.
# Early years in West Yorkshire

> *'Is it not one of [providence's] kind benefits that we were born in a Protestant land, many of us of pious parents? Have none cause to be thankful for some special appearance of it? Others that they were cast in such a town, such a family, under such a minister?'* (John Sutcliff).

When Daniel Defoe (1660-1731), the well-known author of *Robinson Crusoe*, drew up in the mid-1720s an exhaustive account of his various journeys throughout the length and breadth of Britain, his forceful impressions of the West Riding of Yorkshire were among the most memorable portions of the entire narrative. Travelling over the hills and moors from Rochdale to Halifax in mid-August, Defoe related how he and his companions ran into a snowstorm of such violence that at times 'It was impossible to keep our eyes open to see our way.'[1] Although the storm soon abated, negotiating the hilly terrain posed a constant challenge to the travellers. 'As soon as we were at the top of every hill,' Defoe recalled, 'we had it to come down again on the other side; and as soon as we were down we had another to mount, and that immediately; for I do not remember that there was one bottom that had any considerable breadth of plain ground in it, but always a brook in the Valley running from those gulls and deeps between the hills.'[2] The hills which Defoe and his companions were traversing are part of the central portion of the Pennines. Their foundation is millstone grit—visible in the cliffs, towering crags and outcroppings of grey rock. Nestled side by side with these higher reaches of the Pennines are the moors, covered with sturdy grasses and heather such as ling, and dotted with extensive tracts of peat, which here and there have been eroded into huge chocolate-coloured slabs. Deeply dissecting this landscape of hill and moor are, as Defoe discovered, valleys in which flow rivers and becks that can become raging torrents when swollen by winter rains and melting snow in the springtime.

Inhospitable as Defoe found the topography of the West Riding to be, he also discovered, to his astonishment, the steep hillsides 'spread with houses, and that very thick' and villages clustered in the valleys. 'This whole country, however mountainous, and that no sooner we were down one hill but we mounted another, is yet infinitely full of people,' and 'those people all full of business'.[3] Their business, Defoe observed, primarily had to do with the manufacture of various types of cloth. Through the doors of some of these houses the inquisitive Defoe caught sight of 'lusty fellows, some at the dye-vat, some dressing the cloths, some in the loom, some one thing, some another, all hard at work'.[4] Indeed, within a few years of the appearance of these words in print, West Yorkshire was well on its way to establishing itself as England's leading cloth-producing region, a supremacy which remained unchallenged for much of the eighteenth century and which formed the foundation of its immense prosperity in the final decades of that era.[5]

Along with this growing material prosperity during the eighteenth century, West Yorkshire also proved to be fertile ground for religious Nonconformity and small hardy congregations outside of the Church of England. Frank Baker, the historian of early Methodism, attributes this to the 'compact self-sufficiency' of the people of West Yorkshire and their reluctance in the eighteenth century to submit to external authorities.[6] Be this as it may, at mid-century more than half of the Baptist causes which existed in Yorkshire were in the West Riding. Some of them dated back to the opening years of the century when they had been planted through the itinerant evangelism of William Mitchel and David Crosley; others had more recent origins and were the fruit of the Evangelical Revival. The problems, though, that afflicted the Calvinistic Baptist movement nationwide and which have been discussed in the previous chapter did not pass them by — even those congregations that were formed as a result of the revival. William Crabtree (1720-1811), for instance, pastor of the Baptist work in Bradford for fifty years, was a direct product of the revival, but not until he was fairly advanced in years did he overcome his hesitation to offer the grace of God freely to sinners.[7]

## Sutcliff's early years

Such are a few of the contrasts of the West Riding of Georgian Yorkshire at the time of John Sutcliff's birth on 9 August1752 at a farm called Strait Hey, around two miles to the east of the town of Todmorden and not far from the Lancashire border.[8] The now-derelict ruins of the house in which he was born back onto moors that rise up to 1,300 feet above sea level.

The little that is known of his life up to his conversion at the age of fifteen or sixteen is found primarily in two sources: the sermon which Andrew Fuller delivered at Sutcliff's funeral on 28 June1814 and which was published later that year as *The Principles and Prospects of a Servant of Christ*, and the memoirs of Sutcliff's pastor in Yorkshire, John Fawcett (1740-1817), which were published by Fawcett's son, John Fawcett, Jr, the year after his father's death.

Of Sutcliff's early years Fuller simply tells us that Sutcliff's parents, Daniel and Hannah Sutcliff,[9] were both 'pious characters, and remarkable for their strict attention to the instruction and government of their children'.[10] The depth of their spirituality is readily seen in a portion of a letter which they wrote to their son in 1773. After expressing the desire that their son's life be devoted to God and spent for his glory, they encourage him to reflect frequently upon the person of the Lord Jesus and to pray to him 'for light and assistance', for 'This Divine Redeemer's presence is the life and light of thy soul.'[11] The names of only two of their other children have come down to us. There was a daughter named Hannah, who became a member of Wainsgate Baptist Church, just outside of Hebden Bridge, on 28 October 1767; later, in 1779, she joined the Baptist congregation at Rodhill End, near Todmorden. She died at the age of fifty-eight.[12] Then there was another son named Daniel, who was with his brother John in the latter's final days. A letter which Daniel Sutcliff wrote to Fuller after his brother's death, and from which Fuller quoted in his funeral sermon for Sutcliff, clearly indicates that Daniel shared his parents' and brother's faith to the full.[13]

The memoirs of Fawcett are somewhat more informative regarding Sutcliff's early years. This is not surprising, since their author grew up in the same area of West Yorkshire as Sutcliff. We are told that Daniel and Hannah Sutcliff instructed their children in 'the

Strait Hey, near Todmorden, the early home of John Sutcliff
*(Photo courtesy of Rita Butterworth)*

leading truths of Christianity', as well as making sure that they did not build friendships with 'ungodly companions'.[14] Given this solid Christian foundation which Sutcliff received as a young boy, it is not odd to find that among his first literary endeavours was a catechism for children, which proved to be extremely popular and went through at least five editions. On the title page of one of these editions, the third, is Ephesians 6:4: 'Bring up [your children] in the nurture and admonition of the Lord.' Although he never had any children, and, in fact, was not married till he was in his mid-forties, his own experience of Christian nurture as a youngster had obviously made him appreciative of the importance of the apostle Paul's exhortation to Christian parents.

The Fawcett memoirs also inform us that the Sutcliff family used to worship at Rodhill End (or Rodwell End) Baptist Church, which was not far from where they lived. This church had its origins in the evangelistic labours of William Mitchel and David Crosley, who, using their home church at Bacup in the Rossendale valley as a base, had planted numerous branch works or house fellowships throughout the Calder, Aire and Wharfe valleys between the years 1692 and 1705. 1705, though, saw the death of Mitchel and the departure of Crosley for London, and within the space of a dozen years most of the works which they had planted had become independent churches. At Rodhill End a meeting-house had been erected for worship in 1703, but it was not until 1717 that it finally became an independent Baptist church with Thomas Greenwood (d.1742) as its first pastor. Greenwood was succeeded by Richard Thomas (d.1772), who pastored the congregation for thirty years. Not long after Thomas' death, however, the church disbanded in 1783.[15] According to the Fawcett memoirs, there was a worship service at Rodhill End only every other week. On those Sundays when there was no service at Rodhill End, the Sutcliffs attended Wainsgate Baptist Church.[16]

## Wainsgate and the influence of William Grimshaw

Built on a hill overlooking the town of Hebden Bridge, Wainsgate was a somewhat younger church than Rodhill End, and had quite different origins. Its first pastor, Richard Smith (1710-1763), had been converted under the preaching of William Grimshaw (1708-

1763), an Anglican minister and one of the founding fathers of the Methodist movement in Yorkshire.[17]

Grimshaw himself had passed through a long and severe spiritual struggle in the mid-1730s while he was chaplain at Todmorden. His struggle was largely taken up with the search for an answer to the question of how a person can be saved. This struggle is well typified by what took place one Sunday when Grimshaw was leading the Todmorden congregation in worship. Increasingly conscious of his own sinfulness, Grimshaw electrified his congregation by stopping for a few moments in the middle of the service and then abruptly exclaiming, 'My friends, we are all in a damnable state, and I scarcely know how we are to get out of it!'

For Grimshaw the way out came through the agency of a man and a book. The man was an evangelical minister and may well have been Benjamin Ingham (1712-1772), the friend of the Wesleys and an outstanding itinerant evangelist in Lancashire and the West Riding of Yorkshire. Frequently he rebuked Grimshaw for his legalistic approach to salvation. 'Mr Grimshaw, you are a Jew,' he told him, 'you are no believer in Jesus Christ, you are building on the sand.' Grimshaw tried his best to avoid him, but the man's words constantly tugged at his conscience.

The book was *The Doctrine of Justification by Faith* (1677), written by the Puritan divine John Owen (1616-1683). It was aimed at men and women in Grimshaw's exact spiritual plight. As the Puritan theologian assured his readers in the preface, 'I have had no other design but only to inquire diligently into the divine revelation of that way, and those means, with the causes of them, whereby the conscience of a distressed sinner may attain assured peace with God through our Lord Jesus Christ.'[18] In the actual treatise of about thirty thousand words Owen argued that it was not through 'our faith and repentance, the renovation of our natures, inherent habits of grace, and actual works of righteousness which we have done, or may do' that salvation and peace with God come. Rather, as Owen cogently demonstrated from the Scriptures, sinful men and women have but one hope of being absolved from their sins, namely, through God's 'effectual grant and donation of a true, real, perfect righteousness, even that of Christ himself, unto all that do believe'.[19] Grimshaw pored over Owen's treatise till he came to the point where, in his words, 'I was now willing to renounce myself, every degree of fancied merit and ability, and to embrace Christ only for my all in all. O what light and comfort did I now enjoy in my own soul, and what a taste of the pardoning love of God!'[20]

When Grimshaw left Todmorden in 1742 for the curacy of Haworth, he was a changed man and had fully embraced the doctrine of justification by faith alone, which lay at the heart of the Evangelical Revival, then beginning to have an impact on many areas of the British Isles. Almost immediately after Grimshaw's arrival in Haworth, the church there experienced a profound revival. From a mere dozen communicants at the Lord's Table when Grimshaw first conducted the quarterly communion service, there were soon 400 to 500 in the winter and as many as 1,200 in the summer. The force and ferment of this revival can be seen in a description by Joseph Williams (1692-1755), a Dissenter from Kidderminster, of a talk he had with a woman in Halifax: 'She told me she went about Midsummer to spend a Sabbath with Mr G[rimshaw], found a crouded *[sic]* church, which will at least contain a thousand and almost as many without, for whom there was no room within the walls. He spent two hours in expounding the Lord's Prayer that morning, and his word came with power.'[21]

Grimshaw, unlike many of his fellow ministers in the Church of England, regularly preached without notes and in language easily comprehensible by his congregation — 'market language' his critics called it. He was not afraid of using colloquial words in the pulpit, or even of coining new ones. Filled with pithy phrases and striking images, his style of preaching was well suited to drive home the gospel to the hearts of rough and ready Yorkshire men and women. William Crabtree, later to be the Baptist minister of Bradford, was arrested and converted through one such statement: 'One sin would damn a soul as well as a thousand!'[22]

Crabtree was not the only future Baptist among those converted in the early years of the Haworth revival; a goodly number of Grimshaw's converts became Baptists, including such prominent Baptist leaders as Richard Smith, James Hartley (d.1780) and John Parker (1725-1793). Grimshaw took this all in his stride and was even able to joke about it, saying, 'So many of my chickens turn ducks!'[23] Nor was Grimshaw's influence on Baptist life and witness in Yorkshire limited to those directly converted through his preaching. John Fawcett, who had become a Christian through the preaching of George Whitefield,[24] frequently used to trudge the nine or so miles over the moors from Bradford to hear Grimshaw. Moreover,

Fawcett's commitment to the Baptist denomination was derived both from his reading of Scripture and also from his friendship with three of Grimshaw's converts: William Crabtree, who baptized him in 1758 and of whose congregation in Bradford he was a member for six years following his baptism; James Hartley, pastor of the revitalized Baptist cause in Haworth; and Richard Smith, whom he succeeded as pastor of Wainsgate in 1764.[25]

## Fawcett's ministry

Not only were the first two pastors of Wainsgate powerfully influenced by Grimshaw, but many of the early members had come to Christ under his ministry. The church, located a mere five or six miles from Haworth, was thus a direct result of the revival. But when Fawcett came to the church, he found it in a state of disarray, wracked by controversy over the speculations of John Johnson, the Liverpool Baptist with a penchant for theological polemic. The controversy had arisen during the final months of Smith's pastorate, when Smith, a dying man, had been incapable of preaching and leading the church. Fawcett, however, had great personal tact and was a very peace-loving individual — according to his son, he had 'an utter aversion' to controversy.[26] He was thus able to calm the waters and resolve the conflict.

However, Fawcett's dislike of controversy did not prevent him from indicating clearly where he stood with regard to High Calvinism. He had seen first hand in the Bradford church the way in which High Calvinism could foster an atmosphere of morbid introspection and cramp evangelistic outreach. Furthermore, his wide reading of such Puritan authors as John Flavel (*c.*1630-1691), Matthew Henry (1662-1714) and especially Oliver Heywood (1629-1702) made him aware of an alternative to the High Calvinism then prevalent in so many Baptist causes in the north of England. In these pastors and writers from a previous generation he found an evangelical Calvinism that was committed to the proclamation of the gospel to all and sundry.

Help was also received from a few northern Baptist pastors of his own day, men like Alvery Jackson (d.1763), who were forthright in their advocacy of this older version of Calvinism. The pastor of Barnoldswick Baptist Church — now in Lancashire — Jackson was a long-standing critic of the views of High Calvinists such as John Johnson and John Brine. His one major publication was a trenchant refutation of High Calvinism, published in London in 1752.

Finally, the experience of having heard Whitefield's evangelistic preaching had left an indelible impression on Fawcett's mind which 'remained unabated to the end of his life' and laid down the lines upon which he was to pursue his own ministry.[27] Shaped by these various influences, Fawcett's pastoral ministry at Wainsgate, and then later in Hebden Bridge, was distinguished by an untrammelled proclamation of the gospel. Fawcett never argued for his convictions in a polemical fashion, though he did compose a ditty at Wainsgate about them, the last lines of which declared:

> To be brief, my dear friends, you may say what you will,
> I'll ne'er be confined to read nothing but Gill.[28]

In view of these words and Fawcett's decided theological convictions, it is fascinating to note that when Gill, the doyen of High Calvinist Baptist theologians, was ill in the spring of 1771, Fawcett was asked to preach a number of times in his stead and after Gill had died in October that year, Fawcett was the first to be asked to succeed him as pastor, a request he seriously considered but eventually declined.[29]

Fawcett's commitment to evangelical Calvinism began to bear visible fruit during the late 1760s when there was a considerable revival in his congregation. The meeting-house became too small to accommodate the many who came to worship and sit under his preaching. A gallery was consequently erected and the interior of the church altered so as to provide more seating. It was during this period of revival that Sutcliff, in the words of John Fawcett, Jr, was 'brought to a saving knowledge of the truth'.[30] According to Fuller, his conversion took place in 'the sixteenth or seventeenth year of his age,' that is, in either 1767 or 1768.[31] The Fawcett memoirs do not mention the actual time of his conversion. Both sources, though, do specify that it was in 1769 that Sutcliff became a member of the church, presumably upon his having been baptized by Fawcett.[32] Along with five others, three men and two women, he was added to the membership of the Wainsgate congregation on 28 May 1769.[33]

Wainsgate Baptist Church

## Sutcliff's conversion and early spiritual growth

Undoubtedly Sutcliff's family and the preaching of John Fawcett were key factors in Sutcliff's conversion. Mention should also be made, though, of one other individual who appears to have played a role in his becoming a Christian. John Fawcett, Jr tells us that in either 1767 or 1768 Sutcliff 'occasionally assisted the Rev. Dan Taylor, in a school which he had established at Birchcliffe,' on the outskirts of Hebden Bridge.[34] Dan Taylor (1738-1816), a former Wesleyan Methodist, had embraced Baptist principles in 1762, though without shedding his Arminian convictions. He founded the first General (i.e. Arminian) Baptist church in Yorkshire at Birchcliffe the following year, and united himself and the church with the General Baptists, the oldest stream of English Baptists, whose existence went back to the early years of the seventeenth century. For much of that century they had been brimming with evangelistic zeal and energy, but by the mid-eighteenth century they were largely moribund and many of them denied the essential deity of Christ. In the words of Taylor, 'They degraded Jesus Christ, and He degraded them.'[35] As a denomination the General Baptists firmly resisted Taylor's attempts to move them back towards a robust orthodoxy, and so in 1770, together with a few other General Baptist pastors and churches, Taylor formed the New Connection of General Baptists.

Now, during the early years of Taylor's ministry at Birchcliffe, he established a school in order to educate children of the area as well as to augment his income. At the same time he was assiduously meeting with John Fawcett three or four days a week to study theology and classical literature.[36] It was surely in the course of these meetings that Taylor first heard of Sutcliff from Fawcett, and especially of Sutcliff's 'fondness for books' and aptitude for study.[37] Enquiries were made and Sutcliff was taken on as an occasional assistant in Taylor's school. During his time with Taylor, Sutcliff not only gave instruction; he also received it — the General Baptist minister instructing him in the rudiments of Latin grammar and, Fawcett's son states, 'in the best things,' that is, the essential truths of Christianity.[38] Conversation with Taylor about spiritual matters and observation of his tireless zeal for Christ would certainly have left their mark on Sutcliff and helped to reinforce what he had learned in his home and what he was hearing at Wainsgate.

Something of the ardour and seriousness with which Sutcliff approached his new life in Christ is discernible in the earliest pieces of his correspondence that we possess. The first, dated 8 September 1770, was written to him by a close friend named William Thomas (d.1773), who became a member of Wainsgate exactly one year after he had penned this letter and who later described Sutcliff as a 'bosom companion — one that is dear to me as my own soul'.[39] Sutcliff and Thomas had apparently been mulling over whether or not the directive of the Jerusalem Council to Gentile believers to 'abstain from meats offered to idols, and from blood, and from things strangled' (Acts 15:29) was still in force. Thomas was positive that it was not. These items were forbidden by the council, he stated, only because Jewish aversion to them prevented them from conversing freely with any who ate such items. Of course, Thomas concluded, if their churches were in similar circumstances, Christian charity would surely require them to put themselves under the same restraints.[40] The interest of this letter lies not so much in its actual contents as in the fact that it shows us Sutcliff, at this early stage in his Christian life, seriously studying the Scriptures with fellow believers, and pondering their interpretation and proper application for his own generation.

In the days following his conversion Sutcliff not only discovered the fascination of the study of the Scriptures, but also a scriptural emphasis which had long been a hallmark of Reformed teaching: regeneration makes the heart a battlefield between the Holy Spirit who has come to inhabit the believer's heart and the remnants of indwelling sin. Five months after Sutcliff received Thomas's letter, he wrote to Fawcett complaining of this warfare. His pastor responded in a letter dated 9 February 1771: 'That you are still attended with complaints of the power and strength of indwelling sin, is no matter of surprise to me. We find one of the most eminent of Christ's servants crying out on this account, "O wretched man!" (Romans 7:24). Be not discouraged, my dear Brother, Christ was manifested that he might destroy the works of the devil. Carry your sins and lusts to the foot of his cross, lay open your sores, your wounds and bruises before him, and put him in mind that he hath said, "I will in no wise cast out" (John 6:37). Wrestle with him for sin-subduing grace, and lay hold on his strength by the hand of faith. Millions of poor sinners have taken this course, and none ever failed of success. No mean[s] so effectual for the mortification of sin as constant converse with Jesus in this manner. May the good Lord establish your heart with grace and confirm you to the end. Assure yourself of my steady affection for you, as one of the children God has given me.'[41]

Fawcett is not at all surprised at Sutcliff's discovery. Following the traditional Reformed interpretation of Romans 7, he expresses his belief that warfare between the Spirit and indwelling sin is part and parcel of the normal Christian life. His remedy, moreover, is one of which his Calvinistic forebears would have readily approved. Seek to mortify indwelling sin, he tells his young friend, by being honest with Christ about all the struggles and failures, confessing them and pleading for 'sin-subduing grace', which he alone can give. His final assurance of love for Sutcliff would also have encouraged the young man to persevere in his Christian walk.

That April Sutcliff wrote to Fawcett to let him know that he was finding 'a growing pleasure in religious opportunities, and the thought of being deprived of them would be very distressing'. For, the more that he engages in religious exercises, the more he experiences their power and 'the more enjoyment and satisfaction' he derives from them: 'The path of duty is not only the path of safety, but of pleasure.' Nevertheless, he confesses, the affections of his heart are still so easily diverted; his 'heart is perpetually prone to forsake the Lord, and to turn aside to crooked paths'.[42] Fawcett probably would not have been too disconcerted by this confession. His February letter had, after all, encouraged Sutcliff to think of the normal Christian life as one of continual warfare with the flesh, in which victory is found through an ever-increasing reliance on Christ.

Contact between Sutcliff and Fawcett during this period was obviously not restricted to written correspondence. There would have been opportunities to chat on Sundays and Sutcliff, 'having an increasing desire to improve his mind,' frequently visited his pastor during the week.[43] On these latter occasions Fawcett helped him to hone his understanding of English grammar as well as giving him help in the study of classical literature. At one point — probably during the latter months of 1771 — Sutcliff lived for several weeks at a house near the church so that he could better pursue his studies with Fawcett. That Fawcett, amongst his many other labours, made the time to tutor Sutcliff in this way indicates his sure grasp of the vital importance of theological training from the early days of his ministry at Wainsgate. After Sutcliff there was to be a steady stream of ministerial candidates whom he educated in his own home, including William Ward, Carey's distinguished colleague. Fawcett's efforts in this regard paved the way for the formation of the Northern Education Society in 1804 and the establishment of a seminary at Bradford the following year.

Sutcliff's evident hunger for spiritual and academic knowledge, his desire to wed that knowledge to practice, coupled with the fact that he appeared to possess gifts suited to pastoral ministry, eventually led Fawcett and the Wainsgate congregation to recommend him for formal study at the Bristol Baptist Academy, the sole institution at that time in Britain where men could train for the Baptist ministry. Obviously eager to begin such full-time studies, Sutcliff left West Yorkshire for Bristol in January 1772, walking the entire distance of two hundred or so miles in about a week. In total the trip cost him around twenty shillings.[44] The construction of a national network of turnpike roads — a development which was at its height during the 1750s and 1760s — undoubtedly facilitated the journey. If he had attempted the same walk thirty years earlier in the depth of winter it would most likely have been much more costly, both in terms of time and money.

After Sutcliff left his home on that winter's day in January 1772, he would never again be a permanent resident in his native shire. He would be a frequent visitor, both in person and by letter, and the cause of Christ in Yorkshire would never be far from his mind and heart — but henceforth, his home and ministry lay to the south. The north of England, though, had not sent him forth totally unprepared. In Fawcett especially he had had an exceptionally good mentor: as an evangelical Calvinist, a product of the Evangelical Revival and one who was conscious of the vital importance of theological education, Fawcett's influence on Sutcliff cannot be regarded as anything but considerable. As Fuller told him many years later, 'We are indebted to you for … Sutcliff.'[45]

# 3.
# Bristol, 'the metropolis of the West'

> *'Every increase of religious knowledge should not only make me wiser, but better; not only make my head more clear, but purify my heart, influence my affections, and regulate my life'*
> (John Sutcliff).

At the turn of the eighteenth century, Bristol was, in the words of Defoe, 'the greatest, the richest, and the best Port of Trade in Great Britain, London only excepted'.[1] Half a century after Defoe wrote these words, though — at the time when Sutcliff first set eyes on the town — Bristol's position of prominence was being eclipsed. Not only were other towns, like Manchester and Liverpool, outstripping it in terms of population growth, but also its standing as the second most prominent centre of commerce in the nation had clearly been taken by Liverpool. Nevertheless, this decline in relative importance, which continued well into the next century, would probably not have materially affected Sutcliff's impression of Bristol as a bustling metropolis. To many who visited the town throughout the eighteenth century, the streets of Bristol — a good number of them narrow and confining, and dating back to the Middle Ages — appeared to be swarming with people 'all ... in a hurry, running up and down with cloudy looks, and busy faces, loading, carrying and unloading goods and merchandizes of all sorts'.[2] In *A Tour through the South of England* (1791), E. D. Clarke told his readers that in Bristol there might be found 'all the throng and bustle of the metropolis' and 'so exactly the confusion of London that it requires a very slight exertion of the fancy to imagine oneself absolutely in the Strand'.[3] For Sutcliff, living in such a busy metropolis would certainly have been something of a contrast to his early years in West Yorkshire.

In one important respect, however, Bristol was quite similar to West Yorkshire: like Yorkshire it was fertile ground for various forms of religious Nonconformity. As Defoe observed, 'There are in Bristol ... many Meeting-Houses, especially Quakers.'[4] When Defoe made this observation, Dissenters actually comprised close to twenty per cent of Bristol's population; in fact, after London, the town had the largest community of Dissenters in England. Of this twenty per cent, slightly more than a quarter were Quakers, since George Fox (1624-1691), one of the leading figures in early Quakerism, had made Bristol an important base for his activities in the West Country. And after 1739, when both Whitefield and John Wesley found such signal success in open-air preaching to the colliers at Kingswood, which lay on the outskirts of Bristol, the town also became a key centre for Methodism. It was here in Bristol, for instance, that the first distinctively Methodist chapel, the New Room, was erected in 1739. Enlarged ten years later, possibly under the direction of the Quaker architect George Tully, it bears many of the marks of Nonconformist architecture, not least in the fact that it is 'a building beautiful in its simplicity'.[5]

## The Bristol Baptist Academy

The Calvinistic Baptists also put down roots deep into Bristol soil. In the eighteenth century there were two flourishing works in the city, Broadmead and Pithay, both of which had come into existence during the turbulent years of the English Civil War. It was an elder of the Broadmead congregation, Edward Terrill (1634-*c.*1685), who, in his will, had made provision for a fund for the subsistence of one of the ministers at Broadmead, 'an holy man, well skilled in the Greek and Hebrew tongues,' who would be responsible for the ministerial preparation of other men in the context of his own pastoral ministry.[6] It was not, however, until Bernard Foskett (1685-1758) came to be the assistant minister of Broadmead in 1720 and his stipend was paid out of the Terrill Trust that the vision of the seventeenth-century Broadmead elder became a reality in the form of the Bristol Baptist Academy.

No records of the academy exist prior to 1770. The Broadmead minute books, though, do indicate that there was a steady stream of students, mostly from Wales and the West Country, who studied under Foskett and his Welsh assistant, Hugh Evans (1713-1781). John Rippon (1750-1836), who later studied under Evans with Sutcliff and who later still became an influential London pastor, candidly stated that Foskett was not the 'first of tutors', but was a somewhat severe man, whose methods of teaching employed memory work more than reasoning. Yet, Rippon went on to say, 'Some good scholars, and several of the greatest ministers who have adorned our denomination since the days of the reformation, were educated by him.'[7] Among the scholars and ministers whom Rippon had in mind were men such as Benjamin Beddome, John C. Ryland, John Ash (1724-1779) and Benjamin Francis (1734-1799) — and Foskett's own assistant, Hugh Evans. When Foskett died in 1758, Evans succeeded him as pastor of Broadmead and principal of the academy, positions which he ably filled till his death. During most of Evans' tenure as principal, he was assisted in the academy by his son, Caleb Evans (1737-1791), who, following his father's death, was made principal as well as pastor of the church.[8]

Of Hugh Evans it was said by Rippon that 'Every one who sat at his feet recognized in him a friend and a father.'[9] Evans took a keen interest in all of the students who entered the academy and sought to be a genuine father in God to them. It was a relationship, moreover, which he strove to maintain even after the students had passed from under his direct care. As Rippon noted of himself and his fellow-students, 'When we no longer enjoyed the bosom of our Alma Mater, nor rested under his shade, he interested himself in our history: his sympathy lessened our sorrows, and his participation with us increased our joys.'[10] As a preacher, whom the students regularly heard at Broadmead expounding the Scriptures, he was a model of clarity and forthrightness. One who habitually preached without notes, he especially knew how to inform and convince the minds of his audience of the truth of the Scriptures and then, on the basis of the truth, to kindle 'all their noblest passions into a blaze of devotion'.[11] His son, Caleb Evans, remembered how as a young man his father's preaching 'brought [him] into the very dust before the throne of a holy God, and enabled [him] to magnify the riches of free grace'.[12]

Along with this giftedness in preaching Hugh Evans also possessed a gift in prayer which was 'uncommon' and his students thought 'unequalled'. 'In the family,' Rippon recalled, 'at occasional meetings, in the services of the Lord's day, and upon extraordinary occasions, with copiousness, dignity, and warmth of devotion, he poured out his soul unto God; and yet with such variety, that he was seldom, if ever, heard to pray twice alike.'[13]

Rippon's mention of having heard Evans pray 'in the family' is noteworthy, for it is an indication of the fact that students at the academy lived with the principal and tutor in their homes, where they were taught and where they shared in many of the facets of their teachers' daily lives. For a young man like Sutcliff, only nineteen when he arrived in the bustling metropolis of Bristol, this arrangement would certainly have helped to overcome any initial culture shock and feelings of homesickness he might have had. More importantly, it was in the context of an intimate, family atmosphere that Sutcliff was educated in Christian doctrine and ancillary subjects. He saw lived out before him in the lives of Hugh and Caleb Evans the practical application of much of what he was learning. The divorce between doctrine and devotion, between theory and practice, which has so often bedevilled Christian theological education would to some extent have been avoided by such a context of study.

In 1770, two years prior to Sutcliff's arrival, the academy had been reconstituted on a broader and more solid financial foundation with the establishment of the Bristol Education Society. The idea of the society had come from Caleb Evans. As Rippon, who was a student at the time, later recalled regarding the younger Evans' involvement in the origins of this society, 'He devised — he planned — he executed.'[14] The aim of the society was to solicit generous financial support for the academy from Calvinistic Baptist churches throughout Britain in the form of either capital investments or annual subscriptions. In this way, the academy would be able to train a greater number of ministers and thus supply more destitute churches 'with a succession of able and evangelical ministers'.[15] The churches' response to the society's formation was a gratifying success. In the first year of the society's existence £474.19.0 in capital investments were given and £106.1.0 in annual subscriptions.[16] Due to the establishment of this society, the academy enjoyed in subsequent years a substantial degree of financial security and stability.

## Sutcliff's studies at the academy

The young Sutcliff who arrived in Bristol was tall for his day, nearly six feet in height, and thin. During the last twenty years of his life, 'he gathered flesh,' to use the words of Andrew Fuller, though not to the point where he would be considered fat. His silhouette reveals a face characterized by a prominent Roman nose, the source of some amusement for his closest friends. Fuller further tells us that 'His face was grave but cheerful.' Robert Hall, Jr (1764-1831), similarly speaks of the 'mild and placid cheerfulness which marked his countenance and deportment'.

Silhouette of John Sutcliff

The basic goals of the course of study which Sutcliff pursued during his time at Bristol were outlined by Hugh Evans in a sermon which he preached before the Bristol Education Society in 1773. Near the end of the sermon he stated that the academy sought 'to instruct them [i.e. the students] into the knowledge of the languages in which the scriptures were written, to give them a just view of language in general, and of their own in particular, to teach them to express themselves with propriety upon whatever subject they discourse of, and to lead them into an acquaintance with those several branches of literature in general, which may be serviceable to them, with the blessing of God, in the exercise of their ministry. In a word, the design of this institution is to contribute what we can, towards the church and world's having able ministers of the new testament.'[17]

It is not without significance that Evans placed at the head of this list of goals the ability to read the Scriptures in the original Hebrew and Greek. In his opinion this ability enabled the student of the Scriptures to avoid the problem of always having to view them through the 'medium of fallible and varying translations'. Moreover, as his son maintained, without some knowledge of the languages in which the Scriptures were originally written, 'A man must be very poorly qualified indeed to undertake the instruction of others into the meaning, spirit and force of the scriptures, or to defend the truths contained in them.'[18]

As to the details of the curriculum which Sutcliff followed at Bristol, there is a report of his studies in his final year, 1773-1774, which he drew up when he was about to leave the academy in May 1774.[19] According to this report, Sutcliff 'read' and presumably translated the following works into English: some of the speeches of the famous Roman orator Cicero (106-43 B.C.); several books of the Latin epic poem *Aeneid* by Virgil (70-19 B.C.); a number of the Psalms which the Scottish historian George Buchanan (1506-1582) had paraphrased in Latin; *De officio hominis et civis juxta legem naturalem* (The Whole Duty of Man according to the Law of Nature) by Samuel Pufendorf (1632-1694), a German professor of law, which was first published in 1673; certain portions of *On the Truth of the Christian Religion* (1622) by the Dutch theologian and jurist Hugo Grotius (1583-1645); sections of the letters and Gospels of the New Testament; some of the writings of the Greek author Xenophon (*c.*430-*c.*355 B.C.); a number of the Hebrew Psalms and twenty chapters of Genesis in Hebrew. In addition, Sutcliff studied in its entirety *The Principal Rules of Hebrew Grammar,* which

Caleb Ashworth (1722-1775) published in 1763 for the academy at Daventry, where he taught.

A brief glance at this list of books which Sutcliff studied and translated clearly reveals that the student at Bristol received a good grounding in classical and ecclesiastical Latin, classical and New Testament Greek, as well as Hebrew. Like many other academies run by Dissenters in the eighteenth century, what was required of students at Bristol with regard to facility in these classical languages was literally amazing. In Sutcliff's case, his time at Bristol gave him a solid grasp of New Testament and *koiné* Greek such that close to thirty years after leaving Bristol he could produce a fairly good translation of *The Epistle to Diognetus,* a pearl of the patristic era that was written in the second century A.D.

Sutcliff's report on his final year of studies continued by indicating that he had spent some time in the study of philosophy and geography, and had also read Isaac Watts' *Logick: or, the Right Use of Reason in the Enquiry after Truth* (1725) and *Rhetoric; or, a View of its principal Tropes and Figures* (1767) by Thomas Gibbons (1720-1785). Watts' *Logick* was a highly successful attempt to make the study of logic accessible to a wide range of readers in the eighteenth century. It was much admired in its day and served as a text in schools throughout the English-speaking world, including the Universities of Oxford and Cambridge. Thomas Gibbons' *Rhetoric* was not as widely used, but its author was personally known to Caleb Evans, since Gibbons had been his tutor at Mile End Academy in London. Finally, every week Sutcliff had prepared an essay on a passage of Scripture and drawn up an abridgement of various sections of John Gill's *A Body of Doctrinal Divinity,* which had been published only a few years earlier in 1769. Gill's volume seems to have served as the academy's main textbook in dogmatic theology.

A further indication of the sort of reading which Sutcliff would have done during his time at the academy is found in 'A Catalogue of a few useful Books', which Caleb Evans drew up in 1773 for one of the students, probably Thomas Dunscombe (1748-1811), and which John Rippon later published.[20] Evans first gave advice regarding which editions of the Hebrew Old Testament, the Septuagint (the Greek translation of the Old Testament) and the Greek New Testament to purchase, and what were the best available dictionaries and concordances. The 'Catalogue' then lists what Evans considered to be the most valuable commentaries, the best books dealing with revelation and the defence of Christianity against the Deists, various indispensable theological works and collections of sermons. It concludes with a few choice biographies, some significant histories and various miscellaneous books dealing with philosophy and natural science. Isaac Watts and Philip Doddridge, both of them evangelical Calvinists, are the authors most cited. However, John Gill's classic defence of Calvinism, *The Cause of God and Truth* (1735-1738), and his exhaustive nine-volume exposition of the Old and New Testaments, which was published over a twenty-year span from 1746 to 1766, are also given high commendation. Nevertheless, despite this recommendation of Gill's writings — and the use of Gill's *A Body of Doctrinal Divinity* as a textbook in theology — the younger Evans was not prepared to follow him in all things. With many, he noted, Gill is 'the touchstone of orthodoxy'. But evidently not with him; for it was the evangelical Calvinist Jonathan Edwards, not Gill the High Calvinist, to whom he gave the highest praise as being 'the most rational, scriptural divine, and the liveliest Christian, the world was ever blessed with'. Edwards' writings had deeply influenced the younger Evans' thinking, a fact which had great significance for Sutcliff's theological formation.

In his funeral sermon for Sutcliff, Andrew Fuller confessed that he did not know when his friend 'first became acquainted with the writings of President Edwards'.[21] There is a distinct possibility that it was John Fawcett who introduced Sutcliff to Edwards' works, since Fawcett was reading what was available of the New England divine's writings in the 1760s. Caleb Evans' high admiration of Edwards' works would then have reinforced Sutcliff's early exposure to Edwards in West Yorkshire. On the other hand, as the English Baptist historian Roger Hayden has recently argued, it is quite possible that it was Evans who first made Sutcliff aware of the American theologian.[22] Whatever the exact origins of Sutcliff's interest in Edwards' theological perspective, however, there is little doubt that, after the Scriptures, the writings of Edwards exercised the greatest influence in shaping Sutcliff's theology. More than any other eighteenth-century author, Edwards showed Sutcliff, and fellow Baptists like Fawcett and Evans, how to combine a commitment to Calvinism with a passion for revival, fervent evangelism and experiential religion.[23]

## Training men to be 'able ministers'

Alongside this formal study there was also a great emphasis at Bristol on the cultivation of Christian spirituality and on practice in preaching and itinerant evangelism.[24] In an address which Caleb Evans delivered to the students on 12 April 1770, he forthrightly declared at the very beginning of the address that the only proper way to become 'a good and useful Preacher' was to 'learn to be a zealous lover of Christ'. As a means to this end Evans went on to recommend 'reading the word of God with other practical and experimental [i.e. experiential] writings, meditation, self-examination and prayer'. This attention to the cultivation of one's own walk with God, Evans stressed, is the student's first and leading priority. If it came to a conflict between spending time in these spiritual disciplines and fulfilling other priorities, Evans was adamant that the student's other priorities should take second place. For, he said, 'If you are not lively Christians, you are not likely to be either comfortable or useful Ministers.' He hoped that 'One hour at least will be devoted every morning and evening to these exercises.'[25] Sutcliff definitely paid close attention to this advice, which Evans presumably gave to each incoming class of students. In a diary which Sutcliff kept during his time at Bristol, he stated, in words that clearly echo his tutor, Caleb Evans, 'The way to lose the sense of religion upon my heart, is to live in the neglect of private duties.'[26]

The primary goal of the academy, as set forth in the portion of Hugh Evans' sermon of 1773 which was cited above, was to supply the churches of the Calvinistic Baptist denomination with 'able ministers of the new testament'. Understandably, therefore, there was a considerable emphasis placed upon student preaching. The sort of preaching that was encouraged was first of all that which was Christ-centred and Christ-exalting, preaching that focused on the glory of Christ's person and the marvel of his work. 'The grand business ... of a gospel minister,' Caleb Evans told Thomas Dunscombe at the latter's ordination on 4 August 1773, 'must be to preach Christ.'[27] Second, it was preaching that was clearly aimed at drawing men and women to worship and adore the triune God. It was preaching with a distinctly evangelistic thrust. When he preached Christ, Evans told Dunscombe, he must not neglect highlighting 'the *ability* of Christ to save; to save the very chief of sinners, to save unto the *uttermost*, to save *all* that come to God by him. Preach the *willingness* of Christ to save. Tell poor broken-hearted sinners, that the smoking flax he will not quench, the bruised reed he will not break, and that whosoever cometh to him he will in *no wise* cast out.'[28]

During Sutcliff's time at Bristol, a number of students were also involved in itinerant evangelism. For instance, John Geard (1749-1838) — who was originally from Yeovil, Somerset, and was later pastor at Hitchin, Hertfordshire, for fifty-seven years — spent a good deal of the summer of 1773 preaching throughout Cornwall. When he wrote to Sutcliff from Falmouth on 9 August 1773, he told him that in the previous seven weeks he had ridden 600 miles and preached some fifty times. 'May the Lord quicken us,' he concluded his letter, and 'enflame us with a zeal for his glory and with love to immortal souls'.[29]

## Sutcliff preaches at Trowbridge

Sutcliff gained much of his experience in preaching at Trowbridge in Wiltshire, about twenty miles south-east of Bristol. After arriving at Bristol, his first Sundays were presumably spent at Broadmead, where he was admitted to transient communion on 9 February 1772.[30] From 5 July to 30 August of that year, though, he preached every Sunday at Trowbridge, and thereafter was in the Trowbridge pulpit one Sunday out of every month till he left Bristol in May 1774.[31]

Calvinistic Baptists were present in Trowbridge as far back as the late 1660s, when a number of vital Baptist causes were being established in towns and villages along the Wiltshire-Somerset border. Many of the leading members of these nascent works were clothiers, weavers and self-employed artisans, although there were a few who were landed gentry and farmers. By 1669 the conventicle in Trowbridge, which became known as the Conigre Church, was meeting in the house of an Edward Grant and was united with the nearby Southwick congregation as two branches of the same church. Doctrinal differences in the first couple of decades of the eighteenth century, however, began to force these two branches apart. John Davisson (d.1721) was the pastor of the two congregations during these decades, and was 'noted for his zeal, piety, and usefulness'. Yet, a few years before his death, he is said to have embraced Socinianism, a heterodox system of theology with denies the essential deity of Christ.[32] His successor, Thomas Lucas, definitely was a Socinian. The Southwick church consequently refused to recognize Lucas as their pastor, and broke off fellowship with the Trowbridge congregation. As Joseph Ivimey (1773-1834), the nineteenth-century Baptist historian, observed, the embracing of Socinian doctrine by the Conigre Church was somewhat exceptional for a Calvinistic Baptist church in the eighteenth century. 'We have met with but few instances,' he wrote, 'of the particular baptist churches going into the error of Socinianism.'[33]

A further split took place within the Trowbridge congregation in 1736, when a number of members who were faithful to Trinitarian doctrine and Calvinism left to form Back Street Church in Trowbridge (known as Emmanuel Baptist Church after 1902). During the late eighteenth century this congregation experienced strong growth. In 1767 there were seventy-three members — twenty-one men and fifty-two women. Thirty years later, under the leadership of Nathaniel Rawlins (1734-1809), a Bristol graduate, the membership had risen to 135. In fact, during his thirty-seven years as pastor of the church — from 1765 to 1771 and from 1778 to 1809 — Rawlins baptized close to 180 people.

Now, on the occasions when Sutcliff — his name appears as 'Sucleff' or 'Suckleff' in the minute book — preached at Back Street Church, he would ride over from the academy, stable his horse for the day, and then ride back at night. Like those of many budding preachers, his early attempts at preaching were not without their problems. His uncle, William Sutcliff, told him in a letter written on 1 October 1773 that when John preached, his voice was 'some times rather too low'.[34] Benjamin Beddome heard him nearly two years later and he too was somewhat disappointed at the way in which Sutcliff delivered his sermon.[35] Even as late as 1779, William Sutcliff could criticize his nephew's manner of preaching. 'You are some times too low,' he told him, and 'some times rather too high and some times rather too quick that you are not so intelligible as could be desired.'[36]

The Trowbridge congregation, however, did not allow whatever infelicities were present in Sutcliff's early attempts at preaching to prevent them from considering calling him to be their pastor. As Hugh Evans informed John Fawcett in June 1773, Sutcliff's ministry in Trowbridge had been 'much approved of by the church' and they 'had their eye upon him for their pastor'.[37] When the Trowbridge Baptists thought about Sutcliff's preaching, what they remembered most of all was the way it had been instrumental in the conversion of a number in their midst. Sally Grigg, for instance, had been converted when Sutcliff preached the funeral sermon of a certain Mary Larden from Micah 7:9. It was especially a passage from one of the Psalms upon which Sutcliff had focused in the course of the sermon — Psalm 89:30-33, which talks of God's love for and faithfulness to his people despite their sinful ways and his having to chastise them — that caught Sally's attention and resulted in her conversion.[38]

Some of the young people of the Trowbridge church consequently took it upon themselves to write to Sutcliff in the autumn of 1772 to let him know that they deeply missed his ministry week by week. 'Be pleased,' they wrote, 'to let us be favoured with your good company as soon as possible for we stand in great need of your admonitions and reproofs.' The letter finished by praying that God would send Sutcliff to them to be their 'guide and ... leader and director'.[39]

From what we shall see later of the care with which Sutcliff sought God's guidance as to the place of his ministry in late 1774 and early 1775, we can be certain that he must have given deep thought and much prayer to the desire of the congregation at Trowbridge to call him as their pastor. But by the end of 1773, he had definitely come to the conviction that Trowbridge was not to be the place of his future service.

## Friendships with fellow-students

Important in the life of any student are the friends whom he or she makes among his or her classmates. In the three years that Sutcliff studied at Bristol, there were at any one time easily a dozen students. Of these men with whom he studied, Sutcliff — who had a hunger for friendship throughout his life — became especially close to three: John Geard, who has already been mentioned; John Cooper, originally a member of Broadmead, who later became the pastor of the Baptist church at Bratton, not far from Trowbridge; and Thomas Purdy (d. 1820), who, after leaving Bristol, pastored the Baptist congregation at Chipping Norton in the Cotswolds.

There are at least three extant letters from Geard to Sutcliff. Two of them were written during Sutcliff's time at Bristol and relate to Geard's evangelistic tour of Cornwall; a portion of the second of these letters has been quoted above. The first letter, written on 5 July 1773 from Chacewater, provides an excellent insight into the evangelistic spirit which was prevalent at the academy during the principalship of Hugh Evans and with which Sutcliff became imbued. After telling Sutcliff about how he is going to spend his summer preaching in Cornwall, Geard expresses the hope that he and Sutcliff may 'never preach an unfelt gospel but continually feel the power and influence of the truths we deliver unto others upon our own hearts'.[40] Such sentiments — together with the use of the word 'feel' — are frequently encountered in the writings of those associated with the Evangelical Revival. Their presence here in Geard's letter, however, betrays the influence of the spirituality and evangelistic zeal of the Evanses. Caleb Evans, for instance, prayed on one occasion that the students at the academy 'might not be suffer'd to preach an unfelt gospel'.[41] These were sentiments with which Sutcliff was in wholehearted agreement.

Upon leaving Bristol Geard settled in Hitchin, a small market-town not far from Olney where Sutcliff eventually resided. Although Geard was pastor there all the time that Sutcliff lived in Olney, contact between the two men in later years appears to have been fairly limited. Geard's attitude towards High Calvinism may in part be responsible for this relative lack of contact between him and Sutcliff. When Sutcliff and some of his other friends like Andrew Fuller began to question the tenets of High Calvinism and bemoan its destructive effects on the life of their denomination, Geard considered their criticism to be 'little more than a strife of words'. In the ensuing controversy over High Calvinism — discussed in detail in later chapters — he was 'for keeping in with both sides'.[42] Given the seriousness of this controversy, Geard's attitude would have appeared to Sutcliff as highly irresponsible.

The correspondence of John Cooper with Sutcliff which still exists mainly concerns Cooper's bad experience at the Trowbridge church, where he supplied the pulpit for two years following Sutcliff's departure from Bristol. The letters were thus written after Sutcliff's time at the academy, but they do shed some light on his own experience at Trowbridge. In a letter which was written on 1 July 1775 and begins by describing Sutcliff as a 'bosom friend',

Cooper complains that a 'spirit of tattling and disaffection' prevails among the members of the church in Trowbridge. Many of them had 'enthusiastic notions' and were all for basing their Christian lives on their feelings. In particular, Cooper cites a view of preaching which was obviously shared by some members of the congregation, though whether it was prevalent or not is hard to say. According to Cooper, these members refused to sit under preaching that did not deeply stir their affections and emotions.[43] Whatever these observations may imply with regard to Cooper's own preaching, the fact that the Trowbridge congregation was prepared to call Sutcliff as their pastor must mean that they considered *his* preaching as lively and as having an impact not only on the mind, but also on the affections. In fact, a number of years later, Sutcliff was to observe that 'Since man is a compound being of judgement and affections ... each should be addressed in the Gospel Ministry.'[44]

Six months later Cooper wrote again. This time he told Sutcliff that his presence at the church was resented by a significant number of individuals, since they considered him to be theologically unsound. In particular one, William Crook, had taken offence at a statement which Cooper had made in a sermon to the effect that 'It was the duty of all men to pray.' Crook understood Cooper to be asserting that it was the duty of all men, saved or unsaved, to pray 'spiritually', that is, in a manner acceptable to God. Cooper denied this interpretation of his statement. But Crook, according to Cooper, never personally approached him to ask him what he actually meant, but simply spread it around the church that Cooper was 'not sound in principle'. Cooper was concerned because Crook had great influence in the church: 'His word ... goes a good way with many people,' he told Sutcliff. Apparently Caleb Evans had recommended that Cooper go to Trowbridge after Sutcliff had left, but in light of this squabble Cooper regretted ever having come to the church.[45] It appears that Crook and those who supported him may well have had High Calvinist tendencies. Was this one of the reasons why Sutcliff decided against settling in Trowbridge? We do not know, but in the final months of 1776 Cooper left Trowbridge for good and took up residence at Bratton, five miles or so away, where the local church paid him a handsome salary of fifty guineas a year. He was the pastor of this church till 1797.

Sutcliff's closest friend during his days in Bristol was undoubtedly Thomas Purdy, who, on one occasion, told Sutcliff that he considered it a great privilege to have a friend such as Sutcliff to whom he could 'unbosom [his] soul'. Like Geard, and obviously influenced by the Evanses, Purdy was fired with a great passion to participate in the advance of the kingdom of Christ. 'Shall we not,' he once asked Sutcliff, 'spread his [i.e. Christ's] fame from pole to pole? Shall we not wish to spend and be spent that hereby sin-sick souls may hear of him and hastily fly to him for a cure?'[46] Sutcliff had absolutely no hesitation in answering both of these questions with a resounding 'Yes'. As he wrote to Fawcett, his former pastor and early mentor, in November 1773, 'If we cast our eyes around, what a solemn sight! Souls, immortal, souls by multitudes hastening into another world, who have never called seriously to mind why they came into this! Let us cry aloud and not spare, be "instant in season and out of season," "abounding in the work of the Lord" (2 Timothy 4:2; 1 Corinthians 15:58).'[47]

In the year following Sutcliff's departure from the academy, Purdy's friendship would prove to be especially important to Sutcliff, as the Yorkshireman sought to discern exactly where God would have him serve. It was a difficult year for Sutcliff, as we shall see, and Purdy proved to be a marvellous friend to him.

## News of old friends and the first meeting with a new one

Despite the burden of his studies, his involvement in the work at Trowbridge, the time he would have spent with his friends at the academy and occasional bouts of ill-health, Sutcliff did not lose contact with either his family or his friends back in West Yorkshire. For instance, a lengthy letter which his parents wrote at the end of February 1773 in response to a letter from their son informed him about church affairs in the north, the deaths of friends and acquaintances from smallpox, and afforded his parents an opportunity to remind their son that 'There never was a student, there never will be one, that shall prosper in the study of divinity, if he proves cold and indifferent' in his walk with Christ.[48]

Sutcliff also kept up a regular correspondence with John Fawcett, who told him in March 1773 that his 'letters give me more satisfaction than I can express'.[49] Later that year, however, on 29 May, Fawcett had the unenviable task of informing Sutcliff that William Thomas, with whom Sutcliff had enjoyed the study of

Scripture in his early days as a believer, had come down with smallpox.

The leading study on smallpox in eighteenth-century Britain is probably that by Peter E. Razzell, a medical historian. He believes that prior to widespread innoculation in the final three decades of the century most people in England in the eighteenth century would have contracted the disease. Furthermore, he argues that it was the leading cause of death during this period. Razzell's well-documented arguments have not won universal acceptance, however. Smallpox was a virulent killer, of that there is no doubt; but it may not have been as prominent as Razzell contends.[50] However, even if Razzell has exaggerated the number of deaths from smallpox, of all the diseases in the eighteenth century smallpox was the most feared. The onset of 'the speckled monster' — the graphic description given to smallpox by Edward Jenner (1749-1823), the English physician and discoverer of vaccination — in a locality brought terror and torment to those not yet stricken. Of the eight or so strains of the virus, some, like fulminating smallpox, had a 100 per cent mortality rate, while others, like mild smallpox, had a mortality rate of less than one per cent. In the more severe strains there were a variety of symptoms: feverish chills, inflammation of the cornea, torpor, convulsions, vomiting of blood and, of course, the eruption of the dreaded pustules, which, as they suppurated, gave off an offensive, fetid odour. The victims of the disease died either through blood-poisoning or massive haemorrhaging. Roughly one in five who contracted smallpox succumbed to it. Moreover, a good number of the strains of the virus left those who survived its ravages with pock marked faces and the immeasurable psychological scars which accompanied such disfigurement.

Unlike many of his contemporaries, William Thomas, when he discovered that he had smallpox, was able to remain 'serene and well composed in his mind'. For, as Fawcett told Sutcliff in his letter of 29 May, 'His hope is steadfast in Christ.' Fawcett was distressed to think that his young friend might die, but he had to admit to Sutcliff that Thomas had 'appeared for some time like a person ripening for glory.'[51] The day after Fawcett wrote this letter to Sutcliff was the Lord's Day. Fawcett was up early and went to visit Thomas about six o' clock in the morning. But at the very moment he reached the door of Thomas's home, the young man passed away. The previous day Thomas had told Fawcett he expected soon to be in Christ's 'presence where "there is fulness of joy," and at his right hand, where are "pleasures for evermore" (Psalm 16:11).' When Sutcliff learned of his dear friend's death, he wrote on the back of the last letter that he had received from him, 'He died full of comfort and good hope through grace. He left his relatives and friends in the deepest distress. Lord sanctify this affecting stroke!'[52]

The wound caused by his friend's death would still have been fresh when Sutcliff visited his parents later that summer and presumably saw Thomas's family, and maybe even the final resting-place of his friend's body. Leaving Yorkshire in July, Sutcliff returned to Bristol via Northampton and called on a distinguished alumnus of the Bristol Academy, John C. Ryland, pastor of College Lane Baptist Church. The elder Ryland lost little time in asking the young Bristol student if he would preach that evening. Thus, on the evening of Thursday, 22 July, Sutcliff preached in the pulpit of College Lane. The text of his sermon and its contents have not been recorded. But the elder Ryland's son, John Ryland, Jr, did note in his diary this occasion of their first meeting.[53] He was a kindred spirit to Sutcliff and, together with Andrew Fuller, the three men would form an inseparable trio. Sutcliff could not have known it at the time, but in Ryland God was giving him a friend the equal of the one he had lost in William Thomas.

## An invitation to Shrewsbury

One final important event of that summer of 1773 took place in late August, when, on the recommendation of Hugh Evans, the Baptist church in Shrewsbury, Shropshire, extended an invitation to Sutcliff to preach in their empty pulpit. As they indicated to Sutcliff, their church was 'a decaying interest', but they were hopeful that the Lord would 'yet appear for his people' and 'cause a revival to take place'.[54] The Baptist church at Shrewsbury dated from the 1650s, but until the end of the eighteenth century the number of Baptist congregations in the rest of Shropshire was fairly negligible. In 1773 the Shrewsbury congregation received a major blow, when there was a split over the issue of Calvinism. John Pyne, who had been minister of the church since 1762, seceded with a portion of the congregation and formed a General Baptist church in the same town.

Like most church splits, this one was attended with 'much bitterness and spleen', to quote Thomas Phillips (d.1815), a deacon of the church who wrote an important history of Shrewsbury.[55] In fact, Pyne, refusing to let sleeping dogs lie, wrote a number of abusive letters to his former congregation filled with the 'most inveterate language.'[56]

When the Calvinistic Baptists in Shrewsbury first approached Sutcliff, they asked him if he would consider coming 'for a month or two or more'. Sutcliff appears to have put them off; he had, after all, his studies to finish. In October Phillips travelled down to Bristol to see Sutcliff, obviously in an attempt to elicit a commitment from him. Sutcliff agreed to come the following June, after his course of study at Bristol had been completed. When he told Fawcett, the Yorkshire pastor said he was 'well satisfied' with Sutcliff's decision. 'Wherever you are,' he told him, 'I trust I shall be solicitously concerned for your happiness and success.'[57]

Lest it appear that Sutcliff was not concerned about the pastorless state of the Shrewsbury church, it needs to be noted that for much of this final year of Sutcliff's studies a John Sandys was supplying at the church. Sandys had studied under John C. Ryland at the latter's boarding-school for boys, and early in 1773 had been taken on by Fawcett to help in his teaching of ministerial candidates. This arrangement, however, did not work out. As Fawcett's son later observed, while Sandys was clearly possessed of a 'sterling piety', he did not have an aptitude for scholarship and study — in Fawcett's words, 'He does not appear to have been formed for that close, assiduous attention requisite in a seminary.'[58]

In February of the following year, Phillips wrote to Sutcliff and asked if he could possibly come before June, since the Shrewsbury deacon was not at all sure how much longer Sandys would be with them. Despite the split of the previous year, Phillips told Sutcliff that their church was well attended and had good prospects for further increase. Thus, 'The sooner you can come, the better.'[59] In April, Sutcliff let Phillips know that after he had finished his studies that May he was thinking of visiting a few friends on the way to Shrewsbury. Phillips was evidently a little annoyed at this piece of news. As he bluntly told Sutcliff, ''Tis quite necessary that you should come here as soon as [you] be dismissed from Bristol.' True, the congregation had been well supplied by Sandys; but ever since Sutcliff had agreed to come to the church they had literally 'been in a state of suspense', as they awaited his coming.[60] On Tuesday, 17 May, Phillips dispatched a second letter to Sutcliff, imperiously telling him that he expected him to be on his way to Shrewsbury via Oxford in a week or so.

Sutcliff received Phillips' letter as he was packing and making his final preparations to leave Bristol. Despite Phillips' two sharp letters, Sutcliff decided to stick by his original intention of visiting an acquaintance or two on the way from Bristol to Shrewsbury. In particular, he wanted to go to Birmingham, where he hoped to see the pastor of Cannon Street Baptist Church, James Turner, who was originally from the Rossendale Valley and was a friend of Sutcliff's uncle William. Obviously he would have to write and tell Phillips of his intentions. Before he did so, though, he had another important letter to write — the following brief, but heartfelt, letter of thanks to his tutors at the Academy and to the Bristol Education Society: 'Being about to leave the Academy, would beg liberty to return my warmest thanks for all favours conferred me. My situation has been very agreeable and comfortable to myself. Most sincerely wish that all your laudable attempts of this kind to do good, may be crowned with the desired success.'[61]

He did indeed have much for which to be thankful. He had received an education which gave him the linguistic, theological and homiletic tools requisite for a lifetime of pastoral ministry. Moreover, the evangelical Calvinism which he had learned from Fawcett had been strengthened and confirmed in the atmosphere of the academy. This process of strengthening and confirmation had made of him both an heir and a bearer of the rich tradition of evangelical Calvinism which had long prevailed in a number of West Country Baptist churches. Finally, with his tutors — Hugh and Caleb Evans — and with some fellow students — notably Thomas Purdy — he had formed friendships which continued to develop long after he had left the metropolis of the West Country.

Upon leaving Bristol Sutcliff travelled up to Birmingham by way of Evesham to visit — and, as it turned out, to assist briefly — James Turner. When Sutcliff informed Phillips of his whereabouts, the latter immediately wrote to Sutcliff in Birmingham and told him that he would meet him on the evening of 1 June in Wolverhampton, and from there convey him to Shrewsbury, which was about twenty-nine miles away. Sutcliff presumably met Phillips on that summer evening and in his company travelled to the leading town of

Shropshire, where he sincerely hoped he would have a ministry that would advance the glory of God. Before we follow Sutcliff's experience in Shrewsbury, however, something needs to be told of the early life and experience of John Ryland, Jr, whose acquaintance Sutcliff had made the previous summer and who was to play such an important rôle in his life and future ministry.

John Ryland, Jr

# 4.
# Sutcliff's friends: John Ryland, Jr

> *'True friendship is first enkindled by a spark from heaven, and heaven will never suffer it to go out, but it will burn to all eternity'* (Esther Edwards Burr).

John Ryland, Jr came from a long line of Dissenters.[1] His great-grandfather, also called John Ryland, was originally a member of the Baptist church at Hook Norton in Oxfordshire. In 1694 he transferred his membership to the Baptist cause at Alcester, Warwickshire. Of his eight children who survived infancy — all of whom were 'accounted persons of a religious character'[2] — it was his second son, Joseph Ryland (d.1748), who was the grandfather of John Ryland, Jr. The first wife of Joseph Ryland died childless. After her death he married 'a most excellent, religious woman' named Freelove Collett (d.1729), a member of the Baptist church at Bourton on the Water in Gloucestershire.[3] Among her ancestral relatives was reputedly John Colet (*c.* 1466-1519), the famous humanist and friend of Erasmus. Their eldest son was John Collett Ryland, who was born at Bourton-on-the-Water in 1723. Without a doubt one of the most colourful characters to grace the eighteenth-century English Baptist scene, John Collett Ryland had, to use the words of the Anglican evangelical John Newton (1725-1807), 'many particularities which gave him an originality of character'.[4]

### John C. Ryland (John Ryland, Sr)

Until 1741 J. C. Ryland's main pusuits in life were always being dressed in the height of fashion and card-playing. In that year, however, he was soundly converted in a revival which swept the Baptist community of Bourton-on-the-Water. Along with Ryland forty people or so were converted and subsequently received into the church.

Instrumental in this revival was the preaching of a young man who was supplying the pulpit at the time, Benjamin Beddome, only twenty-four years of age.[5] Beddome had studied under Foskett in Bristol, where his father, John Beddome (1674-1757), was the pastor of the Pithay church. Beddome first visited Bourton-on-the-Water in the spring of 1740, and for the next three years supplied both the Baptist pulpit in this extremely attractive Cotswolds village and that in Warwick. Eventually he received a call to be the pastor of the church in Bourton-on-the-Water, where he stayed till his death in 1795. Despite numerous personal trials, he had an extremely fruitful ministry. In 1743, the year of his ordination, there were around 100 members. Twenty or so years later, he had baptized close to 200 individuals and the membership stood at 183.[6] Also noteworthy are some of the men from this church who went into the ministry during Beddome's time as pastor: Nathaniel Rawlins, who has been mentioned in the previous chapter in relationship to the Trowbridge congregation; Richard Haynes (d.1768), who was baptized during the revival at Bourton-on-the-Water in 1741 and probably converted in it as well, had a ministry that was accompanied by great blessing at Bradford-on-Avon from 1750 until his death;[7] John Reynolds (1730-1792), who succeeded the High Calvinist theologian John Brine at Cripplegate Baptist Church in London (of Reynolds' ministry it was said at the time of his death that 'Nothing very remarkable attended' it, yet it was noted that he had a 'solicitude for the conversion of souls'[8]) and John Collett Ryland.

With the encouragement of Beddome, Ryland studied at Bristol from 1744 to 1745. Bristol, as has already been mentioned, was an important centre at this time for the Evangelical Revival. A fascinating diary which Ryland kept during this period reveals that he did not miss the opportunity which Bristol offered of hearing some of the revival's leading lights. For instance, on Tuesday, 2 April 1745 he went to hear Charles Wesley speak on John 5:1-14 at the New Room. He was not impressed. Wesley apparently asserted in the course of his sermon that a believer could lose his or her salvation. Ryland says he was thankful to God that during the course of Wesley's remarks he was able to call to mind a discourse by Elisha

Coles, Sr (*c.*1608-1688) on the perseverance of the saints. The following morning Ryland spent time reading over Coles' discourse, which comprised a section of his *A Practical Discourse of God's Sovereignty* (1673), a minor classic of Dissenting literature, and was encouraged by '7 arguments for and 8 inferences from' this doctrine.[9]

In the autumn of 1745 he received a unanimous invitation from the Baptist church at Warwick to serve as their minister for a year. The year stretched out to four, and in 1750 the church called him to be their pastor. Among the ministers involved in his ordination in the summer of that year was John Brine, who travelled up from London to give the charge to the young pastor from 1 Timothy 4:1-2. In Ryland's opinion, Brine was a theologian of the highest calibre, to be ranked alongside such divines as the Puritans John Owen and Stephen Charnock (1628-1680) and the Dutch author, Herman Witsius (1636-1708). The 'great John Brine' was the way that he once referred to him.[10] His unbounded admiration for Brine is a strong clue to the school of theology towards which Ryland leaned; he definitely favoured the High Calvinism of Brine and Gill. Like Brine he did not think that it was proper to employ the word 'offer' with respect to the preaching of the gospel. 'The gospel is a declaration,' not an offer, 'of the free grace of God,' he asserted and in support of his assertion recommended the perusal of the definitive High Calvinist text on this issue, *God's Operations of Grace: but no Offers of Grace* (1707) by the Cambridge Congregationalist Joseph Hussey (1660-1726), as well as Brine's rejoinder to Alvery Jackson's defence of offering the gospel to the unsaved.[11]

Ryland stayed at Warwick till 1759, when differences between himself and his congregation over the question of who could legitimately partake of the Lord's Supper necessitated his leaving. In the statement of faith which the Warwick church professed, the eleventh article maintained that the only individuals who 'are to be admitted to the communion of the church, and to participate of all ordinances in it' are those 'who have been baptized by immersion'.[12] Presumably Ryland agreed with this article of faith when he became the pastor of the church. By 1759, however, he seems to have become convinced that 'The table is the Lord's; and all who are called by his grace are his guests.'[13] The Lord's Supper was not to be restricted to those who had undergone believer's baptism. Benjamin Beddome, who tended to favour the same position, may have influenced Ryland in this regard.[14] The fact that Ryland had developed friendships with Congregationalist and Anglican evangelicals may also have been a significant factor in the development of his thinking about the Lord's Supper. He corresponded with Philip Doddridge and, on at least one occasion, preached for him. He became very good friends with James Hervey (1714-1758), who had been a member of that circle of men around the Wesleys in Oxford known as the Holy Club. After experiencing an evangelical conversion in 1740, Hervey went on to have a vigorous minstry as the Anglican rector of Weston Favell near Northampton and 'the most popular *littérateur* among the first generation of evangelical [Anglican] clergy'.[15] After Hervey's death in 1758, Ryland published a memoir of his friend, together with sixty-five letters that he had received from him.

The church to which Ryland went after leaving Warwick was the small open communion Baptist congregation at College Lane, Northampton. Over the course of the next twenty years, Ryland saw the church building twice enlarged to accommodate the swelling numbers who came to worship under his ministry and the membership grow from the thirty or so who were there when he came to over two hundred. Actually in the course of those years more than 250 new members were added, many of them converted under the thunderous preaching of the elder Ryland.[16] A good number of these conversions were quite striking, such as that of Eleanor Bibwell, who, prior to her becoming a Christian, was 'an ignorant, profligate swearer and persecutor of her husband', or that of a woman from the nearby village of Hardingstone who for several years had been 'a vain frothy singer of songs'.[17] In Ryland's case, his propensity towards High Calvinism was obviously not a barrier to the numerical growth of his congregation.

It is interesting to note that this growth of the College Lane congregation did not go unnoticed by leaders in the Evangelical Revival. Howel Harris made an observation in his diary in November 1762 about the 'great work done' by Ryland at Northampton, and George Whitefield, whom Ryland had heard preach as a young man in Bristol in 1744, took time to visit him in 1767 during one of the great evangelist's last preaching tours of Britain.[18] Ryland also continued to cultivate friendships with those outside of Calvinistic Baptist circles, such evangelical leaders as Augustus M. Toplady (1740-1778), author of the passionate hymn 'Rock of Ages, cleft for me', John Newton and Rowland Hill (1744-1833), a very popular preacher, though, like Ryland, somewhat eccentric.[19] John Collett Ryland was thus a fascinating blend of theological positions: a High Calvinist who favoured the school of Brine and Gill, yet, because of his open communion stance, very catholic in his friendships. As the Congregationalist William Jay (1769-1853) later commented about Ryland, whom he had come to know fairly well during the latter's last years of life, 'He was intimate with Mr Whitefield and Mr Rowland Hill, and much attached to many other preachers less systematically orthodox than himself; and laboured, as opportunity offered, with them. He was, indeed, a lover of all good men; and, while many talked of candour, he exercised it. Though he was a firm Baptist, he was no friend to bigotry or exclusiveness.'[20]

Though Ryland's son, John Ryland, Jr, would eventually disavow his father's High Calvinism, he was profoundly shaped by his evangelical catholicity and involvement with men closely associated with the Evangelical Revival.

## The conversion of John Ryland, Jr

One of the younger Ryland's earliest memories in fact was of a visit with his parents, when he was only five years of age, to James Hervey at Weston Favell. Ryland distinctly remembered reading the twenty-third Psalm in Hebrew to the Anglican rector. Clearly a rather precocious child, John had been born during his father's first pastorate at Warwick. His conversion took place in the early years of his father's second pastorate at Northampton, not long before that of Sutcliff in Yorkshire. But unlike that of Sutcliff, about which we have next to no details, Ryland's conversion experience was recorded in full in a manuscript of twenty-three pages, which he entitled 'The Experience of Jo/N R.l..d jun^r^ as wrote by himself in a Letter to Tho^s^: R..t dated Feb^y^: 1770.'[21]

In this manuscript the young Ryland recorded how he was led to reflect on his own spiritual state in the autumn of 1766 by the words of a friend who attended a boarding-school which his father ran. This friend, who had experienced a spiritual awakening only a short while before and who had begun to meet with two other teenagers for prayer and fellowship, had been engaged in a conversation one evening with Ryland. Suddenly, in the middle of their conversation the friend — remembering that he had to meet his other two friends for prayer — excused himself from Ryland's company. Ryland was deeply hurt, thinking that his friend no longer wanted to associate with him. The next day Ryland refused to speak to him and gave as his reason his friend's actions the previous night. His friend then explained why he had had to leave so abruptly. 'We were talking of something better,' he told Ryland. This phrase, 'something better,' stuck in the young Ryland's mind. Having been raised in an evangelical environment, he had no trouble guessing what his friend meant by the phrase: 'Jesus Christ and the salvation of their souls.' Ryland began to sense a deep concern about his spiritual condition; his friends were going to heaven and was he to be left behind?

A lengthy period of spiritual struggle now followed, in which he sought for a lasting assurance of salvation and in which heartfelt convictions and fervent prayer alternated with periods of spiritual lukewarmness and 'horrible doubts'. One day he might be full of joy and assurance; the next he could be cast down and convinced that he was not a child of God. Reading through this account, one is reminded of that classic Puritan conversion narrative, *Grace Abounding to the Chief of Sinners* (1666) by John Bunyan (1628-1688).

It was while Ryland was in the midst of this struggle that Whitefield came to visit his father and preached the following day, 8 September 1767, at the Castle Hill Church in Northampton — the church which Philip Doddridge had pastored during his lifetime. Five days later Ryland was baptized by his father in the River Nene, near the foot of the slope upon which Castle Hill Church stood. In those days a roadway led directly from the chapel to the brink of the river, a distance of around 200 yards. It was here, in 1783, that the young Ryland would baptize William Carey. Lasting assurance, though, did not come for Ryland until May 1768. After hearing his father preach from Isaiah 55:1 on the final Sunday of that month and then from Isaiah 40:1-2 later that week in the village of Kingsthorpe, Ryland said he 'was in general freed from doubts' about his salvation.

Over the next three years Ryland was exposed to a number of significant Baptist and evangelical leaders. During the summer of 1768, for instance, his father took him for a month to London, where he heard John Gill preaching on one occasion from John 14:1. He was in London again that October, this time with his mother, and 'with much pleasure' heard Benjamin Beddome preach three times. The following June he and his father made another trip to London. They 'went to see Mr Whitefield' — only three months before Whitefield's final voyage to America — and heard Toplady preaching on a text long familiar to Ryland, Psalm 23. 'I found my soul much melted with a sense of divine love,' was his response to Toplady's exposition. That autumn he was again in the capital. This time he heard Joshua Symonds (1739-1788), the pastor of the Congregational/Baptist church in Bedford which John Bunyan had once pastored (today known as Bunyan Meeting), and three Baptists: Gill, Gill's close friend Benjamin Wallin and Abraham Booth (1734-1806), the pastor of Prescott Street Baptist Church and a strong evangelical Calvinist.[22]

## The influence of John Newton

Of greater moment, though, than all of these experiences — exhilarating as they must have been for a young believer — was the invitation which John Newton extended to Ryland to come and visit him in Olney on 17 January 1768.[23] Newton was nearly three times the age of Ryland. During his forty-two years, he had seen enough adventure and excitement for two or three lifetimes.

The son of a shipmaster in the merchant marine and a godly Congregationalist mother, he had been deprived of his mother's invaluable guidance and counsel before he was seven through her death from consumption. When he turned eleven his father took him to sea for the first time, and for the next eighteen years Newton would know the vicissitudes and 'wild rigours of a life before the mast'.[24]

In 1744, during the War of the Austrian Succession (1740-1748), Newton was press-ganged into the Royal Navy. Seeking his freedom through desertion, he was caught and flogged. Release from the navy was at hand, though, when he was given the opportunity to be transferred from the man of war on which he was serving to a ship engaged in the slave-trade. By this time Newton had become a man who had no fear of God and whose profanity shocked even the most hardened of sailors. Arrriving off the coast of West Africa, Newton joined the service of a slave-dealer, but ended up being a slave himself to the man's African mistress! After more than a year of brutal abuse, ill-treatment and deep humiliations, Newton was rescued by another slave-ship, which, on its homeward passage to England in March of 1748, nearly foundered. During a wild Atlantic storm shipwreck seemed imminent and Newton, not even thinking about what he was saying, called on God to have mercy. This cry for mercy proved to be the critical turning-point of his life. The ship came safely through the storm and Newton 'began to know that there is a God who hears and answers prayer'.[25]

For four more years Newton continued to be involved in the slave-trade, even to the point of captaining a slave-ship. At the time he was not at all troubled by his occupation. However, years later, when reflection and Christian maturity had showed him the iniquitous nature of this traffic in human beings, he was a firm ally of those seeking its abolition. His seafaring days were cut short by a stroke in 1754, when he was only twenty-nine. Although he soon recovered and suffered no lasting ill-effects, the doctors whom he consulted suggested that he find a different occupation. He thus relinquished his command and in 1755 became a tide surveyor in Liverpool.

Shortly before he began his nine years of service as a tide surveyor, Newton heard George Whitefield preach and was subsequently introduced to him. This meeting proved to be another important juncture of his life. 'Never before had I such an idea and foretaste of the business of heaven,' he wrote in his diary after meeting Whitefield.[26] As a tide surveyor, he had a fairly comfortable vocation. But Newton began to sense his heart being stirred in a very different direction, namely, the pastoral ministry.

The question, though, was where to serve — in the Church of England or among the Dissenters? Newton was in frequent attendance at the Liverpool Baptist church pastored by the High Calvinist John Johnson. He was initially impressed with Johnson and actually considered becoming a member of his congregation. When he was later introduced by George Whitefield to John Oulton (d.1780), the pastor of Byrom Street Baptist Church in Liverpool whom Whitefield had termed 'an excellent humble man', Newton became a regular worshipper among the Byrom Street Baptists. However, what Newton termed an 'unprofitable dispute about baptism' with Oulton on Sunday, 18 April 1756 seems to have shut the door once and for all to his joining the Baptists. Serious consideration was also given to serving among the Congregationalists, but this too proved to be a dead end.[27] At last, in 1764 Newton was ordained to the Anglican ministry through the help of William Legge (1731-1801), the second Earl of Dartmouth, who was an evangelical and very supportive of gospel causes. Dartmouth was also instrumental in Newton's being appointed to the curacy of the parish church in Olney later that year.

Newton arrived in Olney in May 1764. The following February, he made an appointment to visit John Collett Ryland in Northampton. Their first meeting, Newton recorded in his diary, was 'an agreeable one'.[28] It was to be the first of a number of visits over the next fifteen years (Newton left Olney in 1780 to become the rector of St Mary, Woolnoth, in the heart of London). Three years later Newton also began to cultivate a friendship with Ryland's son. The younger Ryland had probably seen Newton on the latter's visits to his father, but it was not until 17 January 1768, that, as Ryland puts it, he 'became first acquainted with Mr Newton'.[29] Despite the fact that Newton was old enough to be Ryland's father, in time the two became the firmest of friends. Many years later Ryland would say of the Anglican evangelical that he was one of his 'wisest and most faithful counsellors, in all difficulties'.[30] A good number of the details of their friendship have been preserved for us in a substantial collection of Newton's letters, which Ryland kept and treasured, and most of which today are housed in the archives of Bristol Baptist College.[31] Only a few of these letters, though, have ever been published. Nine of them were published by Newton in his *Cardiphonia* (1781). Newton asked Ryland to loan him these early pieces of their correspondence, which he copied for inclusion in *Cardiphonia* and then returned to his friend. Another ten, or extracts from them, were submitted to *The Baptist Magazine* by Ryland and appeared in 1816. The remaining fifty or so letters exist only in manuscript and await a definitive edition.[32]

The two earliest extant letters both relate to Ryland's early commitment to High Calvinism. Given his father's admiration for John Brine, it is not surprising that Ryland initially 'inclined to Mr Brine's opinion' about avoiding the free offer of the gospel. Either in 1768 or 1769 Ryland spent an entire year reading some of his father's most cherished theological works by divines such as Brine and Gill. At a very impressionable age and young in the Christian faith, Ryland had no resources to evaluate critically what he was reading and he embraced the High Calvinist sentiments of these theologians as his own. The consequence of imbibing these sentiments became quite clear when he received the approval of the College Lane congregation to preach and to assist his father on 10 March 1771. As Ryland admitted seven years before his death, 'When I first entered on the work of the ministry, though I endeavoured to say as much to sinners as my views of this subject would allow, yet I was shackled by adherence to a supposed systematic consistency, and carefully avoided exhorting sinners to come to Christ for salvation.'[33]

Over the course of the next few years Ryland's views underwent a significant change. At the time of his ordination in 1781, he could clearly state that he believed that 'repentance and remission of sins [were] to be preached' in the name of Christ 'among all nations and his gospel to be published to every creature'. Moreover, all men and women, regardless of their spiritual state, had an obligation to obey God's command to repent and embrace Christ as their Saviour; for 'men are still the proper subjects of commands and invitations notwithstanding their moral depravity'.[34]

In listing those things which induced this change of perspective, Ryland mentions a growing acquaintance with the writings of those who preceded Gill and Brine, 'both the old Nonconformists, and the most evangelical Episcopalian writers'. He also specifically makes mention of the Scottish theologian Samuel Rutherford (*c.*1600-1661) and a letter which Rutherford wrote to a certain James Lindsay in 1637. When Ryland read Rutherford's assertion that God has placed the reprobate under an obligation to believe in Christ he began to question seriously what he had imbibed from Gill and Brine.[35] Two New England divines, Jonathan Edwards and John Smalley (1734-1820), are also creditedwith helping Ryland break free from the trammels of High Calvinism — the influence of their writings will be developed in greater detail in chapter 7. Furthermore, Newton made an important contribution to this theological shift in Ryland's views. Unlike the influence of Edwards and Smalley, however, it was not in the realm of tract and treatise, but was in the form of personal conversation and correspondence, more along the lines of Rutherford's letter to Lindsay.

The earliest piece of Newton's correspondence with Ryland which we possess is dated 17 October 1771. It is a lengthy letter, in which Newton very lovingly but firmly reproves Ryland for some faults that he sees in his young friend's life, especially as they relate to a collection of hymns and poems which Ryland had published. In the preface to this collection and in some of the poems themselves Ryland had aired his sentiments regarding eternal justification, a highly controverted doctrine in seventeenth- and eighteenth-century Calvinstic circles.

The early Calvinistic Baptist position regarding eternal justification is best displayed in the *Second London Confession* of 1689. In article 11.4 of this statement of faith, it is expressly declared that 'God did from all eternity decree to justify all the elect ... nevertheless they are not justified personally, until the Holy Spirit, doth in due time actually apply Christ unto them.'[36] In other words, while God had resolved in eternity to justify his elect when, in the realm of time, they put their faith in Christ, they are not actually justified until the Spirit enables them to so embrace Christ. High Calvinists like Gill and Brine diverged from this understanding of justification. For Gill, probably the pre-eminent champion of eternal justification in his day, God's eternal decision to justify the elect has to be regarded as their justification, even as his 'will to elect, is the election of his people'.[37] The will to justify is justification itself. The believer's experience of justification then comes to be interpreteted as his discovery of what God has done for him in and from eternity.

Ryland seems to have dogmatically asserted Gill's viewpoint on this subject, which was somewhat disconcerting to Newton. It was not simply that Newton felt that this perspective on justification was wrong, but that 'For a young man under 18 to pronounce *ex cathedra* upon a point in which a great majority of the most learned, spiritual and humble divines, are of another opinion, was such an offence against decency as grieved me.' Newton was quite willing to admit that the assertion of eternal justification coming from the pen of 'Dr Gill or Mr Brine ... might have been borne with, their years, characters, and experience might have made it less noticed'. Newton thus strongly advised Ryland 'to let a few more years pass over your head, before you take the chair in controversial matters, especially in those, in which the life of faith and the power of religion is no way concerned'. Newton emphasized that his words stem from his love for Ryland and his desire to see the young man prosper in God's service. 'You will perhaps find,' he told him frankly, 'many ready enough to say smooth and pleasing things to your face, but I hope you will know how to value an admonition from a friend.'[38]

Ryland did not immediately answer this loving rebuke. Newton was apprehensive that he had offended him. But Newton had nothing to worry about. Ryland did respond in a letter which no longer exists — it is a shame we have none of Ryland's letters to Newton — and in a humble and teachable spirit. Newton thus told Ryland in the second letter, which is dated 16 January 1772 and which begins the sequence of letters to Ryland in Newton's *Cardiphonia*, 'Henceforward I can converse freely with you.' Ryland had taken Newton's remarks about eternal justification to imply that he was opposing the concept. No, Newton said, 'I did not oppose it; I judge for myself, and am willing others should have the same liberty. If we hold the *head*, and love the Lord, we *agree* in him, and I should think my time ill employed in disputing the point with you. I only meant to except against the positive manner in which you had expressed yourself. My end is answered, and I am satisfied.'[39]

In his collection of hymns and poems Ryland had reflected a style of theologizing that was all too common among High Calvinists. Newton calls it 'positive', by which he means intolerant and dogmatic. It was this style and manner of theological discourse which Newton was taking to task, not so much the theology itself.

In this second letter Newton goes on to talk of another integral aspect of the High Calvinist position, namely, the commitment to the 'Supra-lapsarian scheme'. Supralapsarianism is one interpretation of the order in which God issued the decrees (1) to create the human race; (2) to elect some to eternal blessedness and to reprobate the others to eternal damnation; (3) to permit the entry of sin into human history; (4) to send his Son to save the elect. Central to the supralapsarian interpretation of the order of these decrees is the conviction that the decree to elect or reprobate is logically prior to the decree to permit the Fall. In its most stringent form supralapsarianism places the decree of election or reprobation even before the decree to create the human race.

The infralapsarian interpretation (which Newton calls sublapsarianism) holds the reverse: the decrees to create and to allow the entry of sin into human history logically precede the decree to elect or reprobate.[40] Among seventeenth-century Puritan authors infralapsarianism was certainly the more common of these two perspectives. Their eighteenth-century High Calvinistic Baptist heirs, on the other hand, were by and large committed to the supralapsarian point of view.

While Newton did suggest that there may be a way in which a 'judicious Supra-lapsarian, and a sound Sub-lapsarian ... might safely unite', his primary interest again was not so much the theological issues at stake, but the way in which the theological discourse about these issues was being conducted. There are 'several in the Supra-lapsarian scheme', he stated, 'at whose feet I am willing to sit and learn, and have found their preaching savoury and edifying'. There are many more, though, whose embrace of supralapsarianism — and in the eighteenth-century context this entailed the advocacy of its natural corollary, High Calvinism — had made them 'rather wise than warm, rather positive than humble, rather captious than lively, and more disposed to talk of speculations than experience'. Newton named one author in particular: the High Calvinist Joseph Hussey, whose *God's Operations of Grace: but no Offers of Grace* Ryland's father recommended with regard to the impropriety of talking about the 'offer of the gospel'. The elder Ryland's delight in Hussey was certainly not shared by Newton. When he read Hussey, Newton told the younger Ryland, he rarely found nourishing and palatable food. In Newton's opinion, Hussey's writings contain 'more bones than meat' and are 'seasoned with much of an angry and self-important spirit'. Newton longed to grow in the knowledge of God. But the knowledge of God in which he was interested was not the sort of speculation that often characterized High Calvinist tracts and tomes. 'I want nothing,' he wrote, 'that has not a direct tendency to make sin more hateful, Jesus more precious to my soul.'[41]

These two letters both clearly reveal that Newton was discussing with Ryland the latter's commitment to High Calvinism, and that he was lovingly alerting Ryland to some of the dangers of this theological perspective. Thus Newton seems to have played a significant rôle in the reshaping of Ryland's theology.[42]

## The influence of Hill

Yet another important influence on the thinking of Ryland about these issues was the example he witnessed in evangelical preachers whom his father often invited to preach from the College Lane pulpit. For instance, in 1772 the younger Ryland, presumably at the behest of his father, invited Rowland Hill, frequently described as a second Whitefield, to preach at College Lane: 'Very dear Sir ... we have heard of thee ... and we long to see you and hear from you the Lord's message. You may find room in a dozen houses, a thousand hearts, two Northampton pulpits, our best bed, [and] our large yard, which George Whitefield ... preached in. In very many neighbouring towns and villages, barns, malthouses, and orchards are at your service; and if you would break up neighbouring fallow ground, we will find at any time at least 300 prayers and a dozen men to go with you in spite of devils, stones, or rotten eggs, or any thing else. There will be our friend [John] Newton at Olney, within a dozen miles. In short there will be work enough, and victuals enough, and drink enough, and joy enough.'[43]

Ryland continued by insisting that Hill simply had to come. If he did not heed this appeal, Ryland threatened to write another letter with a hundred signatures, 'for by God's help we are determined you shall preach in Northampton before long'.[44] As it turned out, Hill did respond positively to this invitation. In the spring of the following year he preached with great success at Northampton. Twelve individuals came under deep conviction as a result of his preaching, which bore godly fruit in the lives of at least eight.[45] The next spring, in 1774, Hill returned to Northampton. 'Thousands attended' his preaching, Ryland informed Sutcliff that August. In fact, by 1775 Hill had made three visits to Northampton. Ryland was overjoyed at the number who had been converted through his preaching. As Ryland wrote to Hill in 1775, 'We have vast reason to be thankful that God blessed you so gloriously among us; and I hope the Lord will make it a means of endearing Northampton to you, and of inducing you to visit us oftener.'[46] Though a Calvinist, by no stretch of the imagination could Hill be termed a High Calvinist. In his preaching Ryland would have seen at first-hand a Calvinist unreservedly urging the lost to flee to the only haven of safety from God's wrath, the crucified Christ. Rowland Hill's preaching would certainly have shown Ryland that Calvinism and fervent evangelism are not mutually exclusive.

It was after Hill's second visit to Northampton that Ryland wrote to Sutcliff in Shrewsbury on 26 August 1774 the letter, of which a snippet has been quoted above. It is a fascinating letter, crammed with titbits of information and with solid exhortation, and written in Ryland's lucid handwriting, which he maintained all of his life. He told Sutcliff about Rowland Hill's ministry at Northampton and observed that it was the better part of wisdom 'as well as the duty of the dissenters to be friendly with the orthodox Methodists'. By 'orthodox' Ryland evidently meant Calvinistic, for he went on to state with regard to the followers of the Wesleys: 'Both their doctrine and policy are inimical to the Dissenters and I think contrary to the Word of God.'[47] Despite this qualification, Ryland's remarks display an openness and evangelical catholicity rarely found in Calvinistic Baptist circles prior to this date. After all, at this point in time Hill was a deacon in the established church, which, for many Baptists earlier in the century, 'represented the penultimate step toward Popery'.[48]

## The revival at Shepshed

Ryland also supplied Sutcliff with information about a revival which was taking place in the Baptist church in the village of Shepshed (then spelt 'Sheepshead'), Leicestershire: 'You ask if I have heard of a revival of Sheepshead — I have *seen* it. The instrument is Mr Guy … the plainest rough-hewed preacher you ever saw or heard… 3 sabbaths back 24 gave in their experience there, the Church meeting lasted from 4 in the afternoon till 12 at night. The devil roars woefully there. Guy never spares him in the pulpit and he never spares Guy out of it — the poor man is often distressed almost to death about the greatness of the work, and generally goes up the pulpit stairs in chains, but God owns him abundantly — will you meet me at Sheepshead in a week or two or more?'[49]

William Guy (1739-1783), the central figure in this text, had come to Shepshed Baptist Church in 1774. It was to be his only pastoral charge. Not long after his call to the church it experienced the revival described above. Preaching at Shepshed after Guy's death in 1783, Ryland made the comment that the deceased had had 'an alarming ministry', that is, a ministry greatly used by God to awaken the unsaved to their need of Christ.[50] His preaching set forth God's Word in such a way that his hearers' self-confidence was shaken to the core and they were brought to know themselves as they truly were — sinful and in desperate need of peace with God. But his preaching also made them aware of the mercy and forgiveness that a gracious God freely extends to all who come to him through Christ.

The ongoing impact that this revival had upon Ryland, and presumably Sutcliff, is well seen from a remark Ryland made in a letter quite a number of years later. Writing in 1807 to John Williams (1767-1825), a Welsh Baptist pastor who had emigrated to America, Ryland stated: 'We seldom seem to fish with a net, as you have often done in America. It is very uncommon I mean for an awakening to seem to run through a town or a village. The most similar case to those I have read of, in your country, was the awakening at Sheepshead in Leicestershire near 30 years ago, when my dear friend Guy was first settled there.'[51]

In the way that the Shepshed revival swept beyond the Baptist congregation into the community of the Leicestershire village, it was akin to many of the local manifestations of the First and Second Great Awakenings in America, where, under the press of revival, whole communities were reshaped. It would be too much to claim for the Shepshed revival that it played the leading role in stimulating Ryland's ongoing hunger for revival — a hunger which, as will be seen, Sutcliff shared to the full. But, if Ryland's comments to Williams be a good guide, the revival certainly did leave a lasting impression on him.

That autumn Sutcliff went to see for himself what was transpiring at Shepshed and doubtless came away with a conviction similar to that expressed by Ryland earlier in the year: 'God is with him [i.e. Guy] I am persuaded.'[52] But when Ryland's letter reached him at Shrewsbury, Sutcliff was quite discouraged. He had obviously complained to Ryland of an abiding sense of his insufficiency for the work at Shrewsbury. For in the same letter in which Ryland spoke of Rowland Hill's ministry at Northampton and the Shepshed revival, he urged Sutcliff to remember that the believer's strength is in Christ. The difference between a young believer and a mature Christian, he went on to say, is not that the latter has more inner strength than the former; rather he or she knows where to look for it, namely in the Lord Jesus. 'We are apt to form a wrong idea of growth in grace, and expect to feel an increasing fullness in ourselves instead of a growing sense of our emptiness and Christ's sufficiency.' Sutcliff badly needed such encouragement, for the work in the church at Shrewsbury was not going at all as he had hoped.

# 5.
# Shrewsbury and Birmingham

*'The heart may be as really alive to God, and grace as truly in exercise, when we walk in comparative darkness and see little light, as when the frame of our spirits is more comfortable'* (John Newton).

'Go from Salop [i.e. Shropshire] by all means. Don't stay there. I would sooner go to Yorkshire, into my native obscurity than stay with such a people. Go to the end of the town and borrow a brush and wipe off the dust as an everlasting testimony against them.'[1] Such was the advice that Thomas Purdy gave to Sutcliff on 22 September 1774 with regard to the church at Shrewsbury, and Sutcliff had not even been at the church four months! The problems had started almost as soon as he reached Shrewsbury. About a month after his ministry in the town had commenced, he wrote to Purdy and told him that some of the congregation would have preferred the former interim pastor, John Sandys, to have continued among them. However, Sutcliff told Purdy that he was determined not to allow this state of affairs to unnerve him. Purdy's response was to assure him that after Sandys had been gone some time and Sutcliff 'present with them some time' the situation would surely improve.[2]

For a few weeks it appeared that Purdy was right and that Sutcliff was winning the affection of the Shrewsbury Baptists. By mid-August, though, when Sutcliff wrote to Ryland, he was again feeling discouraged. As we have seen, he felt daunted by the task facing him in Shrewsbury. By the following month he was even more distressed and disconsolate.

It was now very obvious that the majority of the congregation were still hankering after the ministry of Sandys. Purdy's advice, as cited above, was to leave and not look back, but Sutcliff was reluctant to consider this course of action. If he left after so short a time, other churches might assume a major defect in his character, and his reputation might end up being sullied. Purdy replied telling him to let God take care of his reputation: 'O how happy if we could leave ourselves with God and ... seek so that the glory of God may be advanced.' He reminded Sutcliff of a text on which the latter had recently preached: 'The steps of a good man are ordered by the Lord' (Psalm 37:23). 'Your steps are ordered by the Lord. O what a blessed consideration! He knows the end from the beginning and he will order every step for you. And remember the time will come that you shall evidently see it and see how justly that passage is fulfilled in you.'

Purdy concluded by reiterating the advice he had given at the beginning of his letter: 'As to staying there [i.e. at Shrewsbury] I would not, I would remove as soon as I conveniently could,' and expressed the hope that his friend would soon be rid of 'the shackles of Salop'.[3]

On 30 September, the day after this letter from Purdy had arrived, Sutcliff received another piece of mail, this one from James Turner of Birmingham. Evidently Sutcliff had also told Turner the full story of his woes at Shrewsbury. Right at the start of his letter Turner emphasized the same foundational truth which Purdy had developed in connection with Psalm 37:23: God sovereignly rules over every aspect of his creation. Taking an image from the world of shipping and sailing, he told Sutcliff that God is 'an infallible pilot'. He always 'leads by a right way, though at times, a *rough* one'. Nevertheless, as to the details of what Sutcliff should do, Turner was at a loss as to how to advise him. The fact that Turner was unable to sit down with Sutcliff and have a face-to-face discussion with him about his feelings and possible courses of action only added to the difficulty of giving concrete advice. 'I write like one with his head in a bag,' the Birmingham pastor frankly admitted. Turner did suggest that Sutcliff seriously consider coming to Birmingham for 'a month, 3 weeks, or a fortnight'. That way he would have 'time for reflection, consultation and prayer', and so might be able to better decide what he ought to do. Turner was grieved at the way the Shrewsbury church was acting: 'I wish my Shrewsbury friends would read this cutting sentence, "While one saith I am of Paul and

I of Apollos, are ye not carnal?" [cf.1 Corinthians 3:4].'Tis dreadful (but alas! common) for a church to be carnal.'[4]

Over the course of the next few weeks Turner obtained the opinions of a few of his friends, including Sutcliff's uncle William, about the advisability of Sutcliff's coming to Birmingham. Turner then wrote to Sutcliff on Saturday, 12 November, to tell him that all of those whom he had consulted 'heartily approve of the scheme of your coming here for a season'.[5]

The following Friday Sutcliff received yet another letter from Purdy. He too confessed that he did not know how to direct Sutcliff, but he told him, 'You have a better Counsellor, attend to him, and he shall direct you in his own time and way.' He drew Sutcliff's attention to Isaiah 50:10, which Purdy felt was directly applicable to his friend's case: 'Who is among you that feareth the Lord ... that walketh in darkness, and hath no light? Let him trust in the name of the Lord, and stay upon his God.' Purdy was right. This was an appropriate text for Sutcliff's situation — he was in the midst of distressing circumstances, God seemed to be absent, he had no clear direction as to the future and he genuinely felt that he was the object of the Lord's frowns and not his smiles. 'Wait upon him by prayer,' Purdy urged his friend, 'and trust him by faith... Stand still Sutcliff and see the salvation of God.' Sutcliff was thus encouraged to cultivate patience and trust in God — fruits of the Spirit much needed by those in pastoral ministry.

## An invitation to Olney

Purdy went on to mention that exactly two weeks earlier, on 3 November, he had been at College Lane Baptist Church in Northampton, where he had had some discussion about Sutcliff's situation with the younger Ryland. Ryland informed Purdy that he had just written to the church at Olney in Buckinghamshire, which had been without a pastor since 1773, to see if they might be interested in either Sutcliff or another 'lay preacher' whom Purdy did not know supplying their pulpit.[6] Yet, in telling Sutcliff this extremely important piece of news, Purdy was not informing him about something of which he had no prior knowledge. For on 7 November Sutcliff had received the following letter from Mary Andrews (d.1795), a prominent member of the Baptist congregation in Olney:

The Baptist Church here have long been destitute of a stated minister, therefore whenever an opportunity offers for a supply they are glad to embrace it. Receiving a line from our good friend Mr Ryland last night wherein he informs us that you are not like to stay long at Shrewsbury and likewise encouragement that, if applied to, you would kindly think of the case the people here are in and would be prevailed upon to make them a visit, our friends unite in love and beg leave to petition your kind assistance in supplying them for two or three Lord's days. Here's a great number of precious souls that are ready to attend upon the Word and was there an answer of prayer in providing suitable means in a stated way there's reason to hope there would be an increasing number. If the Lord should incline you to think with compassion on the above case and willingly to comply with the earnest request of our friends in paying them a visit, they would be glad if you could make it agreeable to be here the fourth Lord's day in this month and the two following sabbaths. But if that can't be, must leave it for you to fix a time when it will be convenient to you. But hope, sir, you'll not defer it long beyond the time proposed; hope you'll be so kind as to indulge with an answer as soon as possible. I wish you may have direction from the Lord in this and every importunate affair so God's glory may be much advanced and your comforts and consolations abound greatly in the Lord. Though a stranger, I hope, sir, you will excuse the freedom I have taken in writing on the above. 'Tis on the behalf of the needy and distressed sheep of Christ that prevailed upon me to send those lines. That the same motive may excite you to comply with an answer in their favour is the ardent wish of, sir, your sincere friend and humble servant.

Mary Andrews

P.S. If we should be favoured with a line of hope of seeing you soon, shall expect your company at my house.[7]

Sutcliff wrote to Ryland about the state of the Baptist church in Olney as soon as he received this letter; but he delayed till Thursday, 24 November to respond to the letter itself. Why he delayed so long is not known. He was not waiting for a letter from Ryland, for an answer had come from him, which is discussed below, around 15 or 16 November. Most likely Sutcliff was following Purdy's advice and waiting upon God for direction and assurance about his next move.

In his response to Sutcliff, Ryland told him what Purdy would later tell him: it was he who had written to Mary Andrews and encouraged her to invite Sutcliff to supply the Olney pulpit. Ryland stressed that there were many believers in Olney 'of *each* denomination', who were 'excellent people'. In fact, speaking of his own knowledge of the town, he could honestly say that 'There is nothing but gospel in the town.' Unfortunately, though, there was also 'too little love' between the members of the different denominations. Ryland hastened to add that this remark should not be taken to apply to his good friend Newton: 'I believe Mr Newton ... is the freest of a party spirit of any man in Olney nor do I know any man more so in the world.' In Ryland's opinion, the Baptist cause in particular had been hurt by bigotry and 'a party spirit', or what Ryland specified as their 'stiffness'. Nevertheless, their church services were well attended with '300 or 400 people in [the] afternoon and night'. Ryland was personally convinced that 'If a man of a gospel spirit should go there and determine to believe no tales and labour by gentle degrees to undermine a party spirit and try to outdo Mr Newton in candour and love for all that love Christ, I believe he would have *a good* prospect — and would find that the interest would gain more than it lost by the gospel in the Church.'[8] In other words, if the Olney Baptists had as their pastor a man who genuinely loved all that loved the Lord Jesus Christ, they would flourish, even as Newton's congregation had flourished under the preaching of the Word and his winsome leadership. These remarks tell us as much about Ryland as they do about the believers in Olney. His father's wide sympathies and his friendship with Newton had fostered within him an evangelical catholicity, which refused to regard the Calvinistic Baptist cause as the only viable expression of the kingdom of God.

Purdy's advice to Sutcliff was similar: he should seriously consider going to Olney. His reasons were quite different from those of Ryland, though. Olney was not that far from Chipping Norton, and being what he called 'natually selfish', he wanted his friend nearby. 'But all this is conferring with flesh and blood,' he added, 'may the Lord direct you.'[9] Sutcliff's reply to Purdy was written on 24 November, the same day as his response to Mary Andrews. From some pieces of later correspondence, which we shall examine in due course, it is apparent that Sutcliff declined her invitation to visit Olney. Why he declined is not clear, especially in view of the strong encouragement that Ryland had given him to accept the invitation.[10] Probably he was mentally and emotionally exhausted, and unable to contemplate another pastoral situation where he would be the sole pastor.

## Farewell to Shrewsbury

So in the second or third week of January 1775, Sutcliff left Shrewsbury for Birmingham. The following year the Shrewsbury congregation called back John Sandys to be their pastor. He served the church till 1781. During his ministry a new meeting-house was erected in Dog Lane, now Claremont Street but, according to the most recent history of the church, 'Lean years followed, during which the church had to face discouragement, quarrels, and a dwindling congregation.'[11] The situation changed only with the coming of John Palmer (d.1823), pastor from 1794 to 1822, whose energetic, outward-thrusting ministry brought an era of great spiritual prosperity to the church. Between 1796 and 1817 the membership grew steadily from twenty to 195, and at least five new chapels were planted in nearby villages as a direct result of his preaching.[12]

Not all of the Shrewsbury Baptists preferred Sandys' ministry to that of Sutcliff. For instance, Peggy Skrymsher, who kept in contact with Sutcliff after his departure from Shrewsbury, was deeply distressed when he left after only six months or so in the town. 'What joy, what comfort and soul refreshment I have experienced under many of your sermons!' she said in a letter pleading with him to stay in Shrewsbury.[13] In April 1775 she told him that while 'Sandys is very agreeable in company and in the pulpit' and though she greatly esteemed him, 'He will never lessen my regard for Mr Sutcliff; no, I shall still be a lamb of your fold and stand by you in the kingdom of our Father.'

Moreover, by the time that Sutcliff left Shrewsbury, he had come to see his experience in the town as a blessing in disguise, which had taught him 'many a useful lesson'.[14] It is interesting to reflect on the fact that shortly after Sutcliff had first arrived in Shrewsbury, he had received news that back in Yorkshire John Fawcett was ill. In the letter which he wrote to Fawcett on 14 June 1774, he confessed his own need of learning patience in the midst of trials and tribulation: 'Sorry I am to hear of your late affliction; hope the Lord has in mercy to you and your many friends removed his hand. However this be, it is our comfort in the midst of all that "the Lord reigneth" (Psalm 97:1). Our afflictions spring not out of the dust. Our steps in this, as well as in other respects, are "ordered by the Lord" (Psalm 37:23). It is, if need be, that we are "in heaviness through manifold temptations" (1 Peter 1:6). Sanctified strokes of his chastening rod are often some of the choicest proofs of his paternal love. Yet it is hard amidst afflictions to say, the "will of the Lord be done" (Acts 21:14), it requires much grace, but not more than God has to give. The Almighty prepares by the dispensations of providence, as well as by the influences of grace, for the enjoyment of glory. It is in the exercise of faith that we are meetened for an entrance into the kingdom. O that I could practically learn this myself!'[15]

As noted above, Sutcliff had preached a sermon on the second Scripture text which he cites in this letter, Psalm 37:23. His encouragement to his former pastor was, in fact, centred upon the words of this verse. God's sovereign guidance of, and care for, the believer in his or her journey on the road of life extends to every aspect of that journey, rough spots as well as smooth. The rough spots are evidence of God's fatherly love for his children, by means of which he shapes them for their inheritance in glory. As believers exercise 'faith and patience' in the midst of trying circumstances, they are 'meetened for an entrance into the kingdom'. However, the fact that Sutcliff knew this to be the case certainly did not mean that he was a master when it came to faith and patience. In fact, as he confessed, he was more of a novice in such matters. But six months after he had written this letter, when he was preparing to leave Shrewsbury for Birmingham, he had begun to acquire these important fruits of the Spirit and had also learned something of the cost of their acquisition.

## Birmingham — setting the scene

During the latter half of the eighteenth century the town of Birmingham was growing at an extraordinary rate, and was well on its way to becoming one of the leading manufacturing centres in Great Britain. Between 1760 and 1801 the town's population doubled from around 35,000 to 70,000. During the same period it saw the rapid development of a number of important industries, such as the manufacture of gilt buttons and gun-barrels, to name but two. When Sutcliff came to the town in January 1775, he would have been immediately struck by the contrast beween the workshops of his native riding of Yorkshire, which were dispersed along the banks of fast-flowing streams, and those in Birmingham, which were crowded together in the heart of the town.[16] Along with the growth in population and industry came cramped living quarters and long hours of labour at monotonous tasks. The little time left for recreation was often spent by many in drinking and coarse amusements such as cock-fighting. Drunkenness was the besetting sin of urban life in eighteenth-century Britain, and Birmingham was no exception.[17] In the final decades of the century this state of affairs was slowly being alleviated by a variety of influences — charity, education and, one that is frequently overlooked, vital Christianity. And in the impact of the latter, the Calvinistic Baptists had their part to play.

The Baptist congregation in Birmingham met on Cannon Street, where they had been since 1738. When the church had been formed in 1737 it had first met in a room off a yard behind High Street. The following year a friend of the church died and bequeathed a sum of money to the congregation for the express purpose of erecting a meeting-house. A plot of land was purchased for £18 in what had originally been a cherry orchard on Cannon Street and the first meeting-house built. The erection of a meeting-house would usually be attended with sanguine prospects, but the early years of this church failed to fulfil such hopes. The history of the church during this period was particularly gloomy and for a number of years there was no pastor. Matters had reached such a pitch by 1745 that the pastorless congregation was contemplating dissolution.

As it turned out the church did not dissolve, but when James Turner came to the pastorate of this congregation in 1754 there were only fourteen members.[18] Due to his 'faithful and earnest labours' the membership had risen to 140 by 1776, and the meeting-house was twice enlarged, first in 1763 and then again in 1780, the year of his death.[19] The second enlargement cost around £800. According to William Hutton, the Birmingham historian and a leading member of the Presbyterian Old Meeting, there was observable in it 'some beauty, but more conveniency'.[20]

## James Turner

Turner hailed from the Rossendale Valley in Lancashire, having been born near Bacup.[21] Cannon Street was his first and only pastoral charge. His interest in Sutcliff's welfare arose initially from the fact that Sutcliff's uncle William was a personal friend. However, the short time which Sutcliff spent with Turner in May of 1774 helped to provide a foundation on which a solid friendship was established.

From his correspondence with Sutcliff, which spans the final five years of Turner's life, and from his few minor publications one forms a picture of a strong-minded man who was decidedly Calvinistic, a convinced Baptist and unashamedly a Dissenter. His preaching on election in the early years of his ministry caused some to complain that he was 'quite too dogmatical and positive'.[22] The passage of time did nothing to change his convictions regarding the scriptural nature of Calvinistic thought. While retaining, for instance, a sneaking admiration for John Wesley's indefatigability, he viewed his religious opinions with contempt. When it came to religion and theology, Wesley was 'a *nothing*'! His Arminianism was 'trash', which Turner compared to the wood, hay and stubble of 1 Corinthians 3:12. It was certainly not a fit foundation on which to build a pastoral ministry.[23]

On the other hand, he was critical of the virulent manner in which Augustus Toplady censured Wesley in his *magnum opus*, *Historic Proof of the Doctrinal Calvinism of the Church of England,* which appeared in two volumes in 1774. While Turner admired the evidence of Toplady's 'talents and orthodoxy' in the first volume of this work, he strongly disapproved of the 'extreme severity' with which he treated Wesley and Walter Sellon (1715-1792), one of Wesley's Anglican supporters. 'That they are enemies to many of the doctrines of the gospel', he wrote in a postscript to a letter that he sent to Sutcliff in September 1774, 'is evident, but this does not authorize Toplady's severity, in my opinion.'[24]

Nor did he sanction the continuous intramural battling that characterized English-speaking Protestantism: ''Tis a pity that protestants, instead of combatting the common enemy, popery and infidelity, should be for ever battling one another.'[25] Yet this concern for presenting a common front to common foes did not diminish his Baptist convictions. Baptism, for example, he conceded to be a non-essential aspect of the Christian faith, a 'circumstantial'. This concession, however, did not mean that he believed there was no appreciable difference between believer's baptism and infant baptism. The former was established by divine power, but the latter was 'a mere nullity [and] a piece of Romish trumpery'.[26] On the other hand, he was appreciative of the preaching and writing of many non-Baptist evangelicals. When the Anglican evangelical William Romaine (1714-1795) was preaching at St Mary's in Birmingham in October 1776, Turner did not miss the opportunity of going to hear this powerful preacher. On this occasion, though, Turner was somewhat disappointed. As he told Sutcliff, when it came to the content of the sermons, 'John Wesley himself would have found no fault on the score of doctrines.'[27]

Moreover, his genuine appreciation of Church of England evangelicals like Toplady and Romaine did not cause him to waver in his adherence to the cause of the Dissenters. In a statement which, in many ways, goes to the heart of the dispute between the defenders of an established church and those whose consciences led them into the dissenting camp, Turner declared in one of his final letters to Sutcliff, 'If conscience is not left free, there can be no sincerity, consequently no religion.'[28]

While Sutcliff was nowhere near as blunt as Turner in expressing his convictions and probably somewhat broader in his sympathies, he was just as firm in his Calvinism and his loyalty to that group of Dissenters who went under the Baptist name. Of course, earlier mentors such as Fawcett and the Evanses had played crucial roles in instilling these convictions into Sutcliff's heart and mind. But the time he spent with Turner in Birmingham and the regular correspondence that the two men enjoyed after Sutcliff's departure for Olney helped, in their own small way, to reinforce these beliefs.

## Sutcliff's friends offer advice on his future ministry

Sutcliff had declined the offer to visit Olney. But he could not remain in Birmingham indefinitely. While he was there, though, he was proving to be a great asset to Turner, who was ill. The difficult circumstances attending his stay in Shrewsbury were behind him, but he was still in the dark as to where God was leading him. Not that he lacked well-meaning suggestions as to what he should do.

Hugh Evans wrote to him on 28 February and suggested he think seriously about going to Falmouth in Cornwall for '2, 3 or 4 months'. Such a move would give him 'an opportunity of seeing more of the world' and also 'of doing much good'. 'There is a wide door opened in Cornwall,' Evans told him, 'if we could but enter in while it is open.'[29] Prior to this point in time Dissent in general had little hold upon the Cornish people. Sensing a change in this state of affairs and, in particular, an openness to the Baptist position not hitherto present in Cornwall, Evans was eager to make the most of the opportunity. John Geard also thought Sutcliff should go to Cornwall. Hugh Evans had preached at Geard's ordination on 13 April, and had presumably told him of what he had suggested to Sutcliff. Benjamin Francis was currently preaching in Cornwall, and Geard was certain that he could readily give Sutcliff details as to the situation there.[30]

On the other hand, William Wilkins, another friend from Sutcliff's days at the Bristol Academy, told him that as far as he was concerned Sutcliff should take advantage of being young and single. He should thus think of spending some time as an itinerant evangelist 'going from place to place'.[31] His old mentor John Fawcett had no specific advice as to a future course of action, but he did remind Sutcliff of his ongoing concern for his situation. 'Considering your youth, your trials have been singular. Yet,' he wrote, 'hitherto the Lord has helped you, and I trust you will find in the end that all has been ordered for the best.'[32]

It was his good friend Purdy who came up with the most elaborate plan for his future ministry. Benjamin Beddome, who had seen much fruitfulness from his labours at Bourton-on-the-Water, was getting old and due to gout in both of his feet was finding it difficult to get around as he once had done. He had told Purdy, who was only twelve or so miles away in Chipping Norton, that he was seriously thinking of getting an assistant. He had heard a good report of Sutcliff's abilities and asked Purdy whether or not Sutcliff would be available to assist him. However, there was a hitch. Hugh Evans was due to be at Bourton on Sunday, 23 April — Purdy was writing to Sutcliff on Tuesday, 11 April — and undoubtedly they would discuss Beddome's need of an assistant. Evans would probably recommend someone who was studying at the academy, and the result would be that 'Sutcliff will be hooked out.' Purdy therefore suggested the following scheme. If Sutcliff just 'happened' to turn up at Bourton-on-the-Water on Saturday, 15 April, Beddome would undoubtedly ask him to preach the following day. Then, when Evans came the next week, Sutcliff's preaching would still be fresh in Beddome's mind.[33]

But like many of the best-laid schemes of mice and men, this one went astray. Sutcliff's reply to Purdy's letter was not written till the day before Evans was due at Bourton, when it would have been too late to go. Does this mean that he refused to go along with his friend's well-intentioned scheming on his behalf?[34] Not necessarily, for a letter which Purdy wrote to Sutcliff on 9 June clearly indicates that Beddome did hear Sutcliff preach, though when the latter went to Bourton remains uncertain. He may well have suggested a modification of Purdy's plan, and gone to Bourton after Hugh Evans' visit. Be this as it may, in this letter Purdy told his friend that he had just been talking to Beddome, who had remarked that Sutcliff measured up to all of his expectations except in one important area, his preaching. Purdy's scheme had failed.

It is interesting to note that Sutcliff was still wrestling with his preaching style, which had been a problem since the beginning of his public ministry. Not that he was incapable of delivering a good sermon. In this very letter in which Purdy informed Sutcliff of Beddome's comment about his preaching, Purdy mentioned that the Baptists in Chipping Norton were generally appreciative of Sutcliff's ministry from the pulpit.

While Beddome did not see Sutcliff as the assistant for whom he was looking, he did feel, according to Purdy, that Sutcliff 'would have done for Olney very well'.[35] Sutcliff may well have thought that the pastoral charge in Olney was no longer an option, but there were some like Beddome — and, as he would discover the following month, his former tutor Caleb Evans — who strongly thought he should still consider it. There is probably no better example of the strong paternalistic attitude of Hugh and Caleb Evans with regard to the students who had studied under them than the letter which Caleb Evans wrote to Sutcliff on 30 June and which Sutcliff received three days later.[36] The letter began with an earnest and forceful request by Evans on behalf of the Baptists at Olney to visit the Buckinghamshire congregation and supply their pulpit for a few Sundays.

Sutcliff would then be able to determine more easily whether it might be 'the will of providence' that he become their pastor, should of course his ministry 'be approved of by them'. Evans emphasized that in writing in this vein to Sutcliff, he was not merely conveying his own sentiments and those of the Baptist believers at Olney. He was also accurately representing those of Benjamin Beddome and Thomas Dunscombe of Cote, both of whom had been to Olney and spoken with the church there. The Bristol Baptist leader stressed: 'Unless your engagement where you are should be very urgent indeed, we [that is, himself, Beddome and Dunscombe] shall take it unkind if you do not comply with this request.'

A description of the Baptist cause in Olney then followed. From this description and the details about the Olney congregation provided by Ryland the previous year Sutcliff would have had a fair idea of what to expect in the Buckinghamshire town. Evans wrote, 'The interest at Olney is considerable, a good house, a large congregation, and were there an acceptable minister, a prospect of its becoming much larger, an agreeable neighbourhood with respect to other churches and ministers, and many circumstances of a very encouraging nature. With respect to the people, *some* of them are pretty high in their sentiments, and are perhaps too fond of a doctrinal ministry. But in the general, a spiritual, experimental, evangelical minister would be highly acceptable, and I verily believe the people would unite cordially in such a man.'

Like Ryland, Evans underscored the fact that the congregation was of a substantial size with the encouraging prospect of even greater growth. In other words, if Sutcliff was called to Olney he would not be faced with a dwindling congregation as he had been at Shrewsbury. But he would have to cope with some of the Olney Baptists, who were 'pretty high in their sentiments' and 'perhaps too fond of a doctrinal ministry', which was Evans' way of describing their High Calvinism. Evans underlined the word 'some' in order to emphasize that not all of the congregation were High Calvinists. Ryland probably had in mind the same situation when he cautioned Sutcliff about the 'stiffness' of the Olney Baptists. Evans was confident, however, that the presence of such High Calvinism would pose no real problems for a man whose ministry was 'spiritual, experimental, [and] evangelical'. The key word in this trio of adjectives is 'experimental'. It was a favourite term of eighteenth-century evangelicals who used it to describe authentic

Christianity. True Christianity was 'experimental religion', that is, a religion in which one's inward religious experience and affections were found to be genuine by the fruit they bore. 'Our inward acquaintance with God,' Jonathan Edwards wrote in his classic work on Christian experience, *A Treatise concerning Religious Affections,* 'surely belongs to the head of experimental religion: but this, God represents as consisting chiefly in that experience which there is in holy practice.'[37] A ministry, therefore, which stressed the importance of Christian practice, but which was also firmly grounded in evangelical doctrine, would in Evans' opinion be 'highly acceptable' to the Olney congregation, including the High Calvinists. As we shall see, eighteenth-century High Calvinism was sometimes accompanied by doctrinal antinomianism, a point of view which argued that believers did not have to obey God's law as a rule of life. Lest Sutcliff be afraid that the Olney High Calvinists were also doctrinal antinomians, Evans was careful to highlight the fact that an 'experimental' ministry would be quite acceptable to the congregation as a whole. It should also be noted that these remarks by Evans only make sense if he knew that Sutcliff was of the same doctrinal convictions as himself, that is, if Sutcliff were an evangelical Calvinist.

Evans closed the letter with a final admonition to Sutcliff to pay the Olney congregation a visit 'immediately', stay with them as long as he could, and then seek further direction from God. 'Your present duty, as things appear to us [i.e. himself, Beddome, and Dunscombe], seems clear and evident, and it will give us great pain if you refuse to comply with our request.' In a postscript Evans informed Sutcliff that Beddome had 'lately preached from — and do you now practise these words — the king's business requireth haste (cf. 1 Samuel 21:8)'.

This letter well illustrates the way in which Caleb Evans, like his father, unashamedly sought to be a father in God to those whom he had taught. It is a forceful letter, but it appears that it was the very thing Sutcliff needed. If Evans' words and tone had been any less commanding, Sutcliff might have given way to his natural diffidence and the door to Olney would have been left to shut once and for all. As it was, he received Evans' letter on 3 July and three days later he had written to Mary Andrews seeking to arrange a time when he could visit Olney.

# 6.
# Olney

*Jesus, where'er thy people meet,*
*There they behold thy mercy-seat;*
*Where'er they seek thee thou art found,*
*And ev'ry place is hallow'd ground.*

*For thou, within no walls confin'd,*
*Inhabitest the humble mind;*
*Such ever bring thee, where they come,*
*And going, take thee to their home.*

(William Cowper)

Olney is a small market-town situated at the northern end of Buckinghamshire in what is known as the Ouse valley, the Ouse River coiling around the town to the south and to the east.[1] While the earliest written evidence of the town's existence dates from a Saxon charter of 979, archaeological finds have revealed that the area had been occupied for some millennia prior to the Saxons. Since Sutcliff's day, there has been no change to the basic layout of the town: a long, broad street — now High Street — widens into a spacious, three-cornered market-place at the southern end of the town. Standing in the south-east corner of this market-place is the three-storey, red-brick house in which the evangelical poet William Cowper (1731-1800) lived from 1768 to 1786. From his upstairs windows the poet could see the roof of what is now called Sutcliff Baptist Church, which then stood behind a row of shops, part of the western frontage of the market-place. It was here that Sutcliff was to minister and to lead the Baptist congregation in worship for close to thirty-nine years.

By and large the members of the congregation were not well-to-do. Cowper once described them and many of the town's other Christian inhabitants as 'the half-starved and ragged of the Earth', who 'suffer everything that infirmity and poverty can inflict upon them'. 'Living and dying in a state of neglected obscurity,' he observed, yet they 'love God, trust him, they pray to him in secret, and though he means to reward them openly, the day of recompense is delay'd.'[2]

A goodly number of the women of the Baptist congregation, as well as many of their children and a few of their husbands, were involved in the manufacture of lace, the most prevalent form of industrial occupation in the town as well as the county. The average lacemaker would often put in twelve hours of unremitting labour a day. During the short days of winter a single candle perched upon a three-legged stool would have to serve three or four of them in a cottage as they 'wove' the fine thread into intricate patterns of lace. Unable to afford heat from coal during the winter months, the lacemakers would keep their feet warm by putting them on earthenware pots that had been filled with hot charcoal or wood-ash. From an early age children, in groups of twenty to thirty, would be crowded into one of the larger cottages where some of the older women would teach them the trade. John Newton believed that it was this 'poring over ... [lace] pillows for ten to twelve hours every day, and breathing confined air in ... crowded little rooms' that rendered a dozen or so individuals in the town 'disordered in their heads'.[3] Be this as it may, this cottage industry did exact a heavy toll. The very close work that it entailed often meant that those who engaged in this labour for any length of time ran the risk of impaired vision or even its loss. Yet, the women had no choice but to be employed in this domestic industry. The earnings of their husbands, who were for the most part agricultural labourers, were rarely enough to enable their families to subsist. Female and child labour was thus a matter of necessity.[4]

## The story of the Olney Baptists

The Baptist cause in Olney had been planted in the 1660s by John Gibbs (1627-1699), who had been the vicar at nearby Newport Pagnell but was ejected for his Nonconformist convictions in 1662

An Olney lacemaker from Sutcliff's day

following the restoration of Charles II. An early record of this work, from the hostile pen of the Anglican vicar of Olney, described it as an 'Anabaptist' meeting, which gathered 'at the house of Widow Teares; number, about 200 ... meane people; led by Mr Gibbs, one Breedon, and James Rogers, lace buyers, and one Fenne, a hatter'.[5] Gibbs was a good friend of John Bunyan, and like Bunyan believed in both open communion and open membership. Thus, at this point in time the Olney congregation could be well described as an open membership Baptist church. Of the three individuals who shared the leadership of the Olney Baptists with Gibbs, it is noteworthy that two of them, James Rogers and John Fenne, were members of the Bedford congregation which Bunyan pastored from 1672 till his death in 1688.[6] Joan Teare, the widow at whose home the Olney Baptists first met, died in 1672. That same year the Baptists shifted their meeting-place to a barn owned by a certain Joseph Kent, which stood on the present site of Sutcliff Baptist Church. Joseph Kent's barn was subsequently torn down in 1694 to make way for the construction of a proper meeting-house.

Three years prior to the erection of this meeting-house a paedobaptist congregation had also been started in Olney through the preaching of Richard Davis (1658-1714), who had been ordained pastor of the Congregationalist church in Rothwell, Northamptonshire in 1690.[7] A remarkable evangelist with 'a good voice and thundering way of preaching', Davis planted some seven churches within the space of a few years of his ordination. Among these was one at Wellingborough, Northamptonshire, which was formed in 1691 by the dismissal from Rothwell of seventy-two members, forty-five women and twenty-seven men. The Olney congregation was a branch work of the Wellingborough church, becoming a church in its own right in 1718.

Despite the fact that Gibbs practised open membership and open communion, he was not at all favourably disposed towards the Olney Congregationalists. The reasons for Gibbs' attitude were partly theological and partly 'territorial'. Davis was a convinced paedobaptist, while Gibbs' sympathies were definitely baptistic. Davis had also been accused of doctrinal antinominanism, a widespread cause of offence throughout the Midlands. Then, by coming into Olney where there was already a Nonconformist congregation Davis was poaching on Gibbs' territory.

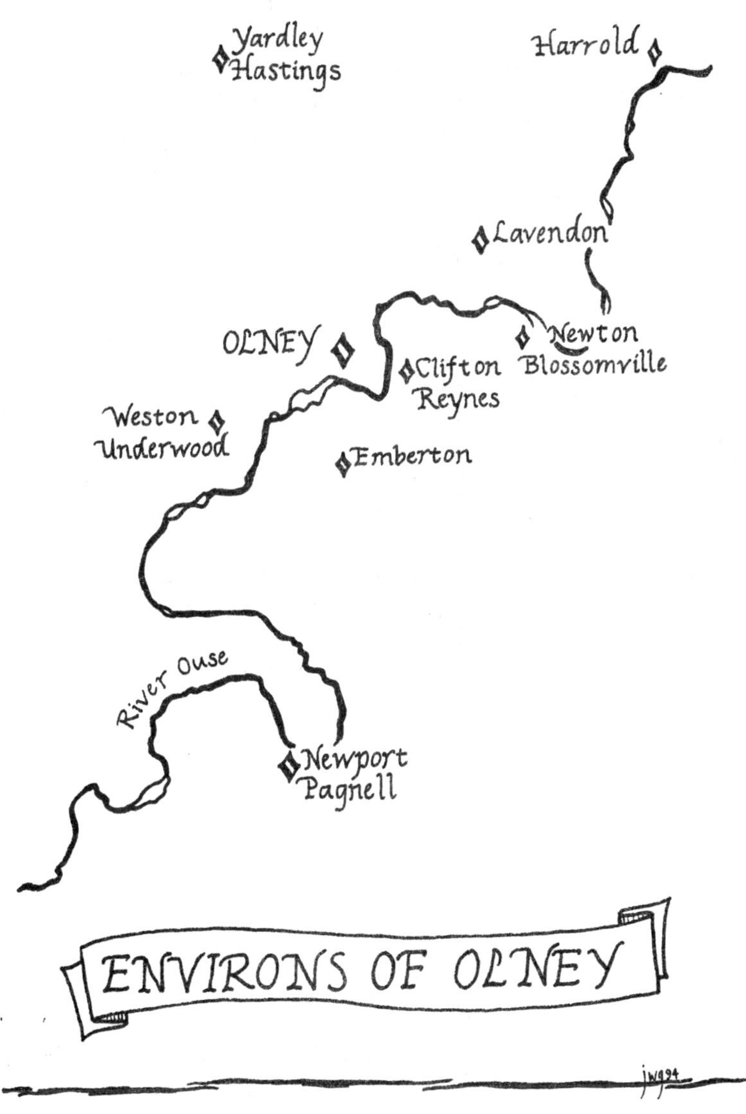


Map 2 — Environs of Olney

Relations between the two congregations further deteriorated in 1713 when Matthias Maurice (1684-1738) came to pastor the congregation Gibbs had gathered together.[8] Maurice, a convinced paedobaptist, had little sympathy with the Baptist position. In a year and a half or so he was able to persuade many in the open membership congregation to abandon the principles upon which Gibbs had founded the church and to take a decided position against working together with Baptists. In November 1714 Maurice left Olney to accept a call to succeed Davis as the pastor of the Rothwell congregation. When he departed, those whom he had influenced left to join the Congregationalist work in the town. This exodus of members was a severe blow to the Olney Baptists and the years immediately following were extremely depressing ones for their cause.

At some point after 1732 — the exact date is not known due to the loss of the minute book — the Baptists in Olney placed themselves under the oversight and care of Walgrave Baptist Church, Northamptonshire, and their pastor, Moses Deacon (d.1773). This arrangement continued until 15 November 1738, when the cause was recognized again as an independent work through the dismissal of thirteen individuals — four men and nine women — to form a closed membership Baptist church. By 1742 this newly reconstituted work had grown to forty-six members and had called a Francis Walker to be their pastor. But Walker served less than a year. Appointed pastor in November 1741, he died the following October. For the next eight years the church did not have a resident pastor, but oversight was given for a few years by a 'Mr Rogers'.

Who was this 'Mr Rogers'? Maurice F. Hewett, who pastored Sutcliff Baptist Church from 1922 to 1931, thought that he was Jacob Rogers, a Church of England clergyman from Bedford who was converted in the 1730s through the witness of two Moravian missionaries and whom George Whitefield met on one occasion in Olney in May 1739. However, Geoffrey F. Nuttall, who is widely recognized as a leading authority on eighteenth-century English Dissenters, has identified him as a certain Charles Rogers (d.1782). For a few months in 1732 and 1733 Rogers had been the pastor of College Lane Baptist Church in Northampton, an open communion cause where John Ryland would later minister. Rogers failed in an attempt to lead this congregation into the adoption of closed communion convictions. He was thus constrained to leave the church along with those who had sided with him and to worship with a closed communion congregation in Northampton which met in a building that fronted on a square known as the Green. Appointed as their pastor in 1733, Rogers stayed with these Baptists until 1738, when he left Northampton for Coventry. After only three years in Coventry he moved to Romsey in Hampshire. He was only a few years in the south before he again moved on, this time to Olney. Upon Nuttall's reckoning, his ministry in Olney lasted a couple of years and then he was gone to Chatham in Kent. An 'inveterate wanderer', he subsequently went through a host of churches prior to his death in 1782.[9] Following Rogers' departure the Olney Baptists were without a pastor for at least a couple of years till the coming of William Walker (d.1792) in 1749.

William Walker had been baptized by Rogers in 1732 at College Lane Baptist Church only a short time before Rogers forsook this congregation for the closed communion church on the Green.[10] Walker went with him and it was this church that called Walker to the ministry in 1735, giving him leave to preach at Olney if the believers there so requested. When Walker came to Olney in 1749, therefore, the congregation had probably known him on and off for fourteen years. Typical of many eighteenth-century Baptist churches, though, the congregation took its time in extending a call to Walker. By the latter months of 1750 he had still not been given a call to the chuch, even though some of the members said that 'A year and a half's stated preaching upon trial is long enough.'[11] The length of this trial period, long even for the 1700s, may have had something to do with the fact that Walker had introduced singing into the church, a controversial issue in not a few Baptist churches of that era. There was an acute division in the church over this innovation in worship, and Walker eventually stated that he would rather 'commit himself to Providence than to labour any longer in the fires of Olney'![12] He thus left Olney, and, after spending some time in London, ended up at neighbouring Newport Pagnell.

However, Walker evidently had a number of keen supporters in Olney, who were determined to have him for their pastor. Despite his earlier statement about labouring in 'the fires of Olney', he was persuaded to return to Olney and began preaching there again in March 1753. That November he was set apart as pastor of the church and the church covenant drawn up anew and signed by all the members. The covenant, Walker wrote, 'is not doctrinal, but practical; it contains not the doctrines we believe but the duties we should do'.[13] Since this covenant was a vital part of the church's life throughout the ministry of Sutcliff, it is appropriate to say a few words about it.

## The church covenant

From the beginning of their history in the mid-seventeenth century Calvinistic Baptists had widely used church covenants, though there were some — for instance, the influential London Baptist leader Hanserd Knollys — who opposed their use. Knollys simply did not believe that the New Testament warranted their usage.[14] Other Baptists disagreed, however. They found covenants especially helpful in creating a sense of community among church members, in emphasizing the place of discipline in local church life and in reminding members of their need for regular patterns of public and private worship — all of which were key aspects of New Testament church life.

The Olney Covenant began with a preamble in which the members of the church declared how God had brought them 'through grace and everlasting love to look unto Him who is the complete Saviour of sinners'. They thus renounced their own righteousness as filthy rags, disavowed any hope of being saved by their own obedience, and in no uncertain terms declared their dependence 'entirely and alone on the sure foundation of Christ, his grace, blood, righteousness, satisfaction, and intercession, for salvation, justification, and acceptance with God'. On this foundation of the 'person, office, authority, Spirit and Word of Christ' the members of the church gave themselves 'up to the Lord, and to one another by the will of God to walk together in a visible church state'. What this walking together entailed was then laid out in thirteen articles. Among other things, these articles pledged those who signed the covenant to make the Scriptures their 'only rule and constant guide in all matters of religion both of faith and practice' (Article I), to defend 'in the face of all opposition whatever the doctrines of free grace' (Article II), to 'hold communion with other churches of the same faith and order' (Article X) and to encourage the development of spiritual gifts in their midst, especially that of preaching — those who exhibited proficiency in this area they hoped to set apart after 'due trial' and to send forth 'to preach the gospel wherever God in the course of divine providence opens a door' (Article XI).

Two major modifications to this covenant occurred during Sutcliff's pastorate. Article XIII, which advocated liberty of conscience regarding singing in public worship, was dropped. This was probably due to the fact that singing was no longer the controversial issue that it had been. Article XII, a blunt declaration of the fact that the members were agreed that 'No woman shall speak in the Church without leave or in answer to any question proposed to her by the Church,' was apparently felt to be too severe as the eighteenth century wore on. It was revised to read that 'A woman is allowed to speak in the Church, yet not in such sort as carries in it direction, instruction, government and authority.'[15] In the seventeenth century and the early decades of the following century, most Baptists would have had no problems with the way that this article had been originally worded. For example, in 1694 the Calvinistic Baptist congregation which met in Fleur de Lys Yard in Southwark, London — later Maze Pond Calvinistic Baptist Church — allowed female members to vote at church meetings by the 'lifting up of their hands', but at the same time insisted that women be excluded 'from prayer, prophesying, and giving of thanks', all of those areas of public church life which involved speech.[16] By the late eighteenth and early nineteenth centuries, though, attitudes were changing.

The shift in attitudes is well seen in the response to an unsigned letter entitled 'On Women Speaking in the Church', which appeared in the April 1815 issue of *The Baptist Magazine*, the monthly paper of the Calvinistic Baptists which had begun publication in 1809. This unsigned letter maintained on the basis of 1 Corinthians 14:34 that it was 'unscriptural for [women] to speak in the church *at all*'. In reply to this letter, one respondent argued that what Paul had in mind in this verse was 'that kind of loquacity, or female inquisitiveness, which, in the early days of Christianity was, perhaps, but too common amongst them, of asking questions in the churches respecting the new doctrine'. In other words, Paul was dealing with a situation specific to the early church and not at all laying down a blanket prohibition for all time. Another respondent, who was probably James Lister (1779-1851), the pastor of Lime Street Baptist Church, Liverpool, argued that there were some specific occasions when it was quite 'proper for females to speak in the presence of the church', for example, when they sang God's praises or gave their profession of faith prior to being received into membership.[17]

The change of attitude in the Olney Covenant as well as in these items from *The Baptist Magazine* is part and parcel of an ever-increasing respect in eighteenth-century English culture for the intellectual capacities of women. While this growing respect was not universal, it is quite evident that in some Baptist circles there was occurring a rethinking of attitudes with regard to the role of women in the life of the church. It should be added, however, that there was never any discussion in eighteenth-century Calvinistic Baptist churches of the possibility of female pastors or elders.

## The meeting-house

Walker's pastorate, which lasted until 1773, was an important period of consolidation for the church after a lengthy period of instability. He laid a solid foundation upon which Sutcliff was to build. During his time as pastor the meeting-house was also enlarged for a cost of £252.13.2, more than half of which was given by Baptist churches near and far. The way in which the enlarged interior appeared in Sutcliff's day is well described by Thomas Wright in his book *The Town of Cowper*.[18] He depicts a typical late eighteenth-century meeting-house. It was oblong in shape and could seat 700. A pulpit with a pedimented back was located in the middle of one of the longer walls, the north wall, 'whilst to the other three walls [were] affixed cumbrous galleries supported by wooden pillars'. The box pews were deep and 'perpendicular-backed', their backs lined with green baize and their doors fastened by wooden buttons. In the tops of the pews were inserted wooden candlesticks to provide light during evening services. Immediately in front of the pulpit was what was known as the Communion or Table Pew, so called because of the table that was placed in that pew for the celebration of the Lord's Supper. As one would expect in a church that had its spiritual roots in the Puritan tradition, there was no ornamentation. In this simplicity and plainness, though, there was a definite beauty.

An early photo of the interior of the Baptist meeting-house at Olney
*(Reproduced by courtesy of the Sutcliff Baptist Church, Olney).*

Chair used by Sutcliff, still in use at the church
*(Reproduced by courtesy of the Sutcliff Baptist Church, Olney)*

## Fellowship with local believers in other denominations

The enlargement of the meeting-house interior took place in 1763. The following year, as we have already noted in chapter 4, John Newton came to the Olney parish church. He lost no time in getting acquainted with his fellow ministers in the neighbourhood. As we have seen, he met with John Collett Ryland in February 1765. The previous July he had gone to the Baptist meeting-house in Olney and heard a sermon by William Grant, the pastor of the open membership Baptist church in Wellingborough. In a letter that Newton wrote to his wife the following day he told her, 'A more excellent sermon I never heard, never was my heart so melted down since the golden days when I first attended Mr Brewer [i.e. Samuel Brewer (1723-1796), a London Congregationalist minister] and Mr [George] Whitefield.'[19] When Brewer came to visit Newton at Christmas 1765, he was asked to preach at both the Baptist and Congregationalist churches in town. Newton went to hear him on both occasions, and then invited William Walker and the Congregationalist minister, John Drake, back to the vicarage to dine with Brewer and himself.[20]

Two years later, on Newton's suggestion, the Baptists, Congregationalists and Anglicans in Olney began to hold what became an annual series of joint services for the town's young people at the beginning of each new year. On 30 December a service was held in the Baptist meeting-house, the following day in that of the Congregationalists, and on New Year's Day Newton himself preached in the parish church. The Christian friendliness that is evident in these reciprocal visits and joint services had been hitherto unknown in Olney,[21] but a tradition had been started which Sutcliff, when he came, would heartily endorse.

## The Northamptonshire Baptist Association

The other major event of Walker's pastorate was his participation in the formation of the Northamptonshire Baptist Association in May 1765. Associations had played a central role in the establishment and advance of the Baptist cause since its inception. *The First London Confession of Faith* (1644), the earliest Calvinistic Baptist statement of faith, which was itself the product of an association of

Calvinistic Baptist churches in the capital, had succintly rejected the view that inter-church fellowship was merely an option for believers. Although 'particular Congregations be distinct and severall Bodies', the framers of this confession declared in Article XLVII, yet 'are they all to walk by one and the same Rule, and by all meanes convenient to have the counsell and help one of another in all needfull affaires of the Church, as members of one body in the common faith under Christ their onely head'.[22] The mutual interdependence envisaged in this text flourished in a number of associations during the mid-seventeenth century, but by the beginning of the following century association life in many parts of the country had begun to wilt and even disappear. One sign of the renewal of the Calvinistic Baptist cause towards the end of that century was either the creation of new associations or the revitalization of ones that had been founded earlier.[23]

Plans were drawn up by Walker and five other pastors on 17 October 1764 for the inaugural meeting of the Northamptonshire Association the following May. Two of these pastors came from Northamptonshire churches, Moses Deacon of Walgrave and John Brown (d.1800) of Kettering, while the other three hailed from Leicestershire: Isaac Woodman of Sutton-in-the-Elms, John Evans of Foxton and Robert Hall, Sr (1728-1791), of Arnesby. Hall, as we shall see, would play a very significant role in the lives of Sutcliff and his close friends. What led these six men to contemplate such an association was undoubtedly a consciousness of their own need of fellowship and a recognition of the great help and support their churches could derive from its existence. But they could hardly have envisaged the way in which their association would be instrumental in meeting the needs of many far from their fields, towns and villages. For it was in this association that the Baptist Missionary Society would be conceived and brought to birth before the end of the century, and in the course of the following century missionaries sent out from this society would take the gospel to such places as far afield as India and Jamaica, China and the Congo.

The first meeting of the association was held at Kettering on 14-15 May 1765, at which time Moses Deacon and William Walker preached.[24] A circular letter was drawn up by John Evans of Foxton to be sent around to the churches who were part of the fledgling association. This first circular letter basically contained a brief report of the substance of Deacon's sermon on Acts 2:42 and that of

Map 3 — The Northamptonshire Baptist Association

Walker on 2 Thessalonians 3:1, as well as informing its readers and hearers of the fact that in meeting together the representatives of the churches had experienced 'much of the Lord's presence', even as he had promised in Matthew 18:20. The letter was signed by twelve ministers. Handwritten copies were presumably made for all of the churches in the association, for this letter was not printed, though all the later ones would be.[25]

The following year, 1766, saw the association hold its annual meetings in Olney. The ministers and messengers sent by the churches stayed at the Bull Inn, which stood on the western frontage of the market-place. It was a convenient place to stay, since it was scarcely twenty yards from the entrance of the Bull Inn to that of the Baptist meeting-house. The meetings began on the evening of Tuesday, 6 May. That evening was taken up with prayer and those present discussing and sharing about their Christian experience. There was also time set apart to read the letters written by the various churches of the association for this very occasion, in which they catalogued their encouragements and discouragements. The following day began with more prayer and sharing. Around 10 o'clock a public service was held at which first Robert Hall and then John Brown preached. The evening of this day was also spent in prayer, further consideration of the state of the churches and the giving of direction to Moses Deacon as he drew up the circular letter to be sent around to the churches that year.

The meetings were again at Olney in 1768. At 10 o'clock in the morning of Wednesday, 15 June, John Gill (1730-1809), the pastor of the Baptist church in St Albans, Hertfordshire, and the nephew of the famous London Baptist divine of the same name, preached on 2 Corinthians 4:1, followed by John Collett Ryland on Revelation 3:11. Abraham Booth, who was at that time living in Sutton-in-Ashfield, Nottinghamshire, and who would become one of the leading lights in the Calvinistic Baptist denomination in the late eighteenth century, preached that evening from Acts 11:26. Newton and Cowper also attended the meetings, Newton having been asked to preach in the evening of 16 June. Cowper later wrote down some of his impressions of the meetings in a letter to his aunt, Judith Madan (1702-1781), the mother of the evangelical clergyman Martin Madan (1725-1790). Cowper especially made mention of the 'excellent endowments' the Lord had given to Booth.[26]

Three years later, in 1771, the association met yet a third time in Olney. It was the last occasion for Walker to help host the meetings of the association in which he had played a prominent role. Early in 1773 he said goodbye to Olney, though he had once entertained hopes of ministering in the town till the end of his earthly life. The final years of Walker's ministry in Olney were marred by contention and bickering. In a blistering farewell letter that he wrote to the church on 4 February 1773, Walker stated that during his time at Olney he had 'laboured in the very fire', recalling words that he had used of the church more than twenty years earlier.[27] His gifts had been abused and 'sadly crushed', and he had found himself 'frequently dispirited'. He had been induced to settle in Olney mainly because of the church's 'willingness and readiness to hear the Word'. But, he continued, if he had known what had awaited him in this pastoral charge, he would never have accepted the church's call to be their pastor. Walker did not spell out in detail the troubles he had faced in the church. Some of it probably had to do with High Calvinism. As we have seen, when Caleb Evans all but ordered Sutcliff to preach at Olney for a number of Sundays, he mentioned that some of the Olney Baptists were 'pretty high in their sentiments' and very fond of 'a doctrinal ministry', which was his way of describing their High Calvinism. And in his farewell letter, Walker told the members of the Olney congregation to 'take heed unto your spirit, be not too dogmatical in sentiment'. Yet, it also appears that Walker's problems had much to do with the attitudes of many in the congregation. They found it next to impossible to overlook non-essential differences, and thus there were 'frequent quarrels and almost incessant variance' in the church. Nor was Walker himself entirely blameless in this conflict between pastor and congregation. He said that he was naturally timid and easily discouraged. But evidently he too had lost his temper on more than one occasion, for he mentioned that some of the members represented him 'sometimes as angry and impatient'. Nevertheless, Walker assured the congregation that he had forgiven them and he urged them to treat his successor differently. The letter closed with a lengthy exhortation, in which Walker pointed out that the church had a dire need to be filled with the Holy Spirit: 'He can soon set all things to right amongst you.'

## Sutcliff arrives in Olney

Despite Walker's encouragement to treat his successor gently, Sutcliff initially had no easy time of it when he came to the church in the summer of 1775. Walker had been gone more than two years, but the church was still characterized by divisions, as a letter from Caleb Evans bears witness. Writing to Sutcliff in late October that year, he lamented, 'Oh what a pity it is that *Brethren* should fall out by the way! When will the breaches at Olney be made up — when will that meek and quiet spirit, which so eminently adorns your pious hostess, universally spread among the people and leaven the whole lump! We are commanded to pray for the peace of Jerusalem (see Psalm 122:6) — when will our prayers be answered with respect to that part of our Jerusalem where you are at present situated?'[28]

The 'pious hostess' whom Evans mentions as possessing an exemplary spirit of meekness was none other than Mary Andrews, who had written to Sutcliff in November 1774, beseeching him to consider supplying the Olney pulpit. He resided in her home till she died in 1795 and he married the following year. Her house, which had been built in 1611, is next door to the meeting-house. It is now known as 'Westlands' and is much altered. Mary traced her early interest in the gospel to a sermon by George Whitefield that she heard when she was only three or four. By the time that she was nine, Sutcliff tells us, 'She frequently attended the ministry of the Word with a peculiar degree of pleasure.' Her sister, Hannah (d.1804), was married to William Bull (1738-1814), the Congregationalist minister of Newport Pagnell and a good friend of William Cowper. She had come to live in Olney in the early 1770s after her husband had been tragically killed in a riding accident. Though she regularly attended the Baptist meeting-house at Olney for the rest of her life she never became a member. When Sutcliff came as pastor, it was arranged that he would be given room and board in return for tutoring her young son, William.[29] This arrangement well suited Sutcliff, since it allowed him to spend a significant amount of his income on books. In the sermon which he preached at Sutcliff's funeral, Fuller mentioned that his deceased friend had had 'a great thirst for reading' and over the course of time had built up 'one of the best libraries in this part of the country'.[30] John Fawcett's son

Westlands, former home of Mary Andrews, where Sutcliff lived for over twenty years, as it appears today. (Both house and church are much altered. In Sutcliff's day there was a row of shops on the High Street in front of the meeting-house and the entrance was on the left-hand side of the building, as seen in this photo.)

noted the same in his memoirs of his father. The latter also emphasized that Sutcliff's love of books did not make of him a literary recluse; on the contrary, his 'conversation on all occasions showed that his mind was richly stored with what he read ... which he readily communicated to others.'[31]

Now, not only were the Olney Baptists divided among themselves, but soon some of them were at odds with Sutcliff. For instance, some disagreed with his refusal to allow unbelievers to be present when prospective members of the church related in the presence of the congregation the way that they had been led to embrace Christ as Saviour and Lord. James Turner fully supported Sutcliff's stance in this regard. Citing Jesus' admonition in Matthew 7:6 not to give what is holy to dogs nor to place pearls before pigs, Turner stated that to him 'It appeared ... that this is done in the most express and literal sense of the words when carnal people are admitted to hear the experiences of the saints before the church.' He then went on to refer Sutcliff to that favourite text of eighteenth-century Baptists, Song of Solomon 4:12: 'Is not the church a *garden enclosed*? Not at all if the ungodly are to mix with them in privileges and duties belonging only to themselves.'[32] Much more serious, though, was a problem which we shall examine in more detail in the next chapter, namely, the concern of the High Calvinists in the congregation that Sutcliff's evangelical Calvinism was a departure from the canons of 'orthodoxy'.

In spite of these initial problems, Sutcliff does not seem to have shown any hesitation in accepting the fact that Olney was the place that God had marked out for him as the future scene of his pastoral ministry. This is noteworthy in view of the deep uncertainty he had experienced regarding the place of his future ministry prior to his coming to Olney. Somewhat reluctant to come to Olney, once he arrived he did not look back. In the autumn of 1775, he wrote to John Fawcett, requesting that his membership at Wainsgate Baptist Church be transferred to Olney. He told Fawcett and the Wainsgate congregation that it was with 'pain and reluctance' that he asked for this transfer of membership, for he counted it a 'great privilege' that God had led him to become a member of that church. He assured the West Yorkshire Baptists that he was not unmindful of them and emphasized that their union with one another was indissoluble, since they were all united to Christ, their 'exalted Head'. But he believed that 'The leadings of Providence evidently point out

Olney' as the place where God wanted him, and for that reason he felt constrained to ask for a dismissal. In a postscript to this letter, Sutcliff indicated that the membership of the church stood at roughly thirty-eight, but that 'Many young persons were waiting to be admitted.'[33]

In the official letter of dismissal to the Olney congregation, signed by the leadership of the Wainsgate church, including Fawcett and William Sutcliff, Sutcliff's uncle, the Wainsgate believers thanked God 'for the grace and gifts bestowed' on Sutcliff and noted that it was without hesitation that they granted Sutcliff's request. May 'the God of Israel bless you in him', the letter concluded, 'make him a blessing to you, and succeed all his labours for your good, give him many seals of his ministry among you, and make him a repairer of your breaches.'[34] It cannot have been a coincidence that the Wainsgate Church asked God to make Sutcliff 'a repairer of [the] breaches' in the Olney congregation. Presumably Sutcliff had communicated something of the situation at Olney to either Fawcett or his family.

Accompanying this official letter of dismissal was also a personal letter from Fawcett to Sutcliff. He told his young friend, 'You have a distinguished place in my affections, and a share in my poor prayers. I am heartily concerned for you, and should be glad to see you. If your ordination should be during the Christmas vacation, I shall be strongly inclined to attend, if possible.'[35] As it turned out, Sutcliff's ordination was not till the following August. Happily, Fawcett was able to make the trip south and participate in this important event in the life of one of his spiritual children.

## The ordination service

Sutcliff was received into membership at Olney on 26 November 1775.[36] His ordination was set for 7 August the following year. It was a red-letter day in the life of the Olney congregation. The previous day Newton had noted in his diary that quite a crowd had come to Olney to either 'assist or be present at Mr Sutcliff's ordination'.[37]

John Evans of Foxton opened the service with prayer, after which Sutcliff read a statement of faith that he had drawn up especially for the occasion and which the other pastors present had already approved. Joshua Symonds, the pastor of what is now called

Bunyan Meeting, Bedford, noted in his diary that it was 'a very full and concise confession of faith'.[38] John Fawcett then asked Sutcliff various questions, which would have related to his personal Christian life, his reasons for believing that he was called of God to pastoral ministry, his doctrinal views and the manner in which he hoped to fulfil the duties of his office. Newton, who attended the ordination, mentioned in his diary that Sutcliff's answers were 'pertinent and modest'.[39] At this point Sutcliff probably knelt down, while the pastors present gathered around him and laid hands on his head as Fawcett prayed over him. In praying Fawcett would have especially commended him to God's keeping and invoked upon him the richest blessings of heaven, in particular, the infilling of God's Spirit of wisdom, power, and holiness.[40]

Caleb Evans, Sutcliff's tutor at Bristol, then preached the first sermon of the day, which was a charge to Sutcliff with regard to the office into which he had entered. Sutcliff may well have received this charge standing, so as to be seen easily by the entire congregation that was assembled.[41] Evans' sermon was based on Hebrews 13:17. In Newton's opinion it was 'sensible and solid'.

Following Evans' sermon, Thomas Pilley (1734-1801), pastor of Luton Baptist Church, led the congregation in prayer, and Thomas Hull (d.1778), the pastor of Carlton Baptist Church, Bedfordshire, and a former member of the Olney Church, delivered a sermon to the Olney Baptists with regard to the duties that they owed to their newly ordained minister. Hull's sermon was taken from Colossians 3:14:'And above all these things put on charity, which is the bond of perfectness' — a very appropriate text in view of the troubles that had plagued the Olney Church. Newton thought it an 'honest and suitable discourse tho' tinctured with a narrowness of spirit'. It appears that there was an element of Baptist triumphalism in the sermon which grated on Newton's evangelical catholicity. As the Anglican went on to state, 'They are thy Servants, My Lord, they love thee and preach thy Gospel, therefore, I will love them and be ready to hear and espouse them notwithstanding they cannot break through the prejudices of Education, which fence them to keep aloof from those who wish them well.'[42] And yet Hull was a good pastor. During his twenty-six years of ministry at Carlton, ninety or so were added to the church and he exercised his office with 'fidelity, affection, and profit' to the congregation.[43] Joshua Symonds closed the service in prayer.

Among the Baptist ministers who had come to Olney for Sutcliff's ordination was Benjamin Beddome from Bourton-on-the-Water. He had been strongly urged to take part in the ordination service, but he declined, being content to sit with the congregation. After the service, though, he was prevailed upon to preach in the evening. For many his sermon that evening was to be long remembered as one of the highlights of the day. Newton was in attendance and heard Beddome as he spoke from Zechariah 11:12, the prophecy about the amount of money Judas received for betraying the Lord Jesus. 'He is an admirable preacher,' Newton later wrote in his diary, 'simple, savoury, weighty.' This was not the first time that Newton had heard one of Beddome's sermons. The previous year, only a few weeks before Sutcliff had come to the town, Newton had heard Beddome preach on 2 Corinthians 1:24. Of that sermon Newton had written, '[It] gave me a pleasure I seldom find in hearing. It was an excellent discourse indeed, and the Lord was pleased to give me some softenings and relentings of heart.'[44] Judging from Newton's diary, Beddome's sermon on 7 August 1776 was equally good.

It was indeed a day, Sutcliff later wrote in the church minutes, 'always to be remembered with joy'.[45] Sutcliff was conscious that the ministry to which he had been called was a solemn task, but he hoped that he would never lose the sheer joy of serving God.

For reasons unknown Sutcliff's old friend James Turner was not able to travel to Olney for the ordination. Sutcliff therefore wrote to him shortly after 7 August and gave him a brief account of the day's activities. Evidently it was not full enough, for Turner wrote back on 28 August with a number of questions which Sutcliff's account had not answered to his satisfaction. Did Sutcliff read his confession of faith? How were the sermons of the day? Were they likely to be printed? After this batch of questions, Turner, knowing Sutcliff's temperament, sought to encourage his friend in his new ministry: 'Well, Sir, now you are married. Permit me to wish you joy! May you prove a good, tender, loving husband; and may your wife be virtuous and fruitful! ... The whole weight of the pastoral office now rests on your shoulders; and I doubt not but you have often cried..., "Who is sufficient for these things?" (2 Corinthians 2:16). You know who has said, "My *grace* is sufficient for thee" (2 Corinthians 12:9) and you know too that nothing short of it is sufficient. I commend you and your Spouse therefore to this grace.'[46]

## Pastoral matters

The clearest record of Sutcliff's exercise of this pastoral office at Olney over the next few years is to be found in the church minutes. A superficial reading might find these minutes dull, lifeless, containing little of importance. Yet, the truth is that such documents are of inestimable value and, when properly questioned, reveal much about the life of the local church that they record. The initial entries of Sutcliff's ministry testify of divisions healed, joy from fruitful labours, the recognition — never pleasant — of human sin, and sadness in the loss of key members of the congregation.

January 1776, for instance, saw the official reinstatement of William Ashburner (d.1777), his wife Sarah and Sarah Jackson, who, the minutes tell us, had 'for many years stood off' from fellowship with the church, a division which undoubtedly occurred during one of the bickerings that Sutcliff's predecessor had mentioned in his farewell letter.[47] The Ashburners had originally become members of the church in 1741, William being appointed deacon that same year.

In addition to their reinstatement, along with that of Sarah Jackson, some thirty new members were received into the church during the first four years of Sutcliff's pastorate. When Sutcliff came to Olney in 1775 the membership stood at thirty-eight. Four years later it had risen to sixty-one. Sutcliff was understandably thrilled at the way in which God was evidently blessing the work at Olney, a fact that he readily communicated to his friends when he had the opportunity. For instance, on 29 April 1777 he wrote to Joshua Llewellyn (1743-1780), who was pastoring a Baptist work in Dublin, that he had just baptized a dozen individuals and that there were 'several others [who] give hopeful evidences of real conversion'. Llewellyn wrote back two months later and told Sutcliff, 'It gave me pleasure to be informed of your success in Olney.'[48]

Sadly, in this same period some members had to be excluded from the fellowship of the church and a few had died. Of the first four received into membership after Sutcliff, for example, three were eventually excluded: Thomas Griggs for lying and criminal deception, Mary Brittain also for lying and Elizabeth Burditt for petty theft.[49] Exclusion of members was not a step that was taken lightly. When Elizabeth Burditt was disfellowshipped, she had been visited at least twice with regard to her conduct — once in March by

Thomas Osborn and William Ashburner, both of whom were deacons, and then again in either late July or early August by Thomas Anderson (d. 1781), also a deacon. Showing neither repentance nor remorse, she was formally excluded at a church meeting on 1 August 1776, only six days before Sutcliff's ordination.

The death of a key member of a church is also a sad experience in the life of any congregation. William Ashburner, whom Sutcliff had the joy of receiving back into the church in January 1776, died suddenly the following year. On 6 August 1777 Sutcliff wrote in the church minute book that the church had 'had a great loss in the sudden death of Mr W. Ashburner, Deacon'. Newton, who mentioned Ashburner's death in his diary, said that he 'was taken away suddenly — well and dead in 5 minutes'.[50] The following January Thomas Osborn was elected 'by a majority of votes' to take his place as deacon. Osborn would faithfully serve in this capacity until compelled to resign the office in 1809 due to physical infirmity.

### Fellowship with other local evangelicals

In addition to his ministry within the Baptist congregation Sutcliff also worked at strengthening the links between evangelicals within the town. For instance, he firmly supported the services held jointly by the Baptists, Congregationalists and Anglicans at the beginning of each new year. As Newton wrote in his diary for 2 January 1776, 'I put off the evening meeting, that the people might hear the sermon to the youth at the Baptist Meeting. The text was Prov. 4:7. I thought Mr Sutcliff spoke well and there seemed a great attention. Do Thou, O Lord, command a blessing.'

And exactly two years later to the day, Newton mentioned in his diary that he had gone to hear Sutcliff preach on the first four words of Proverbs 27:11: 'My son, be wise.' He noted that the young Baptist pastor 'spoke with pertinence and earnestness'.[51] Yet another example of the strong links that were being built between evangelicals in Olney was the fact that when the Olney church hosted the annual meetings of the Northamptonshire Association in May 1776, Newton was cordially invited not only to attend, but also to participate.

From fairly small beginnings these annual association meetings had grown tremendously. In 1774, when the association met in

Carlton, Bedfordshire, the public meetings had been so thronged that the Baptist church could not contain all who wanted to worship and to hear the preaching. The preachers on that occasion had therefore stood in a fairly spacious window from which the glass had been removed, so that the large numbers outside of the meeting-house could also easily hear the sermons. It was a similar situation two years later at Olney. On the first day of the association meetings, Tuesday, 28 May, the representatives of the churches gathered in the Olney meeting-house. Joshua Symonds noted in his diary that there were forty-six ministers present, a clear intimation that the public meetings the following day would be well attended. Sutcliff opened the meeting that evening with a prayer that was, Symonds tells us, 'earnest, lively and fervent — suitable to the occasion'.[52]

The public meetings the following day were indeed thronged. Unlike the Baptist church in Carlton, though, the Olney meeting-house did not have a spacious window-sill which could serve as a makeshift pulpit. So the large congregation was forced to re-assemble under the open sky — *sub dio*, as Newton put it in his diary.[53] An orchard, which backed onto both Cowper's garden and that of the vicarage where Newton lived, served as the place of worship. A platform was set up on which those who were involved in leading the worship and preaching could stand. A few hundred seats were also procured and arranged for the congregation. Even so there was not enough seating for all who were present and several hundred people had to stand.

William Guy, the Baptist pastor from Shepshed whose church and community had recently known revival, began the morning service with what Newton termed 'an earnest and powerful prayer'. Joshua Symonds, who was present on this occasion, also wrote in his diary that Guy prayed 'with astonishing earnestness and power'.[54] John Evans then preached on Psalm 80:19. It was a short sermon and Newton felt that Evans was somewhat flustered by having to preach out of doors. After further prayer, John Ryland, Sr spoke on Romans 3:27 with power, 'originality and zeal'. Newton hoped that 'many were impressed' by the sermon. In the evening, there was yet another sermon, this one by Robert Hall, Sr on Revelation 3:22. Again, the congregation was 'very large and attentive'.

The next day, 30 May, there was in the afternoon a third public service at which Thomas Dunscombe of Cote preached — Newton 'liked him much' — and in the evening Newton himself spoke on

Zechariah 2:10. In his diary Newton said that he wanted his preaching not only to comfort the Baptists present, of whom Sutcliff would certainly have been one, but also to convince them that though he and his fellow Anglicans 'are not gathered exactly in their way', yet God is 'pleased to favor' them with his presence. Newton was convinced that God honoured this desire, for he spoke with liberty and, he felt, 'with acceptance'.[55]

## Hall affirms the doctrine of the Trinity

These annual association gatherings also included more private meetings, at which the representatives of the churches would pray together, share about their Christian experience and listen to the circular letter which had been drawn up for that year. At the 1776 gathering it had been the responsibility of Robert Hall, Sr to write the circular letter that would be printed and then circulated among the churches of the association. The topic that was chosen for 1776 was the doctrine of the Trinity, and as we shall see, Hall's letter proved to be a very timely and popular one.

At the time when he wrote this letter, Hall was the pastor of a small Baptist cause in the village of Arnesby, Leicestershire. He had served in Arnesby since 1753 and it would be his only pastoral charge. He had accepted the call to pastor this work not long after his coming to Baptist convictions. Like John Bunyan, the elder Hall was deeply distressed from a very early age by his own sinfulness. When he was only twelve years old, he was filled with 'black despair ... continually ... accompanied with horrid temptations and blasphemies which ought not to be uttered'.[56] From this state he found no lasting relief until he read Paul's statement in Galatians 4:4-5 that God sent Christ into the world to redeem those who were under the law. This text fully convinced Hall, now in his twenties, that, sinner though he was, he was not outside the bounds of Christ's redemptive work. For some time after his conversion Hall resisted the idea of believer's baptism, but, in 1752, having been convinced of its validity through a reading of Samuel Wilson's *A Scripture Manual* (1750), he was baptized near Hexham, in Northumberland. Five months later he received a call to the ministry and in 1753 was invited to become the pastor of Arnesby Baptist Church.

Throughout Hall's ministry at Arnesby, the church found it

extremely difficult to provide adequate financial support for him, his wife and fourteen children, one of whom would become the famous Baptist preacher, Robert Hall, Jr. The elder Hall often thought that he would have to leave his charge, but as he said later, 'I found my heart so united to the people, that I never durst leave them... It appearing pretty clear to myself and my wife, that we were where God would have us to be, this sense of duty, and a willingness to live honestly, made us resolve in the strength of the Lord, that we would not run into debt, let us live as hardly as we might, which resolution he enabled us to keep.'[57]

To help supplement his income Hall kept a small farm, and on a number of occasions he acknowledged that the Lord undertook for him through generous gifts from friends. For instance, in 1775 John Newton sent him a gift of £10, at which Hall declared: 'This is the Lord's doing and marvellous in my eyes. O to be found worthy of favours!'[58]

Arnesby had been one of the founding churches of the Northamptonshire Association and Hall had been active in its affairs right from the initial meeting which had been held in 1764. By 1776 the Arnesby pastor had become a very valued member of the association. Twice already he had been asked to write a circular letter on key issues: in 1768, when he had penned a refutation of what he termed 'conditional salvation', and in 1772, when he had written on the nature of redemption. His 1776 circular letter on the doctrine of the Trinity was on just as foundational a doctrine.

Near the beginning of the letter, Hall mentioned that it was occasioned by 'awful departures from, and artful oppositions made to, the fundamental doctrine of a Trinity of Persons in the Godhead'.[59] This denial of orthodox trinitarianism was a prominent feature of the religious landscape for most of the eighteenth-century England, and the 1770s were a decade in which anti-trinitarians were especially vociferous. In 1771 an influential group of around 200 Anglican ministers had signed a petition known as the Feathers Tavern Petition, so named after a tavern in London where they had held their meetings. In this petition they called for the abolition of subscription to the Thirty-Nine Articles, the doctrinal basis of the Church of England, in favour of a simple declaration of belief in the Bible. While some of the support for this petition came from clergymen who were definitely trinitarian in belief, it was widely believed that the driving force behind the petition was a group of men who had come to, or were about to, embrace Unitarianism, men such as Theophilus Lindsey (1723-1808). Although the petition was defeated in the House of Commons on 6 February 1772, the debate it had raised did not quickly dissipate.

The following year a number of Dissenters made an abortive attempt to free themselves from the legal obligation of the Toleration Act of 1689, which required that all who dissented from the Church of England and its worship should nevertheless agree with the bulk of the Thirty-Nine Articles. Again the most conspicuous support for this measure came from those who were theologically heterodox, in this case, Presbyterians on the verge of Unitarianism. Unitarianism in fact was to became the leading form of heterodoxy within English Dissent in the last quarter of the eighteenth century.

The Feathers Tavern Petition thus sparked a debate that thrust the doctrine of the Trinity into the public eye, and it is no surprise that the Baptist leaders of the Northamptonshire Association felt that they had to make some sort of statement as to where they stood. Over against those who denied the deity of the Son and the Holy Spirit, Hall asserted on the basis of Scripture that the Son and his Spirit are 'persons properly divine' and, together with the Father, 'are the one living and true God'.[60]

A good idea of the form and manner of his argument may be gained by considering his defence of the Spirit's personality and deity. In seeking to demonstrate that the Holy Spirit is a person Hall turned to those scriptural passages where the Spirit is said to have a mind and a will (Romans 8:27; 1 Corinthians 12:11), where he is said to speak (1 Timothy 4:1; Ezekiel 3:24; Acts 8:29; 10:19-20; 13:2), and where he is spoken of as one with whom believers have fellowship (Ephesians 4:30). That the Spirit is divine Hall showed from the fact that he does what only God can do. For instance, he is involved in the creation of the heavens, the world and its inhabitants (Job 26:13; Genesis 1:2; Job 33:4). In a number of scriptural passages he is also (implicitly) called God (Acts 5:3-4; 1 Corinthians 3:16; 6:19). Furthermore, the attributes which Scripture assigns to him are divine ones: he is depicted as omniscient (1 Corinthians 2:10), omnipresent (Psalm 139:7), and eternal (Hebrews 9:14).[61]

Ending on a practical note, Hall concluded that the believer's 'obligations to the Lord the Spirit are great. He is the author and inditer of your Bible... He is the Lord of the harvest, who prepares and sends forth labourers. He is the author of all edifying gifts to the Church. It is owing to him that you are renewed and strengthened in your minds. Look to him to create in you a clean heart and renew a right spirit within you.'[62]

This small work proved to be of such help to Hall's fellow Baptists that a second edition was soon called for and printed in the same year.

One further event which took place at this meeting of the association in Olney should be noted. Although it was of great significance for the future of the Calvinistic Baptist denomination, it would have merited hardly any attention at the time. It was during these three days of meetings at the end of May 1776 that Sutcliff first made the acquaintance of the one whom C. H. Spurgeon many years later described as 'the greatest theologian' of the nineteenth century, namely, Andrew Fuller.[63]

## Sutcliff on the providence of God

Before we turn to look at Andrew Fuller's early years, however, we should take notice of Sutcliff's first venture into print. Sutcliff had been asked to preach at the 1778 association meetings held in Leicester. He chose to speak on a clause from Revelation 2:1: 'who walketh in the midst of the seven golden candlesticks'. Though his sermon has not survived, his preaching obviously impressed his fellow ministers, for the following year he was asked to draw up the circular letter on the doctrine of providence.

Sutcliff felt overwhelmed by having to write on what was such a vast subject and then to submit it to the approval of his fellow ministers, nearly all of whom had had many years of experience of the ministry. He wrote to both Fawcett and Turner in the early months of 1779, seeking their advice and help. Fawcett's reply was written on 6 April from Liverpool, where he was supplying in the stead of Samuel Medley (1738-1799), the pastor of Byrom Street Baptist Church who was away preaching in London. The Yorkshire pastor confessed that 'Divine providence is indeed awfully mysterious,' and directed Sutcliff to pay close attention to his 'own experience and observation, and the precious treasury of God's Word'. He went on to cite a striking example of the way that divine providence had worked itself out in the life of a certain Mr Liverley, who appears to have been a Liverpool Christian. Liverley had been 'worth some thousands', but was now utterly bankrupt. His catastrophic fall had been used by God for good, though. A number of 'the most respectable, most pious, and most remarkable families for supporting the interest of Christ' in Liverpool had been deeply convinced of the transitory nature of all human wealth and the pressing importance of finding their true riches in Christ. Fawcett concluded by saying that he wished he could be present with Sutcliff at the forthcoming meeting of his association. Not only would he like to hear Sutcliff's circular letter, but he also stated: 'How happy should I be in having another interview with the ministers in your connection!'[64] The ministers whom Fawcett had met at the time of Sutcliff's ordination had obviously made a lasting and favourable impression on him. In fact, on the back of this letter Fawcett asked Sutcliff to especially convey his love to Newton. This request not only says much about Fawcett's admiration for the evangelical Anglican, but also speaks of Sutcliff's friendship with Newton.

Turner's letter was written five days before that of Fawcett and was considerably more helpful in the advice that he gave to his younger friend. Turner began it by chiding Sutcliff for abusing his health. Sutcliff's physical constitution, even in his younger years, was never robust. During the summer of 1777 he had had a bout of serious ill-health.[65] By the following summer he was feeling much better, though his health was still somewhat indifferent.[66] In pursuing his ministry during these early years at Olney, however, Sutcliff tried to ignore these health problems. There seemed to be so much to do. But Turner rightly warned his friend against overworking, wrecking his constitution and rueing it when it was too late. Before answering his enquiries about the doctrine of providence, Turner thus sternly warned Sutcliff: 'Don't tell me, "You had rather wear away, than rust away," extremes are not right on either hand.' It had been the great evangelist George Whitefield who had said only a couple of hours before his death in 1770, 'I had rather wear out than rust out.'[67] But Turner was correct to point out that such unbalanced activism was not right, especially in view of the effects it could have on the physical constitution of one such as Sutcliff.

After this personal warning, Turner turned to the matter about which Sutcliff had sought his advice. He questioned his own ability to help Sutcliff, but then produced a brief sketch of the way in which he would tackle the subject:

1. Providence, what [it is]
2. In whose hands the administration of it
3. The universality of it
4. The equity of it
5. The sovereignty of it
6. The mercy of it
7. The wisdom of it etc.
8. The mystery of it.[68]

Sutcliff did not follow Turner's suggested plan, but the influence of his suggestions can be discerned at various points in the circular letter. For instance, he told Sutcliff to lard the letter well with texts of Scripture and Sutcliff did just that. He convincingly demonstrated that, although the actual term 'providence' never occurs in Scripture, it denotes what is 'plentifully found' in the pages of God's Word. Turner had also suggested that Sutcliff begin by explaining what is the nature of providence. Following this piece of advice, Sutcliff stated near the beginning of the letter that in the world-view of Scripture, providence is 'God's exercise of his divine perfections over all the works of his hands, displayed in [the] preserving of them and directing all their affairs according to his sovereign will, in order, ultimately to manifest his own glory'.[69] This is a fairly broad definition. It permits Sutcliff to subsume under providence not only such things as God's ever-watchful superintendence of the regular events of nature — 'the constant succession of summer and winter; seed-time and harvest; day and night' — but also more 'extraordinary' happenings, such as the fulfilment of prophecy, the miracles of Scripture, and 'the many instances ... of the Lord's hearing and answering prayer'.[70]

This definition of providence is strongly shaped by the Calvinist tradition in which Sutcliff had been reared and which he had come to endorse wholeheartedly. The biblical concept of providence, he asserted, is first and foremost a declaration of God's sovereignty. In his activity in nature and history God's 'omnipotent and irresistible' power is evident as he 'graciously influences' all those activities that are good and 'sovereignly permits' those that are evil.[71] It should be noted that the absolute sovereignty of God over the totality of the created realm is also one of the theological pillars upon which Sutcliff and his friends built their vision of the Christian life.[72] While they were only too aware of the ways in which God's sovereignty had been distorted by High Calvinism, it was none the less one of their mainstays in life — and in death.

Sutcliff's definition of providence also manifests another central concern of the Calvinist tradition, namely, the glorification of God. 'Providence,' Sutcliff maintained, 'proclaims a God, possessed of perfections inconceivably great and glorious.' 'Search we for *wisdom*? Here it shines: shines in colours bright and dazzling. Wisdom infinite and unerring! ... Look we for *power*? Here it appears. Power omnipotent and irresistible! What hand was ever lifted up against the Lord and prospered? ... Do we esteem *truth* and *faithfulness*? Yes, we justly do. These are displayed with a shining brightness among the perfections of our God in his works of providence. Truth immutable! Faithfulness unchangeable! ... Do we admire *goodness*? Here we may trace its breakings-forth with astonishment.'[73]

Sutcliff was conscious that some of his contemporaries would violently dispute his assertion of the biblical view of providence, notably those who had embraced atheism or Deism. The intellectual climate of eighteenth-century Europe was such that many had come to regard human reason as the final arbiter in deciding what was true and what was false. In such an environment, atheism and especially Deism — a rationalistic religion which argued that men and women need only to use their reason to know God — had flourished. The first significant English work to advocate Deism had been *Christianity not Mysterious* by John Toland (1670-1722), which was published in 1696. Toland and other English proponents of Deism, men such as Anthony Collins (1676-1729) and Matthew Tindal (1655-1733), typified an age sick of, and disgusted with, the religious wars and controversies which had convulsed Europe during the previous two centuries. But, in regarding the Bible as the true source of these controversies and wars, these men went much further than most. They sought a religion shorn of its dependence on divine revelation and the miraculous, in which only that which could successfully weather rational criticism need be affirmed as religious truth. The advent of Newtonian physics, with its understandable emphasis on rational enquiry, also tended to bolster this confidence of the Deists in human reason. Sutcliff, however, believed that due consideration of God's providential activity would help to silence these implacable foes of biblical Christianity. Speaking of the world of nature, he asked, 'Can the utmost stretch of charity imagine that person to have any eyes, who can say, that all this beauteous order and undisturbed harmony is the result of blind chance?' Although the providential work of God contains 'depths that we cannot fathom, breadths that we cannot measure' and 'designs that we cannot comprehend,' yet enough is plain and intelligible to 'silence the daring atheist and confront the inconsiderate Deist'.[74] While this argument for God's existence from the harmony of nature was a telling point against atheism, it was not a good argument against Deism, since the Deists did affirm the rationality and harmony of the created order.

Sutcliff concluded this letter on divine providence with a 'few inferences, reflections, advices' with regard to ways in which this doctrine should be practically applied. Belief in providence should lead, for instance, to an awe-filled reverence for God: 'This view of God should fill our minds with holy awe in every place and employment, whether alone or in company, by night or by day.' It should also provide great encouragement and fervency in prayer: 'Does his eye behold our every circumstance, is his ear ready to listen to every cry, and does his hand hold every needful good? Before him let us fall, to him make known our request, and from him expect every supply.'[75] Here, Sutcliff was speaking not only out of his study of Scripture, but also out of his own experience. In 1774 and 1775, when he felt God was no longer listening to his prayers, God was graciously preparing him for a ministry of eternal significance in the Buckinghamshire town of Olney and for lifelong friendships with such neighbouring pastors as John Ryland, Jr and Andrew Fuller.

Andrew Fuller

# 7.
# Sutcliff's friends: Andrew Fuller

*'Christ and his cross be all my theme! Surely I love his name, and wish to make it the centre, in which all the lines of my ministry should meet!'* (Andrew Fuller).

Born on 6 February 1754 in the village of Wicken, Cambridgeshire, Andrew Fuller, like Sutcliff, came from a lower middle-class background.[1] His parents, Robert Fuller (d.1781) and Philippa Gunton (d.1816), rented and worked a succession of small dairy farms. Baptists by conviction, both of his parents had been born into Dissenting families. For instance, Honour Hart, Andrew Fuller's paternal grandmother, had become a Baptist after a number of years as a Congregationalist. His maternal grandmother, Philippa Stevenson, was among the founding members of Soham Baptist Church, where Fuller would later spend his first pastorate.

When Fuller was only seven years of age, his parents moved to the village of Soham, which was about two and a half miles from Wicken. Settled in Soham, they joined themselves to the Calvinistic Baptist work in that locality. Its pastor was John Eve, whom we have already met in chapter 1. He was a High Calvinist, or, as Fuller put it, he was 'tinged with false Calvinism'. His preaching 'was not adapted to awaken [the] conscience', and he 'had little or nothing to say to the unconverted'. Thus, despite the fact that Fuller regularly attended the Baptist meeting-house, he gave little thought or heed to the sermons that he heard. When he was fourteen, though, he began to entertain thoughts about the meaning and purpose of life. He was much affected by passages that he read from Bunyan's *Grace Abounding to the Chief of Sinners,* his *Pilgrim's Progress* and some of the works of Ralph Erskine (1685-1752), a Scottish evangelical minister and poet. These affections were often accompanied by weeping and tears, but they ultimately proved to be transient, there being no radical change of heart.

Now one popular expression of eighteenth-century High Calvinist spirituality was the notion that if a scriptural text forcefully impressed itself upon one's mind, it was to be regarded as a promise from God. One day in 1767 Fuller had such an experience. Romans 6:14, 'Sin shall not have dominion over you: for ye are not under the law, but under grace,' came with such suddenness and force that Fuller naïvely believed that God was telling him that he was in a state of salvation and no longer under the tyranny of sin. But that evening, he later recalled, 'I returned to my former vices with as eager a gusto as ever.' For the next six months, he utterly neglected prayer and was as wedded to his sins as he had been before this experience. When, in the course of 1768, he once again seriously reflected upon his lifestyle, he was conscious that he was still held fast in thraldom to sin. What, then, of his experience with Romans 6:14? Fuller refused to doubt that it was given to him as an indication of his standing with God. He was, he therefore concluded, a converted person, but backslidden. He still lived, though, with never a victory over sin and its temptations, and with a total neglect of prayer. 'The great deep of my heart's depravity had not yet been broken up,' he later commented about these experiences of his mid-teens.

## Conviction and conversion

In the autumn of 1769 he once again came under the conviction that his life was displeasing to God. He could no longer pretend that he was only backslidden. 'The fire and brimstone of the bottomless pit seemed to burn within my bosom,' he later declared. 'I saw that God would be perfectly just in sending me to hell, and that to hell I must go, unless I were saved of mere grace.' Fuller now recognized the way that he had sorely abused God's mercy. He had presumed that he was a converted individual, but all the time he had had no love for God and no desire for his presence, no hunger to be like Christ and no love for his people. On the other hand, he could not bear, he said, 'the thought of plunging myself into endless ruin'. It was at this point that Job's resolution, 'Though he slay me, yet will I trust in him' (Job 13:15), came to mind, and Fuller grew determined to cast himself upon the mercy of the Lord Jesus 'to be both pardoned and purified'.

Yet the High Calvinism which formed the air that he had breathed since his earliest years proved to be a real barrier to his coming to Christ. It maintained that in order to flee to Christ for salvation, the 'warrant' that a person needed to believe that he or she would be accepted by Christ was a subjective one: conviction of one's sinfulness and deep mental anguish because of that conviction were popularly regarded by High Calvinists as such a warrant. From this point of view, these experiences were signs that God was in the process of converting the individual who was going through them. This perspective on conversion was a direct result of the argument made by both Gill and Brine, the principal authors of High Calvinism in the Baptist denomination, that the Scriptures invite only those sinners who are sensible of their sin to believe in Christ.[2] The net effect of this teaching — though unintended by either Gill or Brine — was to place the essence of conversion and faith not in believing the gospel, 'but in a persuasion of our being interested in its benefits'. Instead of attention being directed away from oneself towards Christ, the convicted sinner was turned inwards upon himself or herself to search for evidence that he or she was being converted. Against this perspective Fuller would later argue that the gospel exhortation to believe in Christ was a sufficient enough warrant to come to the Lord Jesus.[3]

Although Fuller was in the throes of a genuine conversion and quite aware of his status as a sinner, he was convinced he had neither the qualifications nor the proper warrant to flee to Christ in order to escape the righteous judgement of God. Upon later reflection, he saw his situation as akin to that of Queen Esther. She went into the presence of her husband, the Persian King Ahasuerus, at the risk of her life, since it was contrary to Persian law to enter the monarch's presence uninvited. Similarly, Fuller decided: 'I will trust my soul, my sinful, lost soul in his [i.e. Christ's] hands — if I perish, I perish!' So it was in November 1769 that Fuller found peace with God and rest for his troubled soul in the cross of Christ. His personal experience prior to and during his conversion taught him three things in particular: the error of those who maintained that a warrant to believe was necessary for salvation; the New Testament concept of faith, whereby faith was understood to be a coming to Christ and putting one's trust in him — it was not a turning inwards upon oneself to see if there was any desire to know Christ and embrace his salvation; and a concept of conversion which was rooted in a radical change of the affections of the heart and manifest in a lifestyle that sought to honour God.[4]

The first time that Fuller witnessed believer's baptism was in March of the following year. He was deeply moved by the event. 'The solemn immersion of a person,' he later wrote, 'on a profession of faith in Christ, carried such conviction with it, that I wept like a child on the occasion.' Fully persuaded 'that this was the primitive way of baptizing', he was himself baptized about a month later and became a member of the Baptist work at Soham. Some new Christians experience halcyon days at the beginning of their walk with Christ, and Fuller appears to have been one of these. He later recalled the summer of 1770 as 'a time of great religious pleasure'.

## Controversy in the church

In the autumn of that year, however, the church was sorely divided over the question of whether or not sinful men and women had 'the power ... to do the will of God and to keep themselves from sin'. The controversy in the Soham church over this issue — which Fuller later described as the 'wormwood and the gall of my youth' — had arisen through Fuller's rebuke of a fellow member who habitually drank alcohol to excess. When confronted by Fuller with regard to his sin, the individual replied that he was not able to prevent himself from sinning in this way and that he was not his own keeper. Fuller told him that 'He *could* keep himself from such sins as these, and that his way of talking was merely to excuse what was inexcusable.' The man answered Fuller by telling him that he was still a young Christian and only in time would he come to know the deceitfulness of the heart. While this member was ultimately disfellowshipped, the theological implications of his answers to Fuller continued to be debated in the church for quite a few months.

Pastor Eve wanted to draw a distinction between 'internal and external power'. While men and women lack the resources to do anything that is spiritually good, they do, nevertheless, possess the power to keep themselves from open acts of sin. In support of his argument, Eve cited the numerous admonitions of Scripture and asked, 'If we had no power to comply with them, why were they given us?' Fuller's fellow members who disagreed with their pastor were more consistent in their High Calvinism. They argued that 'The greatest and best of characters,' both in Scripture and in the history of the church, 'never arrogated to themselves the power of keeping themselves from evil, but constantly prayed for keeping grace.' To support their case, they referred Eve to such texts as Psalm 19:13, where the psalmist asked God to keep him from 'presumptuous sins'. The controversy grew so severe that Eve eventually had to resign from the church in October 1771. Fuller had initially thrown his support behind Eve, but after a few months took the side of Eve's opponents. While Fuller at this time did not come to a satisfactory resolution of this question, it was this controversy which more than anything else led him into 'those views of divine truth' that later made their appearance in his major published works.

## A call to the ministry

From November 1771 to January 1774, the preaching of the Word in the Soham church was mostly undertaken by Joseph Diver (d.1780). Although old enough to be Fuller's father, Diver was a very good friend to Fuller. During the controversy in the Soham church, he had been one of the most earnest advocates of the position opposed to that of Eve. After Eve's departure, he was chosen by the congregation to be a deacon of the church. Fuller also occasionally preached. Although Fuller was quite discouraged by his early preaching attempts, the church as a whole came to the conviction by early 1774 that a call to the pastorate should be extended to him. After a trial period of slightly more than twelve months, Fuller was ordained on 3 May 1775.

During this first year of ministry, Fuller's time was largely taken up with reading and study. He continued to reflect upon the principles at stake in the controversy which had wracked the Soham church a few years earlier. Though a practising High Calvinist — at this point in his life he refused to urge the unconverted to come to Christ — he was increasingly dissatisfied with High Calvinist reasoning. He began to sense that his 'preaching was antiscriptural and defective in many respects'. But as yet he saw no viable alternative. He also read extensively in the area of Christology, particularly focusing on two highly mooted questions of the day: did Christ's human soul exist prior to the incarnation, and is the title 'Son of God' ever given to the pre-incarnate second person of the Godhead? Answering 'No' and 'Yes' respectively to these questions, Fuller later declared that wrestling with these Christological issues at an early stage in his theological career equipped him to be a defender of orthodox Christology later in his life.[5] It should be noted that Christological debates centred around the pre-existence of Christ's human soul and the eternal Sonship raged in High Calvinist circles well into the nineteenth century.[6]

One of the ministers who took part in Fuller's ordination in May 1775 was Robert Hall, Sr. Prior to the ordination, Fuller was asked why Eve had had to leave the church in 1771. After Hall had heard Fuller recount the details of the controversy which had led to Eve's resignation, he recommended that Fuller study 'Edwards on the Will'. Hall intended by this remark Jonathan Edwards' classic work *A Careful and Strict Enquiry Into the Modern Prevailing Notions of the Freedom of Will* (1754). The Arnesby pastor was rightly convinced that this work would help clarify some of Fuller's thinking about the power of sinful men and women to obey God. Fuller had obviously never heard of either the book or its illustrious author, for he subsequently procured *Veritas Redux* by John Edwards (1637-1716), an Anglican clergyman with a high reputation as a Calvinistic divine. Fuller appreciated *Veritas Redux*, but was quite puzzled as to why Hall had recommended it, for the book had next to nothing to say about the question that had been hotly debated at Soham. It was not until 1777, nearly two years later, that he finally discovered his mistake.

Meanwhile Fuller was immersing himself in John Gill's *A Body of Doctrinal Divinity,* various tracts and sermons by John Brine, as well as the works of John Bunyan. He read most of Gill's *A Body of Doctrinal Divinity*, found much that was helpful in it, but was deeply troubled by the evident differences between Gill and Bunyan. Both were ardent Calvinists, but whereas Bunyan recommended 'the free offer of salvation to sinners', Gill did not. Fuller wrongly concluded that though Bunyan was 'a great and good man', he was not as clear as Gill regarding the gospel. Yet, as Fuller perused the writings of other sixteenth- and seventeenth-century authors, in particular those of the Puritan theologian John Owen, he noted that they too 'dealt ... in free invitations to sinners to come to Christ and be saved'. In other words, Fuller had discerned that with regard to the preaching of the gospel there was a definite difference not only between Bunyan and Gill, but more broadly between sixteenth- and seventeenth-century Calvinism and that of the early eighteenth century.

## Sutcliff, Ryland and the influence of Edwards

In 1775 the Soham Church had also decided to join the Northamptonshire Association. The following summer, as we have already noted, Fuller met Sutcliff for the first time at the annual assembly of this association in Olney. Soon after Fuller also made the acquaintance of John Ryland, Jr. 'In them,' Fuller recalled many years later, 'I found familiar and faithful brethren; and who, partly by reflection and partly by reading the writings of Edwards, [Joseph] Bellamy, [David] Brainerd, etc. had begun to doubt of the system of False Calvinism, to which they had been inclined when they first entered on the ministry, or, rather to be decided against it.' For a variety of reasons this statement is one of great importance. First, Fuller indicated that his friendship with Sutcliff and Ryland brought him into contact with men whose thinking about High Calvinism — what Fuller here calls 'False Calvinism' — was moving in directions identical to his own. Second, the key influence — apart from reflection on the Scriptures — which Fuller identified as leading Sutcliff and Ryland to regard High Calvinism as biblically defective was to be found in the writings of the New England divine Jonathan Edwards and the circle of men around him — men such as Joseph Bellamy (1719-1790), for many years the pastor of the Congregationalist church at Bethlehem, Connecticut, and David Brainerd (1718-1747), a missionary to North American natives in New York, Pennsylvania and New Jersey whose biography was written by Edwards. As we have seen, Sutcliff's first contact with Edwards' writings came through either John Fawcett or Caleb Evans. As for Ryland, his father was a great admirer of the New England author and it was probably he who initially introduced the younger Ryland to Edwards.

In chapter 4 we also noted something of the way in which Ryland broke free from the trammels of High Calvinism. By the time that he met Fuller in 1776, Ryland was all but convinced that High

Calvinism was unbiblical in its view of preaching the gospel. Close study of Edwards' *Freedom of Will* had been especially helpful for Ryland.[7] In this treatise Edwards had sought to show that it was scriptural to uphold the responsibility of men and women for their remaining in sin as well as to maintain that human beings are utterly unable in their own strength to turn from their sin and turn to God. A person's possession of natural faculties such as reason and will renders him or her accountable to God for the proper use of them. However, due to the perverse disposition of the human will, men and women in their natural state are unable to use their natural faculties aright. Humanity's consistent failure to live in such a way as to please God stems, then, not from physical inability, but from moral inability. Ryland's perusal of John Smalley's *The Consistency of the Sinner's Inability to comply with the Gospel; with his Inexcusable Guilt in not complying with it, illustrated and confirmed* (1769), which he had borrowed from John Newton and which made the same point as Edwards' treatise, also helped to confirm Ryland's conviction that High Calvinism was unbalanced in its view of human responsibility and divine sovereignty. This distinction between physical and moral inability would later be central to the attack Andrew Fuller made on the canons of High Calvinism in his *The Gospel Worthy of All Acceptation* (1785). Fuller's appropriation of this distinction derived from a direct reading of Edwards. As we have noted, Robert Hall had first drawn Fuller's attention to Edwards' treatise on the human will in 1775, though it was not until 1777 that he actually perused this work. By that time both Sutcliff and Ryland were also strongly encouraging Fuller to read Edwards and in so doing they played a rôle in Fuller's theological formation.[8]

One final comment on Fuller's statement about his first meeting with Sutcliff and Ryland needs to be made. Fuller stated that *both* Sutcliff and Ryland had been 'inclined' towards High Calvinism when they first entered upon pastoral ministry. That this was true of Ryland has been clearly outlined in chapter 4. Yet, it is a very surprising remark about Sutcliff in the light of all that we have seen with regard to his early years. Each of his three early mentors, Fawcett and the two Evanses, were evangelical Calvinists and not at all receptive towards the distinctive features of High Calvinism. In fact, a number of Caleb Evans' comments to Sutcliff in the letter in which the Bristol tutor urged Sutcliff to preach at Olney make little sense if Sutcliff did not share Evans' evangelical Calvinism.

Nor does there appear to be any other evidence to indicate that Sutcliff, like Ryland and Fuller, trod the path from High Calvinism to a full-orbed evangelical Calvinism. How, then, is Fuller's statement to be understood? That he was simply mistaken about Sutcliff seems hard to believe since the two men became extremely close friends. Yet he may have taken Sutcliff's growth in articulating his opposition to High Calvinism in the late 1770s to have also entailed a movement out of High Calvinism towards evangelical Calvinism. Of this growth, which paralleled that of Fuller, there is ample evidence. A couple of letters written by James Turner to Sutcliff in late 1778 and early 1779, for example, reveal something of Sutcliff's struggle to formulate his thoughts.

During the summer of 1778 Sutcliff asked Turner what he thought of the distinction between the physical and the moral inability of the will. Turner wrote back on 9 September to tell him that he hardly knew what to make of it. To him it was a 'new notion', but he felt himself 'too old and too dull' to serve as a theological critic.[9] Understandably Sutcliff was not satisfied with such a terse reply, and he pressed Turner for further particulars regarding his opinion. Cautious by nature, Sutcliff wanted assurance that Edwards' distinction was scripturally based. In later years his caution would be a hallmark of his character. F. A. Cox (1783-1853) could speak of Sutcliff's 'carrying caution and prudence to the utmost'. And J. W. Morris (1763-1836) said that 'caution was so thickly interwoven' into Sutcliff's mind 'as nearly to destroy its elasticity'.[10] At the time that Sutcliff was mulling over the issues relating to High Calvinism, he genuinely wanted the advice of men like Turner, who were older than himself, had more experience in pastoral ministry and were thus more immune to theological fads. Turner, however, was not able to stir himself up to give Sutcliff much of a response. In a letter dated 6 January 1779, he still confessed his inability to know what to say about Sutcliff's remarks 'respecting the natural and moral liberty of the will. It may be as you say,' he continued, 'or it may not. I do intend to give the point a little consideration some time or other.'[11]

If Turner did give this subject more consideration, his thoughts on it are not to be found in any of his further correspondence with Sutcliff. His last letter to Sutcliff was written on 24 November 1779, in which he informed his friend that he had a nasty cold accompanied by a fever.[12] This cold and fever may well have led to further complications, for Turner died on 8 January the following year.[13] He was only fifty-four.

Meanwhile, sixty or so miles away in Soham, Fuller was wrestling with the same theological issue. His enquiry after the truth was in many ways a solitary one. As Ryland wrote in his memoirs of Fuller, 'He had fewer means of assistance from men and books than he might have had elsewhere; but he was obliged to think, and pray, and study the Scriptures, and thus to make his ground good.'[14] A personal memorandum, which Fuller wrote in 1780, spoke of his 'determination to take up no principles at second-hand, but to search for every thing at the pure fountain of [God's] *word*'.[15] Being so far from both Sutcliff and Ryland, he seldom saw either of them. They would, of course, have been together at the annual assemblies of the Northamptonshire Association. By the early 1780s the ministers of the association were also meeting together at various other times of the year for prayer and mutual encouragement. Whether this was also the case during the 1770s is hard to determine. If so, there may have been further opportunities for Fuller to discuss these theological issues with Sutcliff and Ryland.

Nor did he correspond at length with either of them about the issue. Mention should be made, though, of one letter that Fuller wrote to Sutcliff on 28 January 1781, in which he sought to answer a query Sutcliff had put to him regarding the activity of grace in the believer's heart. In answering Sutcliff's question, Fuller distinguished between faith as the gift of God and faith as the believer's act. Fuller was convinced that God gives faith as a principle within the heart. However, its activity, which includes the 'act of believing in Christ ... for salvation', is the believer's own act, though done with the assistance of God.[16] Here, Fuller was seeking to take seriously human responsibility, while at the same time affirming the need of divine enablement to do anything truly good.

## *The Gospel Worthy of All Acceptation*

However, Fuller had been conscious that he needed to think through these issues in a more logical and orderly fashion than was possible in pieces of personal correspondence. Consequently, a few years earlier he had decided to draw up a treatise on the subject, which originally he had no intentions of publishing. A preliminary draft was written in 1777 or 1778.[17] In what was roughly its final form it was completed by 1781.[18]

Published as *The Gospel Worthy of All Acceptation*, the work eventually went through two editions. The first edition, published in Northampton in 1785, was subtitled *The Obligations of Men Fully to Credit, and Cordially to Approve, Whatever God Makes Known, Wherein is Considered the Nature of Faith in Christ, and the Duty of Those where the Gospel Comes in that Matter*. The second edition, which appeared in 1801, was more simply subtitled *The Duty of Sinners to Believe in Jesus Christ*, a subtitle which well expressed the overall theme of the book. There were substantial differences between the two editions, which Fuller freely admitted and which primarily related to the doctrine of particular redemption, but the major theme remained unaltered: 'Faith in Christ is the duty of all men who hear, or have opportunity to hear, the gospel.'[19]

In the first section of the work, Fuller stated the theme of the book and spent some time discussing the nature of saving faith. He especially took to task the popular High Calvinist view of faith as something primarily subjective: 'The Scriptures always represent faith as terminating on something without us; namely, on Christ, and the truths concerning him: but if it consist in a persuasion of our being in a state of salvation, it must terminate principally on something within us; namely, the work of grace in our hearts; for to believe myself interested in Christ is the same thing as to believe myself a subject of special grace.'[20]

Faith is fixed, not on one's interest in being saved by Christ, but on Christ and his willingness to save all who cry to him for mercy and pardon. Here, Fuller's own experience was invaluable in helping him to understand and explain the scriptural concept of faith. A series of biblical texts was then expounded to show that the Scriptures require this type of faith of all who hear the gospel.

When the psalmist in Psalm 2, for instance, admonished the 'kings' and 'judges of the earth' to 'serve the Lord with fear' and to 'kiss the Son' (Psalm 2:10-12), the command was a spiritual one, 'including unfeigned faith in the Messiah'. Fuller pointed out that the introductory verses to this psalm were quoted in Acts 4:25-26, where the 'kings of the earth ... and the rulers' (Psalm 2:2) were identified as Herod and Pontius Pilate, and the 'Anointed' One or Messiah (Psalm 2:2) understood to be the 'holy child Jesus' (Acts 4:27). It is, therefore, Herod and Pilate — these 'enemies of Christ

[and] unregenerate sinners' — who are commanded to 'kiss the Son', that is, embrace Christ's 'word and ordinances, and bow to his sceptre'. In other words, what is required of unbelievers in Psalm 2 is nothing less than a 'holy fear of Christ's majesty, and a humble confidence in his mercy'.[21] Fuller discerns similar emphases in other Old Testament texts, passages like Isaiah 55:1-7 and Jeremiah 4:16-19. Obviously, even more explicit proof was to be found in the New Testament, where faith in Jesus Christ is 'constantly held up as the duty of all to whom the gospel is preached'.[22]

John 12:36, for instance, contains an exhortation of the Lord Jesus to a crowd of men and women to 'believe in the light' that they might be the children of light. Working from the context, Fuller argued that Jesus was urging his hearers to put their faith in him. He is the 'light' in whom faith is to be placed, that faith which issues in salvation (John 12:46). Those whom Christ commanded to exercise such faith, however, were rank unbelievers, of whom it is said earlier that 'They believed not on him' (John 12:37).[23]

Again, in John 5:23 we read that all men and women are to 'honour the Son, even as they honour the Father'. Giving honour to the Son entails, Fuller rightly reasoned, 'holy, hearty love to him' and adoration of every aspect of his person. It 'necessarily supposes faith in him'. Christ has shown himself to be an infallible teacher, a holy advocate who pleads the case of his erring people, a physician who offers health to the spiritually sick and a supreme monarch. Honouring him in these various aspects of his ministry requires faith and trust: 'To honour an infallible teacher is to place an implicit and unbounded confidence in all he says; to honour an advocate is to commit our cause to him; to honour a physician is to trust our lives in his hands; and to honour a king is to bow to his sceptre, and cheerfully obey his laws.'[24]

In sum, the Scriptures, especially those of the New Testament, abound with exhortations 'to *hear* the word of God, to *hearken* to his counsel, to *wait* on him, to seek his favour, etc., all which imply saving faith'.[25]

Fuller further maintained that though the gospel is a message of pure grace, not a new law, nevertheless, it 'requires obedience, and such an obedience as includes saving faith'. In this respect, Fuller referred to passages in Paul's letter to the Romans where the apostle mentions being obedient to the faith and to the gospel (see Romans 1:5; 10:16). As has been mentioned earlier, in the 1770s Fuller was reading widely in the works of John Owen. Drawing upon this reading, he now cited a relevant passage from Owen's earliest work, *A Display of Arminianism* (1642), in which the Puritan theologian commented on a phrase from 2 Corinthians 5:20: 'We pray you in Christ's stead, be ye reconciled to God.' '"When the Apostle beseecheth us to be 'reconciled' to God, I would know," says Dr Owen, "whether it be not a part of our duty to yield obedience? If not, the exhortation is frivolous and vain."'[26]

From the fact that the lack of faith in Christ is considered a 'heinous sin' in the Scriptures, Fuller also reasoned that trust in Christ is required of all who sit under the preaching of the Word. Men and women are never reproved for their not being among the elect, for election is solely God's work. But 'Sinners are reproved for not believing,' as is evident from John 16:8-9. There, listed among the tasks of the Spirit of Christ is that of reproving the world of its sin of unbelief. 'But unbelief cannot be a sin if faith were not a duty.'[27] Similarly, Fuller took the fact of God's past and threatened future judgements upon those who refuse to believe in the Lord Jesus as proof of his thesis. Here, Fuller was drawing upon texts like 'He that believeth not shall be damned' (Mark 16:16) and 'He that believeth not is condemned already' (John 3:18), where unbelief is regarded as a sin which merits punishment.[28]

The final section of *The Gospel Worthy of All Acceptation* marshalled answers to various objections to Fuller's position. Prominent amongst these objections was that sinners are unable to do anything spiritually good, and thus are under no obligation to exercise faith in Christ. This objection was a common one posed by High Calvinists and supported by reference to such texts as John 6:44 and 1 Corinthians 2:14. The inability of which these passages speak, Fuller contended in response, is a moral inability, which is rooted in the sinful disposition of the heart. They are not speaking of a physical inability — such as insanity or mental retardation — which excuses its subject of blame.[29] Thus, although God requires faith of all who hear the gospel, only those who are given faith by the Spirit of God can comply with their duty. 'Repentance and faith, therefore, may be duties, notwithstanding their being the gifts of God.'[30] In making this distinction between physical and moral inability, which Fuller derived from Jonathan Edwards, Fuller was seeking to affirm a scriptural paradox: sinful men and women are utterly powerless to turn to God except through the regenerative work of God's Holy Spirit, yet this powerlessness is the result of their own sinful hearts.[31]

It should be noted that this distinction between physical and moral inability has not gone without criticism from various theologians in the Reformed tradition. For example, in this century Louis Berkhof (1873-1957), the Dutch Reformed theologian, has pointed out that this distinction gives the impression that fallen men and women, while lacking the moral strength to do what pleases God, do possess unimpaired all of the other natural faculties that are required for doing spiritual good. In other words, the use of this distinction to stress that the fallenness of men and women lies essentially in their wills appears to undercut the doctrine of total depravity.[32] Fuller, however, was quite clear as to the effects of the Fall on human nature. 'Men are totally alienated from God' and in every aspect of the human mind, its 'various passions and propensities', there is to be found 'a marked aversion from the true God'. As such, 'Turning a sinner's heart [to God] must be altogether of God and of free grace.'[33]

The reason for Fuller's heavy use of Edwards' distinction was to help him rebut the assertion of popular High Calvinism that men and women are physically and constitutionally unable to exercise saving faith. Human wickedness, in the perspective of this system, was ultimately grounded in the way in which men and women had been created. John Brine, for example, could argue that Adam, in his pre-Fall existence, was neither required nor equipped to exercise repentance and saving faith. If the father of the human race had not possessed such endowments, it followed that his posterity naturally lacked such capacities.[34] While Edwards' distinction between physical and moral inability is not without ambiguity and is even somewhat misleading, it did help Fuller to assert the truth that human fallenness lies not in the human constitution as such, but 'in the corrupt moral state of the faculties, and of the disposition of the heart'.[35]

There were two main practical conclusions to Fuller's arguments. First, sinners have every encouragement to trust in the Lord Jesus for the salvation of their souls. They do not need to spend time dallying to see if they are among God's elect or if God is at work in their hearts by his Spirit. Moreover, they can no longer sit at ease under the sound of the gospel and excuse their unbelief by asserting that faith is the gift of God.[36] Second, ministers of the Word *must* earnestly exhort their hearers to commit themselves to Christ and that without delay. In so doing they will be faithful imitators of Christ and his apostles, who 'warned, admonished, and entreated' sinners to repent, to believe, and to be reconciled to God. Many High Calvinist ministers of Fuller's day were too much like John Eve and had next to nothing to say to the unconverted in their congregations, because they believed that these men and women were 'poor, impotent ... creatures'. Faith was beyond such men and women, and could not be pressed upon them as an immediate, present duty. Fuller was convinced that this way of conducting a pulpit ministry was unbiblical and simply helped the unconverted to remain in their sin.

## The advice of Fuller's friends

As we have noted, Fuller originally wrote this treatise to help clarify his own thinking. It was not intended initially for public consumption. Nevertheless, in September 1782 — only a few weeks before he left Soham to accept a call to pastor the Calvinistic Baptist church which met in Gold Street, Kettering, Northamptonshire — Fuller sent the treatise to Sutcliff. Read it over, he said, and 'make remarks on a separate paper where you see any mistakes or defects'. He asked Sutcliff to send these remarks to him and then to pass the treatise on to Ryland, who presumably was also asked to correct any deficiencies that he found.[37] Although Fuller was a self-taught theologian, it was a blessing that he had peers to whom he could turn for counsel and help. A very real danger for those who are self-taught is that they become so accustomed to relying upon their own judgement that they become impervious to the advice of others.[38]

As Sutcliff and Ryland perused Fuller's manuscript they would have recognized its importance and outstanding value for their day. Along with Robert Hall, who was also asked to read it over, they encouraged Fuller to consider seriously its publication. Hall, it seems, was particularly insistent that Fuller have it published.[39]

Hall himself had recently had published a vigorous attack on High Calvinism entitled *Help to Zion's Travellers*. This treatise had begun life as a sermon that Hall had preached at the annual assembly of the Northamptonshire Association in 1779, the same meeting for which Sutcliff had written his circular letter on providence. Hall's text had been Isaiah 57:14: 'Cast ye up, cast ye up, prepare the way, take up the stumbling-block out of the way of my people.' Hall's sermon so resonated with the thinking of Fuller, Sutcliff and Ryland, that they, along with the others present at the meeting, recommended that Hall have it printed with 'what circumstantial alterations or enlargements he might think proper'.[40] Due to the great variety and scope of material that Hall wanted to discuss, he was advised to expand the sermon into a book and have it printed by subscription. Its appearance in 1781 was made possible by 468 subscribers. Hall plainly declared, in words that Fuller would later echo, that there is 'no preventive bar in the sinner's way to the Saviour, but what arises from a carnal heart'. The way to Christ is 'graciously laid open for every one who chooses to come to him' and 'free for *whosoever will*' make this choice. Hall clearly intended that the preaching of the gospel should not be restricted in any way, but that people everywhere and in every condition be exhorted to repent and believe on Christ for salvation.[41]

Much more reticent than Hall to venture into print, Fuller long delayed publishing his manuscript. He honestly feared that it might injure the cause of Christ. He was also afraid of the controversy that it would engender. This latter fear was only alleviated by the conviction that his argument for the obligation of men and women to believe in Christ was indeed of vital importance. Finally, in October 1781 Fuller took the plunge and made the decision to publish. The following month he walked the thirteen or so miles from Kettering to Northampton to deliver it into the hands of Thomas Dicey (1742-?), a wealthy Northampton printer whose father and grandfather had made the family money through the sale of ephemeral popular literature.[42]

## Reactions to the teaching

When Fuller's book appeared the following year, it was indeed an epoch-making work. It provided a theology for many others in the Baptist denomination whose thinking was moving in the same direction and developing along the same lines. There were, for instance, in addition to Fuller's close friends in the Northamptonshire Association, men like Thomas Steevens (1745-1802), the pastor of Colchester Baptist Church, Essex, from 1774 until his death in the first decade of the next century. Henry Spyvee, who has recently been appointed Historical Adviser to the Essex Baptist Association, has described Steevens as 'a "Fullerite" before Fuller'.[43] In other words, before Fuller ever enunciated his theological views in print, Steevens had come to an evangelical Calvinist position.

A few months after the publication of *The Gospel Worthy of All Acceptation* Sutcliff in fact had written to Steevens, asking him what he thought of Fuller's work. Steevens' response reached Sutcliff on the final day of November 1785. The Colchester Baptist found much to admire in the book and admitted that since 1777 he had been coming over to Fuller's point of view, though he was unaware, he said, 'that I had any partners'. He was hopeful that 'some who cannot fully adopt his [i.e. Fuller's] views, will yet so far profit by it as to address their fellow sinners more in the style of Scripture'. He drew Sutcliff's attention, though, to the fact that many of the Baptists with whom he was personally acquainted would have nothing to do with the book. 'Some of them,' he further informed Sutcliff, 'already deem me an Arminian for only attempting to explain to them the meaning of the phrases moral and natural inability.'[44] The county of Suffolk, to the immediate north of Colchester, was a bastion of High Calvinism and many of the Baptists of whom Steevens spoke in this letter were almost definitely from this area of East Anglia. Conflict, as Fuller had foreseen, was inevitable.

Of the various early written attacks against Fuller's position there were two major ones, both of them by London High Calvinists. The first, by William Button (1754-1821), pastor of Dean Street Baptist Church, appeared in 1785. The second, by John Martin (1741-1820), who pastored Grafton Street Baptist Church, was published in three parts between the years 1788 and 1791.[45] It is noteworthy that despite their attacks on Fuller, both Button and Martin subsequently had friendly relations with him. Button, for instance, was a firm supporter of the Baptist Missionary Society from its early years until his death. And Martin, in 1797, could speak of his sincere respect for Fuller.[46]

Martin would eventually distance himself from Fuller, as well as from most of his other Calvinistic Baptist brethren — but the estrangement was due to politics, not theology. In 1798, in the midst of Britain's war with revolutionary France, Martin, a political conservative, publicly — and, it should be added, falsely — accused his fellow Dissenters of harbouring republican tendencies which would probably lead them to support the French if the latter invaded England. Asked to retract this accusation by his fellow London Baptists, Martin refused and was subsequently shunned by most Baptists in the capital.

Far less significant than these theological responses of Button and Martin, but probably more irksome, was the petty sniping and ostracism to which Fuller was subjected. Rushden Baptist Church was about ten miles south of Kettering. From 1785 to 1794, though, relations between Fuller's church and that in Rushden were quite acrimonious. In the summer of 1785, a Mrs Wright, who was a member of the Rushden church but was now living in Weekley, just north of Kettering, requested a letter of dismissal from Rushden to Kettering. The pastor of Rushden, William Knowles (d.1794), refused to give her one, because, he said, 'The church at Kettering had gone off from their former principles.'

After a while Mrs Wright again sought a letter of dismissal from Rushden, but to no avail. On behalf of the Kettering congregation, Fuller then wrote to the Rushden work and asserted that they still held to those truths 'commonly called Calvinistical', which were 'the source of all our salvation and all our hope'. A response from Rushden was a long time coming. Eventually on 22 December 1785 the Rushden Baptists wrote back and accused the Kettering congregation of lording it over their church. 'Have we not,' they wrote, 'an undoubted right to dismiss or not to dismiss a member at [our] discretion without being compelled thereto?' Nevertheless, they said, if the Kettering church wanted to receive Mrs Wright as a member, they were free to do so, but it would have to be without a letter of dismissal. Indeed, at this point, the Kettering Baptists were prepared to accept her without such a letter.

The Kettering church also acknowledged that there was indeed one difference between them and the Rushden believers. It was obviously this one difference which had led to the strained relations between the two churches. 'We consider,' Fuller wrote in the minute book of the Kettering congregation, 'the doctrines of grace as entirely consistent with a free address to every sinner, and with an universal obligation on all men where the gospel is preached to repent of their sins and turn to God through Jesus Christ.'

However, Mrs Wright, being of a timid disposition, was unprepared to leave the Rushden fellowship with ill-feeling. She thus stayed in the Rushden church until Knowles died in 1794, and finally, on 16 February 1796, she was given an honourable dismissal to Kettering.[47]

Sutcliff also ran into criticism and opposition in the late 1770s when the High Calvinists in his congregation began to be deeply disturbed by his evangelical Calvinism, and to become critical of his evangelistic preaching. Not content with urging the lost to come to Christ at Sunday worship services in Olney, Sutcliff was constantly employed preaching on weekdays in the small villages surrounding Olney, of which there were a number, places like Lavendon and Emberton.[48] In the latter part of 1779, as the discontent of the High Calvinists began to worsen, Sutcliff sought Fuller's advice. Fuller did not know what to advise concerning the state of affairs at Olney beyond prayer. He himself prayed that Sutcliff would 'be directed to acknowledge the Lord in all [his] steps' and that he be kept from 'brashness or impatience'.[49]

When Sutcliff showed no sign of accommodating their views, the Olney High Calvinists, judging their pastor to be no longer 'orthodox', began to absent themselves from the congregational celebration of the Lord's Table.[50] Sutcliff, with a patience that was becoming characteristic of the man, did not publicly raise the issue until that December. When, at that month's church meeting, the dissidents — John Rogers, James Johnston, John Tapp, William Walker, John Marriott and Sarah Davey — were asked the cause of their conduct, the reason that they gave was 'dissatisfaction with the ministry'. After a lengthy debate, the congregation 'unanimously agreed to let the dispute rest' for four months. If the High Calvinists took their places at the Lord's Table within that space of time, the matter was to be quietly forgotten.[51] The gentle and generous way that this opposition was dealt with owed much to Sutcliff's character and his heeding the advice given to him a number of years before by Ryland. The latter, the reader will recall, had told Sutcliff that the Olney Baptists needed a pastor who would labour amongst them with love, gentleness and candour.[52]

A month later none of the High Calvinists had sat down at the monthly celebration of the Lord's Supper, though Sutcliff had undoubtedly visited them and prayed for them. Yet Fuller was full of encouragement when he wrote to his friend on 28 January 1781: 'I know it is a very difficult thing in perplexing controversy to keep our heads or hearts free from confusion and when opponents abuse truth it's often a temptation to us to desert [the truth], or at least to think the worst of it. May the Lord keep you, my dear brother, in an hour of temptation which is come to try you!'[53]

The Lord did keep Sutcliff, for though it took more than four months, Sutcliff, 'by patience, calmness, and prudent perseverance,' eventually won over all of the dissidents.[54] One by one they were reconciled to the church and to Sutcliff's evangelical Calvinism: John Tapp stopped absenting himself from the Lord's Supper on 4 February 1781, William Walker and John Marriott on 4 March, James Johnston on 1 April, John Rogers — who was before and after this incident a leading member in the congregation — on 1 July and, finally, Sarah Davey — after deacon Thomas Osborn had visited her in her home in December 1781 — on 27 January1782. Yet, in the midst of these very trying and painful circumstances, God was blessing Sutcliff's preaching in very evident ways. A 'remarkable seriousness' gripped many in the congregation and weeping was not infrequent as they met for worship.[55] From Sutcliff's point of view, God was honouring his truth.

Later opponents of the evangelical Calvinism which characterized Sutcliff's preaching and teaching would dub it 'Fullerism'. In some ways this term obscures the fact that Fuller's doctrinal perspective in *The Gospel Worthy of All Acceptation* produced the impact that it did simply because it made explicit what a goodly number in the denomination implicitly held. On the other hand, this term does bear witness to Fuller's theological genius. Fuller had no formal theological training and looked 'the very picture of a blacksmith', as William Wilberforce (1759-1833) once graphically put it,[56] but he became the 'soundest and most creatively useful theologian' in the history of the English Calvinistic Baptists.[57] And that soundness and usefulness is nowhere more evident than in *The Gospel Worthy of All Acceptation.*

# 8.
# The Prayer Call of 1784

*'Whenever a long wished for revival of religion takes place, it certainly will be effected by the abundant outpouring of the Holy Spirit. This blessed event, we have reason to believe, will be preceded, or rather its near approach evidenced, by a spirit of prayer among the churches'* (John Sutcliff).

In 1783, the year after the last of the Olney High Calvinists was received back into the church, Sutcliff publicly declared his commitment to evangelical Calvinism in *The First Principles of the Oracles of God, represented in a Plain and Familiar Catechism, For the Use of Children.* Reprinted in at least five editions over the next forty years, this catechism would be used far beyond Olney and its neighbouring villages.[1] It was of this small catechism that Fuller later commented that Sutcliff's 'views of the gospel may be seen' clearly in it.[2]

Embedded in the catechism was a series of questions on moral and physical inability as well as a lengthy footnote explaining the difference between the two. To anyone who had read Jonathan Edwards' treatise on the will, the source of Sutcliff's distinction between these two types of inability and of the conclusions that he drew from it was patent. Although it is not at all surprising that this theological issue made its appearance in the catechism — it was after all very much on the minds of Sutcliff and his friends at this time — Sutcliff certainly did not compose the catechism simply to propagate 'Fullerism'. Raised in a solid Christian home and having in his early years a pastor, John Fawcett, who had a genuine concern for the Christian nurture of children and teenagers, Sutcliff was understandably convinced that the 'proper education of youth is a matter of the highest importance'.[3]

Sutcliff may also have been aroused to the task of writing this catechism by the decision taken by the Northamptonshire Association to 'encourage the catechizing of children' at its annual assembly in 1779.[4] Sutcliff was the moderator of the assembly in this particular year and may well have been instrumental in urging the association to make this decision. In fact, the previous year he had received a letter from Thomas Purdy that had drawn his attention to this very subject. Writing on 19 April 1778, Purdy mentioned in passing that he had again begun 'to catechize the children on the sabbath day as no other is convenient'. Then he asked, 'Do you do anything of this kind?'[5] Whether Sutcliff did or did not at this point in time we do not know. Following the decision of the Northamptonshire Association to encourage such catechizing there is every likelihood that he did, the evidence for which lies in the catechism that he issued in 1783.

## The influence of Jonathan Edwards

As we have just noted, the catechism bears the imprint of Edwards. Indeed, at this juncture in his life, Sutcliff was voraciously reading everything that he could find by the New England writer. Thinking, for instance, that Fuller had a copy of Edwards' memoirs of David Brainerd, Sutcliff wrote to him at Soham in late 1780 and asked if he could borrow it. Fuller had to disappoint him. 'I cannot tell,' he wrote to Sutcliff on 28 January 1781, 'how you come to think of my having had Brainerd's Life. I have never seen it, nor don't know any likelihood of coming at it.'[6] Sutcliff, Fuller later declared in his funeral sermon for his friend, 'drank deeply' of Edwards and his New England disciples. They gave Sutcliff a clear view about 'the harmony between the law and the gospel — between the obligations of men to love God with all their hearts and their actual enmity against him — and between the duty of ministers to call on sinners to repent and believe in Christ for salvation, and the necessity of omnipotent grace to render the call effectual'.[7]

Edwards also gave Sutcliff an 'optimistic eschatology'. In the words of Fuller, Sutcliff derived from the American theologian 'a largeness of heart that led him to expect much from the promises of God to the church in the latter days'.[8] Edwards, like the Calvinistic Baptists for whom he was a mentor, was a firm believer in what has been termed the 'latter-day glory'. This perspective on the future held that there would be a time of great spiritual prosperity for the church prior to the return of Christ. The immediate harbinger of this 'latter-day glory' would be the conversion of the Jewish people. Then the Muslim and heathen nations of the world would be enlightened to the truth of the gospel and there would be an unparalleled ingathering of men and women into Christ's kingdom. What would ensue would be a glorious time when the entire earth would be 'blessed with honourable tokens of God's presence, not only as the Land of Canaan, but as the Temple; yea, as the holy of holies and the ark that had God's glory upon it'.[9] Edwards wisely refused to identify the Evangelical Revival that he had witnessed in his own lifetime as the start of this period of millennial blessing for the church. Nevertheless, he did hope that this revival would be the forerunner of even greater displays of the Spirit's power and ultimately of that stupendous outpouring of the Spirit in the final age of history.

Timothy George, a Southern Baptist historian who has recently written an excellent biography of Sutcliff's friend Carey, has noted that Sutcliff did not endorse every aspect of Edwards' eschatology. Yet, following Edwards and like Fuller and Ryland, Sutcliff did believe that he was living on the verge of great things. His was a day in which the Holy Spirit was greatly advancing the kingdom of Christ.[10]

## The fulfilment of prophecy

Sutcliff's *The Divinity of the Christian Religion Considered and Proved*, which was composed in 1797 as a circular letter for the Northamptonshire Association, argued at some length that earth-shaking prophecies were in the process of being fulfilled. According to Sutcliff, the book of Revelation, though obscure in many of its sections, had clearly predicted 'a grand apostasy from the truth'. This had been fulfilled in the emergence of Roman Catholicism. Yet its downfall had also been prophesied in this final book of the New Testament. The fulfilment of this prophecy, Sutcliff believed, was now happening before his and his contemporaries' very eyes. 'Concerning the fall of popery,' Sutcliff wrote, 'it is an object of general expectation. Even papists themselves are said to have strong apprehensions on this head.'[11] Sutcliff is here referring to the invasion of the papal states in Italy in early 1797 by the French army under the command of Napoleon Bonaparte (1769-1821). The pope, Pius VI (1717-1799), was subsequently forced to hand over to the French a vast amount of money and valuable art treasures, as well as to cede to French control significant portions of his territory. The situation further deteriorated over the next three years, as the French deposed Pius as the head of the papal states and eventually transferred him as a prisoner to the French citadel of Valence, where he died in 1799. Quite understandably, Sutcliff was not the only one who assumed that these momentous events spelled the final destruction of the papacy.

As the influence of Roman Catholicism waned, Sutcliff was confident that the power of the church would wax. 'The heavens and the earth are shaking,' Sutcliff said of his day at the close of *The Divinity of the Christian Religion Considered and Proved*, but 'The cause of Christ shall prosper, and his kingdom shall rise.'[12] Six years earlier he had expressed a similar sentiment: Satan's 'power [will] be broken, his policy confounded; while the empire of Jesus shall advance, his kingdom arise, and the crown flourish upon his head'.[13]

The same God-centred optimism was present in his final published piece, *On Reading the Word of God* (1813). In what is basically a pastiche of scriptural quotations and allusions, he stated, 'The period is not far distant, the day has already dawned, in which those who sit in the region of darkness and the valley of the shadow of death shall see the light of life; for the sun of righteousness is arising with healing under his wings. All shall know the Lord from the least unto the greatest... Whatever dispensations affect the world or the church, still the Lord reigns. The Lord is in his holy temple; the Lord's throne is in heaven. By faith view Jesus as head over all things to the church. He who was dead is alive, and his hands hold the keys of hell and of death. Seated upon his throne, at the head of the universal empire, he opens the sealed book. New scenes arise, which astonish heaven and earth, all tending to bring on that glorious day, when the kingdoms of this world shall become the kingdoms of our Lord and of his Christ; and he shall reign for ever and ever.'[14]

## The importance of corporate prayer

How, then, should God's people live in the midst of such times? Well, first and foremost, they must be devoted to corporate prayer.

'Anxious to see the advancement of the Redeemer's kingdom,' Sutcliff wrote of believers in tune with what God was doing in his world, 'you will give vent to your fervent desires by warm addresses at a throne of grace.'[15]

Early on in his Christian life Sutcliff had learned from his study of Scripture and the history of the church to prize prayer as vital for a life of communion with God and usefulness in the advance of his kingdom. For instance, it was probably during his time at Bristol Baptist Academy or at the beginning of his pastorate in Olney that Sutcliff first read the mini-biography of the New England divine Thomas Hooker (*c.*1586-1647) in Cotton Mather's *Magnalia Christi Americana: or, The Ecclesiastical History of New England* (1702). Converted at Emmanuel College, Cambridge, Hooker became a fairly well-known Puritan preacher in England during the 1620s. In 1629 he fell into disfavour with William Laud (1573-1645), the future Archbishop of Canterbury and an implacable foe of Puritanism. Suspended from his ministry within the Church of England and in danger of imprisonment, Hooker fled to the Netherlands in 1630. In the spring of 1633 he moved again, this time to New England, where he became a leading advocate of congregational church government.

What especially impressed Sutcliff about Hooker was the fact that the latter was above all a man devoted to prayer. Writing in a diary that he kept in his younger years, Sutcliff said after having read the story of Hooker's life, 'How did the gifts and graces of God shine in him! I remark in him, and all other eminent men of God and of great usefulness, that they did abound much in prayer. Lord, may I follow the example.' Other portions of this diary reveal that Sutcliff's aspiration to 'abound much in prayer' was not a passing fancy, for he often lamented the times when he neglected private prayer.[16] It is noteworthy that in *A View of the Doctrine of Divine Providence,* Sutcliff argued for the reality of God's providential dealings with the world from the fact that 'saints ... in all ages, have sought unto God' in prayer and God has answered them.[17]

Fuller and Ryland completely concurred with Sutcliff's conviction in this regard. In the statement of faith which Fuller gave at the time of his formal induction into the pastorate at Kettering in 1783, he firmly declared that he believed that 'The kingdom of Christ will yet be gloriously extended, by the pouring out of God's Spirit upon the ministry of the word,' and that it was therefore incumbent upon 'all God's servants and churches most ardently to pray' for it.[18] And the very first item which Fuller had published, the sermon 'The Nature and Importance of Walking by Faith,' which appeared in 1784, argued that 'A life of faith will ever be a life of prayer.'[19] Ryland could also bemoan the fact that he had not been 'more importunate and constant in prayer'. 'Of all the evils that infest me,' he confessed in 1790, 'I think a formal attendance on this duty, with too frequent neglect of it, is the worst.'[20] Evident in all of these passages is a very high esteem of prayer, an esteem that would bear rich fruit in the 1780s and the succeeding decades.

## The *Humble Attempt* and the concert of prayer

On 23 April 1784 Ryland received in the mail a treatise by Jonathan Edwards dealing with corporate prayer and revival, which had been sent to him by the Scottish Presbyterian minister John Erskine (1721-1803). When Erskine was in his mid-twenties he had entered into regular correspondence with Edwards, and had become part of a close-knit, letter-writing network of Scottish, English and American ministers committed to the promotion of the Evangelical Revival. Long after Edwards' death in 1758 Erskine had continued to uphold the theological perspectives of this network of ministers and to recommend heartily books that they had written, especially those by Edwards.

Well described as 'the paradigm of Scottish evangelical missionary interest through the last half of the eighteenth century',[21] Erskine regularly corresponded with both Sutcliff and Ryland from 1780 till his death in 1803, sending them not only letters, but also on occasion bundles of interesting books and tracts which he was seeking to promote.[22] Thus it was in mid-April of 1784 that Erskine mailed to Ryland a copy of Edwards' *An Humble Attempt to Promote Explicit Agreement and Visible Union of God's People in Extraordinary Prayer for the Revival of Religion and the Advancement of Christ's Kingdom on Earth, pursuant to Scripture Promises and Prophecies concerning the Last Time* (henceforth referred to as the *Humble Attempt*). Knowing the affection that Sutcliff and Fuller had for Edwards' writings, Ryland lost no time in sharing this treatise with his two friends.

The treatise had been inspired by a transatlantic movement of regular prayer meetings for revival which had sprung up in the early

1740s. There had been advocates for such meetings from the early years of the eighteenth century. For instance, in 1712 a group of London Dissenters had issued 'A Serious Call from the City to the Country', in which it was urged that an extra hour be set aside every week to beseech God to 'appear for the deliverance and enlargement of his Church'. And in 1757, after the outbreak of the Seven Years' War (1756-1763), the Anglican William Romaine had published a similar call in which he urged the 'friends of the Established Church' to set apart 'one hour of every week for prayer and supplication, during the present troublesome times'.[23]

What became known as the 'Concert of Prayer', though, had its actual beginnings in Lowland Scotland. It was there, in October 1744, that a number of Scottish evangelical ministers — including such regular correspondents of Edwards as John McLaurin (1693-1754) of the Ramshorn Church, Glasgow; William McCulloch (1691-1771) of Cambuslang; James Robe (1688-1753) of Kilsyth; and Erskine, then of Kirkintilloch — had committed themselves, together with their congregations, to pray regularly and corporately for revival. A part of Saturday evening and Sunday morning each week, as well as the first Tuesday of February, May, August and November, were to be spent in prayer to God for 'an abundant effusion of his Holy Spirit' so as to 'revive true religion in all parts of Christendom', to 'deliver all nations from their great and manifold spiritual calamities and miseries,' and to 'fill the whole earth with his glory'.[24]

This concert of prayer ran for an initial two years, and then was renewed for a further seven. When Edwards was sent information regarding it, he quickly sought to implement a similar concert of prayer in the New England colonies. He encouraged his own congregation to get involved, and also communicated the concept of such a prayer union to neighbouring ministers who he felt would be receptive to the idea. Although the idea initially met with a poor response, Edwards was not to be put off. In a sermon given in February 1747 on Zechariah 8:20-22, he sought to demonstrate how the text supported his call for a union of praying Christians. Within the year a revised and greatly expanded version of this sermon was ready for publication as the *Humble Attempt.*

The *Humble Attempt* was divided into three parts. The first section opened with a number of observations on Zechariah 8:20-22 and then went on to provide a description of the origin of the concert of prayer in Scotland. From the text in Zechariah Edwards inferred that a spirit of prayer would be given to God's people in various places of North America, 'disposing them to come into an express agreement, unitedly to pray to God in an extraordinary manner, that he would appear for the help of his church, and in mercy to mankind, and pour out his Spirit, revive his work, and advance his spiritual kingdom in the world, as he has promised'.[25] Edwards thus concluded that it was a duty well-pleasing to God and incumbent upon God's people in America to assemble and, with 'extraordinary, speedy, fervent and constant prayer', pray for those 'great effusions of the Holy Spirit' which would dramatically advance the kingdom of Christ.[26]

Part II of the treatise cited a number of reasons for participating in the concert of prayer. Our Lord Jesus shed his blood and tears, and poured out his prayers to secure the blessed presence of his Spirit for his people. The sum of the blessings which Christ sought in his work of redemption was the gift of the Holy Spirit. In 'his indwelling, his influences and fruits, is the sum of all grace, holiness, comfort and joy, or in one word, of all the spiritual good Christ purchased for men in this world: and is also the sum of all perfection, glory and eternal joy, that he purchased for them in another world.'[27] The inference that Edwards drew from this fact would have strongly impressed Sutcliff and his friends: if the gift of the Spirit is what Christ did so much desire and set his heart upon, and for which which he suffered so much, then his followers 'should also earnestly seek it, and be much and earnest in prayer for it'.[28]

Scripture, moreover, is replete with commands, incentives and illustrations regarding prayer for the Holy Spirit. There is, for example, the encouragement given in Luke 11:13: 'If ye then, being evil, know how to give good gifts unto your children: how much more shall your heavenly Father give the Holy Spirit to them that ask him?' These words of Christ, Edwards observed, imply that prayer for the Holy Spirit is one request that God the Father is particularly pleased to answer in the affirmative.[29] Or one might consider the example of the early disciples who devoted themselves to 'united fervent prayer and supplication ... till the Spirit came down in a wonderful manner upon them,' as is related in Acts 1-2.[30]

Additional incentives to take part in the concert of prayer were provided by 'the spiritual calamities and miseries of the present time'. Among the calamities which Edwards listed were King

George's War (1744-1748), the disastrous attempt by Charles Edward Stuart (1720-1788), the 'Young Pretender', to seize the British throne for his father only a couple of years before in 1745-1746, the persecution of the Huguenots in France, the decay of vital piety, the deluge of vice and immorality, the loss of respect for those in vocational ministry and the prevalence of religious fanaticism.[31]

Moreover, Edwards found in the drift of the intellectual and theological currents of his day a further reason for prayer, as men and women rejected Reformation and Puritan theology so as to embrace theologies shaped by the world-view of the Enlightenment. Sutcliff, who was well aware of the challenge posed to biblical Christianity by many Enlightenment values, would have recognized in the following passage an accurate picture of his day:

> Never was an age wherein so many learned and elaborate treatises have been written, in proof of the truth and divinity of the Christian religion; yet never were there so many infidels, among those that were brought up under the light of the gospel. It is an age, as is supposed, of great light, freedom of thought, and discovery of truth in matters of religion, and detection of the weakness and bigotry of our ancestors, and of the folly and absurdity of the notions of those that were accounted eminent divines in former generations ... and yet vice and wickedness did never so prevail, like an overflowing deluge. 'Tis an age wherein those mean and stingy principles (as they are called) of our forefathers, which (as is supposed) deformed religion, and led to unworthy thoughts of God, are very much discarded, and grown out of credit, and supposed more free, noble and generous thoughts of the nature of religion, and of the Christian scheme, are entertained; but yet never was an age, wherein religion in general was so much despised and trampled on, and Jesus Christ and God Almighty so blasphemed and treated with open daring contempt.[32]

Yet Edwards also listed a number of events which showed that, though his time was a 'day of great apostasy', it was also a 'day of the wonderful works of God; wonders of power and mercy' that should move believers to united prayer just as much as the distresses and calamities.[33] Edwards especially highlighted such 'wonders of power and mercy' as God's granting of military success to the British against the French in North America, and various spiritual revivals on the European continent, in Great Britain, and among the New England colonies. In particular, these 'late remarkable religious awakenings ... may justly encourage us in prayer for the promised glorious and universal outpouring of the Spirit of God'.[34] The inclusion of military and political events alongside those more specifically 'religious' reveals Edwards' belief that God directs the course of history in its most minute details.[35] Edwards and most of his fellow New England preachers had 'a deep-seated conviction ... that if they did not know their history they did not know God'.[36]

The beauty and benefits involved in a visible union for prayer formed yet another motive that Edwards gave for complying with his proposal. Unity, Edwards maintained, is regarded by the Scriptures as 'the peculiar beauty of the church of Christ'.[37] In support of this statement, he referred his readers to the Song of Songs 6:9, Psalm 122:3 and Ephesians 4:3-6,16. Union in prayer would also prove to be beneficial for the church in that it would tend to promote closer rapport, 'mututal affection and endearment' between the members of different denominational bodies.[38] Edwards' argument at this juncture would have been especially attractive to Sutcliff, who, as we have noted, never dreamt of restricting his friendships simply to men and women of his own denomination.

Part III, the longest portion of the *Humble Attempt,* was devoted to answering various objections to the idea of a concert of prayer. These objections ranged from the charge that the concert was something previously unknown in the history of the church and therefore suspect, to the assertion that certain eschatological conditions needed to be fulfilled before God would answer prayer for such an abundant outpouring of the Spirit as Edwards was longing to see. This latter objection launched Edwards into a detailed and lengthy exposition of his perspective on the course of history and its outcome, a perspective that has been briefly outlined earlier in this chapter.

A significant number of congregations in America and Scotland observed the concert of prayer throughout the 1750s. Especially during the French and Indian War (1755-1760), the concert enjoyed 'a considerable vogue among American Calvinists'.[39] In 1759, for instance, Robert Smith informed fellow Presbyterians in Pennsylvania that the concert of prayer would prove to be far more effective in hastening the 'brightest period of the militant Church's glory' than the military victories won by British forces.[40] Yet, as we shall see, the *Humble Attempt* would bear much of its greatest fruit long after the death of its author. As Iain H. Murray has noted in his biography of Edwards, 'It is arguable that no such tract on the hidden source of all true evangelistic success, namely, prayer for the Spirit of God, has ever been so widely used as this one.'[41]

## The Prayer Call is issued

Reading Edwards' *Humble Attempt* in the final week of April 1784 evidently had a profound impact on Ryland. As we have mentioned, he immediately shared it with Fuller and Sutcliff, on whom it had a similar effect. Within a few days of reading Edwards' treatise, these three Baptist pastors, together with a few other ministerial colleagues, had committed themselves to meeting the second Tuesday in every other month 'to seek the revival of real religion, and the extension of Christ's kingdom in the world'.[42]

Fuller was to preach that June at the annual meeting of the Northamptonshire Association in Nottingham. As described in chapter 1, he discovered on his way there that the spring rains had inundated many areas of the roads on which he was travelling. One particular area appeared to be so deeply flooded that Fuller was sure that he would have to turn back, but a man who knew the area told him to urge his horse on. Although the water came up to Fuller's saddle, all turned out well. This experience prompted Fuller to preach on 2 Corinthians 5:7 at the association meeting: 'We walk by faith, not by sight.'[43] During the course of this sermon, which he entitled 'The Nature and Importance of Walking by Faith,' Fuller clearly revealed the impression that Edwards' *Humble Attempt* had made upon his thinking when he appealed to his hearers to engage in 'earnest and united prayer' to God for 'an outpouring of God's Spirit upon our ministers and churches, and not upon those only of our own connexion and denomination, but upon "all that in every place call upon the name of Jesus Christ our Lord, both theirs and ours" (1 Corinthians 1:2).'[44]

Hard on the heels of Fuller's sermon Sutcliff proposed that they as an association heed what the Spirit was saying to them through their brother's stirring appeal. The churches of the association should, Sutcliff said, establish monthly prayer meetings for the outpouring of God's Holy Spirit and the consequent revival of the churches of Great Britain. His proposal was met with wholehearted approval by the representatives of the sixteen churches at the meeting and on the last page of the circular letter sent out that year to the churches of the association there was a call for them 'to wrestle with God for the effusion of his Holy Spirit.'[45] After recommending that there be corporate prayer for one hour on the first Monday evening of the month, the call, which was most likely drafted by Sutcliff himself, continued:

> The grand object in prayer is to be, that the Holy Spirit may be poured down on our ministers and churches, that sinners may be converted, the saints edified, the interest of religion revived, and the name of God glorified. At the same time remember, we trust you will not confine your requests to your own societies [i.e. churches], or to your own immediate connection [i.e. denomination]; let the whole interest of the Redeemer be affectionately remembered, and the spread of the gospel to the most distant parts of the habitable globe be the object of your most fervent requests. — We shall rejoice if any other Christian societies of our own or other denomination will unite with us, and do now invite them most cordially to join heart and hand in the attempt.
>
> Who can tell what the consequences of such an united effort in prayer may be! Let us plead with God the many gracious promises of his word, which relate to the future success of his gospel. He has said, 'I will yet for this be enquired of by the house of Israel, to do it for them, I will increase them with men like a flock' (Ezekiel 36:37). Surely we have love enough for Zion to set apart one hour at a time, twelve times in a year, to seek her welfare.[46]

There are at least four noteworthy points about this Prayer Call. First, very much in evidence in this statement, as well as in the extract from Fuller's sermon, was the conviction that any renewal of the Calvinistic Baptist cause could not be accomplished by mere human zeal, but must be effected by the Spirit of God. As Sutcliff noted later in tones strongly reminiscent of Jonathan Edwards, 'The outpouring of the divine Spirit ... is the grand promise of the New Testament.' Without his power 'Divine ordinances are empty cisterns, and spiritual graces are withering flowers.' Without his enablement, 'The greatest human abilities labour in vain, and the noblest efforts fail of success.'[47]

Secondly, there was the catholicity that was recommended with regard to the subjects of prayer. As the Calvinistic Baptists of the Northamptonshire Association gathered together to pray they were encouraged not to think simply of their own churches and their own denomination, but they were to embrace in prayer believers of other denominational bodies. The kingdom of God consists of more than Calvinistic Baptists! In fact, churches of other denominations, as well as Baptist churches in other associations, were encouraged to join with them in praying for revival. This evangelical catholicity, as we have had cause to remark a number of times already, was a hallmark of Sutcliff's circle of friends.

Thirdly, there was the distinct missionary emphasis of the Prayer Call: the members of the association churches were urged to pray that the gospel be spread 'to the most distant parts of the habitable globe'. Little did these Baptists realize how God would begin to fulfil these very prayers within the space of less than a decade.

Finally, the sole foundation for praying for revival was located in the Scriptures. Only one text, Ezekiel 36:37, was actually quoted, but those issuing this call to prayer were aware of 'many gracious promises' in God's Word which speak of the successful advance of his kingdom. At first glance this passage from Ezekiel hardly seems the best text to support the Prayer Call. Yet Edwards had cited this very verse in his *Humble Attempt* and said the following with regard to it:

> The Scriptures don't only direct and encourage us in general to pray for the Holy Spirit above all things else, but it is the expressly revealed will of God, that his church should be very much in prayer for that glorious outpouring of the Spirit that is to be in the latter days, and the things that shall be accomplished by it. God speaking of that blessed event (Ezek. 36), under the figure of 'cleansing the house of Israel from all their iniquities, planting and building their waste and ruined places, and making them to become like the Garden of

> Eden, and filling them with men like a flock, like the holy flock, the flock of Jerusalem in her solemn feasts' (vv. 33-38) (wherein he doubtless has respect to the same glorious restoration and advancement of his church that is spoken of in the next chapter, and in all the following chapters to the end of the book) he says, v. 37, 'Thus saith the Lord, I will yet for this be inquired of by the house of Israel, to do it for them.' Which doubtless implies, that it is the will of God that extraordinary prayerfulness in his people for this mercy should precede the bestowment of it.[48]

Here, Edwards was seeking to interpret Ezekiel 36:37 in the light of the larger context of Ezekiel 37-48. According to Edwards, since these chapters speak prophetically of the latter-day glory of the church — that millennial period in which 'Love will abound, and glorifying God by word and deed will be characteristic'[49] — then Ezekiel 36:37 must refer to the united prayers of God's people that will usher in this glorious period of the church's history. Edwards had directed his own congregation to 'observe what you read [in the Scriptures]. Observe how things come in. Take notice of the drift of the discourse...'[50] Here, in the *Humble Attempt,* he was merely practising what he preached.

Now, while Edwards' particular interpretation of these passages from Ezekiel was open to debate, as Sutcliff later admitted, the principle that he drew from Ezekiel 36:37 was not, namely, that times of revival and striking extensions of Christ's kingdom are invariably preceded by the concerted and constant prayers of Christians. And it is clearly this principle which those who issued the Prayer Call of 1784 wanted to stress, although most of them probably concurred with Edwards' postmillennial vision. The proof of this statement may be found in the 'Preface' that Sutcliff wrote for the edition of Edwards' *Humble Attempt* which he brought out in 1789. By republishing Edwards' work, he stated, he did not consider himself as 'answerable for every sentiment it contains', since an 'Author and an Editor are very distinct characters'. Some might disagree with some of Edwards' prophetic views, but Sutcliff was hopeful that they would nevertheless approve of 'the general design' of the work, namely, Edwards' argument that corporate prayer for the outpouring of the Spirit is vital to the advance of Christ's kingdom.[51]

**The response to the Prayer Call**

The association meetings at which this Prayer Call was issued were held on 2 and 3 June. At the end of that month, on 29 June, the Olney church resolved to establish a 'monthly meeting for prayer ... to seek for a revival of religion'.[52] The following month Fuller noted in his diary that he had read to members of his congregation in Kettering 'a part of Mr Edwards' *Attempt to promote Prayer for the Revival of Religion* [a reference to the *Humble Attempt*], to excite them to the like practice.'

From this point on there occur a goodly number of entries in Fuller's diary relating to this subject. For instance, on 12 July 1784 he wrote, 'Lord Jesus, set up thy glorious, peaceful kingdom all over the world! Found earnest desire, this morning, in prayer, that God would ... hear our prayers, in which the churches agree to unite, for the spread of Christ's kingdom.'

On 6 December of the same year, there is the following entry in his diary: 'An affecting meeting of prayer, this evening, for the revival of real religion: found much pleasure in singing, and freedom with God in prayer.'[53]

Again, on 2 May 1785 he wrote of the monthly meeting for prayer in Kettering, 'This evening, I felt tender all the time of the prayer-meeting for the revival of religion; but, in hearing Mr Beeby Wallis [a deacon in the church] pray for me, I was overcome: his having a better opinion of me than I deserve, cuts me to heart! Went to prayer myself, and found my mind engaged more than ordinarily in praying for the revival of religion. I had felt many sceptical thoughts; as though there were room to ask — What profit shall I have if I pray to God? for which I was much grieved. Find a great satisfaction in these monthly meetings: even supposing our requests should not be granted, yet prayer to God is its own reward.'[54]

When the Northamptonshire Association met later that month in Oakham, then in Rutlandshire, it resolved 'without any hesitation, to continue the meetings of prayer on the first Monday evening in every calendar month'. The resolution then continued in language very similar to the above entry from Fuller's diary: 'We have heard with pleasure that several churches not in the association, and some of other denominations, have united with us in this matter. May God give us all hearts to persevere. If our petitions are not answered by any remarkable out pourings of the Spirit, they may by a more gradual work; or if not in our time, they may in time to come; or if not at all, there is profit enough in the exercise itself to be its own reward. But God hath never yet said to the seed of Jacob, seek ye my face in vain.'[55]

Sutcliff, Fuller and Ryland and their colleagues in the Northamptonshire Association shared Edwards' opinion that genuine revival is generally preceded by prayer. Thomas Blundel, Sr (*c.* 1752-1824), a member of Fuller's congregation in Kettering and later Robert Hall's successor at the Baptist church in Arnesby, summed up their conviction well in a sermon on 2 Thessalonians 3:1: 'It is chiefly in answer to prayer that God has carried on his cause in the world; he could work without any such means, but he does not, neither will he.'[56] As the Oakham resolution wisely recognized, however, it is certainly fallacious to perceive this connection between prayer and revival in terms of the following equation: prayer plus perseverance equals revival. Those who stood behind this resolution were strongly committed to the sovereignty of God: the power to effect revival lay in his hands, not theirs. Moreover, as this resolution bore witness, they were vividly aware that prayer is to be valued not simply for the answers it obtains, but also for the communion it secures with God.

The following year, 1786, Sutcliff gave a progress report and exhortation to the association regarding the prayer meetings that had been established. Monthly meetings of prayer for the spread of the gospel were being 'kept up with some degree of spirit'. Many other churches in various parts of England, and some of them from other denominations, had also responded positively to the Prayer Call. Sutcliff then went on to invite 'all who love truth and holiness, into whose hands our letter may fall, to unite their help. Let societies, let families, let individuals, who are friends to the cause of Christ unite with us, not only daily, but in a particular manner, at the appointed season.'[57] Like his mentor Edwards, Sutcliff was convinced that not simply the individual prayers of God's people presaged revival, but the prayers of God's people when they gathered together to pray in unison.[58] As Sutcliff went on to indicate, God was already answering their prayers by providing 'an open door in many places for the preaching of the gospel'.[59]

The passing years did not diminish the zeal of Sutcliff, Fuller, or Ryland in praying for revival and stirring up such prayer. For instance, Ryland wrote in his diary for 21 January 1788, 'Brethren

Fuller, Sutcliff, Carey, and I, kept this day as a private fast, in my study: read the Epistles to Timothy and Titus; [Abraham] Booth's charge to [Thomas] Hopkins; [Richard] Blackerby's Life, in [John] Gillies; and [John] Rogers of Dedham's Sixty Memorials for a Godly Life: and each prayed twice — Carey with singular enlargement and pungency. Our chief design was to implore a revival of godliness in our own souls, in our churches, and in the church at large.'[60] This is a fascinating entry, for it well displays the kind of literature which Sutcliff and his circle of friends were reading to encourage themselves in praying for revival. Besides the Pastoral Epistles, they were reading their older contemporary and fellow Calvinistic Baptist minister, Abraham Booth. His charge to Thomas Hopkins (1759-1787), when the latter was ordained pastor of Eagle Street Baptist Church, London in 1784, contained the following admonition, which would not have been lost on Sutcliff and his friends: 'With humility, with prayer, and with expectation, the assistance of the Holy Spirit should be daily regarded.'[61] Richard Blackerby (1574-1648) and John Rogers (d.1636) were both Puritan authors. The book of John Gillies (1712-1796), the son-in-law of John McLaurin, one of the initiators of the concert of prayer in Scotland, is his *Historical Collections Relating to Remarkable Periods of the Success of the Gospel, and Eminent Instruments Employed in Promoting It* (1754). This book is reputedly the earliest history of revivals.

By 1789 the number of prayer meetings for revival had grown to such an extent that Sutcliff decided to bring out an edition of Edwards' *Humble Attempt* to encourage further those meeting for prayer. Containing 168 pages, and measuring only six and a quarter inches long, and three and three-quarter inches wide, this version was clearly designed to be a handy, pocket-size edition. In his 'Preface' to this version Sutcliff re-emphasized that the Prayer Call issued by the Northamptonshire Association five years earlier was not intended for simply Calvinistic Baptists:

> Rather they ardently wished it might become general among the real friends of truth and holiness. The advocates of error are indefatigable in their endeavours to overthrow the distinguishing and interesting doctrines of Christianity; those doctrines which are the grounds of our hope, and sources of our joy. Surely, it becomes the followers of Christ, to use

> every effort, in order to strengthen the things which remain... In the present imperfect state, we may reasonably expect a diversity of sentiments upon religious matters. Each ought to think for himself; and every one has a right, on proper occasions, to show his opinion. Yet all should remember, that there are but two parties in the world, each engaged in opposite causes: the cause of God and of Satan; of holiness and sin; of heaven and hell. The advancement of the one, and the downfall of the other, must appear exceedingly desirable to every real friend of God and man. If such in some respects entertain different sentiments, and practice distinguishing modes of worship, surely they may unite in the above business. O for thousands upon thousands, divided into small bands in their respective cities, towns, villages and neighbourhood, all met at the same time, and in pursuit of one end, offering up their united prayers, like so many ascending clouds of incense before the Most High! — May He shower down blessings on all the scattered tribes of Zion![62]

In this text Sutcliff positioned the Prayer Call of 1784 on the broad canvas of history, in which God and Satan are waging war for the souls of men and women. Prayer, because it was a weapon common to all who are 'friends of truth and holiness', was one sphere in which Christians can present a fully united front against Satan. Sutcliff was well aware that evangelicals in his day held differing theological positions and worshipped in different ways. He himself was a convinced Baptist — convinced in particular that the Scriptures fully supported congregational polity and believer's baptism — yet, he emphasized in the 'Preface' quoted above that such convictions should not prevent believers, committed to the foundational truths of Christianity, from uniting together to pray for revival.

The date on which Sutcliff wrote this preface was 4 May 1789. The following day, on the other side of the English Channel, the Estates-General, an assembly consisting of representatives drawn from the three principal social orders in France — the Roman Catholic clergy, the nobility and the commoners — met for the first time since 1614. Many in France were hopeful that the meeting of these representatives signalled the beginning of much-needed, peaceful reform in the political and economic spheres. As it turned out, the convening of the Estates-General actually marked the commencement of the French Revolution, which would plunge Europe into an epoch of turmoil and war. In the midst of this revolutionary and violent epoch, Sutcliff, Ryland, Fuller, along with fellow Baptists and evangelicals in other denominations, persevered in prayer for revival, conscious that for Christians, 'Days of crisis must always be days of increased expectancy, days which call for renewed dedication to the work of the Lord.'[63]

# 9.
# Sutcliff's friends: William Carey

> *'Carey was the living model of [Jonathan] Edwards' theology, or rather of pure Christianity. His was not a theology which left out the backbone and strength of religion — not a theology, on the other hand, all bones and skeleton, a lifeless thing without a soul: his theology was full-orbed Calvinism, high as you please, but practical godliness so low that many called it legal'* (C .H. Spurgeon).

In contrast to the significant influx of members which the Olney church had welcomed during the first four years of Sutcliff's ministry, the 1780s were a period when things appeared to be at a standstill. The number of members in 1780 stood at fifty-nine. Four years later, when the association issued the Prayer Call on Sutcliff's suggestion, the membership of the church had slipped to forty-eight. That year, as Sutcliff drafted the report of the church for the annual assembly of the association, he was somewhat disheartened as he stated, 'Things in general are but low,' for the 'work of conversion seems greatly at a stand.'[1]

Speaking on the basis of this experience, Sutcliff later said that 'Unsuccessfulness in our ministerial work is indeed a heavy trial... To publish our report from sabbath to sabbath, from year to year, and yet to be compelled to return lamenting, "Who hath believed our report, and to whom is the arm of the Lord revealed?" (Isaiah 53:1) is distressing.'[2]

Nevertheless, the following year he was more encouraged. Even though the membership had grown by only one, he could write that the congregation 'seems to be in an increasing state'.[3] Here, Sutcliff is probably referring to a growth in the number of 'hearers'. These were people who regularly attended the services in the Baptist meeting-house, but for one reason or another were unwilling to become members. When Sutcliff came to Olney, it will be recalled that there were anywhere between three to four hundred attending the services Sunday by Sunday. This would mean that there were between 250 and 350 hearers. The remaining years of the decade saw little actual growth in numbers of members — in 1789 there were fifty-three in the membership of the church — yet, the reports sent to the annual assembly of the association were on the whole pervaded with a spirit of optimism. The monthly prayer meetings for revival undoubtedly helped to foment such a spirit. Sutcliff reported, for instance, in 1788 that these meetings were 'tolerably well attended, and frequently spoken of as comfortable seasons'.[4] Also deeply encouraging to Sutcliff was the reception into membership during the 1780s of two individuals in particular: William Wilson (d.1831) and William Carey.

## William Wilson

William Wilson was the town's barber, hairdresser and wigmaker. His house, built just to the south-east of the Baptist meeting-house, faced onto the market-place. A close friend of Cowper, Wilson was regarded by the poet as among the 'men of best intelligence' in Olney.[5] While he seems to have been an adequate barber and hairdresser, as a wigmaker he left much to be desired. In the words of the younger Ryland, 'Good Mr Wilson, of Olney, is an excellent Christian; but one of the ugliest wigmakers that ever was born'![6] The only portrait that we actually possess of Sutcliff is of him from the side with a wig perched on his head, presumably that of Wilson's making.[7] According to Ryland, Wilson made the identical shape of wig for Sutcliff as he did for Carey and Fuller, without any consideration for the differences in their respective cranial structures. No wonder Carey threw his wig overboard into the sea on the voyage out to India in 1793![8]

During Newton's time in Olney, Wilson evidently attended the parish church, where he greatly enjoyed Newton's evangelical ministry. Newton, however, left Olney early in 1780 to become the rector of St Mary Woolnoth, an influential church in the heart of the city of London. A minister named Benjamin Page was appointed curate in his stead. His brief ministry at Olney was neither a happy nor a successful one. When Newton enquired of William Cowper about Page's ministry in either late March or early April 1780, Cowper told him candidly that as a preacher, Page was 'much liked by some and as much disliked by others'. The more judicious, he added, were among the latter group of hearers. The problem had more to do with his style of preaching than the content: 'frequent repetitions of the same thing, references to what he said on a former occasion,' and a 'great proneness' to quibble with the English translation of the Scriptures without 'giving sufficient or indeed any reason to suppose that he understands the original'.[9] After a few months of this sort of preaching, Wilson came to the conclusion that a regular diet of Page's sermons would leave him spiritually emaciated. The Baptist meeting-house was only a few feet from his home, and it was only natural that he decide to see what worship was like there.

When Newton was informed that Wilson was regularly attending the meeting-house, he was apprehensive lest Wilson take what he called 'a trip to the river', that is, get publicly baptized in the River Ouse. Like most Baptist churches of this era, there was no baptistery within the meeting-house at Olney. Sutcliff baptized believers in the Ouse, even as other Baptists throughout the country baptized in local streams, rivers and mill-ponds. In this way, baptism was very much a public testimony of one's commitment to Christ.

Cowper shared Newton's fears with Wilson, as well as freely telling the Olney barber that he himself thought it would be a mistake for Wilson to join the Baptists. Wilson, according to Cowper, reassured him that he was quite aware of the 'narrowness and bigotry' of the Baptists. What the barber was anxious to have was spiritual nourishment, 'the Substance [rather] than the sign'.[10] The fact that Wilson did indeed take 'a trip to the river' Ouse on Saturday, 21 June 1782, says much about what he found among the Baptists. Obviously he became convinced that believer's baptism was the scriptural way of carrying out this ordinance. Moreover, he must have appreciated Sutcliff's preaching, which had a similar evangelical thrust and content to that of Newton.

Sutcliff, as we have seen, had problems with his preaching in his early years. As he became more experienced, though, his preaching greatly improved. For instance, when his friend John Ryland heard him preach on Psalm 51:3 at the annual association in May 1788, he noted in his diary that Sutcliff's 'sermon was very good'.[11] His sermons became characterized by 'a savour of experimental piety' and a simplicity of expression. According to John Robinson, the son of a member of Sutcliff's congregation, Sutcliff's sermons were 'plain and simple', but chock-full of 'solid matter, and evidently the productions of deep and prayerful study'. Robert Hall, Jr tells us that Sutcliff had a deep aversion to ostentation and made a point of never parading his learning in the pulpit. He seems to have developed the lack of self-confidence which marked him in his younger years into what Hall called 'a sweet humility'. Sutcliff would also speak slowly in order to enable all of his hearers, even the most illiterate, to grasp the 'great truths and doctrines of the gospel'.[12]

It also says much about Wilson's Christian maturity that within four years of his being baptized he was elected deacon, an office that he held for many years, and appointed a trustee of the meeting-house.[13] A good illustration of Wilson's value to the church occurred during the year prior to his being elected deacon. Wilson, along with Thomas Osborn and John Rogers — Rogers had been among Sutcliff's High Calvinist critics — were appointed to visit another member of the congregation, William Peace, to ascertain the truth of a very serious charge that had been levelled against Peace. According to the church minutes, 'A scandalous report having been raised of Wm. Peace, he was suspended' on Thursday, 23 December 1784.[14]

Our knowledge of what exactly was entailed by this 'scandalous report' is derived from one of Cowper's letters to Newton. Writing on Christmas Eve, 1784, the day following Peace's suspension, Cowper informed his friend that for more than six months a report about Peace had been 'current in this place in the way of whisper, but lately with much noise and clamour', namely, that Peace had been involved in pederasty.[15] Apparently, he had either sexually molested two boys or attempted to do so. Cowper identified the boys merely by their surnames: 'one called Butcher, and the other Beryl'. These two boys may well have been James Butcher and Jonathan Berril, who became members of the Baptist church in 1799 and 1792 respectively.[16]

When Peace was initially confronted with the charge by one of the boys in the presence of his wife, his reply was a 'clenched fist and a thrust [of the boy] into the street'. The boys refused to let the matter drop and presumably took it to Sutcliff. It was raised with Peace, almost certainly by Sutcliff, either on the last Sunday in November or one of the first three Sundays of December. Peace, according to Cowper, 'denied it with the most solemn asseverations'. Peace was told, however, that the church needed more satisfactory proof of his innocence than simply his word, especially in view of the fact that knowledge of the matter was all over town. Peace refused to try to clear his name. Sutcliff had no choice but to take it to the church at the next monthly business meeting on 23 December. It was at this meeting that Peace's privileges as a member were suspended, and Wilson, Osborn and Rogers delegated to visit him. Wilson's first impressions, which he communicated to Cowper, were that Peace was indeed guilty, his refusal to attempt to clear his name evincing rather 'a hardness of heart, than a consciousness of innocence'.

At the next monthly business meeting, held on 20 January 1785, Wilson, Osborn and Rogers reported that they had met with Peace and his accusers separately. The boys' 'testimony appeared credible', but Peace refused to face the boys, though he vehemently denied their charge. After some deliberation, the church was convinced that Peace's whole attitude to the affair bespoke his guilt and he was 'immediately excluded'.[17] In disciplining Peace in this manner the Olney church would have been hopeful that exclusion would shock Peace into genuine repentance and a reformed life. There is no evidence, though, that it did. In a later letter to Newton, Cowper recorded the aftermath of this affair. Thomas Osborn felt that he should officially notify Peace of the church's decision. But, meeting Peace accidentally in the street one day, he decided to let the matter drop. Peace's demeanour and facial expression revealed, Cowper wrote, 'a temper that it might not be safe to irritate'![18] The service, albeit small, which Wilson rendered to the church in this disagreeable affair was but the first of many which led him to become, in the words of William Hawkins (1790-1853), 'Sutcliff's right hand'.[19]

## William Carey and the Olney church

William Carey's membership in the church was nowhere near as long as Wilson's, yet his two years in the congregation were

William Carey

arguably just as influential. His friendship with Sutcliff reinforced and solidified the latter's missionary vision, which would eventually lead to Sutcliff's becoming one of the founding fathers of the Baptist Missionary Society. Sutcliff's involvement in this society changed for ever the tenor of the Olney church. The congregation became vitally interested in missions, even sending some of its own members overseas, and regularly supporting these and others who went. Moreover, Sutcliff's parsonage academy, which we shall look at in chapter 11, had its roots in his association with Carey. Carey was the first of a goodly number of students whom Sutcliff would tutor. All of these students were involved in the Olney church, which had a lasting and salutary impact on the congregation's life.

## Early influences in Carey's life

Carey was born of poor parents, Edmund Carey (d.1816) and Elizabeth Wells (d.1787), in 1761 in a tiny village called Paulerspury in the county of Northamptonshire. Edmund Carey was a weaver, who worked at a handloom in his own cottage to produce a type of woollen cloth known in the district as 'tammy'. When Carey was six years of age, his father was appointed the Parish Clerk of Paulerspury as well as the schoolmaster of the village. According to William Cowper, the parish clerk had to 'pronounce the *Amen* to prayers and announce the sermon', lead the chants and responses during the service, keep the church register of baptisms, marriages and burials, and chase 'dogs out of church' and force 'unwilling youngsters in'.[20]

Thus, young William was regularly taken to the parish church. Carey later stated with regard to this early acquaintance with the Church of England that he was 'accustomed from ... infancy to read the Scriptures', and 'had a considerable acquaintance therewith, especially with the historical parts'. Without a doubt, he said, 'The constant reading of the Psalms, Lessons, etc. in the parish church, which I was obliged to attend regularly, tended to furnish my mind with a general Scripture knowledge.' But, he underscored the fact that 'Of real experimental religion I scarcely heard anything till I was fourteen years of age.'[21]

Also living in Paulerspury was William's uncle, Peter Carey. Peter had served with James Wolfe (1727-1759) in Canada during the Seven Years' War and participated in the capture of Quebec in 1759, two years before William was born. Peter subsequently returned to England and worked in Paulerspury as a gardener. His tales of Canada and his experiences there awakened William's interest in far-off lands and gave him a longing to travel. Moreover, Peter implanted in young William a love of gardens and flowers which remained with him all his life. William's younger sister Mary (1767-1842) later recalled: 'He often took me over the dirtiest roads to get at a plant or an insect. He never walked out, I think ... without observation on the hedges as he passed; and when he took up a plant of any kind he always observed it with care.'[22] When, years later, Carey was established in India, he was continually asking his friends and correspondents to enclose seeds and bulbs with their letters. In fact, at Serampore in India, Carey had five acres of garden under cultivation. His garden and gardening served as a welcome means of relaxation from the stresses and strains of ministry in India. It was of this garden that his son Jonathan said, 'Here he enjoyed his most pleasant moments of secret meditation and devotion.'[23]

So much did young Carey love gardening that he longed to become a gardener like his Uncle Peter. At this point in his life, however, Carey suffered from a painful skin disease which prevented him from spending large amounts of time in the full sun. Thus, at the age of fourteen, his father apprenticed him to a shoemaker named Clarke Nichols, who lived in Piddington, some eight miles away. This apprenticeship was to have very significant consequences for William, because Nichols' other apprentice was a Christian and a Dissenter. His name was John Warr and he was a Congregationalist. As Warr shared his faith with Carey, the latter was regularly exposed for the first time in his life to what he called 'real experimental religion'.

It was known for a long time that Carey's conversion had been triggered by the witness of his fellow-apprentice. Until the First World War, however, the name of this apprentice had been completely lost. During this war it was discovered in a letter of Carey's which had only then come to light.[24] It is a powerful illustration of how the faithful witness of one believer can have the profoundest of consequences.

At first, when Warr spoke with Carey about Christ, Carey resisted the force of his arguments. Carey was the product of a staunch Anglican home and had come to despise anyone who was not a member of this denomination. As Thomas Scott (1747-1821), an evangelical Anglican minister whose preaching was a great help to Carey at one point in his life, commented concerning the Anglican disdain for Dissenters, 'We imbibe this prejudice with the first rudiments of instruction, and are taught by our whole education to consider it as meritorious.'[25] But as Warr continued to witness to Carey, the latter felt 'a growing uneasiness and stings of conscience gradually increasing'. Warr lent him books which began to effect a change in his thinking, but also increased his 'inward uneasiness'. Warr also persuaded him to attend a prayer meeting with him in nearby Hackleton, where a number of Congregationalists gathered mid-week for prayer and Bible study. Carey subsequently tried to reform his life: to give up lying and swearing and to take up prayer. But, he later said, he had no idea that 'nothing but a complete change of heart' could do him any real and lasting good.[26] Incidentally, it is interesting that Carey mentioned swearing as one of the major sins that dogged his life prior to his conversion. Other Europeans in the eighteenth century often noted that the English in general were addicted to swearing. Even cultured, upper-class women habitually swore. When John Newton, for example, was converted in 1748, he observed that he was 'freed from the habit of swearing which seems to have been deeply rooted in me as a second nature'.[27]

Coupled with Warr's testimony was the powerful impression made by a traumatic incident that took place at Christmas 1777. It was customary for apprentices at that time of the year to be given small sums of money from the tradespeople with whom their masters had business. Carey was in Northampton making some purchases for Nichols as well as for himself. At one particular shop, that of the ironmonger called Hall, he was personally given a counterfeit shilling as a joke. When Carey discovered the worthless coin he decided, not without some qualms of conscience, to pass it off to his employer. Appropriating a good shilling from the money which Nichols had given him, he included the counterfeit shilling among the change for his master. On the way back to Piddington, he even prayed to God that if God enabled his dishonesty to go undetected he would break with sin from that time forth! But, Carey commented in a letter written to Fuller many years later, 'A gracious God did not get me through.'[28] Carey's dishonesty was discovered, he was covered with shame and disgrace, afraid even to go abroad in the village for fear of what others were thinking. By this means,

Carey was led, he subsequently said, 'to see much more of myself than I had ever done before, and to seek for mercy with greater earnestness'.[29] That mercy he found as over the next two years he came to 'depend on a crucified Saviour for pardon and salvation, and to seek a system of doctrines in the Word of God'.[30]

## Hackleton and Earls Barton

Carey continued to go with Warr to the prayer meetings in Hackleton, but it was not until early 1779 that he attended a worship service. Four years earlier the British colonies in North America — except for the Canadian Maritimes — had, for a variety of reasons, decided to seek political independence from their mother country. War broke out and, although many English Dissenters were pro-American, they ardently prayed for peace. At the beginning of the war, for instance, Sutcliff told one of his correspondents that they ought to 'be earnest at the throne of grace', for God 'alone can interpose for the bringing about a substantial and lasting peace'.[31] Thus, when days of national fasting and prayer were proclaimed from time to time during the war by the British government the Dissenters entered into them without any hesitation. Due to various British reverses and losses, such a day was set for 10 February 1779. Warr asked Carey to accompany him to Hackleton, where, in addition to prayer, there was to be a sermon by Thomas Chater (d.1811), a resident of Olney.

Chater's family had had a long association with the Congregationalists in Olney, though he himself was not able to find a home among either of the town's Dissenting causes. In fact, according to Cowper, Chater was hoping to start a third Dissenting chapel in Olney in the early 1780s, where 'the dissatisfied of all denominations may possibly be united under his standard'.[32] Any such plans came to nought, yet his sermon that winter's day in Hackleton made a lasting impression on the young Carey. The biblical text on which Chater based his sermon has not been recorded, but in the course of his preaching he quoted that powerful exhortation in Hebrews 13:13: 'Let us go forth therefore unto him [i.e. Jesus] without the camp, bearing his reproach.' Chater employed this verse to urge upon his hearers 'the necessity of following Christ entirely'. As Carey listened to Chater's exhortation, the interpretation that he made of this text and Chater's words was one that he later described as 'very crude'. He felt that God was calling him to quit the Church of England, where in his particular parish church he was sitting under 'a lifeless, carnal ministry', and to join a Dissenting congregation. Since the Church of England was established by the law of the land, he reasoned, its members were 'protected from the scandal of the cross'.[33] So Carey became what he had long despised — a Dissenter.

When the Congregationalists in Hackleton decided to form themselves into a church on 19 May 1781, Carey was among the founders of what would eventually become Hackleton Baptist Church. Three weeks later he was married to Dorothy Plackett (1756-1807), the daughter of a key member of the Hackleton congregation and a woman whose life has recently received a just and sympathetic account from James R. Beck, a professor at Denver Conservative Baptist Seminary.[34] For the first four years of their married life, William and Dorothy lived in Hackleton, where Carey had begun to preach in the Hackleton church.

During the summer of 1782, Chater encouraged the Baptists in Earls Barton, a village six miles' walk from Hackleton, to ask Carey to preach in their meeting-house, which has been described as 'a paltry thatched cottage'. Though the believers there could not pay him enough even to replace the shoes that he would wear out in walking back and forth between Hackleton and Earls Barton, this one visit led to his preaching there once every fortnight for the next three and a half years.[35]

## First meeting with Fuller and Sutcliff

The summer that he first preached in Earls Barton was also the time when he first laid eyes on Fuller and Sutcliff. The annual assembly of the Northamptonshire Association that year was at Olney. Carey, quite used to walking considerable distances, easily tramped the five and a half miles to Olney in the early hours of Wednesday, 5 June. That morning he heard sermons by William Guy and Richard Hopper, the pastor of Friar Lane Baptist Church, Nottingham; that evening Fuller spoke from 1 Corinthians 14:20. It was a good introduction to the life of this association, for Guy and Fuller were both powerful preachers. We have already had occasion to notice

Guy's preaching.[36] With regard to Fuller's preaching, we are told that he was not 'the exact model of an orator' and had 'none of that eloquence which consists in a felicitous selection of terms'. Nonetheless, his presence in the pulpit was imposing and solemn, 'tending to inspire awe,' and his delivery marked by boldness and a 'great force of expression'. He would be 'deeply impressed with his subject, and anxious to produce a similar impression on his hearers'. Few who heard him did so without satisfaction: 'If the heart were not at all times affected, yet the judgment would be informed.'[37] Carey long remembered the sermons of Guy and Fuller, as well as the fact that he fasted the entire day because he had no money to purchase a midday meal. All through his years at Hackleton Carey laboured at the trade for which he had been trained, but his shoemaking provided only the slenderest of incomes, and certainly left nothing for eating out.[38]

**His baptism**

During these first few years after his conversion, Carey was struggling to crystallize his Christian faith and to establish foundations on which he could build a life of devotion to God. 'Having so slight an acquaintance with ministers,' he later told Fuller, 'I was obliged to draw all from the Bible alone.'[39] He received help at one point during these years from reading the elder Hall's *Help to Zion's Travellers*. Carey noted that some — presumably High Calvinists — called the book 'poison'. But, Carey admitted, 'It was so sweet to me that I drank it greedily to the bottom of the cup.' He pored over it with 'raptures' and many years later assured Fuller that its 'doctrines are the choice of my heart to this day'.[40]

His study of the Bible soon led to the conviction that infant baptism, as practised by Anglicans and Congregationalists, had no scriptural authority behind it. So it was in the course of 1783 that he approached John Collett Ryland of Northampton for baptism. Ryland, who was sixty years of age, turned him over to his son, by whom Carey was baptized in the River Nene in the early hours of the morning of Sunday, 5 October 1783. It was the same river in which the younger Ryland himself had been baptized sixteen years earlier by his father. Only a handful gathered with the younger Ryland and three of the College Lane deacons that morning to witness Carey's baptism. He was the sole individual being baptized and in any case he was not becoming a member of the Northampton church. In a sermon that he gave in 1812, Ryland recalled his baptizing of Carey and frankly admitted that he had had no inkling of the shape that the future would take for him and Carey, how they would become the firmest of friends and co-labourers in a great work of God.[41]

## Birth of a missionary vision

Around the time of his baptism Carey came across the published journals of Captain James Cook (1728-1779) recounting his voyages in the Pacific, which involved, among other things, the discovery of Tahiti and the charting of the unknown shores of New Zealand and Australia. 'The end of Cook's geographical feat,' it has been rightly said, was 'the beginning of missionary enterprise'.[42] Carey, it will be recalled, already had a longing to see other climes and shores beyond his own, sparked by listening to the tales that Peter Carey had told him of Canada. Now, however, his reading a borrowed copy of these journals nurtured something greater than the passion to see the world and to gaze upon fields other than those of Northamptonshire. Carey put it this way: 'Reading Cook's voyages was the first thing that engaged my mind to think of missions.'[43] Through Cook's journals Carey was drawn to reflect on the spiritual plight of those who lived in the countries that Cook had discovered. Many of them had no written language, certainly none of them had the Scriptures in their own tongues, and there were neither local churches nor resident ministers to share with them the good news of God's salvation. 'Pity, therefore, humanity, and much more Christianity,' he wrote only a few years after reading Cook's journals, called 'loudly for every possible exertion to introduce the gospel amongst them.'[44] Over the next eight years one of his main preoccupations was the collection of information, especially geographical and religious, about these nations, including the many other nations of the world that had never heard a word of the gospel.

Carey's growing passion for the evangelization of nations outside of Europe did not cause him to forget the need of the many on his own doorstep. Through his witness, for example, his two sisters, Mary and Ann, were won to Christ. As is often the case with the members of one's own family, William had not found it at all easy to speak to them concerning their need of Christ. But he persevered in praying for them, and when Mary Carey thought back on this period of her life, she could only exclaim, 'O what a privilege to have praying relations, and what a mercy to have a God that waits to be gracious!'[45]

## Membership of Olney and a call to the ministry

After three and a half years of preaching at Earls Barton, Carey was asked by the Baptists who met in that village to consider becoming their pastor as they were desirous of forming themsleves into a regular church. Sutcliff was asked to give them advice about this decision. He accordingly arranged to ride over to Earls Barton early in 1785, where he spoke with the leading individuals of the work in the village, including Carey, and later in the day preached a sermon for them. After the sermon Sutcliff spent some time alone with Carey. Instead of encouraging Carey to become the pastor of the Earls Barton congregation, Sutcliff told him 'very affectionately' that he should join 'some respectable church'. Sutcliff advised him in this manner, not out of disdain for the smallness of the cause in Earls Barton, but out of a concern that Carey be sent into the ministry from a more solidly established work.[46]

Carey pondered Sutcliff's advice, saw the wisdom of it, and in June 1785 applied for membership in the Baptist church at Olney. By this time he and Dorothy were living in Moulton, a small village four miles north-east of Northampton on the way to Kettering. They had moved to the village on 25 March of that year, and taken up residence in a cottage originally built for a shoemaker. Carey had gone there in order to start a school, which he did, but he soon became intimately involved with the Baptist cause in the village, which was next door to his cottage. Incidentally, this cottage still stands and houses a small museum dedicated to Carey memorabilia.

At their monthly meeting in June, the Olney Baptist Church discussed Carey's request for admission as a member. Sutcliff mentioned the fact that Carey's membership was still with the Hackleton church and that he had been preaching with some acceptance in various places. He also pointed out to the members there that night that Carey was 'desirous of being sent out from some reputable and orderly church of Christ into the work of the ministry'.

The main question that the Olney Baptists had to determine, though, was whether Carey was to be received on the basis of a letter from the Hackleton church or on his verbal testimony. The discussion of these alternatives dragged on without any sign of resolution, and so it was decided to postpone the matter to another meeting. There is no mention in the church minutes of another meeting at which this question was resolved. Yet, there must have been one at which the decision was taken to ask Carey to give his personal testimony before the church. For the next minute in the Olney Church Book, that of Thursday, 14 July, recorded Carey's being accepted as a member of the church on the basis of his 'having given a satisfactory account of the work of God upon his soul'.[47]

In order to enable them to decide whether or not they could immediately recommend Carey for pastoral ministry, Sutcliff asked Carey to preach before the Olney congregation the following Sunday evening, 17 July. Carey did so, but he made a poor impression. His great-grandson, S. Pearce Carey, speculates that Carey was 'overawed at this ordeal and perhaps at the presence of the dignified pastor', that is, Sutcliff.[48] Be this as it may, that evening the church encouraged Carey to continue preaching at Earls Barton and resolved that he be invited to preach again at Olney 'in order that further trial may be made of his ministerial gifts'.[49]

In addition to his ministry at Earls Barton, Carey was soon engaged in preaching in the village where he now resided. The Baptist witness in Moulton belonged to the General Baptist stream and reached back into the previous century. For much of the eighteenth century it had been led by members of the Stanger family who, in the words of the Baptist historian Ernest A. Payne, were 'pillars of the General Baptists in the Midlands'.[50] William Stanger (1669-1740) and his son Thomas had had vigorous ministries in the village, but after the death of the latter in 1768 the work fell into serious decline. By the time that Carey came to the village, the Baptist meeting-house had fallen into a fairly dilapidated state and it seemed to epitomize the condition of the congregation. Despite the fact that the Moulton Baptists were Arminians and Carey was a Calvinist, his coming to the village would mean renewal for this struggling work. The Sundays that Carey was not engaged at Earls Barton he began to spend preaching in Moulton. During the week he strove to be a schoolmaster, but with little success, which meant that he also had to carry on his trade as a shoemaker.

As the Moulton work began to flourish, Carey felt he had to make a choice between spending every second week away at Earls Barton or giving all his spare time to the work in Moulton. On 30 December 1785 he wrote to Sutcliff and asked his advice as to where he should commit himself. Apparently the Baptists at Earls Barton were in something of a divided state, and Carey felt that the situation there was such that he could be of little help to them. Those at Moulton, on the other hand, were 'like sheep without a shepherd'. Moreover, the Moulton work was growing and Carey believed that it could be established as a 'church upon evangelical principles', which from Carey's perspective were Calvinistic ones. Yet, he assured Sutcliff as his pastor that he would not dream of encouraging the Moulton Baptists to re-establish themselves as a church without Sutcliff's 'advice and concurrence'.

Carey also requested from Sutcliff 'the outlines of a covenant, which, if strict in practical, and not too high in doctrinal, points,' he was convinced would be endorsed by 'all the old members of the church' — presumably, these were the former members of the General Baptist cause — and with such a foundation, he added, he thought 'eight or ten more would join in a little time'.

Carey concluded his letter with one final request. Would Sutcliff enquire as to whether or not the Baptists in Olney were satisfied as to his gifts for pastoral ministry? Of course, Carey added, 'If they want more trial of my gifts, I shall be willing to wait till they are satisfied.'[51] This final request was met the following June, when the Olney church unanimously decided with regard to Carey that it would 'call him to the ministry at the proper time'.[52] Carey had preached at least once more before the Olney congregation. He later considered it a 'weak and crude' sermon, but the Olney Baptists obviously felt that it showed promise and revealed God's calling for his life. Indeed, when Ryland heard Carey preach around this time, he wrote in his diary, 'Oh that I had much of the like deep sense of divine truth!'[53] Two months after the decision made by the Olney church, Sutcliff noted in the Olney Church Book that on 10 August 1786 Carey had been 'called to the work of the ministry, and sent out by the Church to preach the gospel, wherever God in his providence might call him'.[54]

Sutcliff's advice regarding whether Carey should continue at Earls Barton or devote himself to the work at Moulton has not been recorded, but he must have encouraged Carey to give himself to the

Baptists in the village that he now called home. For that November Carey was invited by the Moulton believers to become their pastor and three months later — after prayer and presumably discussion with Sutcliff — Carey accepted. It has also not been recorded whether or not Sutcliff sent Carey 'the outlines of a covenant'. Most probably he did, for, following Carey's acceptance of the Moulton pastorate, the church was officially established upon the basis of a covenant that their new pastor had drawn up.

The church not only needed spiritual and doctrinal renewal, though; the meeting-house also needed to be completely renovated. By April 1787 it was apparent to Carey and the deacons of the church that one of the walls of the meeting-house had become so ruinous that the entire building was in danger of collapse. Every time that they worshipped in it they literally ran the risk of being buried in the ruins of the building. Since the Moulton Baptists were far too poor to finance the renovation of their meeting-house, an appeal was sent out seeking donations. Some monies came in, but not enough to cover all of the costs. So the remaining amount had to be borrowed. It was in this newly rebuilt meeting-house that Carey was ordained pastor of the Moulton church that August.

The ordination was held on the morning of Wednesday, 1 August. Ryland, Sutcliff and Fuller each took a part in the service. Ryland opened the service and received Carey's confession of faith, which, he noted in his diary that evening, was 'sound and sensible'.[55] Sutcliff gave the charge to Carey, a message based on a clause from 2 Timothy 4:5: 'Make full proof of thy ministry.' Appropriately, the preceding clauses are exhortations to 'endure afflictions' and to 'do the work of an evangelist'. Carey's life and ministry would give fresh meaning to the latter of these exhortations, but it would not be without much suffering and affliction. The charge to the church was given by Fuller.

Also taking part in the service was John Stanger (1742-1823), the son and grandson of the two previous pastors of the Moulton church. Stanger had been born in Moulton, but was now the pastor of a General Baptist church in Bessels Green, Kent. He and Carey had been corresponding with one another for a few months, when Carey invited the General Baptist pastor to take part in his ordination. It may well have been because of Stanger's family connections with Moulton that Carey made this decision. Whatever Carey's reason, Stanger was delighted to come and to join in the rejoicing of the

Moulton Baptists over what God was doing in their midst. He prayed for and laid hands on Carey after the latter had given his confession of faith. Stanger's exposure to the evangelical Calvinism of Carey and his friends had, it should be noted, an impact on the future course of his ministry back in Kent. Within four years, Stanger had led his church at Bessels Green to leave the General Baptists and throw in their lot with the Kent and Sussex Calvinistic Baptist Association.[56]

Carey pastored the Moulton work until the summer of 1789. These were difficult years for the Careys. The church could not afford to support him full-time, so that he had to supplement his income through schoolteaching and his trade of shoemaking. At neither occupation did he earn enough to supply his family regularly with good meals.[57] This was a dire predicament since at Moulton his family had grown to include three sons. Yet there was also much to rejoice about. The boys — Felix (1786-1822), William (1788?-1853) and Peter (1789-1794) — would have brought much pleasure to the Carey home. Dorothy Carey submitted to believer's baptism at her husband's hands in early October 1787. The congregation was growing both spiritually and numerically. And Carey was discovering his gift for languages. According to Fuller, Carey was 'much occupied in acquiring the learned languages' while at Moulton.[58] 'The learned languages' certainly included Latin, Greek and Hebrew. Sutcliff was especially helpful in Carey's acquiring a working knowledge of Latin. He lent him a Latin grammar and helped him with its rudiments.[59] If, as is most likely, Sutcliff gave Carey help with Greek and Hebrew, the former's training in these languages at Bristol would have proved quite useful.[60] On his own Carey learned Dutch, as well as, according to Ryland, French and Italian.[61]

## The *Enquiry*

Alongside these linguistic studies Carey was continuing his research into the nations of the world. This research soon began to take shape as a book that would prove to be as seminal a work as Fuller's *The Gospel Worthy of All Acceptation*. In a brief memoir that he wrote of Carey, Fuller related that it was while Carey was at Moulton that he wrote what was afterwards printed as *An Enquiry into the Obligations of Christians, to use Means for the Conversion of the Heathens* (1792).[62] With a minimum of emotional colouring and rhetoric, this tract argued that the mandate which Christ laid upon the church in Matthew 28:18-20 to evangelize the nations of the world was binding for all time. It was thus incumbent upon local churches of Carey's day to determine what were the appropriate means for accomplishing the task. While it does not appear to have been a best seller at the time of its publication, this tract has been aptly described as 'the classical presentation of the argument for the World Mission of the Church'.[63]

When the tract was published in 1792, it contained five sections. In the first, Carey tackled head-on the theological objections raised by High Calvinists to the evangelization of other nations. Some argued that the mandate to evangelize the nations of the world as found in Matthew 28 was required only of the apostles and they had actually fulfilled it in their lifetime. In fact, this line of argument was not uncommon in various European Protestant circles, where it was supported by reference to proof texts like Romans 10:18; Mark 16:20, and Colossians 1:23. Even an author as astute as the Puritan John Owen asserted that no local church has the authority to 'ordain men ministers for the conversion of infidels'. Since the cessation of the apostolic office, Owen maintained, only God, by an act of 'divine providence', could send men overseas to establish churches in those lands where the gospel was not known.[64] A more pragmatic line of reasoning also declared that there was 'enough to do to attend to the salvation of our own countrymen' without sailing to the ends of the earth.[65]

Carey's response to the first of these arguments was drawn directly from Matthew 28:18-20. If the commission with regard to evangelism that Christ gave in this passage applied only to the apostles, should not this also be the case for the direction to baptize those who became his disciples? Since Carey's tract had as its principal audience fellow Baptists who obviously took very seriously the command to baptize, this would have been a telling point. Then, what of those individuals who have gone to other nations and planted local churches? If the High Calvinists were correct, they must have gone without God's authorization. Yet, as Carey would show in Section II of the tract, God has been with these men and women, and blessed their efforts. Finally, Christ's promise to be with his church till the end of time made little sense if the command to evangelize the world was to be completed by the end of the first century A.D.

Turning to the argument that there was enough to do at home, Carey readily agreed that there were 'thousands in our own land as far from God as possible'. This state of affairs ought to spur the Baptists on to yet greater efforts to plant local churches throughout Great Britain from which the gospel could be faithfully proclaimed and these thousands reached. Yet it still remained a fact that most of the nations of the world of that day had no copies of the Scriptures in their own tongues and no means of hearing the faithful proclamation of the Word.[66] In this section of the tract, Carey showed that missionary work was not reserved for a bygone era, but was the present duty of the church. As one of the keywords of the tract's title stated, Christians had an *obligation* to engage in mission.

Section II of the tract then traced the history of missions down to Carey's own day, which demonstrated that God had blessed missionary endeavours beyond the apostolic era.

Following this was a section primarily composed of a statistical table of all the countries of the then-known world, detailing their length and breadth in miles, the size of their respective populations and the religious affiliation of the majority of their inhabitants. None of this was guesswork. It was the fruit of many hours spent scouring the latest geographical handbooks and the *Northampton Mercury*, the local newspaper, for facts and notices about the nations of the world.[67] From this spare table of facts and figures, Carey concluded that the vast majority of the world was sunk in 'the most deplorable state of heathen darkness, without any means of knowing the true God, except what are afforded them by the works of nature' and 'utterly destitute of the knowledge of the gospel of Christ'.[68]

The fourth section of the tract demolished the practical obstacles that Carey's contemporaries were wont to raise in response to what he was proposing. Confronting the problems posed by keeping life going in other nations of the world, their distance from Great Britain, their different languages, their supposed 'barbarism' and purported treatment of Europeans, Carey cogently argued that none of these rendered the evangelization of these nations impracticable.

Section V, the final section of the tract, concentrated on outlining what was entailed in the other keyword of the work's title, 'means'. First in importance among these means was 'fervent and united prayer': 'However the influence of the Holy Spirit may be set at nought, and run down by many, it will be found upon trial, that all means which we can use, without it, will be ineffectual. If a temple is raised for God in the heathen world, it will not be *by might, nor by power,* nor by the authority of the magistrate, or the eloquence of the orator; *but by my Spirit, saith the Lord of Hosts.* We must therefore be in real earnest in supplicating his blessing upon our labours.'[69]

As Andrew F. Walls, who teaches at the University of Edinburgh, has noted, this text cannot be fully appreciated apart from the background of prayer meetings that had been going on since 1784 in the circles in which Carey was now moving, and which we have examined at length in the previous chapter. Carey, like Sutcliff and their other friends, was thoroughly convinced from the record of Scripture and the history of the church that 'The most glorious works of grace that ever took place, have been in answer to prayer.'[70] Prayer therefore had to be the first resource, or means, that the church used to fulfil Christ's mandate.

Prayer was vital but, Carey argued, there were also other means which Christians could employ. Turning to the world of eighteenth-century commerce for an analogy, Carey noted the way in which merchants would form trading companies, outfit ships with care and then, venturing all, 'cross the widest and most tempestuous seas,' face inhospitable climates, fears and other hardships to successfully secure material wealth. They do such things 'because their souls enter into the spirit of the project, and their happiness in a manner depends on its success'. The truest interest of Christians, on the other hand, lies in the extension of their Lord's kingdom. Carey thus made the following suggestion: 'Suppose a company of serious Christians, ministers and private persons, were to form themselves into a society, and make a number of rules respecting the regulation of the plan, and the persons who are to be employed as missionaries, the means of defraying the expense, etc., etc. This society must consist of persons whose hearts are in the work, men of serious religion, and possessing a spirit of perseverance; there must be a determination not to admit any person who is not of this description, or to retain him longer than he answers to it.'[71]

Out of the members of this society a small committee could be established which would oversee such things as the gathering of information and the collection of funds, the selection of missionaries and the equipping of them for missions overseas. 'All of this sounds so trite today,' Walls comments, 'because we are used to the paraphernalia of committees and councils of reference and subscriptions and donations.' To Baptist churches in the eighteenth century, however, all of this would have been quite new and, in some ways, quite extraordinary. Carey had no desire at all to subvert the primacy of the local church, but he had grasped the simple fact that the way that Baptist congregations were then organized made it next to impossible for them to engage effectively in missions overseas.[72]

As we have seen, Carey's tract was far from being a best seller in his day. Yet, it was a significant milestone on the road to the formation of a voluntary society that would enable the Calvinistic Baptists to do their part in fulfilling their Lord's command to make disciples from all the nations of the earth.

## Fellowship and opposition

Pastoring in Moulton also meant that Carey was now able to enjoy the fellowship of neighbouring ministers. He certainly spent time with Sutcliff, who became one of his mentors. He also regularly visited the elder Hall at Arnesby in the company of John Webster Morris, the pastor of the Baptist work in Clipston, Northamptonshire.

According to Carey's nephew, Eustace Carey (1791-1855), Carey never spoke of his friendship with Hall without 'the deepest emotion, such as often impeded his utterance'. Hall became like a spiritual father to the budding pastor, helping him with the composition of his sermons and giving him advice about pastoral ministry and his own personal walk with God. Hall's friendship, Carey later remarked after the Arnesby pastor was dead, was 'a jewel I could not too highly prize'.[73]

Carey's closest friendship, however, was with Fuller. In the words of Eustace Carey, it was a friendship which continued for nearly thirty years 'without abatement and without alloy'. Carey often told his nephew that nothing so weaned him from pining for England as Fuller's death in 1815.[74] Although Carey saw Fuller for the first time in Olney in 1782, it was not until three or four years later that he and Fuller met face to face at one of the periodical meetings held during the year for ministers in the Northamptonshire Association. Carey had been asked to preach on the occasion, and, after hearing him, Fuller made his way to where Carey was standing beside the pulpit, seized his hand and told Carey that he hoped that they would be able to get to know one another better. That hope was more than abundantly fulfilled over the next three decades.

Now, it was in this forum of ministerial meetings that Carey first tested his ideas concerning the obligation of believers to be involved in evangelism outside of Britain. Fuller tells us that at several of the meetings between 1787 and 1790, Carey's convictions were the topic of conversation. 'Some of our most aged and respectable ministers,' Fuller added, thought that 'it was a wild and impracticable scheme that he [i.e. Carey] had got in his mind, and therefore gave him no encouragement.'[75] Fuller did not specify which of the association's 'most aged and respectable ministers' pooh-poohed Carey's ideas. Tradition, on the other hand, has especially attributed this disdain for Carey's vision to John Collett Ryland, the father of Carey's close friend.

The first writer to mention the elder Ryland's name in this connection was John Webster Morris. In the first edition of his memoirs of Andrew Fuller, published in 1816, Morris claimed that 'before the end of 1786' Carey and 'another minister of the same age and standing' — in his account Morris does not indicate that this other minister was actually himself — attended a ministerial meeting in Northampton. That evening, as a number of the ministers were chatting, the elder Ryland 'imperiously demanded' that Carey and the other minister each propose a topic for discussion. After much hesitation, Carey suggested the topic on which he had been long ruminating: 'Whether the command given to the apostles to "teach all nations" was not obligatory on all succeeding ministers to the end of the world, seeing that the accompanying promise was of equal extent?' Carey's question had obviously grown out of his reflections on Matthew 28:18-20. The promise he had in mind is clearly that given by the Lord Jesus in verse 20, and the command that in the first part of verse 19. If, Carey reasoned, Christ's promise of his presence is for all time (v. 20), what of his command (v. 19)? As we have seen, this sort of reasoning was later made the subject of an extensive rebuttal in the first section of Carey's *Enquiry*. In Morris's narration of this event, Ryland promptly responded to Carey that 'Nothing could be done before another Pentecost, when an effusion of miraculous gifts, including the gift of tongues, would give effect to the commission of Christ as at first.' Moreover, according to Morris, Ryland gruffly told Carey that he was 'a most miserable enthusiast for asking such a question'! However, in Morris's second edition of the Fuller memoirs, which appeared in 1826, he suggested that all of Ryland's remarks may simply have been 'a piece of pleasantry', or even 'intended as ironical'.[76]

Eustace Carey, when he recounted this event in his 1836 biography of his uncle, identified Morris as having been present on the occasion and said that Carey himself had mentioned the event to him not long after Eustace arrived in India in 1814. Eustace Carey did not remember the exact words that his uncle said were spoken to him, but he did 'distinctly recollect that some strong epithet was said to have been used'. Even though Eustace knew that his uncle questioned the accuracy of Morris's recollection when it first appeared in print, he was prepared to believe Morris's version of the event, because of 'the characteristic vehemence' of the elder Ryland and the novelty of foreign missions at the time when the event is said to have taken place.[77]

Yet a third account comes from the hand of John C. Marshman (1794-1877), the son of Carey's co-worker in India, Joshua Marshman. Writing in 1859, he stated that when the elder Ryland heard Carey's proposed topic, he 'denounced the proposition with a frown' and told Carey in no uncertain terms: 'Young man, sit down. When God pleases to convert the heathen, he will do it without your aid or mine'[78]

Understandably, John Ryland, Jr denied that his father ever uttered such sentiments. In a lengthy footnote which appeared in both editions of his life of Fuller, that of 1816 and that of 1818, Ryland questioned Morris's dating of the event as having taken place 'before the end of 1786'. Ryland stated that his father had left Northampton for Enfield, just outside of London, before any of the ministerial meetings in 1786. This is confirmed by Ryland's diary, in which it is stated that his father left Northampton on 11 November 1785 and never returned during his entire sojourn at Enfield, where he died in 1792.[79] This narrows the event down to 1785. In addition to the annual assembly that year, there was a ministerial meeting in Northampton on 30 September. Fuller, Sutcliff and Thomas Skinner (d.1795), the Baptist minister at Towcester, preached during the day. That evening there was discussion between the pastors which centred on two questions: 'To what causes, in ministers, may much of their want of success be imputed?' and 'What was a sufficient call, to attempt introducing village-preaching into places where it had not been usual before?'[80] Since this meeting was in Northampton, the elder Ryland would almost certainly have been present. But his son, who was also present, claimed that the first time he heard of what his father purportedly said to Carey was when Morris published his life of Fuller in 1816. Moreover, Ryland maintained, the words that Morris attributed to his father did not sound at all like his father! 'No man prayed and preached about the latter-day glory, more than my father,' Ryland said. In other words, the elder Ryland longed for the day when the knowledge of Christ would fill the earth. In sum, the younger Ryland said, it was an 'ill-natured anecdote'.

Yet, two years before his death in 1834, Carey spent an evening reminiscing with his old co-worker Joshua Marshman about the early days of their missionary enterprise. According to a letter that Marshman wrote in the early hours of the following morning, 23 May 1832, Carey made particular mention of the way in which God had kept alive his feelings about overseas missionary work when 'good old John Ryland (the Doctor's father) denounced them as unscriptural'.[81] Thus, despite the younger Ryland's defence of his father, the evidence would seem to indicate that the elder Ryland, who had definite High Calvinist predilections and who could express himself quite vehemently at times, did indeed administer a sizzling rebuke to Carey during the evening of 30 September 1785.

The elder Ryland's reaction to what had become for Carey a burning passion was not unique to him. It is noteworthy that the younger Ryland could record in his diary for 8 July 1788 the following response among some of his congregation to Carey's preaching: 'Asked Brother Carey to preach. Some of our people who are wise above what is written, would not hear him, called him an Arminian, and discovered a strange spirit. Lord pity us! I am almost worn out with grief at these foolish cavils against some of the best of my brethren, men of God, who are only hated because of their zeal.'[82]

It was indeed a good thing that Carey had friends like Ryland, Sutcliff and Fuller to whom he could turn for encouragement and wisdom as he encountered such opposition. Yet initially even they were somewhat hesitant when it came to actually seeking to implement Carey's vision. Around the time that Ryland had invited him to preach to his Northampton congregation, Carey travelled to Cannon Street Baptist Church in Birmingham, where James Turner, Sutcliff's old friend, had been the pastor. Carey went there in order to solicit funds to help pay off the loan that had been taken out for the rebuilding of the meeting-house in Moulton.

While he was in Birmingham, he met one of the younger members of the church named Thomas Potts, who would eventually become a well-respected citizen and merchant in the city. Ordained to the office of deacon in August 1790, he served in this office with great distinction for forty-three years. Potts engaged Carey in a conversation on the subject of missions and told him that the concept of foreign missions was something novel that the 'religious public' would not be prepared to support. In response, Carey mentioned the fact that he had actually written 'a piece on the state of the heathen world', which would, he hoped, awaken an interest in this vital issue. Potts asked him, 'Why don't you publish it?' 'For the best of all reasons,' Carey replied, 'I have not the means.' Potts then adamantly told him, 'We will have it published by all means. I had rather bear the expense of printing it myself, than the public should be deprived of the opportunity of considering so important a subject.'[83]

Despite this encouragement, Carey believed himself quite inadequate to write about missions. After his return to Moulton, he met with Sutcliff, Fuller and Ryland in Ryland's study in Northampton. He urged one of them to publish something on the subject. By this point, the three friends had each published a number of pieces — sermons, treatises, circular letters, even poems in the case of Ryland. They were the accomplished authors, not Carey. But none of the three was willing to do what Carey asked. They certainly approved of much of what he was proposing, but still thought there was so much to be done in Great Britain. Failing to convince any of his closest friends to write on the subject of missions, Carey 'said he must tell the whole truth'. Sutcliff, along with Fuller and Ryland, then encouraged him: 'Do, by all means, write your thoughts down, as soon as you can; but be not in a hurry to print them; let us look over them, and see if any thing need be omitted, altered, or added.' When Carey eventually showed them the manuscript that was later published as the *Enquiry,* there was very little that they thought needed to be corrected.[84]

Throughout this period when Carey was striving to convince others to engage in missions overseas, his character as a 'plodder' played a vital role in enabling him to persevere. There was not only outright opposition from the High Calvinists, but even his friends had their doubts about the wisdom and feasibility of his vision. Yet, as he once said to his nephew Eustace, 'I can plod. I can persevere in any definite pursuit. To this I owe everything.'[85] It should also be noted that once Sutcliff, Fuller and Ryland came to share Carey's vision, they did so with a wholeheartedness that fully matched that of Carey himself.

# 10. The Baptist Missionary Society

> *'Christ has much more yet to do in the world; and, numerous as his enemies yet are and few his friends, his heart does not fail him; nor shall it, till he has spread salvation throughout the earth'* (Andrew Fuller).

Near the end of William Carey's *Enquiry*, where he reflected on the prime importance of corporate prayer for the outpouring of the Spirit, he mentioned some of the ways in which God had answered the prayers of those attending the Northamptonshire Association's monthly prayer meetings. 'The churches', he wrote, 'that have engaged in the practice have in general since that time been evidently on the increase.' Moreover, there were 'calls to preach the gospel in many places where it has not been usually published'. This is a clear reference to the expansion of the Baptists by means of itinerant preaching into small towns, villages and hamlets where previously they had been unrepresented. Yes, Carey continued, 'A glorious door is opened, and is likely to be opened wider and wider, by the spread of civil and religious liberty.'[1] In a number of New Testament texts (e.g. Acts 14:27; 1 Corinthians 16:9; 2 Corinthians 2:12; Revelation 3:8) the metaphor of an 'open door' conveys, in the words of John Gill, 'an uncommon opportunity of preaching the gospel ... with great success, which it won't be in the power of any creature to stop or hinder.'[2] Here, Carey used this metaphor to refer to the rapid and vigorous spread of village preaching by Baptist itinerants. Yet, he believed, subserving this evangelistic expansion of the Baptists was the growth of 'religious and civil liberty'. 'Civil liberty' was a phrase that was much used, and in the eyes of some much abused, in Dissenting circles during the few years following 1789. The start of the French Revolution in that year provided a great incentive for those English Dissenters who were agitating for political reform and the removal of the civil disabilites that still remained in place against them. Carey, in his statement about the growth of civil and religious liberty, reflected the hopes of many Dissenters that this agitation for reform would issue in complete civil freedom, which, in turn, would further the expansion of Christ's kingdom.

## Discrimination against Dissenters

Two of the main legal barriers confronting the Dissenting community were the Corporation and Test Acts, which had been passed in 1661 and 1673 respectively. The Corporation Act required, among other things, all magistrates, officers and members of municipal corporations to take an oath of allegiance to the crown and to affirm that in the preceding year they had received the Lord's Supper according to the rites of the Church of England. The Test Act, which was primarily aimed at Roman Catholics, required all officers who held civil or military posts to swear their allegiance to the crown, to partake of the Lord's Supper according to the rites of the established church and to deny the veracity of the Roman Catholic doctrine of transubstantiation. Both acts were still in force during the the late eighteenth century.

Some Dissenters were actually prepared to take the Lord's Supper in an Anglican church in order to qualify for political or military office. While such an act of compromise, known as occasional conformity, was tolerated in some Presbyterian circles, among the Calvinistic Baptists it was roundly and consistently denounced. Calvinistic Baptists who compromised themselves in this manner would be excluded from membership in their local church. Yet, even though the Dissenters disagreed among themselves with regard to the practice of occasional conformity, they were of one opinion about using the Lord's Supper as a necessary requirement for civil and military office — it was an abhorrent scandal.[3]

Around the time of the French Revolution, three successive attempts were made to have the Corporation and Test Acts repealed. These three attempts — made in 1787, 1789 and 1790 — all failed.

The near success of the one in 1789, which was defeated in the House of Commons by the small margin of twenty votes, inspired 'an all-out assault' in 1790.[4] That year Sutcliff and the Olney church registered their full approval of this attempt to secure a repeal of these two acts. At a public meeting held in the Baptist meeting-house on 22 September 1790, a resolution was passed indicating their complete approval and appointing a delegate to a county-wide meeting on the issue.[5] This 'all-out assault' was a disappointing failure, though, as the bill for repeal was soundly defeated by a crushing 189 votes.

Many of those in political office who voted against the repeal of these acts in 1790 were alarmed at the way that most of the Dissenters, Calvinistic Baptists included, had expressed sympathy with the French Revolution in its earliest stages. When these expressions of sympathy were coupled with the beginnings of a vigorous movement of growth in the Baptist and the Congregationalist communities, fears were aroused among the religious and political establishments that the Dissenters might have similar designs to those of the revolutionaries in France. Of course, within a year or so, the tyranny and bloodshed of the revolution had turned the vast majority of Dissenters firmly against what was happening on the other side of the Channel. Yet throughout the 1790s the English Establishment, with its bastion of support among those loyal to the Church of England, viewed the ranks of Dissent as a source of potential revolution.

There were attacks against the Dissenters in print and, on occasion, more physical shows of hostility. At Christmas 1792 the Baptist meeting-house in Guilsborough, about eight miles north of Northampton, was burned to the ground by incendiaries hostile to the Baptists in particular and to Dissent in general. It was reopened the following May, when Sutcliff was one of the preachers.[6]

A year later, on 18 May 1794, James Hinton (1760-1823), the pastor of New Road Baptist Church in Oxford and an acquaintance of Sutcliff, made a visit with a few companions to the nearby village of Woodstock to preach in a private home. Not long after Hinton had begun preaching, a mob of some three to four hundred people appeared, many of them armed with bludgeons and stones. Storming the house, they violently attacked Hinton and his companions, who had to defend themselves from repeated blows to their heads. Not content with driving Hinton and his companions out of

Woodstock, the mob pursued them hurling insults and howling for blood. One of Hinton's companions, a Mr Barnard, was knocked to the ground 'ten or twelve times succesively, the mob just giving him time to rise, in order to have the brutal pleasure of knocking him down again'. Deaf to his cries for mercy, the mob eventually dumped his bludgeoned body into a ditch, where they left him for dead. Hinton later discovered him and another of his companions, senseless and covered in blood.[7]

It is against this background of suspicion of and at times violent hostility towards the Dissenters that the important events in which Sutcliff and his friends participated in the 1790s have to be viewed.

## The Northamptonshire Association meets at Olney

The annual meeting of the Northamptonshire Association was once again at Olney in 1790. On Tuesday evening, 1 June, the messengers from the churches gathered in the meeting-house at six o'clock and read out loud their respective letters which described the state and condition of their churches. The Olney letter, which Sutcliff had drafted and which had been signed by, among others, William Wilson, gave a good report about the vitality of the monthly prayer meetings and declared that the spread of civil and religious freedom in France 'afforded us no small satisfaction'. Yet, the letter went on to state, recent reports about Protestant believers in France indicated that they badly needed the prayers of English believers. The letter also registered a concern regarding the rumours of war that were flying around the country. It suggested that the preservation of peace in Europe should be made a matter of urgent prayer.[8] The last time that Britain had been at war was the American Revolution, when Sutcliff was in his twenties. During that war he had earnestly prayed for peace, though his sympathies were most likely with the Americans. Hostilities would break out again in 1793, this time with France, and apart from a few months of peace in 1802, the rest of Sutcliff's life would be spent under the clouds of war. His suggestion in 1790 on behalf of his congregation that the churches of the association spend time on their knees, imploring God to spare them the horrors of war, was a foreshadowing of what would became his practice during these years of war, as he daily prayed for peace.[9]

The following day began with a prayer meeting at six in the

morning. Later that morning, at 10:30, there was a public worship service. As in previous years at Olney and other sites where the association had held its meetings, the meeting-house was filled to capacity and there were several hundred who had to sit and worship outside in an adjacent yard. A movable pulpit was placed near the window closest to the yard so that those outside might be able to hear. There was much singing that morning, after which Fuller preached from 2 John 8. Then Robert Hall, Sr preached from Acts 20:24: 'But none of these things move me, neither count I my life dear unto myself, so that I might finish my course with joy, and the ministry, which I have received of the Lord Jesus, to testify the gospel of the grace of God.' It was a very fitting text, for this was the last association assembly that he would ever attend. He died rather suddenly on 13 March the following year.

At six that evening there was another service. Leading in prayer was William Vidler (1758-1816), who had travelled all the way from his pastorate in Battle, Sussex, for the occasion. Vidler's fame as a speaker had spread far beyond Battle, and it is not surprising that he was invited to take part in this annual assembly of the Northamptonshire Association. Unknown to his audience that evening, Vidler was passing through some very deep waters, from which he would not emerge unscathed. For a number of years he had wrestled with doubts about Calvinism — 'an unfeeling creed' was the way that he eventually came to describe it — and the doctrine of the everlasting punishment of the wicked. He was slowly inclining towards the view that the future punishment of the wicked is not eternal, but merely temporary and purgative. In other words, he was coming to hold that ultimately all men and women will be saved. When he prayed before the congregation assembled at Olney that summer evening there were probably none present who knew of these struggles. Within two years, however, he had capitulated to his doubts and openly declared himself a Universalist. It was not long before this drift into heterodoxy led him to question other key doctrines. By the early 1800s he had come to deny Christ's essential deity and thus to embrace Unitarianism.[10]

The assembly concluded the following morning, Thursday, 3 June. Among the resolutions passed that morning was an agreement to provide money for the preaching of the Word at Burton-upon-Trent in Staffordshire where, it was said, 'A door is of late providentially opened ... with a pleasing prospect of usefulness.'[11] During the seventeenth and eighteenth centuries Burton-upon-Trent was a haven for Dissenters. It is not surprising that within two years a church had been established in this town and it had joined the Northamptonshire Association. As the concluding pages of Carey's *Enquiry* bear witness, the establishment of this congregation would have been seen by Carey, Sutcliff and their friends as a clear answer to the corporate prayers at the monthly prayer meetings for revival.

Immediately after the conclusion of this yearly gathering of the churches, Sutcliff set off for a couple of weeks in Yorkshire to visit his family and friends. From correspondence that he carried on with John Fawcett and Thomas Stutterd (1752-1815) — a commercial traveller for a woollen manufacturer based in Huddersfield and a gifted lay preacher — it is evident that though Sutcliff no longer made his home in the north, he remained vitally interested in the progress of the gospel and the Baptist cause in that part of England.[12] This year Sutcliff spent only about two weeks in the north and was back at Olney before the end of the month. When he arrived home there was a letter waiting for him from Thomas Langdon (1755-1824), a Bristol graduate who was pastoring in Leeds. Langdon, who wrote to Sutcliff on 17 June, was disappointed that Sutcliff had not paid him a visit on his recent trip to Yorkshire.[13] Unlike some of Sutcliff's other visits north, this one was a very short one, and he had time only to visit family and very close friends, like Fawcett.

## The ordination of Samuel Pearce

The highlight of the summer that year was in August, when, on the 18th of that month, Sutcliff no doubt attended the ordination of Samuel Pearce as pastor of Cannon Street Baptist Church in Birmingham.[14] The 'seraphic' Pearce, as Ryland styled him,[15] is scarcely remembered today, but in his own day, both within and without Baptist circles, he was deeply respected for the power of his preaching and the depth of his spirituality. William Jay (1769-1853), the Congregationalist minister of Bath and no mean judge of character, once wrote of Pearce's preaching, 'When I have endeavoured to form an image of our Lord as a preacher, Pearce has oftener presented himself to my mind than any other I have been acquainted with.' And referring to the last time that he saw Pearce alive, Jay had this comment: 'What a savour does communion with such a man leave upon the spirit!'[16] As we shall see, his preaching and spirituality would be vital to the establishment of the Particular Baptist Society for Propagating the Gospel among the Heathen (henceforth simply termed the Baptist Missionary Society, which it came to be called before the end of the eighteenth century).

Pearce was born at Plymouth on 20 July 1766 to devout Baptist parents.[17] Despite a godly upbringing, it was not until he was around sixteen years of age that he experienced the joy of conversion. According to Pearce's own words, he now had the Spirit's witness within his heart and 'was filled with peace and joy unspeakable'. Fellow-members in the Baptist congregation at Plymouth soon perceived the potential for ministry that Pearce possessed and in November 1785 extended a call to him to enter into pastoral ministry. The church subsequently recommended that he study and receive further training at Bristol Baptist Academy. Pearce left for Bristol the following summer, and stayed there till 1789, when he became the pastor of Cannon Street Baptist Church in Birmingham, where James Turner had been the pastor.

Since Turner's death in 1780 the Birmingham Baptists had had their ups and downs. It took them two years to find a pastor after Turner, a man named Henry Taylor. Taylor had begun his Christian life as a Methodist, but after a while had declared himself a convinced Calvinist and shortly thereafter a Baptist.[18] After his call to the pastorate of Cannon Street in 1782, things went well in his ministry until June 1788, when he informed the church that he could no longer continue as their pastor since he had reverted to his Methodist convictions. Sutcliff, who had kept up his contact with the church, met with him later that summer and discovered that Taylor had been reading a work of his old employer, the General Baptist Dan Taylor, as well as some of the writings of the Methodist leader John Fletcher (1729-1785). It was these books, Sutcliff believed, that 'had a hand in unhinging his mind' from Calvinism.[19]

On the recommendation of Robert Hall, Jr, Pearce's tutor at Bristol, Pearce had supplied the Cannon Street pulpit that summer after Taylor's departure. Despite his youth, he so impressed the congregation that he was asked to spend his Christmas vacation with them, to which he readily agreed. His ministry there that Christmas was again deeply appreciated. The church consequently begged him to return the following summer after he had finished his studies at Bristol. They proposed that there be a year's probation, at the end of which they were hopeful that the Lord 'would incline his heart to take the pastoral care over them'.[20] Pearce's ministry began in June 1789 and indeed, after a year's trial, he was duly called to the pastorate of the church and publicly ordained.

Sutcliff took no part in Pearce's ordination, though most of his closest friends were involved. His former tutor, Caleb Evans, delivered the charge to Pearce; Fuller laid his hands on Pearce and prayed for God's richest blessing on his ministry; Ryland laid his hands on five men who had been elected to the office of deacon and who were being set apart at the same time; Robert Hall, Sr reminded the members of the church of their responsibilities to their new pastor from a text in Deuteronomy. Even Thomas Purdy, Sutcliff's good friend from Chipping Norton, was involved in the service.[21] For Sutcliff, whose soul 'was formed for friendship',[22] it would have been a tremendous opportunity to renew old friendships, like those of Evans, Purdy and Ryland, and to deepen newer ones, like that of Pearce.

## The loss of two old friends

Pearce's ordination was also the last time that Sutcliff saw either Hall or Evans alive. As has already been mentioned, Hall died quite suddenly the following spring. His death occurred in the late afternoon of Sunday, 13 March, after he had preached a sermon that morning on John 4:10. The date of the funeral was originally set for the Wednesday of that week. Fuller and Ryland were both asked to speak at the funeral. Sutcliff, however, was not informed about his friend's death till after Hall had been buried. Fuller had had no opportunity to let Sutcliff know of Hall's death till the actual day of the funeral. Just as Fuller was setting off for Arnesby that morning between nine and ten o'clock, he received a letter telling him that the funeral had been postponed till the following day. In a letter that Fuller wrote to Sutcliff the following month, he confessed that if he had been thinking straight he could have written Sutcliff a note at that point to tell him of Hall's death and the funeral the next day. A mutual friend who was travelling to Wellingborough — about ten miles from Olney — would have taken the note that far and ensured that it went the rest of the distance that day. As it was, Fuller could only wish that Sutcliff had been there. 'I wished for your company at Arnesby,' he plaintively wrote to him.[23]

Fuller delivered a short talk at Hall's actual interment after Ryland had preached a sermon from John 19:30. The number of people who came to the funeral was so great that Ryland had to preach outside the Arnesby meeting-house in an adjoining yard. He had great difficulty speaking as he was reduced to tears for much of the sermon. Ryland had regarded Hall as one of his two leading mentors during his early years, the other being John Newton, and he was not ashamed to show his affection for his deceased counsellor and friend.[24]

Caleb Evans died a few months later on 9 August. Contact between him and Sutcliff had been very limited in the years immediately prior to his death, which upset Sutcliff, who obviously had a deep affection for Evans. When in 1786, for example, Sutcliff mentioned to the elder Robert Hall that he never received a letter from Evans, the latter promptly informed Evans of Sutcliff's grievance. Evans' reply was that his love for Sutcliff was not at all diminished, but his numerous engagements simply left him next to no time at all to write.[25] Whether or not this satisfied Sutcliff, we do not know. The Olney pastor was himself increasingly a busy man, yet he managed to sustain a very large correspondence with a good number of individuals. One key difference between his situation and that of Evans, though, was that Evans was married with a family and had all of the responsibilities that this entails, while Sutcliff was still a bachelor.

### Sutcliff's sermon on 'Jealousy for the Lord of hosts'

Now sandwiched between the deaths of these two 'burning and shining lights' was an event of great moment. The ministers of the Northamptonshire Association were in the habit, as we have mentioned, of meeting for single days of preaching, worship and mutual encouragement at times other than the annual assembly which usually occurred during the week after Whit Sunday.[26] In 1791 one such meeting was scheduled for Wednesday, 27 April at Clipston, where J. Webster Morris was the pastor of the Baptist congregation. Two of the association's ministers were asked to preach on this eventful day: Sutcliff and Fuller. During his forty years as pastor at Olney Sutcliff rarely missed either a ministers' meeting or the annual assembly. Those times that he was absent seemed, as Robert

Hall, Jr remarked, 'essentially defective', for his 'appearance among us was hailed as a certain presage of harmony and love'.[27]

Of the many sermons that Sutcliff preached during his long ministry, the one that he gave that April morning is the only one to have survived in a complete form.[28] Entitled 'Jealousy for the Lord of Hosts illustrated', Sutcliff's sermon was based on 1 Kings 19:10, in particular Elijah's statement:'I have been very jealous for the Lord God of hosts.' The subject of 'divine jealousy' had long been on his mind. Ten years previously he had written a letter to Fuller in which he had expressed some of his thoughts on the subject, and had said that to him it was 'a source of many reflections'.[29] The ministerial meeting in Clipston provided him with the perfect opportunity finally to gather together these reflections and share them with others.

Sutcliff first drew a distinction between jealousy *for* and jealousy *of* an object. While the latter is not at all a desirable sentiment, the former 'implies love to and tender concern for' the object towards which it is directed. When Elijah therefore spoke of his being 'very jealous for the Lord God of hosts', he was declaring that he was gripped by a love and concern for God's 'honour and interest'.[30]

Sutcliff then went on to detail three attitudes which are intimate companions of such jealousy for God: a reverent obedience to the Scriptures as an 'infallible guide', 'a spirit of universal benevolence' and a habitual concern for the cause of Christ.[31] Particularly noteworthy are Sutcliff's remarks about the first and second of these attitudes. He laid great stress on the vital importance of bringing the whole of one's beliefs and life into conformity with the revealed will of God as found in the Scriptures. True jealousy for God is accompanied by unmitigated obedience to these ancient, yet ever new, texts. They are an 'infallible guide' and 'unerring rule', Sutcliff reminded his hearers, by means of which a believer can test the reality of his faith and the purity of his doctrine, experience, worship and lifestyle. Sutcliff clearly regarded the Word of God as critical in transforming the lives and thoughts of sinful men and women.

Then genuine jealousy for God is conscious of the needs of others — all others and not merely those of one's own circle of friends and intimate associates. Drawing upon Paul's statement in 1 Corinthians 6:17 — which Sutcliff rendered as 'He that is joined to the Lord is one spirit with him' — Sutcliff argued that Christians bear a resemblance to their Lord. Even as he shows benevolence to all of humanity, so 'Saints feel a similar temper.' Their benevolence seeks the temporal, and especially the eternal good, of their neighbours. And, Sutcliff reminded his hearers that day, included among their neighbours were not only to be those of 'your own society, or those inclosed in the small circle of your personal acquaintance', but 'every member of the human race', wherever she or he may be found. For such love and benevolence 'can embrace a globe. It can stretch its arms like seas, and grasp in all the habitable shores. — And what is its language? What are the sentiments it utters? Listen, listen to the enchanting sound: "Let the earth be filled with the knowledge of the glory of the Lord, as the waters cover the sea" (cf. Habbakuk 2:14).'[32]

Given the way in which Sutcliff developed his understanding of 'a spirit of universal benevolence' as an inseparable corollary of jealousy for God, it is not at all surprising that, as he then sought to apply his remarks to his hearers' lives, he focused upon prayer and evangelism. Those who are jealous for God, and who consequently possess 'a spirit of universal benevolence', should give themselves to 'fervent prayer for the outpouring of the divine Spirit' that they might 'see the advancement of the Redeemer's kingdom'. Without the empowering of the Spirit of God, 'The greatest human abilites labour in vain, and the noblest efforts fail of success.'[33] Shaping these remarks, of course, was the Prayer Call of 1784 and the vigorous movement of monthly prayer meetings that it had brought into being.

Moreover, Sutcliff argued in his sermon, jealousy for God results in an evangelistic lifestyle. He described this lifestyle by means of Jesus' declaration in the Sermon on the Mount that the people of God are the salt of the earth and the light of the world: 'Are they [i.e. God's people] not the *salt* of the earth? It is not proper that the *salt* should lie all in one heap. It should be scattered abroad. Are they not the *light* of the world? These taken collectively should, like the sun, endeavour to enlighten the whole earth. As all the rays, however, that each can emit, are limited in their extent, let them be dispersed, that thus the whole globe may be illuminated. Are they not *witnesses* for God? It is necessary they be distributed upon every hill, and every mountain, in order that their sound may go into all the earth, and their words unto the end of the world.'[34] God's intention for the local congregation of believers is that it be an aggresive evangelistic body, seeking 'to enlighten the whole earth'.

In commending this balance of ardent prayer and vigorous evangelistic effort Sutcliff was not only describing what he regarded as characteristics of genuine Christianity, but he was also outlining measures he considered essential for the revival of the Calvinistic Baptist cause in England. When these marks of true jealousy for God are present, he concluded, 'This will tend to promote the interests of religion in the world. The cause of Christ will prosper; he must increase; his kingdom shall come.' Yes, he reiterated, when God's people pray and evangelize, 'The empire of Jesus shall advance, his kingdom arise, and the crown flourish upon his head.'[35] If this sermon was typical of Sutcliff's preaching, it is a pity that none of his other sermons have survived.

Finally, one way in which this sermon reflects Sutcliff's debt to the theology of Jonathan Edwards and his New England followers needs to be noted. As has been mentioned in earlier chapters, Sutcliff's theological reflection as a whole was greatly influenced by the thinking of these American divines.[36] The Olney pastor would have heartily concurred with the sentiments of the younger Ryland when the latter told Joseph Kinghorn (1766-1832) that, were he 'forced to part with all mere human compositions but three', the last that he would let go would be two books by Edwards and one by Joseph Bellamy.[37] Now, this debt to the theology of Edwards is especially evident in *Jealousy for the Lord of Hosts illustrated* when Sutcliff comments on what has come to be described as 'disinterested love'.

Very much in line with Edwards and his New England followers, Sutcliff was insistent that 'Right ideas of the divine character lie at the bottom of all true religion.'[38] The Scriptures, Sutcliff frequently emphasized, depict God as 'the greatest and best of beings,' inherently beautiful because of his moral excellence and his 'perfections inconceivably great and glorious': infinite and unerrring wisdom, power that is irresistible and omnipotent, faithfulness and truth unaffected by the impermanence of our world, goodness that knows no limits.[39] As such, he is to be loved and relished primarily for who he is in himself and not for what he does for mortal, sinful humans. Consequently, Sutcliff warned professing Christians in *Jealousy for the Lord of Hosts illustrated* to be 'sensible of the danger of corrupt mixtures, the danger of pride and self-seeking being the real principles that influence your conduct, instead of a single eye to the divine honour'.

As he went on to exhort them, 'Carefully inspect your hearts and examine with severity the springs of action that lie hid from every human eye... Put the query home, "Is love, genuine love to God, an ingredient in my religion? Is the true beauty of his character the ground of my esteem, or do I only love him from some mean and selfish consideration? Do I love him for what he is in himself, as infinitely amiable in every discovery of his moral character, or only because I look upon him as my friend and consider myself as interested in his favour?" Brethren, beware of self-love under the disguise of professed love to God.'[40]

Here Sutcliff is faithfully echoing what Jonathan Edwards had stressed in *The Religious Affections*, that classic work on the nature of authentic Christian spirituality. If the love of professing Christians for God is based upon the benefits that they receive from God, then ultimately their spirituality revolves around themselves. They love God, not because he is altogether lovely, but because he saves them from the anguish and torment of an eternal hell. Thus their religion becomes the ultimate expression of self-love. While Edwards never demanded that self-love be entirely absent from one's love for God, he did insist that the former cannot form the mainspring of one's spiritual life. Only a love that is 'disinterested' can compose the soil in which genuine Christianity can flourish.[41]

## Fuller warns against delay

'The pernicious Influence of Delay' was the intriguing title that Fuller later gave to the sermon that he preached after that of his friend.[42] Fuller took as his text Haggai 1:2: 'Thus speaketh the Lord of hosts, saying, This people say, The time is not come, the time that the Lord's house should be built.' After sketching the historical context of this verse, namely, the refusal of the Israelites to get to work on the rebuilding of the temple after their return from the Babylonian Exile, Fuller noted that the main problem which afflicted the Israelites was a 'procrastinating spirit'. It was not, however, a problem unique to them, but hampered both unbelievers and believers in his own day. With regard to the latter, it prevented them from 'undertaking any great or good work for the cause of Christ, or the good of mankind'.[43] It was a good thing, Fuller declared in an illustration of his point, that Martin Luther (1483-1546), the great German Reformer, was free from this tendency. If he had not been, he and his fellow Reformers would never have undertaken 'the glorious work of the Reformation' and the house of the Lord 'might have lain waste to this day'.[44] Fuller, like Sutcliff and his other friends, was assured that the ministry of the Reformers in word and print had been honoured by the Spirit of God for the blessing of many in the sixteenth and later centuries.[45] The example of Luther was thus an appropriate one to bring forward to encourage his hearers to break out of the grip of a 'procrastinating spirit'.

The Reformation was undoubtedly a watershed in the history of Christianity. The rise of what has been termed the modern missionary movement at the end of the eighteenth century — in which Fuller, Sutcliff, Carey and their colleagues played a critical role — was certainly another. From our standpoint at the end of the twentieth century, it is fascinating to see these two events linked together as Fuller pressed home his point regarding the debilitating effect of procrastination on the church of his day immediately after he had mentioned the example of Luther. His hearers should seriously ponder, he urged, whether it was this tendency to procrastinate which had resulted in 'so few and so feeble efforts' being 'made for the propagation of the gospel in the world'. According to Matthew 28:19-20 and Mark 16:15, Christ gave his apostolic band a command to evangelize the nations, something which they had sought to do with 'assiduity and fidelity'.

But, he continued, 'Since their days, we seem to sit down half contented that the greater part of the world should still remain in ignorance and idolatry. Some noble efforts have indeed been made; but they are small in number, when compared with the magnitude of the object... We *pray* for the conversion and salvation of the world, and yet *neglect the ordinary means* by which those ends have been used to be accomplished. It pleased God, heretofore, by the foolishness of preaching, to save them that believed; and there is reason to think it will still please God to work by that distinguished means. Ought we not then at least to try by some means to convey more of the good news of salvation to the world around us than has hitherto been conveyed?'[46]

By this time, we need to recall, Fuller had read Carey's *Enquiry*, which gave him a fair idea of the size of the evangelistic task that still lay before the church, as well as a summary understanding of the history of missions. As this portion of his sermon indicates, he had obviously been deeply challenged by his reading of it.

Furthermore, ever since the Prayer Call of 1784 he — along with his friends and fellow Baptists in the Northamptonshire Association — had been praying for 'the spread of the gospel to the most distant parts of the habitable globe'. Were he and his hearers in earnest when they prayed this request? If so, how could they continue to pray along these lines without giving serious thought to its fulfilment? Its fulfilment would come, Fuller contended, through God's time-honoured method of planting churches and winning the lost — preaching.

Undoubtedly these remarks on preaching reflect the high place accorded to the preaching of the Word in the Calvinistic Baptist tradition. What Michael J. Walker, a lecturer in Christian doctrine at the South Wales Baptist College, once said regarding preaching among the Nonconformists of the nineteenth century is true also of that in the late eighteenth. The pulpit, Walker pointed out, was nothing less than a means of grace: 'a place of nurture, of fire and light, from which words gave wings to the religious aspirations of the hearers, bringing them, they felt, to the gates of heaven'.[47] Yet Fuller was cognizant that Scripture also gave preaching a place of primacy in evangelism. Immediately after the concluding question in the passage quoted above he cited Romans 10:13-15a, in which the apostle Paul shows that it is impossible for either Jew or Gentile to embrace Christ as Saviour without hearing the proclamation of the gospel. And, what was especially germane to Fuller's argument, Paul asks how shall such preaching take place unless preachers be sent.

## The results of the day's meeting

After hearing these two sermons, those gathered in the Clipston meeting-house were sobered and deeply convicted. Close to twenty-five years later, Morris could still recall the way in which the meeting-house was pervaded with a 'deep solemnity' and how the entire congregation was overwhelmed by what it had heard. Ryland and all with whom he talked afterwards felt a profound conviction of their 'greater need for zeal, and of the evil of negligence and procrastination'.[48] Carey, who had been pastoring Harvey Lane Baptist Church in Leicester since early 1789, must have been thrilled by what he had just heard and was determined to strike while the iron was hot. After dinner at midday, he forcefully urged those present to make some decision concerning 'a society for propagating the gospel among the heathen'. A discussion then ensued which lasted most of the afternoon. Ryland had to leave partway through, since he had a preaching engagement that evening at a place fourteen miles away. In the discussion Carey obviously would have emphasized that the logical implication of what Fuller and Sutcliff had said in the morning was what he had urged in the conclusion of his yet unpublished *Enquiry*: they should form a missionary society for taking the gospel to lands overseas. Carey's friends and fellow ministers were not averse to what he was pressing upon them, but they felt that forming such a society was, in Fuller's words, 'something too great, and too much like grasping at an object utterly beyond their reach'.[49]

Sutcliff in particular, we are told, cautioned against haste.[50] Is it not ironic that Sutcliff, who only that morning had called for aggressive evangelism, urged caution at the end of the day when Carey's plan to implement such evangelism was placed on the table? What undoubtedly caused Sutcliff to be so cautious was not the issue of evangelism *per se* — he himself had been involved in village preaching for more than a decade — but the question of support from their sister churches. Would the Baptist churches in the association and throughout the nation, few of them wealthy, influential establishments, *be able* and *willing* to implement Carey's vision? Sutcliff and his friends could expect, of course, some degree of opposition from those still solidly entrenched in High Calvinism. It should be noted, though, that a number of this persuasion, for example, William Button, would wholeheartedly throw their weight behind Sutcliff and his friends when the time for launching a missionary society came. But it would not have been the disapproval from these quarters that made Sutcliff hesitate when it came to implementing Carey's vision. It was the concerns that would be expressed by those who shared his and Carey's evangelical Calvinism. Such concerns were typified by Benjamin Beddome's reaction to the decision to engage in missions overseas. Writing to Fuller in 1793, he told him that his 'scheme' — i.e., the formation of a missionary society — was definitely ill-advised. 'Considering the paucity of well-qualified ministers,' he reckoned that it had a 'very unfavourable aspect with respect to destitute churches' in Britain, where, after all, he said, 'charity ought to begin'.[51] Now, S. Pearce

Carey has expressed the opinion that of 'all the Association's young leaders none exercised a weightier influence' than Sutcliff.[52] Definitely that afternoon in Clipston his advice to wait was followed. The only decision that was taken was to recommend that Carey revise the *Enquiry* with a view to publication, which would, it was hoped, help to sound out the attitude of the 'religious public' regarding a missionary endeavour.[53]

A number of the ministers stayed in the Clipston manse that night. Carey, Fuller, Morris and possibly Sutcliff sat up chatting to well after midnight. The implementation of Carey's vision and the way that God had spoken through the preaching gave them much to talk about. Despite the fact that they had already had supper, around one o'clock Fuller felt hungry and asked Morris if he had any more meat. When Morris replied that he did, Fuller told him to get it and they would roast it in the fire that was still blazing on the hearth. As the meat sizzled and cooked, the Baptist pastors continued to chat and listen to Carey elaborate on his vision of a missionary society. The decision of the afternoon was not modified by this late-night discussion and nocturnal repast, but what took place in the manse that night was long remembered as a fitting conclusion to an eventful day.[54].

Seven weeks later, at the annual assembly of the association, which was held that year in Oakham, Rutland, it was announced that plans had been made to have the two sermons preached at Clipston printed. They were sent to London to be printed by William Button, who was a bookseller and printer in addition to being pastor of Dean Street Baptist Church. How many copies Button printed is not known, but one of them found its way into the hands of William Steadman (1764-1837), then pastor of the Calvinistic Baptist cause at Broughton, Hampshire. Steadman — 'rough, witty, of sharp intellect and prodigious memory', whom Ryland was wont to call 'that great lump of goodness'[55] — had been at Bristol with Samuel Pearce, where the two men had become close friends. Sharing as he did a similar yearning for the advance of Christ's kingdom among the nations of the world, Pearce may well have told Steadman about the sermons by Sutcliff and Fuller and urged him to get hold of a copy of them. In a diary that Steadman kept, he recorded his reading of the Clipston sermons on 22 November 1792. Both of them, especially that by Sutcliff, 'did me good,' he wrote. He also noted that Fuller's sermon, which closed with a warm appeal for the unconverted in the congregation to accept God's offer of salvation

Composite portrait of distinguished Baptist ministers.
Standing (from left to right): Marshman, Ward, Knibb, Burchell, Rippon, Taylor, Steadman and Pearce.
Seated: Carey, Kinghorn, Ryland, Fuller and Foster.
*(Reproduced by courtesy of the Evangelical Library.)*

in Christ 'without delay', was well calculated to eradicate the 'pernicious ideas' of Gill and Brine about the nature of saving faith.[56]

## Carey's challenge

The formation of a missionary society, for which Carey had cogently argued at the conclusion of his *Enquiry*, had been delayed, but it could not be put off indefinitely. When the association met the following year, 1792, at Friar Lane Baptist Church, Nottingham, Carey's *Enquiry* was in print and gave added force to his pleadings that the asscociation brook no further delay.

The association had never met this far north before, and for some of the delegates to the assembly it meant a horse ride of sixty or seventy miles. Due to this distance some of the churches, including Olney, sent only their pastor to represent them.[57] The church building in which they met was Nottingham's sole Calvinistic Baptist meeting-house. It was a plain, white building, well lit and spacious, able to seat around 230 people.[58] Unlike some of the settings for earlier association meetings the meeting-house this year was able to accommodate comfortably the congregation that assembled for the public services. Because of the location, the number of those attending was definitely down from previous years. This building would be sold in 1815 and in the course of the nineteenth century came to be used as a secondhand furniture store. It has since been demolished.

On Tuesday evening, 29 May, John Ryland, Jr was chosen as the moderator for the assembly that year. He proceeded to chair that evening's meeting in which the letters from the churches were read. For the most part, they were very encouraging. As Ryland summed them up in the circular letter that the association sent out that year, 'Several of your letters and messengers attested the happy effects of engaging in extraordinary prayer with more vigour and earnestness than before; and we hope these promising appearances of a revival will encourage those churches to go on, and engage others to adopt the same method... Surely the state both of the world and of church calls loudly upon us all to persist in wrestling instantly with God for greater effusions of his Holy Spirit.'[59]

The first public meeting of the assembly was at ten o'clock the following morning. Sutcliff outlined the day's agenda, led in prayer, and then Carey came to the pulpit to preach. The text on which he had chosen to speak was Isaiah 54:2-3, which reads thus: 'Enlarge the place of thy tent, and let them stretch forth the curtains of thine habitations: spare not, lengthen thy cords, and strengthen thy stakes; for thou shalt break forth on the right hand and on the left; and thy seed shall inherit the Gentiles, and make the desolate cities to be inhabited.' Exactly how Carey came to choose this text is not known. Iain H. Murray has recently echoed the plausible suggestion that William Cowper's hymn 'Jesus, where'er thy people meet', which was composed in late March or early April 1769, had drawn Carey's attention to this text. Believers in the Midlands had been singing this hymn since 1779, of which the fifth stanza runs:

Behold! at thy commanding word,
We stretch the curtain and the cord;
Come thou, and fill this wider space,
And bless us with a large increase.[60]

Although we do not know for certain what led Carey to this passage, the verses from Isaiah had a message for his day and his circle of friends. They needed to trust God and venture forth to the nations with the message of the gospel, confident that God would bless that message and extend his kingdom. Nor do we know the details of the sermon that Carey preached, since no copy of the sermon exists. What we do know are the two main divisions of his message that morning: 'Let us *expect* great things. Let us *attempt* great things.' This is the way that Andrew Fuller referred to the substance of Carey's sermon in what is the earliest written reference to it, a letter to John Fawcett dated 30 August 1793.[61] These two divisons would later be embellished as 'Expect great things from God. Attempt great things for God.' However, as A. Christopher Smith, who is in the process of preparing a life of Carey, has shown, his original challenge was simply: 'Expect great things; attempt great things.'[62] His close friends — Sutcliff, Fuller and Ryland — were quite prepared to 'expect great things' from God's hand. As the sermons that Sutcliff and Fuller gave in April 1791 at Clipston reveal, they were also ready to talk about attempting 'great things' for the glory of God. But Carey knew that Scripture (e.g. James 1:22) would have them move beyond words to action. They had actually to 'attempt great things'.

The effect of Carey's sermon was both shattering and considerable. He convinced his friends of 'the criminality of [their] supineness in the cause of God'. If the entire congregation had broken into profuse weeping, Ryland said he would not have been surprised.[63] The meeting the following morning was held at six, not long after sunrise. There was as usual a time of sharing Christian experience, in which, as Fuller put it, they 'yearned to feel each other's spirits'.[64] Afterwards there was the business meeting of the assembly. It was decided to give five guineas to those seeking to secure 'the abolition of the inhuman and ungodly trade in the persons of men'. Only that March, Sutcliff, together with James Bean and Thomas Hillyard (d.1828), the Anglican and Congregationalist ministers of Olney respectively, had worked side by side in the town to obtain signatures on a national petition calling for the abolition of the slave trade.[65] Then some money was given to help defray the expenses of four of the messengers to the association who came from 'distant and poorer churches'. Finally, monies were provided to support the preaching of the gospel in Derby and Braybrooke, a village eight or so miles north-west of Kettering.

Imagine Carey's surprise when, despite the impact that his sermon had wrought the day before, Ryland was prepared to close the assembly at this point without pressing for any decisive action to be taken with regard to missions overseas. According to John Clark Marshman, the son of Joshua Marshman, Carey's valued colleague at Serampore, a deeply distressed Carey turned to Fuller, seized him by the hand and asked whether they were going to disperse once again without doing anything? Whatever further reservations Fuller or, for that matter, Sutcliff and Ryland, may have had, they were once for all swept away in this 'catalytic moment'. In the depths of their hearts the three men knew that they could not put Carey off any longer. Before they left that day, they and the other messengers to the association had resolved to draw up plans at the ministerial meeting that October for forming a 'Baptist society for propagating the gospel among the heathens'.[66]

## The meeting at the home of Martha Wallis

This ministerial meeting was held in Kettering on 2 October. The previous evening and all that day the weather had been signalling the approach of winter. William Cowper, now living about twenty miles away in Weston Underwood, wrote that day of the 'sky all in sables'.[67] The inclement weather, though, did nothing to dampen the ardour of those ministers who gathered that day in Kettering.

Fuller's mind, for one, was certainly not on the weather. The months since the association meetings in Nottingham had been very trying ones for him personally. A few days after he got back from Nottingham, his wife Sarah (1756-1792) began to experience bouts of insanity, till by July she was 'as destitute of reason as an infant'. She became convinced that Fuller was not her husband, that he was an 'imposter, who had entered the house, and taken possession of every place, and of all that belonged to her and her husband'. Moreover, she was persuaded that she was no longer at home, but was in the house of strangers. The doors of the house had to be kept locked, since she tried to 'escape' a number of times. She was thus reduced to walking up and down through the house, bemoaning her lot, and crying out that she was lost and ruined. All this time she was pregnant. About two weeks before the birth of the child, a daughter whom Fuller called Bathoni, she recovered her senses for a little over twelve hours. Then, suddenly, while they were eating dinner at midday, her mind was gone again and in that state she remained till her death a few hours after giving birth on 23 August. The baby lived less than a month.[68]

Beset with grief over the deaths of his wife and child, Fuller found himself having to provide leadership for what was an unprecedented step among Calvinistic Baptists, the formation of a missionary society. After the public services of 2 October were concluded, Fuller and thirteen other men — eleven pastors, a deacon from Fuller's congregation, and a ministerial student — crowded into the back parlour of the home of a Martha Wallis, a long-standing member of the Kettering church. Her back parlour measured twelve feet by ten, ample space for three or four men to sit in and stretch out their legs, but quite a tight squeeze for fourteen! Her home, though, was no stranger to numerous guests. Over the years so many preachers had stayed there that Carey appropriately dubbed the house the 'Gospel Inn'.

In those happy days she would have been helped by her husband Beeby, as she took care of their guests — but not that night, for he had died the previous April. He had grown up in the Kettering church — his great-grandfather, William Wallis (d. *c.*1712), and grandfather, Thomas Wallis (d. 1726), having been the first and second pastors of the congregation. For twenty-four years he had served in the church as an esteemed and valued deacon, and his death was deeply felt by the congregation. For Fuller and his friends there would have been a pang of regret as they entered the Wallis home and Beeby was not there to welcome them.

## The men who were present

In addition to Fuller, Ryland, Sutcliff and Carey that night, there was also Pearce, whose church belonged to the Midland Association, but whom Fuller had invited to be one of the preachers that day. He had not been able to make it to Nottingham the previous May, since the day that Carey preached he had been preaching before the Midland Association in the village of Upton-upon-Severn, Worcestershire. No doubt either Fuller or Carey had filled Pearce in on the details of what had transpired at the Nottingham meetings.

Of the seven other pastors who were wedged into the Wallis back parlour that night, they were, as S. Pearce Carey frankly put it, the 'pastors of obscure little village causes', men 'of no fame and of scantiest salary'.[69] The following paragraphs on these men certainly bear out this description — they were indeed pastors of 'obscure little village causes'. Yet this is not the only thing that stands out about these men. For the most part, they were also faithful to their calling and laboured for God's approval, not that of men. The seven pastors were: Reynold Hogg (1752-1843), Abraham Greenwood (1749-1827), Edward Sharman, Joshua Burton (*c.* 1747-1830), John Ayer (1741-1821),[70] William Heighton (1752-1827) and Thomas Blundel.

At the time of the formation of the Baptist Missionary Society, the 'distinguished-looking' Reynold Hogg was pastoring the Baptist work in Thrapston, a village eight miles due east of Kettering. This church was not actually formed till 1797, though Hogg had been preaching to a small body of believers in the village since 1790. Hogg pastored this work until 1807, when he moved to Kimbolton, a few miles away in Huntingdonshire. He continued to preach in a number of locations, until ill health in the early 1820s forced him to retire from regular ministry. Throughout his long life he was a zealous promoter of the Baptist Missionary Society and gave generously to its support.[71]

Abraham Greenwood was a Yorkshireman like Sutcliff. And, like Sutcliff, he had studied with John Fawcett at Hebden Bridge. In 1786, when the Baptist work at Oakham was looking for a pastor, Sutcliff recommended Greenwood, who preached for a year and was then appointed in 1787. He ministered there until 1796, when the congregation asked him to leave, because of what the church minutes described as his 'habit of indulging himself in low vulgarity in the pulpit' and his use of 'personal invective' in his sermons. Arthur S. Langley, an English Baptist historian of this century, thinks that these statements simply mean that Greenwood's preaching was too vigorous and lively for his staid congregation.[72] Whatever the nature of his problems at Oakham, they certainly did not stand in the way of his getting another pastorate, this time at South Killingholme, Lincolnshire. Here he laboured faithfully till his death. He exercised a widespread ministry and, according to Langley, 'North-east Lincolnshire everywhere felt his power.'[73]

Edward Sharman was from the charming hamlet of Cottesbrooke, Northamptonshire. He became Carey's successor at Moulton, but eventually turned against those with whom he had founded the Baptist Missionary Society. By 1800 he had become a Unitarian and that year he wrote an open letter against Fuller, in which he sought to defend the Unitarian position.[74]

Joshua Burton, another Yorkshireman, was the pastor of Foxton Baptist Church, which had been among the six founding churches of the Northamptonshire Association. Burton was set apart as their pastor at a special service in December 1791, in which Sutcliff had taken a part. Burton's ministry at Foxton was not a remarkable one. When he died in 1830, the church had only four more members than it had had when he had begun preaching there — twenty-two. Nevertheless, Burton remained vitally interested in missions throughout these years and lived to see one of his grandsons become a missionary.

John Ayer was the eldest of the men there that night. A native of Kettering, he had been baptized in 1770 by Moses Deacon, the pastor of Walgrave Baptist Church. When Deacon became infirm in his later years, he asked Ayer to preach for him. Ayer would walk the six or so miles from Kettering to Walgrave on the Saturday afternoon, preach on the Sunday and then return to Kettering on Monday morning. After Deacon's death, Ayer was unanimously invited by the Walgrave Baptists to become their pastor. Encouraged by John Collett Ryland and Robert Hall, Sr to accept this invitation, he was ordained as the pastor of the Walgrave congregation in 1773. Here he resided for the next twelve years. In 1785 he left Walgrave owing to a dispute over his preaching. Between then and 1792 he pastored in Leicestershire. A number of months before the ministerial meeting at Kettering, he had moved to Braybrooke, where he preached until his death. He was never formally set apart as the pastor of this small work, and thus often preached at other small causes on the Leicestershire-Northamptonshire border. Preaching was a delight to him, and he thought nothing of walking twenty miles to a preaching engagement. This often meant that when he returned home he did so in the dark. On a couple of occasions, according to his good friend Joshua Burton, he lost his way and ended up wandering in the fields for much of the night! Once he fell into a gravel-pit, and narrowly escaped being drowned. But nothing could convince Ayer to give up these preaching excursions while he still had the strength to walk and to talk.[75]

William Heighton pastored Roade Baptist Church, Northamptonshire, which had been founded in the seventeenth century. Converted under the ministry of the evangelical Anglican Thomas Haweis (1734-1820), Heighton was typical of a generation in the final decades of the eighteenth century who were converted through individuals closely associated with the Evangelical Revival and who eventually found their way into the ranks of the Baptists or Congregationalists. In 1777 Heighton became a member of the Baptist congregation in Kettering. As the members of this church became acquainted with Heighton, they recognized that he definitely possessed gifts for pastoral ministry. Encouraged to use these gifts in the Kettering church, he was set apart for the ministry during the early years of Fuller's pastorate. Heighton's first pastoral charge was at Winwick, Huntingdonshire. On 19-20 October 1784, a new church had been formed in this village and he was the church's first pastor. He stayed only two years, though, for in 1786 he moved to Roade, where he was to remain for the next forty years. The church, which had been languishing prior to his coming, flourished under his ministry. Though he was of a quiet and retiring disposition, 173 people joined the church during his pastorate at Roade. The meeting-house was consequently enlarged in 1793, and in 1802 entirely reconstructed so as to hold four to five hundred people. The epitaph on the tablet to his memory in Roade Chapel well describes him: 'In doctrine sound, in devotion ardent, in life holy and in death happy.'[76]

Thomas Blundel had also been a member of the Kettering

congregation, having been baptized by Fuller seven years previously, to the very day. A weaver by trade, Blundel was encouraged by Fuller and the church to develop his spiritual gifts not long after his baptism. In 1790 the church decided to send him to Bristol Baptist Academy for a year of full-time study. It lasted only a year, since Blundel had a wife and a family of four to support. A fifth child was born while he was at Bristol. The following year Blundel was given the opportunity to preach at Arnesby, where the pastor, the elder Robert Hall, had just died. Blundel supplied the church for two years before he was asked to assume the pastorate of the church. He stayed at Arnesby till 1804, when he left to become the pastor of the Baptist cause in Luton, Bedfordshire. During his time at Arnesby he became a good friend of Sutcliff — the Olney pastor had preached on the occasion of Blundel's ordination at Arnesby in 1793. 'Eloquent and impressive in the pulpit,' he became a keen and useful advocate of the cause of missions.[77]

There were also two laymen present that night in Martha Wallis's parlour. Joseph Timms (d.1827), a wool-stapler, was one of the youngest deacons in the Kettering church.[78] The other layman, William Staughton (1770-1829), was a ministerial student at the time. Staughton had been baptized in 1786 by Henry Taylor, Pearce's predecessor at Cannon Street. Five years later he went to the Baptist Academy in Bristol to begin training for pastoral ministry. For a number of Sundays during September and October 1792 Staughton was preaching in Northampton, and thus was able to attend the ministerial meeting at Kettering on 2 October. A year later a love affair caused him to leave England for the United States, where he eventually had two outstanding pastorates in the city of Philadelphia and later served as the first president of Columbian College (known since 1903 as George Washington College) from 1822 to 1827. A tireless advocate of missions, he stayed in touch with Carey throughout his life, which Carey deeply appreciated. Writing to Staughton in November 1817, Carey told him, 'You are dear to me, and have been ever since we first met together, a little before my first sailing to this country.'[79]

## Funds are raised for the work

Crammed into Martha Wallis's parlour, these fourteen men resolved to form what they called 'The Particular Baptist Society for

Propagating the Gospel amongst the Heathen'. In order to help finance the new venture, they each pledged to give a small sum, Fuller collecting the pledges in his snuff-box. With a representation of the apostle Paul's conversion finely embossed upon its lid, the snuff-box must have seemed a fitting repository for the pledges. None of the men present that night was wealthy, but they promised to give sacrificially.[80] Even then the pledges amounted only to £13.2.6, a paltry sum on which to launch a missionary enterprise. It was truly a case of God choosing the 'weak things of the world to shame the strong' (1 Corinthians 1:27, NIV).

An executive committee consisting of Ryland, Carey, Sutcliff, Fuller as secretary and Hogg as treasurer was also appointed. Within three years, Hogg, obviously feeling that his pastoral responsibilites were more than enough for his time and strength, asked that another be appointed in his stead. Fuller, though, would remain as secretary till his death in 1815. So heartily did he give himself to the work of the society that after his death J. Webster Morris said that 'He lived and died a martyr to the mission.'[81]

What were Sutcliff's thoughts that night as he rode home to Olney? It is unlikely that he had any regrets. The sermon that he had preached at Clipston nearly a year and a half before had commended a zeal for God that took seriously the evangelization of the world. The resolutions taken in Martha Wallis's parlour were simply putting teeth to his words and convictions. Given his prudent nature, had he not been convinced that God was behind this venture, he would not have dared to sign his name to the resolutions and certainly would not have agreed to be on the executive committee.[82]

The next meeting of the society took place at the end of October. On 31 October, the members of the society met at College Lane in Northampton. Neither Fuller, who was ill, nor Carey could attend the meeting. The other three members of the executive — Sutcliff, Ryland and Hogg — were present, however, as Pearce triumphantly presented the society with a gift of £70! In his own words, Pearce had returned home to Birmingham from the previous meeting at Kettering 'resolved to lay [himself] out in this cause'. That Sunday, 7 October, he had preached on the duty of believers to exert themselves in the spread of the gospel. The following Tuesday an auxiliary society of the Missionary Society was formed in Birmingham, with Pearce as its secretary and Thomas Potts as one of the seven other members of its executive. By the end of the month the

her death to be an occasion which undid all that she had spent her life cultivating. Sutcliff felt her cultivation of 'privacy in the exercise of charity' to be a little unbalanced, but nevertheless he honoured her request.[10]

When Sutcliff informed William Bull, the friend of Newton and Mary's brother-in-law, of her death, Bull wrote Sutcliff a brief note, praying that God would be his 'support and strength'. Despite its brevity, this note is a clear indication that Sutcliff had treasured Mary Andrews' friendship and counsel over the twenty years he had lived in her home. This fact finds further confirmation in a letter written to Sutcliff by Samuel Greatheed (d. 1823), who had studied under Bull and was the minister of the Congregationalist church at Woburn, Bedfordshire. Greatheed wrote to Sutcliff the day after Bull and sympathized with him in 'the loss of a cordial friend and pious housemate of so long standing'.[11] Sutcliff had come to her house when still a young man of twenty-two, and in many ways she had been like a mother to him. His own father had died the previous year in 1794 — his mother seems to have predeceased his father — and thus Mary Andrews' death would have been doubly affecting.[12] Despite his grief, Sutcliff also found time to let Fuller know of her decease. When Fuller read the contents of his friend's letter, he saw in it a reminder of the brevity of their lives and thus a stimulus 'to work while it is today!'[13]

## Concern voiced over some of Carey's activities

On 7 April, a month or so after Mary Andrews' death, Sutcliff attended a meeting of the executive committee of the Baptist Missionary Society at Arnesby. Now both he and Fuller were opposed in principle to having an extensive number of committee meetings. To the end of their lives they had a deep mistrust of what Fuller once described as 'speechifying committees' and a 'multiplying of rules and resolutions'.[14] Fuller would frequently consult with either Sutcliff or Ryland in person or by letter, but both he and they sought to keep the number of committee meetings to a minimum. Sutcliff summed up their attitude well in a letter that he wrote at the end of April 1795. Fuller had asked him whether they should have another full-fledged committee meeting to discuss various pressing matters so soon after the one at Arnesby. 'Call a committee meeting?

No. The matter is self-evident,' Sutcliff wrote to his friend. 'If you do call one, appoint some proper place on the turnpike road, at such a milestone, fix the hour and minute; let us meet and set our horses' heads together, pass a vote, and part again in 2 minutes.'[15] In 1795 there were only three formal meetings of the executive committee: one at Guilsborough on 18 March, which Fuller strongly encouraged Sutcliff to attend despite the latter's recent bereavement; one at Arnesby on 7 April; and one at Birmingham on 16 September.

The one at Arnesby wrestled with a concern that had surfaced when Carey informed his friends in England that he had accepted an offer to supervise a plantation in the village of Mudnabatti in northern Bengal that manufactured indigo dyes.[16] Although the production of the indigo dye was a complicated process, it required his full-time supervision for only three to four months of the year. This left him free to pursue his calling and also released the money collected by the society in England for other missionary endeavours. In England, though, his decision was greeted by some with dismay and concern. Was he intent on becoming a businessman? The meeting at Arnesby, at which Fuller was not present due to illness, consequently composed a letter to Carey in which he was urged to 'engage not deeply in [the] affairs of this life'.[17]

In the same letter that he informed the society of his intention to become the manager of this indigo works Carey also asked for various gardening tools — 'scythes, sickles, plough-wheels' — and 'a yearly assortment of all garden and flowering seeds, and seeds of fruit-trees'. When Sutcliff read this request, he could only think of that statement in Luke 9:60, where the Lord Jesus solemnly declared that his disciples should 'let the dead bury their dead', but they are to 'go and preach the kingdom of God'. Surely, he reasoned, the dream of being a gardener was something Carey should have given up a long time ago. When Thomas read Sutcliff's remarks in a letter from Fuller, he stood up for his fellow missionary. Yes, he said, Carey had a garden, but it was no bar at all to his ministry. If he had to, he would think nothing of giving it up.[18]

Sutcliff does not appear to have ever understood this avocation of Carey. In later years Carey made numerous requests of his friends and family in England and the United States to send him seeds, roots and bulbs. He asked Sutcliff on one occasion to send him 'a few tulips, daffodils, snowdrops, lilies'. When Sutcliff dragged his feet about collecting them, Carey chided him: 'Were you to give a boy a penny a day to gather seeds of cowslips, violets, daisies, crowfoots, etc., and to dig up the roots of bluebells, after they have flowered, you might fill me a box each quarter. My American friends are twenty times more communicative in this respect than my English. Do try to mend a little.'[19] For Carey, gardening was, among other things, an important means of relaxation, which Sutcliff does not seem to have realized. A far more bookish individual, Sutcliff seems to have spent his few moments of leisure in his study, reading and poring over books. He was thus always eager to send Carey books that he and his other friends had appreciated. As he told Fuller a week after the meeting in Arnesby, 'Should [Carey] live and prosper, and I live too, [I] shall take a pleasure in furnishing him with a library.'[20]

## Proposals for a work in Sierra Leone

The other main item on the agenda at the Arnesby meeting was to discuss whether or not there were any further openings for missionary endeavours around the world. A year and a half earlier at another committee meeting the same question had been raised and among the possibilities mentioned at that time were Sierra Leone and 'the back parts of Canada'.[21] This time Sierra Leone was the only site seriously considered. A few years earlier a company had been founded in England to establish a settlement in this part of West Africa with the aim of introducing Christianity and European culture to the continent, providing a source of employment for destitute blacks living in London and creating an environment in which blacks and whites could live as equals.

The attention of the Calvinistic Baptists meeting at Arnesby in 1795 was especially drawn to consider this settlement as a viable site for a missionary endeavour because of their recent contacts with the Baptist preacher and church planter David George (1743-1810).[22] George, a former slave from Virginia, had gathered the first all-black Baptist congregation in the United States. From 1782 to 1792 he had lived in Shelburne, Nova Scotia, where he planted and subsequently pastored another Calvinistic Baptist church. At the end of this ten-year period, George, with his family and most of his congregation, sailed for Sierra Leone, where he lost no time in founding yet another Calvinistic Baptist work, this time in

Freetown, the site of the British colony. It was on a visit to England in 1793 that he had made the acquaintance of a number of leading Baptists, including Samuel Pearce and John Ryland. Naturally, when the question was raised as to what other locale besides India might best serve as a site for a missionary enterprise, Ryland and Pearce recommended Sierra Leone, for there the missionaries would have the help of George.

Right from the beginning of his time as principal of the Baptist Academy in Bristol, Ryland had urged the claims of the Baptist Missionary Society upon his students. Thus, when the executive committee decided to send missionaries to Sierra Leone, there was at hand one of Ryland's students, Jacob Grigg (1769-1835), who was willing to go. Within a couple of months, James Rodway, who had also studied at Bristol but was at that time pastoring the nascent work at Burton-upon-Trent, had volunteered his services as a missionary. A meeting was then held at Cannon Street in Birmingham on 16 September, where they were set apart 'to the work of the Lord amongst the Africans'.[23]

Sutcliff was not present for this service. A few weeks before he had been driving a single chaise when it turned over. His injuries were minor except for those to one of his arms. Although he eventually recovered its use, he was not well enough to travel to Birmingham for the commissioning service. Sutcliff would have loved to have been present on this occasion, but he was thankful that his injuries were not worse. As Fuller told him when he heard of his accident, 'These overturnings in single chaises have often been attended with fatal effects.' His arm was evidently still troubling him a month and a half after this meeting in Birmingham, for in a church minute dated 30 October we read of Fuller having to baptize five new members of the Olney church.[24]

Grigg and Rodway sailed from England with high hopes that November and reached Sierra Leone on 1 December. Their hopes were soon dashed, however, as Rodway was plagued with sickness, which compelled his return to England in September 1796, and Grigg ran into opposition from the Governor of Freetown, Zachary Macaulay (1768-1838), an evangelical Anglican. Grigg, like many of his fellow Baptists, including Sutcliff, was strongly opposed to slavery, and was not slow in making his views known in Sierra Leone where slave-traders were still active. Unlike Sutcliff, though, Grigg's radicalism extended far beyond his opinion about the slave-trade and the institution of slavery. A sympathizer with the French Revolution, he regarded the English government as the rule of what he called 'tyrants'. He clashed time and again with Macaulay, and was constantly stirring up trouble in the colony. When news of his conduct reached Fuller in England, the Kettering pastor was understandably concerned. The 1790s, as we noted in the previous chapter, were a decade in which the hearts of many in the political establishment were gripped by a deep suspicion of the Dissenters' political ideology, aims and motives. Grigg's attitude and activities would only help to confirm such suspicions. As soon as he received word of Grigg's imprudent activities, he fired off a letter to Sutcliff on Monday, 3 October 1796: 'There is great danger of the African Mission being utterly destroyed through Grigg's imprudence. I must call a small committee at Guilsborough next Thursday. Your company is absolutely necessary.'[25]

The seriousness of the situation is revealed by the fact that Fuller, who had a hearty dislike for committee meetings, felt compelled to call one. The consensus reached at this meeting was expressed by Fuller in a letter that he wrote to Carey the following week. 'The African Mission,' he told Carey, 'has utterly failed, partly through the affliction of Rodway, who could not stand the climate, and ... partly owing to Grigg's imprudence, who has interfered in the disputes of the colony, and stirred up the people to oppose the Governor.'[26] Eventually in early 1797 Macaulay issued Grigg an ultimatum: either go back to England or sail for America. Grigg chose the latter.

## John Fountain and the risks of political involvement

For Fuller and Sutcliff, their experience with Grigg forced them to recognize that the missionaries sent out by the society needed clear instruction to 'confine themselves to their work and not meddle in politics'.[27] Until the episode with Grigg, they had naïvely assumed that missionaries sent overseas would indeed be single-minded in their proclamation of the gospel, be respectful to those in political authority and not get entangled in the rectifying of political wrongs in the countries to which they had been sent. They had failed to take into consideration the fact that the England of their day was going through great turbulence and upheaval, in which the ideologies of the American and French Revolutions were helping to foster political radicalism, especially among some of the Dissenters.[28] The need to give explicit instruction about what Fuller and Sutcliff regarded as the snare of politics was reinforced by the attitude of the next missionary whom the society appointed to India, John Fountain (1767-1800).

According to John Clark Marshman, Fountain 'was a man of small stature and small mind; he possessed no energy of character, and added little to the strength of the infant cause' of the mission in India. This severe judgement stems in part from Fountain's political views and his unwillingness, once he arrived in India, to keep his mouth shut about them. As Marshman went on to say, before Fountain left England for India in 1796, 'He had caught the contagion of that democratic frenzy which the French revolution had diffused, and adopted sentiments hostile to the existing institutions of government.'[29]

Fountain was originally from Oakham, but when Sutcliff met him he had been living in London for a couple of years, where he was working for a benevolent society for the poor. He had called on Fuller at Kettering on 23 January 1796 and, as Fuller later told Sutcliff, Fountain was interested in going out to India to work with Carey, learn Bengali and eventually 'converse with the poor heathens about Christ'. At that point, Fuller determined to find out more about Fountain, solicit the opinions of Ryland, Pearce and Morris, and invite him to attend a meeting of the executive in Kettering on 1 February, which was a Monday.

Sutcliff rode over to Kettering early that day in order to have dinner with Fuller at Martha Wallis's and confer privately before the meeting later that afternoon, which may well have taken place in Mrs Wallis's home.[30] Over dinner Fuller would have been especially interested in Sutcliff's reaction to some information about Fountain that Morris had sent to Fuller. According to Morris, Fountain had had to leave Oakham because his radical ideas had enraged the local Anglican Tories. In fact, Fountain was well known in Oakham as 'dealing in politics'.[31] This news would have been worrying to both Fuller and Sutcliff, and they would have been determined to ferret out exactly where Fountain now stood with regard to his past politics.

At the meeting, therefore, Fountain was not only asked about his motives in wanting to go out to India as a missionary, but he was also explicitly questioned about his political views: in particular, did he 'not think it the duty of individuals, especially of a Christian missionary, to be obedient to any form of government' under which they found themselves?[32] Whatever answer Fountain gave to the committee that afternoon must have satisfied them, for that spring he sailed to India with their blessing. Shortly before he left, Fuller pointedly told him, 'All political concerns are only affairs of this life with which he that will please him, who hath chosen him to be a soldier, must not entangle himself.'[33] Did Fuller suspect that Fountain's political concerns were not a thing of the past?

Whatever the case, when Fountain got to India, his radical political pronouncements in his letters back home deeply troubled Fuller and Sutcliff. In a letter that Fountain wrote to Morris in May 1798 he mentioned the fact that he had loaned out his copy of William Godwin's *An Enquiry Concerning Political Justice* (1793), a work that had established Godwin (1756-1836) as one of the outstanding radical thinkers of his day. In this substantial and complex work, Godwin advanced a position of philosophical anarchism by arguing that in a justly ordered society there is no place for political and social inequalities, which he believed arose from economic inequality. He thus attacked the institution of private property, as well as the monarchy, the rule of law and retributive punishment. Fountain seems to have imbibed some of Godwin's views and it set him, in Fuller's words, 'spouting against kings' and advocating revolution.[34]

By April 1799 Fuller felt he had to write 'a very pointed letter' to Fountain, in which he frankly told him that if he could not desist from airing his political views the society would 'be under the painful necessity of disowning him'. 'I tremble for the Ark,' he confided in Sutcliff. For Fuller, as for Sutcliff, devotion to Christ and a revolutionary spirit were mutually exclusive.[35]

Sutcliff seems to have allowed Fuller to handle the correspondence with Fountain, for that autumn he received a letter from Fountain, in which the latter said he would love to hear from Sutcliff. Fountain quoted a statement Sutcliff had made three years earlier when he had first met Fountain at Kettering. On that occasion Sutcliff had observed that those on the executive committee always talked 'about Mr Carey as if there was no such man as *John Thomas* in existence'. Now, Fountain wrote to Sutcliff, 'It appears you write to Mr Carey, as if there was no such man as *John Fountain* in existence.'[36] In fact, Fountain complained to Fuller around the same time that in the three years he had been in India he had not received one personal letter from Sutcliff or, for that matter, any from Ryland, Morris, Blundel or Hogg.[37]

In defence of Sutcliff, it could be said that he hardly knew Fountain before the latter sailed from England, whereas he was on intimate terms with Carey before the latter ever saw the shores of India. It is also a fact worth noting that Sutcliff was increasingly having difficulty in writing. As early as 1793, John Rippon alludes to Sutcliff's not being able to write extensively on account of problems with the hand with which he wrote, which was his right hand. In a letter that Ryland wrote to Sutcliff on 28 January 1795, he also mentioned that the latter had a 'slight paralytic affection' of the hand. Sutcliff's accident in August 1795 may have made his problems in this regard worse, if it was his right arm that was damaged. Examination of Sutcliff's signatures between the years 1786 and 1812 led Kenneth W. H. Howard to remark that there was a marked deterioration in Sutcliff's handwriting around the year 1803. Close perusal of the church burial register that he kept would actually place this deterioration a few years earlier, around 1799. Moreover, up till that year Sutcliff always wrote the letters for the annual assembly of the Northamptonshire Association. After 1799 they have been clearly written by hands other than his.[38] Nevertheless, if Sutcliff could find the strength to write to Carey, he could have at least written a brief note to Fountain. Thus, while there were some extenuating circumstances for Sutcliff's not having written to Fountain, there was legitimate reason for Fountain to ask why he had never heard from the Olney pastor.

Sutcliff and Fuller were spared the pain that would have been involved in a public disowning of Fountain by his death the following year. In May 1800 he contracted dysentery, from which he died on 20 August.[39] The following year, when the Olney church prepared its yearly report for the Northamptonshire Association assembly, Sutcliff made sure that there was included a small notice concerning Fountain's death. 'We much regret the loss of Mr Fountain,' it read.[40] Whatever differences Sutcliff may have had with Fountain over political issues, however much he questioned the wisdom of the way in which Fountain made known his views and whatever the reasons for his not writing to Fountain, he genuinely mourned his death.

## Sutcliff's marriage

The last four years of the 1790s also saw a couple of major changes in Sutcliff's life and ministry in Olney. First of all, in 1796 he married. His bride, Jane Johnston (d. 1814), had become a member of the church in 1781, some six years after Sutcliff had settled in Olney.

The Johnston family had originally come to Olney from Scotland, possibly in the late seventeenth century. Jane's father, Simon Johnston (1707-1787), had been born in Olney and was christened in the parish church on 23 December 1707. Married at twenty-two, he lost his first wife, Francis Milley, after only seven years of marriage. Six years later he married Ruth Herbert (d.1781), who was a member of the Baptist church. Simon Johnston thus began to attend the Baptist meeting-house with his wife, though it was not until December 1752 that he was actually baptized and became a member. The following year he was appointed deacon. For reasons unknown he resigned from this office within eight months. Thirteen years later he withdrew from the fellowship of the church. Kenneth W. H. Howard has suggested that Jane's father was at heart an Anglican, and was never comfortable in the Baptist fold. Be this as it may, he and Ruth had three children, all of whom joined the Baptist church: Jane, James and Sarah. James married a Mary Harrison and had several children. Sarah never married and continued to live with her sister after the latter's marriage to Sutcliff.[41]

Very little is known about their marriage. In his funeral sermon for Sutcliff, Fuller tells us simply that their marriage 'appears to have added much to his comfort. For eighteen years they lived together, as fellow helpers to each other in the ways of God.'[42] Howard was persuaded that there was 'a perfect love match between them'. And there is some evidence that points in this direction. When Sutcliff was dying, he told his wife, 'Our separation will not be long; and I think I shall often be with you.' These words evince the deep pleasure that Sutcliff had known in being married to Jane, as well as the belief that the saints in glory take an interest in what is transpiring on earth. Jane survived her husband only just over ten weeks. Since there is no indication that she was ill at the time of his death, it is quite possible that her deep grief at her husband's passing literally precipitated her death.[43]

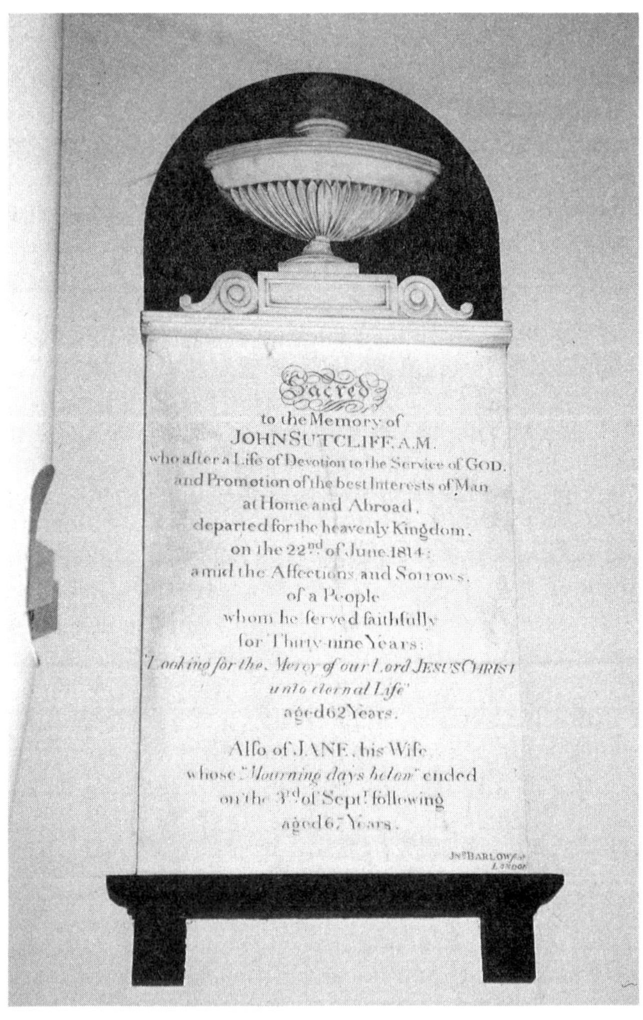


Memorial tablet to John Sutcliff and his wife Jane, Sutcliff Baptist Church, Olney

The only story known about their marriage is one that is more quaint than significant. On Fuller's first visit to the Sutcliffs after their marriage, he is said to have brought a note from his wife requesting Jane to give him a large bowl of bread and milk of such consistency that a spoon could stand upright in it. Jane complied, and after Fuller had quickly consumed all that was in the bowl, he asked for more. He had, after all, ridden eighteen miles or so from Kettering that day and was hungry. After a few further trips to her larder, she is said to have exclaimed, 'My word! What a lot you men eat!'[44]

At the time of their marriage Sutcliff and his bride rented the house that is now 21 High Street from the Olney lawyer John Garrard. By 1810 they had accumulated sufficient funds to purchase it from him. After their deaths in 1814 it remained in the Johnston family for a good number of years.[45] Two years after moving into what is 21 High Street, Sutcliff also began to rent the house to the immediate north, 23 High Street, with the express purpose of using it as a parsonage seminary for missionary and ministerial students.

## The seminary at Olney

Possibly as a result of their experience with Fountain, who had had no formal pastoral training at all, the executive committee of the Missionary Society made the decision at a meeting held on 20 September 1798 in Northampton to place henceforth prospective missionaries who not had a suitable education under the tutelage of Sutcliff. The Olney pastor was the logical individual to choose for such an undertaking. He himself had had a formal theological education. Also, as we have noted, he had a genuine love of books and a predilection for reading. In fact, over the years his wide reading had kept him abreast of developments in the world of theology. One of the members of Olney Baptist Church remarked after Sutcliff's death that 'His knowledge of books was very extensive' and that 'He appeared to have a facility in extracting the substance of them in a short time, as a bee extracts the honey from the expanded flower.'[46] His outstanding scholastic abilites had been recognized five years earlier when Providence College, Rhode Island, awarded him an honorary Master of Arts degree.[47] On the other hand, Sutcliff was well grounded in the faith, had close to a quarter of a century's experience as a pastor, and was deeply trusted by his peers. As Robert Hall, Sr had said of him many years before, 'Brother Sutcliff is a safe man; you never need fear that he will say or do an improper thing.'[48]

Sutcliff and his fellow Calvinistic Baptists were well aware that at the heart of the spiritual and theological decline of some of the Dissenters in their own century had been centres of theological education. The English Presbyterians, who, at the time of the restoration of Charles II in 1660, had been the most significant body of Dissenters, sadly drifted into heterodoxy over the course of the next century, with most of their ministers embracing Arianism, a fourth-century heresy that denied the full deity of Christ, or Unitarianism. And leading the way in this decline had been their academies or seminaries. Even the Congregationalists, who had remained largely orthodox during the eighteenth century, had not been immmune from the contagion of heterodox ideas.

One of the most important Congregationalist academies, which would have been well known to Sutcliff and his friends, was that begun by Philip Doddridge at Northampton, continued by Caleb Ashworth in Daventry, and eventually presided over by John Horsey (1754-1827) when it returned to Northampton in 1789. 'The greatest freedom of inquiry' characterized the studies at this school, and although Doddridge and Ashworth remained free of heresy, many of their fellow teachers and pupils did not. In fact, in the very year that Sutcliff's parsonage seminary was launched, Horsey had to be relieved of his duties for espousing Unitarian beliefs. The suspicion with which Calvinistic Baptists viewed Doddridge's academy is well seen in the following snatch of conversation that reportedly took place in 1805 between a Calvinistic Baptist and another passenger in a Northampton stage-coach. The name of Doddrige having been mentioned, the Baptist commented, 'A great and good man, but a very bad tutor... A very bad tutor ... he gave both sides of the question... What better proof can you have of his pernicious mode of tuition, than that most of his divinity students turned out Arians or Socinians?'[49] The recommendation that Sutcliff begin a parsonage seminary in Olney would probably have had as much to do with his academic abilities as with his reputation for theological soundness and stability.

The first students that he received were Daniel Brunsdon (1777-1801) and John Chamberlain (1777-1821).[50] Brunsdon originally hailed from Defford, a village near Pershore, Worcestershire. His mother regularly attended the Baptist church at Pershore, though his father was a member of the Church of England. Around the age of fourteen he had an 'alarming dream', in which he was taken to hell by the devil. While the effects of this dream were not lasting, it was not long after that a sermon from Revelation 4:5-6 proved to be the means that God used to awaken him to his need of salvation. Nevertheless, he put off making a commitment to Christ. On the final day of 1792, he moved to the city of Bristol to find employment as a linendraper's assistant. Two and a half years later, in July 1795, he began to attend Broadmead Baptist Church, where he was finally converted, was baptized by Ryland and became a member of the church. A sermon by Ryland towards the end of July 1798 having awakened in him the desire to serve God as a missionary, he sought Ryland's advice, who suggested that he attend the committee meeting in Northampton that September. There it was recommended that he study with Sutcliff till the society deemed him prepared for service in India.

Chamberlain, on the other hand, was from the Midlands, having been born and raised at Welton, Northamptonshire, a village roughly twelve miles west of the county town. Converted in 1795, he was baptized the following year at Guilsborough. In October of that year he first heard of Carey's and Thomas's labours in India, and he began to hope that he could join them there. His name was brought to the attention of the executive committee of the society, which resolved that he too should study with Sutcliff for a period of time till he was ready to go overseas.

Thus Brunsdon and Chamberlain came to live with Sutcliff in Olney, where he gave them instruction in theology, the biblical languages and the interpetation of the Scriptures. Among the theological works that Sutcliff gave them to study were some from the pen of Edwards and his New Divinity disciples Joseph Bellamy and Timothy Dwight (1752-1817), as well as *The Reformed Pastor* (1656), the classic on pastoral ministry by the Puritan divine Richard Baxter (1615-1691).[51] He also had them read Christian biographies in order to give them a firm grounding in evangelical spirituality. Sutcliff gave them opportunities to preach in some of the surrounding villages, such as Clifton Reynes and Denton. Moreover, as they observed Sutcliff in his daily round of activities, he exemplified for them what ministry entailed. On two occasions

Chamberlain noted in his diary that he was present at the bedside of someone who was ill or near death. It would appear that Sutcliff took Brunsdon and Chamberlain with him as he went to minister to the sick and dying.[52] Finally, Sutcliff spoke to them about their personal experience as Christians. For both Brunsdon and Chamberlain their time with Sutcliff was a humbling time. They grew in their knowledge of themselves, and their ever-constant need to lean on God. Brunsdon, for one, had come to Olney expecting to 'grow wiser and better'. Instead, he later told Sutcliff, 'I saw myself more wicked and more ignorant than ever I did before.' Day by day he saw more of 'the dreadful depravity' of his heart.[53] Sutcliff himself had trodden this path many years before. From his own experience and his reading of Scripture, he was convinced that knowledge of oneself as a sinner and spiritually needy was utterly vital to Christian maturity. In his discussions with Brunsdon and Chamberlain about their experience, there is little doubt that Sutcliff would have taken the opportunity to press home this truth.

Two months after Brunsdon and Chamberlain came to reside in Olney, Sutcliff reported to the society's executive when they met at Guilsborough that both of them were progressing well. A decision as to when to send them to India, however, was deferred until the following April.[53] By February 1799, though, it was apparent to Sutcliff that Brunsdon would be ready to sail to India that year, but not Chamberlain. The Northamptonshire native was a man of deep devotion, as is evident from extracts of his diary that have been preserved, and was gifted academically, but he was 'a total stranger to discipline' and quarrelsome to a fault.[54] When Sutcliff told Fuller that in his opinion Chamberlain needed more preparation, Fuller was concerned that if Brunsdon was sent and Chamberlain was not, the latter might take it amiss.[55] Nevertheless, when Sutcliff met with Fuller and Thomas Blundel at Wellingborough on 25 February, they decided that of the two students in the Olney seminary only Brunsdon would be sent to India that year.[56]

## Ward, Marshman and Grant join the team for India

Accompanying Brunsdon were to be three other men and their families who had been accepted for missionary service: William Ward, Joshua Marshman and William Grant (d. 1799). The first two of these three, of course, would become Carey's close-knit colleagues and with him form what has come to be called the Serampore Trio. As A. Christopher Smith has observed, 'For several decades they complemented one another in an intricate way. Indeed, very few people in Britain ever realized how dependent Carey was on his partners for insight and a wide range of initiatives.'[57]

Ward was born in Derby and apprenticed at a young age to a printer named John Drewry. In Drewry's printing shop Ward became a skilled printer and editor of the *Derby Mercury*. It was in this capacity as editor of a weekly newspaper that Ward became an 'outspoken, and at times daring proponent of social and political reform'.[58] The earliest religious influences in his life were from the Wesleyan Methodists, but around 1792 he began to have fellowship with Derby's Calvinistic Baptists, who were members of the Calvinistic Baptist cause in Nottingham. It was at the annual meeting of the Northamptonshire Baptist Association in 1792, when Carey preached his famous sermon, that a sum of money had been especially allocated for the preaching of the gospel in Derby. This money bore fruit two years later when a chapel was opened in the town. On this occasion Ward may well have heard Samuel Pearce, who participated in the chapel's opening.

In 1795 Ward moved to Hull to take up the position of full-time editor of the *Hull Advertiser and Exchange Gazette*. This post only lasted nine months, when, for reasons unknown, he was dismissed. His dismissal came a month after his baptism on 28 August 1796 and may possibly have been a result of this step of commitment.

The following year Ward was back in Derby, where he was to have one final and dramatic fling with radical reform. He arranged for John Thelwall (1764-1836), a demagogue who was sympathetic to the left-wing ideology spawned by the French Revolution, to give a public lecture in the Calvinistic Baptist chapel on the night of 20 March. A loyalist mob gathered outside the meeting-house with the intent of drowning out Thelwall with drums and horns. Things soon turned ugly as the mob smashed in the windows of the chapel and wounded several of those inside with bricks and stones. Thelwall made his escape with a drawn pistol, threatening to shoot anyone who molested him. This riot could have landed Ward in jail. As it was, he emerged unscathed, though not unchanged. Never again would he be involved in political radicalism.

The late summer of 1797 found him in Yorkshire, studying with John Fawcett. It was here that Sutcliff probably met him and, with Fawcett, encouraged him to contemplate the possibility of missions. Ward had been thinking of pastoral ministry in England, but by the early autumn of 1798 he decided to apply to the society for service in India. He was formally accepted by the society at a ministerial meeting of the Northamptonshire Association that was held at Kettering on 16 October. Pearce was one of the preachers for the occasion and, as Fuller remarked, he preached 'like an Apostle'. Ward later wrote to Carey that Pearce's preaching 'set the whole meeting in a flame'. 'The missionary spirit was all alive' and, Ward added, had more missionaries been needed, 'We might have had a cargo immediately.'[59]

Neither Marshman nor Grant was afflicted with 'any thing of the political mania', to use the words of Fuller on one occasion to Sutcliff.[60] In fact, when Ward was plunging into the world of radical politics, Marshman was living a life which, according to his son, was positively 'monotonous'.[61] Marshman grew up in Westbury Leigh, Wiltshire, where he eventually became a weaver like his father. From a very early age he had an irrepressible thirst for reading, devouring anything he could borrow or lay his hands on. By his teens, this hunger for knowledge was such that he would often read while working a hand-loom in his father's home. Contrary to his own beliefs, his conversion was neither sudden nor accompanied by a period of despair and 'fearful exercises of mind'. As he regularly attended the Baptist meeting-house of Westbury Leigh with his parents, 'Gradually ... the light of divine truth shone into his mind, and he was able to put his entire dependence for acceptance with God, and his hope of eternal salvation, on the all meritorious atonement of Christ.' After his conversion, which occurred in his late teens, his insatiable reading did not cease, but it now became focused and turned in a different direction. He read through Luther's commentary on Galatians in its entirety, as well as devouring the tomes of the leading Puritan writers of the previous century. His son noted that 'There was scarcely a treatise of that period [i.e. the seventeenth century] of any note, with the arguments and sentiments of which he did not become perfectly familiar.'

In 1794 he took a position as schoolmaster in a school in Bristol that was supported by the congregation of Broadmead. That same year he was baptized by Ryland and became a member of the members of the church had gathered together their gift of £70 to be presented to the society. In view of the fact that the church paid Pearce £100 per annum, it was indeed a substantial gift.[83] Given this zeal for the cause of the society, it is not surprising that Pearce was immediately appointed to the society's executive.

## John Thomas appears on the scene

The third meeting of the society was held on 13 November, also at Northampton. The minutes of this meeting record that there was a lengthy discussion as to where exactly in the world the society should begin its missionary outreach. Carey, obviously influenced by his reading of James Cook's narrative of his voyages in the South Pacific, had been thinking of Tahiti. However, shortly before this meeting, he had received a letter from a man named John Thomas (1757-1800), who was a surgeon and had been a missionary in Bengal, India. Thomas had been raised in a Baptist family in Fairford, Gloucestershire, where his father was a deacon who sometimes entertained the well-known Benjamin Beddome in his home. Thomas did not come to Christ in Gloucestershire, though, but in the heart of the metropolis of London under the preaching of Samuel Stennett (1727-1795), the pastor of Little Wild Street Baptist Church. His early Christian experience was a series of emotional ups and downs; impulsive and imprudent by nature, he never seems to have developed regular patterns of Christian discipline. In this, he was completely unlike Carey, his future colleague, who, if he was anything, was methodical and disciplined. Yet, one thing the two men shared: a passion to see Christ exalted among the nations.

On his second visit to India in 1786 Thomas had become friends with Charles Grant (1746-1823), an evangelical who was on the Board of Trade in Calcutta. In the Indian subcontinent and in England Grant was to become in later years an influential force in both politics and the life of the church. Grant helped Thomas to start a missionary enterprise in Bengal, where Thomas began to learn Bengali and to translate the Scriptures into that tongue. For a variety of reasons, not the least of which was Thomas's proneness to getting into debt and his irascibility, by 1790 the friendship between the two men had soured to the point where Grant, in the later words of Carey, 'cut off all his [i.e. Thomas's] supplies, and left him to shift for himself in a foreign land'. Thomas, enmeshed in debt, was thus forced to return to England in the early months of 1792 to secure funds to undergird his missionary work in Bengal and if at all possible find a like-minded companion for his work in India.[84]

While in India Thomas had been in correspondence with Samuel Stennett and Abraham Booth, two of the key Baptist leaders in London. Upon his landing in England on 8 July he lost no time in going to hear Stennett and Booth preach, and then making known to them his desire with regard to a mission in India. Booth put Thomas in touch with Carey, for whom, as for his friends, Thomas was a complete unknown.

When Carey's information concerning Thomas was made known to the society, Fuller, who was planning a trip to London, was asked to find out more about the man. Fuller met with Booth, who was wholeheartedly behind the cause of the Missionary Society and who gave Thomas a good recommendation. Fuller also had an opportunity to interview Thomas, who described himself as a Calvinist to Fuller. When Fuller probed further as to what exactly Thomas meant by this term, Thomas's perspective appeared to be identical to that of Fuller himself. According to Fuller, Thomas's views 'very much corresponded ... with those of President Edwards in his treatise on the *Affections*, and with those of Bellamy in his *True Religion Delineated*.'[85] Edwards, as we have seen, was Fuller's favourite author, and Bellamy a close second or third. Thomas's reply would undoubtedly have made Fuller warm to the man. Yet Fuller would not have allowed such shared doctrinal convictions to cloud his estimation of the man. E. F. Clipsham, who has done extensive work on Andrew Fuller and his theology, has noted with regard to Fuller's selection of missionary recruits for the society that Fuller was 'rarely, if ever overgenerous in his estimate of a candidate'.[86] Why, then, did Thomas's pecuniary difficulties and other character defects not disqualify him in the eyes of Fuller? Well, there was the recommendation from Booth and Thomas's own assurance that he was trying to satisfy his creditors. There was also the timing of his arrival. To Fuller and to his friends, his coming upon the scene at the exact moment that they were debating where to begin a missionary enterprise seemed positively providential.[87]

Thomas was accordingly invited to meet with the rest of the society at Kettering on 9 January 1793. Fuller wrote to Sutcliff a week before the meeting to inform him of the date, the fact that the meeting would be accompanied by 'fasting and prayer', and to ask him if he could ride over to Kettering the day before, so that they could have some time before the meeting to have fellowship and discuss the events of the following day. Hoping to give Thomas as much exposure to the Calvinistic Baptist community in the Midlands as possible, Fuller also told Sutcliff that he had arranged for Thomas to preach at Northampton the Sunday after the meeting and then at Biggleswade the following week. But he cautioned Sutcliff against expecting too much from Thomas as a speaker: 'Though he seems well adapted to reason and talk with the Hindoos, he is not capable, I am told, of preaching a set discourse to an English audience to advantage.'[88]

## The decision to sail to India

The following Tuesday came and went without any sign of Sutcliff. Nor, to Fuller's distress, was he at the meeting the following day. It seems that he was prevented from coming 'by a very troublesome boil'.[89] Nor was Ryland there. Earlier that year, Broadmead Baptist Church in Bristol, which had been without a pastor since the death of Caleb Evans the previous summer, had approached Ryland with a view to his becoming their pastor. Due to the fact that this position also entailed serving as the principal of the Bristol Baptist Academy, Ryland was indeed faced with a weighty decision. He eventually accepted the Broadmead call, but it took him a full twenty months to do so.[90] In the course of coming to this decision, Ryland spent a number of months away from Northampton in Bristol. The last week in 1792 and the first three weeks of January 1793 were among these. He thus missed this important meeting at Kettering. His absence and that of Sutcliff, Fuller later told Ryland, 'threw a great weight upon me'.[91] This simple remark well reveals the way that Fuller relied on Sutcliff and Ryland for their advice even at this early stage of the Missionary Society's history.

To add to Fuller's consternation, when the meeting began in the morning Thomas was not there. The society spent much time in prayer and then there was a sermon preached by Carey. Evening came and they were about to disperse when Thomas came limping in. He had been delayed, he told the members of the society, by a foot injury that he had incurred on the way north from London. After some discussion the society invited Thomas to return to India under their auspices. Carey, who had long dreamed of this opportunity, immediately offered himself as a companion for Thomas. Fuller was a little amazed at the rapid pace at which things were unfolding. As he wrote to Ryland, 'Things of great consequence are in train. My heart fears, while it is enlarged... It is a great undertaking; yet, surely it is right.'

The day that he wrote these words to Ryland, Fuller rode down to Olney to let Sutcliff know what had happened and to ask him if he would go with him on 23 January to Leicester to 'conciliate the church there and sound Mrs Carey's mind, whether she will go and take the family'.[92] Carey, as James Beck has observed, must have told Fuller and his friends that his wife was not at all pleased about the prospect of leaving England. Her reluctance about going overseas had not yet been put to the test, and Fuller was not sure if Dorothy Carey would actually refuse to accompany her husband to India. It is also noteworthy, Beck points out, that Fuller was willing to allow Dorothy to make her own decision. He and Sutcliff were going to 'sound' out her mind, not talk her into going. In Beck's words, 'Fuller treated Dorothy as a responsible woman who had a monumental decision to make.'[93]

When Fuller and Sutcliff arrived at Carey's Leicester cottage the following week, Dorothy told them that she simply was not prepared to go to India. Why she refused to go is not known. Beck has canvassed various possibilites, such as the fact that she was five months pregnant when Fuller and Sutcliff came to visit her, or that she might have been a fearful individual, but in the final analysis we do not know why she was adamant in her decision to stay in England.[94]

A substantial number of the Leicester congregation, a third of them converted through Carey's ministry, were also resistant to Carey's going to India and leaving them. Unlike Dorothy, they soon changed their minds. As they wrote in their letter to the annual assembly of the Northamptonshire Association that year, 'We had been long praying for the gospel to be sent [overseas], and now providence opened a way.'[95]

Dorothy was not to be moved, however, which caused deep anguish of heart for both Carey and his friends. If William went without her and his children, then, as Fuller wrote, 'There would not

Portraits of Thomas, Fuller, Carey, Ward and Marshman.
*(Reproduced by courtesy of the Sutcliff Baptist Church, Olney.)*

only be a great outcry against it from worldly men, but even many religious people, who had thought but little on the subject, would join in the general censure.'[96] Over the next few weeks Carey thought through various alternative plans till he eventually decided, with Dorothy's consent, to take their eldest boy, Felix, with him. He would get established in India and then return for his family in three to four years.[97]

## Fuller's activity on behalf of the mission and its results

Meanwhile, the strain of these events, coupled with the death of his wife the previous year, told especially on Fuller. On 26 January, the Saturday after he and Sutcliff had ridden to Leicester to see Dorothy Carey, Fuller began to experience a numbness in his lips. The following day he noticed that as he preached he had problems saying words which began with the letter 'p'. By Tuesday, one side of his face was completely paralysed. The paralysis eventually wore off, but he was left with continual headaches. As Fuller wrote to John Fawcett, 'I cannot read, write, or think closely for two hours without bringing on the head-ache.' Then, reflecting on what had happened and why: 'I suppose it was a slight paralytic stroke, probably occasioned by great fatigue, care, and much writing.'[98] Over the space of a couple of weeks Fuller had stayed up night after night, writing numerous letters to fellow Baptists throughout England, encouraging them to throw their support and money behind the mission to India.

Fawcett entered into the endeavour with his whole heart and with unremitting ardour sought to garner support in the north. 'Blessed be God,' Fawcett wrote to Fuller, 'that I have lived to see so much love to Christ. I account it one of the greatest blessings of my life to have assisted in so glorious and disinterested an undertaking.' The fact that his spiritual son, Sutcliff, was right at the heart of this enterprise would have given Fawcett added pleasure.

William Crabtree of Bradford, who had been converted under William Grimshaw nearly fifty years before and was now upwards of seventy years of age, went from house to house in Bradford seeking donations for the mission. 'He could not sleep for joy,' Fuller told Thomas Steevens of Colchester. According to Fuller, Crabtree had told Fawcett, 'My heart has been so much in this work that it has almost been too much for my old body.'[99]

In East Anglia, Steevens and Joseph Kinghorn of Norwich both received letters from Fuller, and both responded positively to his request for support. Kinghorn was personally of the opinion that the difficulties facing the mission to India were considerable, but he heartily wished the endeavour 'superior to [his] hopes'.[100]

Some ministers were far more reticent to help. Benjamin Beddome, in a letter from which we have already quoted, thought the mission to India ill-advised. As for Carey, he told Fuller that 'I had the pleasure once to see and hear Mr Carey. It struck me that he was the most suitable person in the kingdom, at least whom I knew, to supply my place and make up my great deficiencies when either disabled or removed. A different plan is formed and pursued, and I fear that the great and good man, though influenced by the most excellent motives, will meet with a disappointment. However, God hath his ends and whoever is disappointed he will not [be], he cannot be so. My unbelieving heart is ready to suggest with the Jews of old that "the time is not come that the Lord's house should be built" (Haggai 1:2).'[101]

Beddome had serious reservations about Carey's going to India, but he was prepared to admit that he might be wrong, that God's plans might be quite different from what he envisaged. He also confessed that the prophet Haggai's censure of the Jews of his day for unbelief might well be applied to him. It is fascinating that this confession contained an allusion to the very passage on which Fuller had preached a couple of years earlier at Clipston, when he called upon his fellow Baptists to exercise a deeper trust in God. Had Beddome read Fuller's sermon and was he indicating how it applied to him?

Nor were many of the London Baptist leaders that supportive. Booth endorsed the project, as did John Rippon, James Dore (1764-1825), the successor of Benjamin Wallin at Maze Pond, and Timothy Thomas (1753-1827), the pastor of Devonshire Square Baptist Church, which had been gathered under the ministry of William Kiffin in the 1640s and was one of the oldest Calvinistic Baptist churches in England. It is noteworthy that Rippon, Dore and Thomas had all been educated at Bristol Baptist Academy. But the majority of the London Baptists initially heeded the advice of Samuel Stennett, who urged extreme caution. 'The mission,' he said, 'will come to nothing from this cause — people may contribute ... for once in a fit of zeal, but how is it to be [continually] supported?'

Fuller's response to Stennett's scepticism was to declare that his trust was not in human support and resources, but in God. As he wrote to Thomas Steevens, 'For my part, I believe in God, and have not much doubt but that a matter, begun as this was, will meet his approbation, and that he who has inclined the hearts of our brethren hitherto so much beyond our expectations will go on to incline their hearts "not to lose the things which they have wrought." I confess I feel sanguine in my hopes, but they are fixed in God.'[102] By the early nineteenth century, the society was regularly receiving £3,000 or more a year.[103] Fuller's hope had not been misplaced.

## Farewell services for the missionaries

Wednesday, 20 March was the day assigned for Carey's farewell from Leicester. The previous Monday Sutcliff had ridden from Olney to meet Thomas and William Staughton at Kettering, where the three of them stayed overnight, possibly at Martha Wallis's. The next morning they were up early for the ride to Leicester.[104]

The Wednesday morning was given to prayer. As Timothy George has written, their prayers were 'not routine or perfunctory', but were 'wrenched from their souls', as they earnestly entreated God's fullest blessing on Carey, Thomas and their families. In the afternoon Thomas preached and in the evening Reynold Hogg delivered a message from Acts 21:14, after which Fuller gave an emotional address to the missionaries based on John 20:21: 'Peace be unto you: even as my Father sent me, so send I you.' Fuller reminded them that the great objects of their mission in India were to be the same as those of Christ during his incarnate life and ministry: 'To glorify God, and to seek and to save lost souls.' He thus encouraged them to give themselves wholly to living God-glorifying lives and to preaching the gospel. Despite the difficulties that they were bound to encounter in doing this, they had to remember that Christ had promised his presence as support — here Fuller was thinking of Matthew 28:20, a text very familiar to Carey — and a glorious reward: joy in heaven and 'crowns of glory'. 'Go then,' he concluded, 'stimulated by such prospects.' And he added with deep emotion: 'We shall meet again.' In saying this, he was not thinking of the projected return of Carey to England, but of their eventual reunion in heaven. This evening service was, as Fuller later told

Fawcett, 'a solemn and affectionate meeting! O, my dear sir, thousands of tears of joy have been shed.'[105]

The rest of that week was spent helping Dorothy Carey and her children get packed and settled in a cottage back at Hackleton. The Careys said goodbye to one another the following Tuesday, 26 March. This parting could not have been easy for either of them. Dorothy had no idea when she would see her husband and eldest boy again. William would have had the added worry of leaving Dorothy alone when she was about to give birth. Happily, Dorothy's youngest sister Kitty had agreed to live with her and the other children during the remainder of Dorothy's pregnancy and after the birth of her child.

From Hackleton, Carey, Thomas and Pearce, who was going with them to London, rode over to Olney. There Carey was to speak at an evening service that Sutcliff had especially planned as a farewell service in a congregation that had come to mean so much to Carey. It was here that Carey had first set eyes on both Sutcliff and Fuller, now among the dearest of his friends. As Carey wrote to Sutcliff a number of years later when he was established in India, 'I don't know a person in England whom I esteem more than yourself.'[106] Here he had come to treasure Sutcliff's counsel. And it was here in Olney that he had been set apart for the ministry of God's Word.

A very succint account of the service that evening has been recorded by the Olney schoolmaster, Samuel Teedon (d.1798), an Anglican, who also used to attend the Baptist Meeting on occasion. Teedon was an occasional visitor in Sutcliff's home and vice versa. Such visits he often recorded in his diary with the laconic statement: 'Mr Sutcliff smoked a pipe with us'![107] According to his diary for that day, Teedon went to the Baptist meeting-house and heard 'Mr Carey preach, the missionary to go to the Hindus with his son about ten years of age [Felix was actually eight]. A collection was made. I gave 6d. It amounted to almost £10. The Lord prosper the work!'[108]

## The missionaries embark

Eleven days later Carey and Felix, Thomas, his wife and their daughter boarded the *Earl of Oxford* on the Thames and set sail for India. Due to the fact that Great Britain was now at war with France

— war had been declared on February 11 — the captain of the vessel, a Captain White, decided to anchor off the Isle of Wight to await the gathering of a convoy of vessels. There was, he reasoned, safety in numbers.

It was while they were anchored here that Thomas's past caught up with him. One of his creditors called at their lodgings in Ryde on the Isle of Wight with 'a writ and bailiff, to arrest him for £100 or less'. Thomas was away at the time and so was not apprehended, but Carey now realized, probably for the first time, the full extent of his companion's debts. A few weeks later, in the middle of May, when the convoy of ships had assembled and the *Earl of Oxford* was at last ready to sail, Captain White received an anonymous letter signed 'Verax' — probably one of Thomas's creditors — informing him that he had on board his ship 'a person' who should not be allowed to sail to India. If he took this individual to India, he was told in no uncertain terms that he would be risking his command.

Because no name was actually given, Captain White, wanting to be safe, ordered both Carey and Thomas to disembark. Mrs Thomas and her daughter were allowed to stay on board and to sail, which they did, but Carey, Felix and Thomas had to get off at Ryde. It was from there, on 21 May, that a chastened and tearful Carey wrote to Fuller about what had happened. Although he was deeply disappointed, he was not devastated. As he told his friend, 'All I can say in this affair is that however mysterious the leadings of providence are, I have no doubt but they are superintended by an infinitely wise God.'[109]

These 'leadings of providence' soon began to be manifest. In a few days they were able to book passage on a Danish boat, the *Kron Princessa Maria*. Carey, who still entertained a hope that his wife might reconsider and sail with them, decided to make one last attempt to persuade her. After booking passage, they took an overnight coach from London to Northampton, and then walked the five or so miles to Hackleton, arriving in time for breakfast. Dorothy had given birth to a baby boy, Jabez, three weeks before, and this was the first time that Carey had set eyes upon his son. Carey pleaded once again with his wife to go with them, but, to his sorrow, she refused. Thomas also tried to persuade her, but to no avail. They thus decided to leave and head back to Northampton, where they hoped to see Ryland. On the way there, Thomas felt he could convince Dorothy to come with them. Carey thought he was wasting time, but told him, 'Do as you think proper.' Thomas went back, and bluntly told Dorothy that if she did not accompany her husband 'her family would be dispersed and divided for ever' and 'she would repent of it as long as she lived'. These words of Thomas struck home, and in a matter of minutes, Dorothy had agreed to come on the condition that her sister go with her.[110] William understandably was thrilled. 'To my great joy and astonishment she consented ... to go,' Carey wrote hastily in a note to Sutcliff that very day, 24 May. As they were all off to London the next day, and he had no time to sell the furniture of the house and the belongings that were being left behind, Carey also asked Sutcliff if he could dispose of these items.[111] Three weeks later Carey, his family and Thomas finally sailed aboard the *Kron Princessa Maria*. There was no fear of attack by the French, for the Danish were neutral in the war now raging in Europe.

Sutcliff, Fuller and Ryland marvelled at the way things had worked out. As Fuller informed John Saffery (1763-1825), the pastor of Brown Street Baptist Church in Salisbury and a keen supporter of the mission from the moment that he heard of its inception, 'O brother! Tears of joyful adoration are but a small tribute for such mercies! All is well! ... Carey's heart is happy, having his family with him... Had not Carey taken his family he must have come home again in a few years. Now there will be no need of that. He will live and die in the midst of hundreds of millions of heathens, for whose salvation I am sure he is ready to sacrifice his life, and a thousand lives if he had them.'[112]

# 11.
# 'He gave some to be pastors and teachers'

> *'He who converts a soul draws water from a fountain; but he who trains a soul-winner digs a well from which thousands may drink to life eternal'* (C. H. Spurgeon).

Carey had been in India close on nine months before his first letter to Sutcliff, dated 3 January 1794, reached Olney. Sutcliff received it on 29 July, and with eager anticipation unfolded it and read of Carey's first days in Calcutta after their safe arrival in November 1793, their early problems, most of which were caused by Thomas's ongoing indebtedness, and their first illnesses in India. Right at the outset of the letter Carey made plain his love for Sutcliff when he told him, 'I think I should be wanting in friendship if I neglected to write to you — especially considering the ties of Christian affection by which I am bound to you.'[1]

Sutcliff lost no time in replying. Two days later he had written to Carey a letter that presumably reached the missionary in India the following year. The length of time it took for correspondence to pass between Carey and his friends in England was exacerbated by the war between France and England, which hindered ships from sailing on time and frequently required them to stay put in the safety of a harbour. This reply has not survived, and so we have no exact idea of what Sutcliff told Carey.

A letter that Samuel Pearce wrote to Carey and Thomas around the same time has come down to us and may well contain some of the things that Sutcliff might have related to his friend in India.[2] Pearce reaffirmed his affection for Carey and Thomas — 'I feel the most affectionate attachment to your persons' — and told them of the 'thousands of prayers' that had been offered to God on their behalf. He informed them of the ways in which the Holy Spirit was at work in the churches of the Northamptonshire Association: for instance, at Harvey Lane in Leicester, which was still without a pastor, Pearce himself had baptized a dozen individuals; at Walgrave there were 'near twenty young people under hopeful concern'; and at Earls Barton, where Carey had preached for three and a half years, 'the dear Redeemer's cause' appeared 'to be considerably advancing'.

Pearce also told Carey a little about the opening of a new Baptist meeting-house at Guilsborough in May 1794. The previous meeting-house, it will be recalled from the last chapter, had been destroyed by incendiaries at Christmas 1792. When it was rebuilt, it was capable of seating 600 people. In order to celebrate the opening of the new meeting-house, Pearce, Sutcliff and Thomas Blundel were asked to preach. Pearce told Carey the texts that they preached on — Pearce spoke on Psalm 76:10, Sutcliff on Psalm 118:25 and Blundel on Judges 5:31 — and that he had also preached the following morning at 5 o' clock to more than 200 people. What he did not tell Carey, and what Sutcliff probably would have told him, was the particular circumstance that led Pearce to preach so early the following morning and what transpired during his sermon at that time.

Pearce and Sutcliff had preached during the morning, and at the midday meal a good number of the persons present were discussing Pearce's sermon as they ate. Although Sutcliff was by this time a good preacher, Pearce excelled in the pulpit. 'At times,' F. A. Cox wrote, 'he would rise into raptures, and glow like a seraph; and notwithstanding the disadvantage of a voice which failed him in his most animated moments, his oratory was irresistible.'[3] As the discussion went back and forth that day at Guilsborough regarding Pearce's sermon, a certain individual decided to ask Pearce if he would preach early the following morning. 'If you will find a congregation,' Pearce replied, 'I will find a sermon.' The hour was set for 5 o'clock in order to accommodate the farm labourers who would have to be at their tasks early in the day.

After the sermon, as Pearce, Sutcliff, Fuller and a few others were having breakfast, Fuller told Pearce how much he was pleased with what he had heard that morning. Then, with the freedom that friends can employ, he mentioned that in his opinion Pearce's sermon had been oddly structured. 'I thought,' he told Pearce, 'you did not seem to close when you had really finished. I wondered that, contrary to what is usual with you, you seemed, as it were, to begin again at the end — how was it?' Pearce said tersely, 'It was so; but I had my reason.' 'Well then, come, let us have it,' Fuller jocularly replied. Pearce was reluctant to give his reason, but after Fuller had once again entreated him to share it, he said, 'Well, my brother, you shall have the secret, if it must be so. Just at the moment I was about to resume my seat, thinking I had finished, the door opened, and I saw a poor man enter, of the working class; and from the sweat on his brow, and the symptoms of his fatigue, I conjectured that he had walked some miles to this early service, but that he had been unable to reach the place till the close. A momentary thought glanced through my mind — here may be a man who never heard the gospel, or it may be he is one that regards it as a feast of fat things; in either case, the effort on his part demands one on mine. So with the hope of doing him good, I resolved at once to forget all else, and, in despite of criticism, and the apprehension of being thought tedious, to give him a quarter of an hour.'[4]

As Fuller, Sutcliff and the others present heard this simple explanation, they were profoundly impressed by Pearce's love for souls and his self-sacrificing spirit. Pearce, by his own admission, was a man naturally prone to pride.[5] But his ardour for the spiritual welfare of others compelled his pride to give way as he ministered to this 'poor man' and to put aside the thought of what others, especially his fellow ministers, would think of his homiletical skills.

## Death of Mary Andrews

That autumn Mary Andrews, in whose home Sutcliff had been living since his coming to Olney, was not at all well. Living in her home had been a very pleasant situation for Sutcliff. Largely free from the cares that go along with sustaining a house, Sutcliff had time for his pastoral ministry and his library, which was becoming more and more impressive year by year. Moreover, Mary Andrews had been an excellent hostess for the many guests whom Sutcliff had entertained over the years. Not a few of his friends who corresponded with him asked to be remembered to 'Mrs Andrews'. John Fawcett spoke for them all when, at the end of the 1770s, he asked friendly to say, than to pass by your Letter in entire silence. — Mrs. Andrews enjoys a very poor state of Health. She unites with me in kind respects. Thro' mercy, I am pretty well myself. Nothing material in our religious affairs. We are in peace. Lately have had several breaches by death, but on the whole do not decline. Long to see a more abundant revival. I rest,

Your cordial well-wisher in Gospel Bonds,

John Sutcliff.

Olney, 6. May. 1794.

An example of Sutcliff's handwriting at this period, (before it deteriorated): part of a letter to Lawrence Butterworth of Evesham, dated May 1794, in which he mentions the poor state of health enjoyed by 'Mrs Andrews' and includes a greeting from her.

*(Reproduced by courtesy of the National Library of Wales.)*

Sutcliff to tell her, 'I bear an affectionate remembrance of her, and should be happy to lodge once more under her hospitable roof.'[6]

She was an ardent believer, and thus Sutcliff had no fears about her eternal state, but her ill health did cause him alarm, as his correspondence bears witness. In September Fuller, speaking with almost prophetic urgency, urged Sutcliff to beseech her 'not to go out of the world without befriending' the Missionary Society. 'Tell her from me that were I in her place I should tremble to meet the Judge of all without having befriended it.'[7] A couple of months later, she was still quite ill and unable to leave her bed. Fuller wrote on 19 November and asked his friend for news on Mary's condition. When Morris wrote to Sutcliff a few days before Fuller, he was 'sorry', he said, 'to find Mrs Andrews is no better'. Sutcliff's concern for Mrs Andrews continued throughout the winter. When Fuller wrote to his friend on 22 January of the new year, he especially asked him to 'drop a line' about her, 'be it ever so brief'.[8]

By February it was obvious to Sutcliff that Mary Andrews was dying. Her final days were wracked with pain, yet spiritually she was at peace. As Sutcliff later wrote, 'Her views of interest in Christ were clear, and her fears of death removed,' and 'Her comforts and joys carried her often above her pains and distresses.' When Sutcliff told Fuller of her state, the Kettering pastor asked to be remembered 'affectionately' to her and then said, 'The Lord prepare her for what is before her!'[9]

Mary Andrews was prepared. She fervently told Sutcliff a number of times that she longed to depart to 'be with Jesus and his saints above'. Often she would repeat in his hearing the lines of a hymn written by John Mason (d. 1694), who for more than twenty years was the rector of Water Stratford, Buckinghamshire:

My dearest friends, they dwell above,
Them will I go and see;
And all my friends in Christ below
Shall soon come after me.

She died on 9 March. Before she died she had asked Sutcliff to promise her that he would not preach a funeral sermon for her. For most of her Christian life she had made it a point, in accordance with her reading of Christ's statement in Matthew 6:1, to conceal as far as possible her good deeds from public knowledge. She did not want

Broadmead Church. For the next five years, alongside his responsibilities as schoolmaster, he studied at the Bristol Academy, where he especially excelled in Greek, Hebrew and Syriac. As in the case of Chamberlain, the accounts that he read of Carey in India turned his mind to thoughts of missionary service. When his friend and fellow-student William Grant offered his services to the Baptist Missionary Society, Marshman resolved to do the same.

Prior to his offering himself for missionary service William Grant had had a singular career.[62] In his teens he began to read with a friend the work of the French Deist Voltaire (1694-1778), which led him to ridicule the followers of Christ as fanatics. From Deism he eventually plunged into atheism and, he afterwards observed with sorrow, 'There was no sin which I could not commit without remorse.' His conversion came as the result of meeting Marshman in a bookshop — given Marshman's avidity for reading, bookshops were probably a natural haunt of his. Seeing Marshman pick up a Latin dictionary to peruse, Grant asked him if he could read Latin. Finding that he could, Grant asked Marshman if he could get some instruction in the language. Thus they became acquainted, and inevitably when together their conversation turned to the Christian faith and Calvinism. Grant particularly ridiculed the atonement and sneered at what he called 'the absurdities of Calvinism', but Marshman's firm and loving avowal of Christianity — he told Grant that his only hope rested on Christ's death for sinners — drew Grant to the point where he began to attend Broadmead with his new friend. The preaching of the Word, in particular a sermon on Psalm 14:1, and repeated discussions with Marshman eventually led Grant 'to acknowledge the divinity of the Holy Scriptures, to abhor himself as in dust and ashes, and to believe in the Lord Jesus Christ for the salvation of his soul'.

He had been converted less than a year when he told Ryland that he was interested in becoming a missionary with the society. Grant's being a new convert gave Fuller some concern. 'Would it not be advisable that he ... should be tried a little longer?', he queried in a letter that he wrote to Sutcliff in mid-February 1799.[63] Sutcliff probably would have been cautious and would have recommended that Grant wait. However, Ryland spoke highly of Grant, and his opinion convinced Fuller. By the beginning of April it was settled that Grant would sail to India with Brunsdon, Ward and Marshman that May.

## The commissioning services

Brunsdon, Ward, Marshman and Grant were commissioned for service at two separate meetings: Brunsdon and Ward in the meeting-house in Olney on Tuesday, 7 May 1799; Marshman and Grant the previous Friday at Broadmead. Originally Fuller had planned to have the service at Olney on 24 May. But in late April he was informed that the ship in which the new missionaires were to sail, an American vessel called the *Criterion*, was scheduled to depart from London on 9 May. Fuller therefore had to advance the date of the commissioning service by just over two weeks. He told Sutcliff that they would have the service in the morning and leave Olney at one o'clock to drive down to London, where they would meet Marshman, Grant and their families. Sutcliff made arrangements to hire two post-chaises from nearby Newport Pagnell that would take them to London.[64]

The meeting-house could seat around 700 and that morning it was packed to overflowing. The service began with Reynold Hogg reading some appropriate passages from Scripture relating to missions and evangelism. Fuller then asked both Brunsdon and Ward why they were going to India and what was the message that they would seek to proclaim there. Only the essence of Ward's reply has been preserved. The motivation taking him to India, he told the congregation assembled that day, was based on two scriptural passages, Mark 16:15 and Matthew 28:20. These texts contained a command, he said, that was still binding on believers, 'since the promise of Christ's presence reaches to the utmost corner of the earth and to the utmost boundaries of time'. The similarity between Ward's reasoning and that of Carey in the first section of his *Enquiry* is striking. Ward had obviously read Carey's classic apology for missions and made its arguments his own. As for the doctrines that he believed and would seek to inculcate in the hearts of Indians, he made particular mention of 'the being and attributes of God, the total depravity of man, free and full salvation by the grace of God through a mediator, the deity of Christ, and the final salvation of believers'. In other words, at the heart of his preaching would be the teachings of classical Calvinism. And, he added, he was looking to 'the doctrine of the cross ... for success in the conversion of the heathen.'[65] After Brunsdon and Ward had given their answers, they knelt down and, as Fuller prayed over them, other pastors who were present came forward and laid their hands on them.

Sutcliff had been asked to give an exhortation to Ward, Brunsdon and his wife of only a week or so. He chose to direct their thoughts to Ephesians 3:8: 'Unto me, who am less than the least of all saints, is this grace given, that I should preach among the Gentiles the unsearchable riches of Christ.' The Olney pastor began by noticing the similarity between Paul's situation and that of Ward and the Brunsdons. Paul and the three individuals being commissioned for service in India all had the privilege of preaching Christ to ears that had never heard his name before. He then went on to recommend three things in particular to their attention.

First, there was the nature of the work itself: *preaching Christ.* Sutcliff spent time focusing his hearers' thoughts on the unsearchable riches of Christ's person, work and ongoing ministry — in a word, 'the treasures of divine mercy deposited in the hands of the Redeemer to be dispensed to poor sinners'.

He then examined the way in which Paul viewed this central aspect of the ministry: it was *a 'grace given'*. Whatever hardships they might experience, whatever reproaches they might be exposed to, they had to recall constantly the honour that had been conferred upon them. They were co-workers with God, 'carrying into execution the gracious purposes of God, fulfilling Scripture prophecy, acting in fellowship with Christ and the best of men in every age'.

Finally, Sutcliff looked at the mind-set with which Paul carried out his commission and with which they should carry out theirs: in 'a spirit of deep humility'. Only in the soil of humility would 'every other grace or holy disposition of the heart' grow. Sutcliff's thought here is identical to that of his theological mentor, Jonathan Edwards who, in *The Religious Affections*, had distinctly stated that it is only out of a heart 'governed by a truly gracious humility' that 'all truly holy affections ... flow'.[66]

As a concluding encouragement, Sutcliff pointed the Brunsdons and Ward to the promise of Christ to be an ever-present source of help for his people, to the sustaining prayers of those whom they would be leaving back in England, and to 'the prospects of a glorious reward'.[67]

Another exhortation, which had been drawn up by Ryland, who was not able to be present, was then read. Since Ryland had written it in advance without any knowledge of what Sutcliff would say in his address, there were some marked areas of overlap between the two speakers. For instance, Ryland emphasized that he and his friends had not the least hope of the success of those whom they were sending out to India unless the latter were kept little in their own eyes and sensible of their weakness. Yet Christ would be ever with them, 'all-sufficient to protect' and to give them success. One thing Ryland did dwell on that Sutcliff does not appear to have mentioned is that in their own interest and that of the mission they must 'keep at the utmost distance from intermeddling with any political concerns'. In fact, Ryland said, definitely speaking not for only himself, but also for Fuller and Sutcliff, 'We certainly would sooner hear of any one of you sinking in the ocean, than of his becoming a busybody in political affairs.'[68] Nothing now could be taken for granted in the light of the Grigg fiasco and Fountain's behaviour in India.

Ryland was not the only leading figure of the society who could not be present at Olney. Pearce was also absent. At the time of the Olney meeting he was lying ill at Tamerton Foliot, a village just outside Plymouth. The previous October, after preaching at the Kettering meeting that had seen the acceptance of Ward as a missionary, he had been overtaken by a rainstorm while returning home to Birmingham. By the time that he reached his home he was drenched to the skin. That evening he felt the onset of a chill. He neglected it and it got worse. Thinking that preaching and what he called 'pulpit sweats' would cure it, he continued to preach not only at Cannon Street but also in villages surrounding Birmingham. These acts of imprudence led to an inflammation of his lungs and orders from his doctor to take complete rest. By mid-December he could hardly converse for five minutes without losing his breath. In February he felt well enough to ride to the opening of a Baptist meeting-house at Bedworth. Fuller saw him there but, as he later informed Sutcliff, Pearce looked 'sadly'. The Sunday after Pearce returned from Bedworth, he attempted to speak a little at the conclusion of the morning sermon, which had been preached by Francis Franklin (1772-1852) of Coventry, but the effort sparked a fresh inflammation of his lungs, 'produced phlegm, coughing, and spitting of blood'. This was to be the last time that Pearce stood before his beloved Cannon Street congregation. By now it was obvious that he had pulmonary tuberculosis. In late March, he set off for Plymouth in the hope that the climate there would help him to recuperate.[69]

It was from Tamerton Foliot that he wrote to Fuller on 2 May the following words for the missionaries being set apart at Olney and at

Bristol: 'Oh that the Lord, who is unconfined by place or condition, may copiously pour out upon you all the rich effusions of his Holy Spirit on the approaching day [i.e. the day of their departure to India]! ... Happy men! Happy women! You are going to be fellow-labourers with Christ himself! ... Oh what promises are yours, and what a reward! Surely heaven is filled with double joy, and resounds with unusual acclamation at the arrival of each missionary there. Oh be faithful, my dear brethren, my dear sisters, be faithful unto death, and all this joy is yours! Long as I live, my imagination will be hovering over you in Bengal; and should I die, if separate spirits be allowed a visit to the world they have left, methinks mine would soon be at Mudnabatti, watching your labours, your conflicts, and your pleasures, whilst you are always abounding in the work of the Lord.'[70] With this portion of the letter acting as it were as a benediction, many of those present, upon hearing Fuller read these lines, were deeply moved and wept openly.

## A deep union and its practical expression

After the service was over, there would have been time for a quick bite to eat, the saying of final goodbyes, and then it was off to London. At London they met up with the Marshmans and the Grants and, Fuller later wrote, 'presently felt themselves to be of one heart and of one soul'.[71]

The *Criterion* did not, as it turned out, sail on 9 May but was detained for a couple of weeks. This delay turned out well, though. It gave an opportunity for a few of the London churches and their pastors to demonstrate practically their support for the society. A service was held on 10 May at the Little Prescott Street Church, where Abraham Booth was the pastor. Booth preached and four other London pastors took part in the service: William Button, Timothy Thomas, John Rippon and Thomas Thomas (1759-1819). Moreover, there was time to baptize William Grant's wife, who had not previously undergone believer's baptism. And there were also opportunities for prayer and worship together. For instance, in the course of a letter that Ward wrote to Pearce on Monday, 13 May, he mentioned such an occasion which was going to take place that evening when the missionaries, with Fuller and Sutcliff, were going to 'pray together and to commemorate our Saviour's death'.[72]

Fuller also took advantage of this time in the capital to collect donations for the society. Sutcliff helped him for a few days, but then had to head back to Olney soon after 13 May in order to prepare for the annual gathering of the Northamptonshire Association, which that year was to be held at Olney. 21-23 May were the days scheduled for the assembly at Olney and Sutcliff had to act as moderator for the second time in three years. At the conclusion of the assembly, Sutcliff and Fuller — Fuller had had to preach at one of the sessions — returned as fast as they could to London. They saw the missionaries on the morning of Saturday, 25 May, and, thinking that the *Criterion* would not sail before Monday, left them, hoping to say their final farewells at that time. That afternoon, however, a favourable wind sprang up, and the *Criterion* set sail. The following day Sutcliff and Fuller were informed that the ship had already sailed.

Knowing that ships outward bound from London stopped at Gravesend to victual, they and William Button (had they been worshipping with Button at Dean Street Baptist Church?) left the city for Gravesend following the evening service. They reached it soon after midnight and found a boat that would take them out to the *Criterion*, which they reached around two in the morning. They only had time to say a personal farewell to each of the men and their wives and 'commit them to him in whose cause they were embarked'.

Returning to land, they were able to view the ship for a few miles till eventually it disappeared from view. Ward, for one, was deeply affected at having to say goodbye to Sutcliff and Fuller. Their affection for one another and for Ryland, and the friendship of these three men now with him, he saw as 'a three-fold cord binding him to his native land'.[73]

When Sutcliff and his two friends arrived back in the city, it would have been morning. Fuller had been away from home for most of the month, and thus only a few days later he told Sutcliff that he would head back to Kettering. He asked Sutcliff to spend a couple more weeks in the London area, collecting for the society. Sutcliff readily agreed, and stayed until 14 June at which time he had collected £1168.16.0![74] Most of the London pastors, following the advice of Samuel Stennett, had refused to support the society, but obviously there were many in the city whose hearts and purses were behind what Sutcliff, Fuller and their friends were about.

## Death of Samuel Pearce

That summer Pearce's condition worsened. Fuller, riding home to Kettering by himself, thought much about his dear friend 'wasting away at Plymouth'. Not a man given to tears, he rode mile after mile weeping and praying, 'Let the God of Samuel Pearce be my God.'[75]

When Fuller wrote to Sutcliff the following month he told him that Pearce was planning to return to Birmingham so as to die at home. After an exhausting journey that had to be done by stages, Pearce reached Birmingham on 19 July. The following day he wrote to Ryland, with whom he had spent some time in Bristol on his way home. Thanking him and his wife for the way that they had cared for him, he frankly admitted that he was 'getting weaker and weaker'. Nevertheless, he had no cause for complaint, for he was safe in Christ. 'Blessed be his dear name who shed his blood for me,' he added, 'he helps me to rejoice at times with joy unspeakable.' Now, he confessed, he saw 'the value of the religion of the cross. It is a religion for a dying sinner.' [76]

Pearce died on 10 October. Before the close of the following year Fuller had written an account of his friend's life and ministry. As Morris commented, it is 'one of the best specimens of Christian biography' in the church's history and one of the most useful works to come from Fuller's pen.[77] The final chapter of this memoir, in which Fuller sketched the leading features of Pearce's character, is revealing not only for what it tells us of Pearce, but also for the light that it sheds on the circle of friends around him. There is little doubt that Fuller has given us a true description of Pearce, but the aspects of his character and ministry to which he drew attention speak loudly of what he himself, and friends like Sutcliff, held dear.

The governing principle of Pearce's life, Fuller emphasized, was 'holy love'. Pearce was a lover of God: he delighted in adoring him and contemplating his glorious perfections. He was a lover of the gospel: 'Christ crucified was his darling theme,' from the start of his public ministry to the time of his death. Fuller pointed out that 'Pearce's affection to the doctrine of the cross was not merely, nor principally, on account of its being a system which secured his own safety.' If that had been the case, the root of his faith would have been self-love — a love of God for what he got from God. Fuller stressed that Pearce's love of the gospel was rooted in the fact that it upheld the righteousness of God. God saved men and women, not by winking at their sin, but by giving his dear Son to be punished in their stead. God thus revealed himself as 'the just God and the Saviour'. As we shall see, at the heart of Sutcliff's thinking about the cross was a similar emphasis. Pearce was a 'lover of good men'. He was a Dissenter and a convinced Baptist, Fuller noted, but 'His spirit was truly catholic; he loved all who loved the Lord Jesus Christ in sincerity.' Finally, Pearce was a lover of sinful men and women. It was this that motivated him 'to labour in season and out of season for the salvation of sinners'.[78] This love of God for who he is, this emphasis on the revelation of his holiness in the cross, this evangelical catholicity that embraces all who are in Christ and this passion to see sinners saved were leading features not only of the spirituality of Pearce, but also of that of Fuller and Sutcliff.

## Fund-raising in Scotland

Neither Fuller nor Sutcliff was at home when Pearce died. Eight days earlier Fuller had set off for Scotland for a month to collect funds for the Baptist Missionary Society. It would be the first of five trips north of the border. Sutcliff had agreed to go with Fuller on this first trip, and met him at Newcastle on 8 October. Brian Stanley has recently noted that 'Nowhere were Fuller's travels more profitable than in Scotland.'[79] Yet in a diary that Fuller kept of this first trip, he openly admitted that the prospect of going to Scotland daunted him. Unlike the fund-raising trips that he had taken in England, where he was moving mostly in Baptist circles with which he was more or less familiar, Scotland was unknown territory.[80] Moreover, the Baptists in Scotland were what is known as 'Scotch Baptists', with whom Fuller and his friends had important differences.

The early leaders of the Scotch Baptists, of whom Archibald McLean (1733-1812) was the most prominent, had come out of a movement of dissent headed by John Glas (1695-1773).[81] Glas and his followers had been expelled from the Church of Scotland in 1730 for pugnacious advocacy of the idea that churches should be composed of believers only. Glas further believed that the New Testament contained a detailed blueprint of church order. This conviction led him to advocate such things as footwashing, weekly celebration of the Lord's Supper and the plurality of elders in a local congregation.

Moreover, while Glas was a Calvinist, he had a peculiar understanding of the nature of faith. Faith, for him, was essentially intellectual consent, mere belief in the facts of the gospel. This 'simple, unfussy view of gospel truth' was widely disseminated throughout the British Isles by Glas's son-in-law, Robert Sandeman (1718-1771).[82] In fact, in England and Wales Glas's views were known by the name of 'Sandemanianism'. To Fuller and Sutcliff the Sandemanian view of faith tended to 'quench the religion of the heart'. Sutcliff asked a Scotch Baptist who was under the influence of Sandemanianism, whether his conception of faith allowed 'a proper and scriptural place for the exercise of the affections'. If not, Sutcliff could only conclude that it was a defective view by New Testament standards.[83]

Archibald McLean was a member of the Glasite congregation in Glasgow for a few years before becoming convinced of believer's baptism and becoming an elder in a Baptist work in Edinburgh that had been founded in 1765. His Glasite roots were manifest in his commitment to the distinctive features of Glasite congregational life as well as Glas's particular conception of the nature of faith. Although Fuller would later hammer McLean's view of faith in his *Strictures on Sandemanianism, in Twelve Letters to a Friend* (1810), he was not averse to accepting Scotch Baptist support for the Baptist Missionary Society.

From Newcastle Fuller and Sutcliff travelled to Edinburgh, where they met, among others, McLean, John Erskine, the evangelical Presbyterian with whom both Sutcliff and Ryland had long maintained a correspondence, and the Haldane brothers. Robert (1764-1842) and James Alexander Haldane (1768-1851) were extraordinary individuals whose family background was one of wealth and privilege and who had both experienced an evangelical conversion in the mid-1790s.[84] They subsequently devoted themselves and their money to tireless, itinerant evangelism, especially in the Scottish Highlands, and the planting of preaching centres. The first of these centres was in Edinburgh. Initially located in Little King Street in what was known as the Circus, a former theatre, after 1801 it relocated to a newly erected structure on Leith Walk and was named the Tabernacle.

Up till 1799, the Haldanes had worked within the Church of Scotland. Tensions had been building, though, as they frequently criticized Church of Scotland ministers who failed to support their evangelistic efforts. The definitive breach with the established church came in 1799 when James was ordained pastor of the Circus congregation and it was organized on congregational principles. In response, the General Assembly of the Church of Scotland denounced their evangelistic efforts as furthering 'religious and political anarchy'.[85] Sutcliff and Fuller, however, were impressed by the Haldanes. They 'appear to be excellent men', the latter wrote in his diary, 'free from the extravagance and nonsense which infect some of the Calvinistic Methodists in England; and yet trying to imbibe and communicate their zeal and affection'.[86]

From Edinburgh they went to Glasgow, where they both preached to another Haldane-supported congregation at the newly opened Tabernacle. Neither of them had ever preached to such a large gathering. Fuller estimated that he preached to around 4,000 people in the morning, and Sutcliff to even more in the afternoon. That evening the congregation was even larger. About 5,000 managed to crowd into the Tabernacle. 'It was said,' Fuller later jotted down in his diary, 'that many hundreds went away for want of room. It was the largest audience I ever saw.'[87] The generosity of these Scottish congregations matched their size. Fuller and Sutcliff returned home with no less than £900 which would have been tremendously encouraging for the two Englishmen.[88]

In the midst of all this encouragement there was one sorrowful note. While they were in Glasgow they learned of Pearce's death. That same day, 19 October, Fuller wrote to Pearce's widow, Sarah. Alluding to David's lament for his friend Jonathan, he said with obvious anguish of heart, 'O Jonathan, thou wast slain upon thy high places! I am distressed for thee, my brother Jonathan.'[89]

Fuller went back to Scotland four more times — in 1802, 1805, 1808 and 1813 — and was received with ever-increasing affection and generosity.[90] Although fund-raising was not at all to his liking, he turned out to be, as William Button remarked to Sutcliff, 'a prosperous beggar'.[91] Sutcliff returned to Scotland only once, in 1811, when Fuller was ill and Sutcliff was accompanied by Ryland.

## Growth at home

Since neither Fuller nor Sutcliff was available to speak at Pearce's funeral, the responsibility fell to Ryland. When he arrived back at

Bristol on 22 October he found a letter from John Saffery waiting for him. Saffery told Ryland of the zeal that many in Salisbury and Wiltshire were displaying in support of the society. Ryland rejoiced to hear this welcome news and prayed that 'the Lord [might] inflame that of others'. Ryland then informed Saffery of the fact that Fuller and Sutcliff were both in Scotland. 'They are so much out,' he said, 'that their people begin to complain. Others therefore must bestir themselves.'[92]

During the course of 1799 Sutcliff had been away from Olney for probably the better part of two months. Understandably, the Olney congregation was concerned. In later years, however, Sutcliff did not spend nearly as much time away from Olney collecting for the society. Nor did the cause in Olney appear to be appreciably weakened by his absence during 1799. In fact, the many years of sowing and nurture were now beginning to bear a rich harvest. It will be recalled that throughout the 1780s the membership of the church had hovered in the fifties. By 1793 it had reached sixty. Three years later it was up to seventy. By 1799 it had risen to seventy-nine. In the early 1800s it was around eighty, then shot up to 101 in 1808.[93]

Daniel Brunsdon gave a good picture of the congregation's state of health in a letter that he wrote to Ryland early in 1799: 'I think the church here is in a very flourishing state. There are a great many serious people in the congregation who have not joined. Some of them, I hope, will come forward soon. There seems to be a spirit of hearing (at least) in the villages around [Olney]; they pay very great attention and places are generally filled.'[94]

A second testimony, albeit much more personal, provides another revealing glimpse of the congregation at this time. It comes from the hand of a Hannah Smith (1779-1804), who sat under Sutcliff's ministry for three years before she was baptized on 21 March 1799 and became a member of the church. Three years later, on 29 April 1802, she married John Chamberlain and within a couple of weeks was on her way to India with him. Writing to Sutcliff shortly before her departure, she thanked him for the 'many acts of kindness' she had received from him. 'Under many of your sermons,' she further told him, 'I have been much impressed with the importance of religion, and have been so delighted with its beauty and excellence, that I have esteemed it the greatest happiness I could enjoy, to live to God and be devoted to his service.'[95]

Hannah seems to have been one of the 'many serious people' in the Olney congregation of whom Brunsdon spoke. For her, as presumably for many of the others, Christianity had come to be seen as pre-eminently a religion of wholehearted devotion to God. With such sentiments gripping the hearts of many who came to listen to Sutcliff's preaching, congregational life could not be anything but healthy.

# 12.
# Other friends, other ministries[1]

*'A spirit of strong personal attachment, as existing among two or three individual Christians only, when seeking the kingdom and glory of God, may illustrate the vast importance of its prevailing throughout the church: for oh how much of moral good has been achieved by only two or three individuals as the result of such attachment!'*

(Christopher Anderson).

John Chamberlain studied with Sutcliff until 1 July 1799, when he went to Bristol to receive further training. As we have seen in the previous chapter, he was eventually sent out to India in 1802 with his new wife, the fomer Hannah Smith. He went as a replacement for Grant and Brunsdon, both of whom had died — Grant of cholera and dysentery less than a month after his arrival in 1799, and Brunsdon on 3 July 1801.

In one of Brunsdon's last communications to Sutcliff he told the Olney pastor about the baptism of the society's first convert, Krishna Pal (1764-1822) on 28 December 1800. 'This is the first Hindu,' Brunsdon jubilantly informed Sutcliff, 'who has trampled on his caste for Christ's sake, and joined the standard of the cross... Thus you see, my dear brother, the Lord is doing great things for us and the poor Hindus.'[2] Brunsdon's account would have thrilled Sutcliff as he read it in his home in Olney. At last they were seeing answers to their prayers.

Within five months of writing these lines, however, Brunsdon was dead. He never saw the way that Krishna Pal matured and became, in Carey's words, 'a steady, zealous, well-informed, and...

eloquent minister of the gospel'.[3] Nor did he see the letter that Sutcliff, together with other members of the committee of the Baptist Missionary Society, wrote six weeks later, on 19 August to Krishna Pal and a few others who had been newly converted. Rejoicing in the fellowship that they had with them, though separated by many miles, they declared in words that reflected a deeply held conviction: 'The gospel breaks down every middle wall of partition, making us of one heart and of one soul. Neither distance of situation, difference of customs, language or colour, shall prevent a union of the spirit.'[4]

In India, one manifestation of this unity was the way that Carey, Ward and Marshman, three quite different individuals, were able to work together harmoniously for the advance of the gospel. As Carey informed Sutcliff, 'I have very great pleasure in all my brethren and sisters here. They are of the right sort; and perhaps as striking a proof as ever was exhibited of the possibility of persons of different tempers and abilities being able to live in one family in the exercise of Christian love. Probably there has seldom been a greater diversity in natural disposition and temper; yet this diversity serves for mutual correction. We really love one another.'[5]

Stephen Neill, a recognized authority on the history of missions, has observed that this partnership between Carey, Ward and Marshman is one 'to which there are few parallels in Christian history'.[6] The quality of the friendship between these three men takes on added lustre when it is recognized that it flourished in the midst of setbacks and challenges, and at times definite tension between them.

One of the first challenges that it faced was the arrival of Chamberlain. Despite his Christian ardour and facility with languages, Chamberlain became known as an extremely contentious individual, who absolutely refused to follow the advice of Carey and his co-workers. In a very revealing letter, William Ward, writing on behalf of his colleagues, told Chamberlain in 1807, 'We are led sometimes to wish that you were more entirely given up to God in your *temper.*' Ward went on to speak of the 'asperities' that still clung to Chamberlain's character, his egotism and his 'want of more real, vital religion'. On one occasion Chamberlain's temper got the better of him, and he physically struck a young Brahmin who was heckling him while he was preaching. To Sutcliff, Chamberlain's behaviour would have been a deep disappointment, for he firmly believed that division among Christian co-workers and a lack of 'cordial union' would inevitably hamper the advance of the gospel.[7] It is noteworthy, though, that Chamberlain cherished a deep respect for Sutcliff, of which there is no better proof than the fact that he named one of his sons John Sutcliff Chamberlain (1803-1804) and often addressed Sutcliff in his letters to him as 'my dear Father Sutcliff'.[8]

## More students for Sutcliff's seminary

The year that Chamberlain left for India, Sutcliff received four more students for his academy: Joshua Rowe (1781-1824), William Moore (1777-1844), Richard Mardon (1776-1812) and John Biss (1776-1807). All four of these men studied at Olney for nearly a year. Though each of them was married by the time they went out to India early in 1804, it would appear that only Biss was married during their time with Sutcliff. In fact, he and his wife Hannah had a baby girl, Mary, born to them during their stay at Olney. Apparently Jane Sutcliff, who never had a child of her own, was deeply attached to this little girl.[9]

In a letter that Mardon wrote to Ryland in February 1803 we see something of the spirit that reigned in Sutcliff's seminary: 'I trust we are all of one heart and one soul, and walk in love. Mr Sutcliff is very kind and affectionate. Our welfare, I believe, lies near his heart. He acts, I think, in every respect a father's part.' Mardon was but one of many that made mention of this characteristic kindness of Sutcliff. William Moore justified his addressing Sutcliff as 'my dear Father' in a letter that he wrote in 1805 because, he said, 'I can find no terms so congenial with my feelings as these. You have certainly manifested the tender affection of an indulgent parent towards me.'[10]

Close to forty years later, F. A. Cox, who had known Sutcliff well, vividly recalled another occasion when Sutcliff displayed this quality. Cox and Fuller had been the preachers at Walgrave one particular morning. When dinner was served at midday, it being customary for those who had preached to sit at the head of the table, Cox was invited to take his place beside Fuller. But Cox was young and timid and somewhat reluctant to sit next to such an august figure as Fuller, and so he indicated that he would sit further down the table. At this Fuller 'knitted his brows' and in a manner, Cox recalled, that 'no one would wish to tempt a second time', said to the young preacher, 'Come, sir, I like every man to take his proper place; what do you hesitate for?' After dinner, Sutcliff went up to Cox, tapped him on the shoulder and whispered, 'I want to speak to you.' They left the room and Sutcliff asked Cox whether or not it was true that his feelings had been hurt by Fuller's peremptory manner. Cox admitted it was. 'Well,' returned Sutcliff, 'don't be disconcerted or discouraged. It is his manner; he does not mean anything unkind; he really loves you. My brother Fuller serves me just the same: he speaks, on a sudden, perhaps very harshly; but I know him, and let it pass; and he will soon be as confiding and affectionate as ever.'[11] Such kindness and sensitivity were obvious assets for Sutcliff's role as a Christian teacher and were probably a further reason for his having been asked to open a seminary in Olney.

On Thursday, 1 December 1803 Rowe, Moore, Mardon and Biss were set apart as missionaries at a morning service in Broadmead Church, Bristol. Sutcliff and Fuller had ridden down by coach the previous Monday for the occasion. Fuller had not known whether he would be able to attend, since his wife was pregnant.[12]

Two years after the death of his first wife, Fuller had married Ann Coles (d. 1825), a daughter of the manse. At the time of her marriage to Fuller, her father, William Coles (1735-1809), was the pastor of the Baptist work in Maulden, Bedfordshire.[13] As it turned out, Ann gave birth to a daughter the week before the commissioning service and was well enough for Fuller to leave her for a few days. Due to Ann Fuller's condition, her husband was unable to oversee many of the last-minute details that needed to be done before the missionaries sailed. He thus had to entrust them to Sutcliff. For instance, on 14 November, Sutcliff had to ride up to London to make arrangements for each of the missionaries and their wives to get fitted for new clothes before their departure.[14]

At the actual service, Sutcliff also played a major role. After an opening prayer and after John Saffery, who was Joshua Rowe's pastor, had read Isaiah 6, Sutcliff asked each of the missionaries to give a brief account of their religious convictions and why they were going overseas. He then came down from the pulpit and, as the four men knelt down in front of the pulpit, prayed for them, while he and the other pastors who were present laid their hands on them. Fuller then gave an address, based on Genesis 28:3-4, which recounts Isaac's parting blessing of Jacob when he sent him to north-west Mesopotamia to find a wife.

Just over a month later, on 3 January 1804, the missionaries sailed from Bristol. Of these four missionaries, Biss was dead within a few years, and of the other three only Rowe did not cause Carey, Marshman and Ward 'considerable headache'.[15] Like Chamberlain, Mardon and Moore were quite unwilling to be told by their senior brethren at Serampore where they should labour in India and south-east Asia. The result was that their presence in India turned out to be more of a liability than an asset.

## William Robinson

By the summer of 1804 Sutcliff had another student in the person of William Robinson (1784-1853).[16] Robinson was a native of Olney whose family connections with the Olney Baptists went back three generations. His father, John Robinson (d. 1836), was a lacemaker, but he himself was apprenticed to a shoemaker at an early age. Raised under the preaching of Sutcliff, he was only a young boy when he became 'deeply sensible of his sinfulness' and fearful of dying outside of Christ. He dated his conversion from the summer of 1801. The following year, on 14 March, after John Chamberlain had preached in the morning, he was baptized in the Ouse by Sutcliff and became a member of the church.

Looking back on this period of his life many years later, Robinson counted his membership in the Olney church as one of the highest privileges of his life. 'It is a great advantage to have such friends as those at Olney,' he wrote to a brother still living in Olney. 'I often think my Olney friends were the best I ever met with, and the time that I spent among them, the happiest period of my life.'

Within two years of joining the church, Robinson expressed to Sutcliff a desire to be a missionary. Sutcliff was quick to point out to him the difficulties of such a calling, and advised him to get hold of a copy of David Brainerd's life and to read it. By the early nineteenth century Jonathan Edwards' life of the American missionary had become an immensely influential book. Judging from the number of editions and reprints that it went through during this period of time, it was the most popular of the works written by the New England divine.[17] To Carey, the book was 'almost a second Bible', and Ryland was so impressed by Brainerd's life that he named one of his sons David Brainerd Ryland.[18] Sutcliff presumably recommended it to Robinson's perusal, because the Olney pastor saw Brainerd's example of prayer and self-denial, unremitting labour and endurance as instructive for what faced the would-be missionary.

Robinson was not daunted, however. On 23 February and again on 22 March 1804, Sutcliff asked him to preach before the congregation. After the latter date, he was given the sanction of the church to preach in the villages surrounding Olney, and was subsequently the means of gathering together a small church in Astwood, a village that lies on the road from Newport Pagnell to Bedford.[19]

The Baptist Missionary Society formally placed Robinson under Sutcliff's tutelage in June 1804. In the thirteen months that he studied with Sutcliff, he found the Olney pastor to be, in his own words, 'a wise and judicious tutor, and a faithful and affectionate friend'. Robinson's course of study appears to have included Latin in addition to the other subjects that Sutcliff taught him.[20] Sutcliff also gave him plenty of opportunities to preach, either at Olney or in surrounding villages.[21]

One area in which he later wished Sutcliff had given him some instruction was history. For a person to be 'well acquainted with men and things', he wrote to Sutcliff in 1807, 'he must have a knowledge of history,' at least to a moderate extent. While at Olney, Sutcliff, reflecting his own interests and priorities, had urged upon Robinson 'the study of the prophecies'. Yet, it appeared to Robinson that 'The knowledge of history is a necessary prerequisite to this study.'[22] Robinson's implicit criticism of Sutcliff at this point identifies the leading weakness of the 'parsonage seminary' model of theological education: the inability of one man, no matter how gifted, to possess the expertise needed in all of the main areas of theological study.[23]

## Christopher Anderson

Studying with Sutcliff for part of the time that Robinson was in the Olney seminary was the Scottish Baptist Christopher Anderson.[24] Anderson had been born in Edinburgh and taken as a child to a congregation of evangelical Dissenters known as the Old Scots Independents. The men who pastored amongst this small group of believers were worthy men, but largely uneducated and unable to retain or attract those who had enquiring minds like Anderson. One by one his older brothers had left this congregation in search of something more satisfying, and Anderson was not slow to follow their example when he reached his teen years. He ended up at the Circus, where he was strongly attracted to the preaching of James Alexander Haldane. Here he was converted in the summer of 1799 and subsequently became a member.

It was not long after Anderson's conversion that Fuller and Sutcliff made their first trip to Scotland. The cause of the Baptist Missionary Society, and Fuller in particular, left an indelible impression on the young believer's mind and heart. He longed, he wrote on 20 August 1801 in a private diary, 'to go out and join Messrs Carey and Thomas in their labours in the East Indies'. By this time he had come to Baptist convictions, had been baptized, and as a result had been excluded from the Circus. It is ironical to note that by 1808 the Haldanes had also come to similar convictions.

Anderson and a few others of like sentiments tried to start a Baptist fellowship modelled on the Baptist churches south of the border. He specifically did not attempt to join the Scotch Baptists. Though he honoured them, he felt they were lacking in evangelistic zeal and unduly preoccupied with ecclesiological minutiae. Anderson's new venture failed, however, and he eventually associated himself with a Baptist work in Glasgow pastored by the Glaswegian James Lister.

During Fuller's second trip to Scotland in 1802, Anderson had an opportunity to meet him for about half an hour. Anderson told Fuller of his desire to serve with Carey and Thomas in India. Fuller's response is not recorded, but it appears to have been encouraging, since further journal entries in Anderson's diary continue to speak of this desire to go to India as a missionary. Correspondence with Fuller in 1804 and 1805 led to Fuller recommending that Anderson study for a while with Sutcliff at Olney. When he spoke to Sutcliff about it, the latter replied, 'Let him [i.e. Anderson] come. We will make him as happy as we can. If his mind be in it we may employ him occasionally in preaching Christ in the villages. When he has been here a while both he and we may better understand the path of future duty.'[25]

Of course, neither Sutcliff nor Fuller had any idea of Anderson's academic attainments. But even if it turned out that he had no need of instruction in this area, there were 'various other things', Fuller told Anderson, in which Sutcliff 'may be of use to you'. Fuller did not specify what these 'other things' were. Presumably what he had in mind were some of the other essentials of pastoral ministry: the dynamics of preaching and evangelism, personal spirituality and one's walk with God.

Therefore, in May 1805 Anderson sailed from Leith for London. After a short stay in the metropolis, where he met John Newton and Rowland Hill, he made his way down to Olney, arriving there in the middle of June. As it turned out, he spent only four and a half months with Sutcliff before going to study with Ryland at Bristol for close to eight months. We possess a good sketch of Anderson's time in Olney, since he kept a diary of his experiences there.[26] Though the entries are brief and succinct, a number of them are very illuminating.

Anderson was given numerous opportunities to preach during his time with Sutcliff: at Lavendon and Clifton Reynes, where Sutcliff had established preaching centres; for Fuller at Kettering; at Castle Hill in Northampton, where Philip Doddridge had once pastored. On one occasion he preached at Harrold, a village six miles or so north-east of Olney. At that time, according to Anderson, there were about a thousand inhabitants in the village and surrounding countryside. There was a Baptist work in the village, but the pastor was a High Calvinist, who strongly disapproved of 'calls to the unconverted', and on this account would not let men like Sutcliff or Fuller enter his pulpit.[27]

Anderson also occasionally preached for Sutcliff at Olney. On Friday, 6 October, for example, he preached at the evening service from 2 Peter 1:5 after Sutcliff had baptized eight young women in the slowly flowing Ouse, one of whom, Martha Boon, was among those brought in through the ministry at Lavendon.[28] Anderson noted in his diary that the service was attended by a 'crowded house', which would have meant 700 or more people. On his last Sunday at Olney, 17 October, he again preached for Sutcliff at all three services — morning, afternoon and evening. In the evening, he noted, it was 'to a full and very attentive house'.

A friendship was struck up with William Wilson, who regaled Anderson with stories of Cowper, while giving him guided tours of sites associated with the evangelical poet. Sutcliff's ongoing warmth towards fellow evangelicals, no matter what their church connection, is also evident in one entry from Anderson's diary, that of 2 July. John Ryland and his wife had called on the Sutcliffs and had been asked to stay for dinner. Along with Robinson and Anderson, Sutcliff also decided to invite the vicar of the parish church, Christopher Stephenson, and his curate to dinner that evening. Afterwards, Anderson noted in his diary, 'All went to meeting' to hear Ryland preach a sermon on Isaiah 49:7.

Anderson also gives us a glimpse of Sutcliff the man. In one of his letters to his family back home in Scotland, he mentions that Sutcliff 'is very much afflicted with a nervous affection. His hand shakes so violently, that it is a great burden to him to write a few words.'[29] Sutcliff's right hand had now deteriorated to the point where he could hardly write. To a man who spent much of his day absorbed in the printed word this must have been agony. One senses his inner pain in a statement that he made in one of his letters to Joshua Rowe the year after Anderson had left Olney. 'If I could write freely,' he told Rowe early in 1806, 'I would pour out my heart on sheets of paper.' By 1808, Sutcliff had to rely upon his students to help him with extensive pieces of writing.[30]

Despite the fact that Anderson was with Sutcliff for only a brief period of time the two men became quite close. Years later, in a letter that Anderson wrote to Carey, he mentioned that he had had 'the happiness of being the bosom friend both of Sutcliff and Fuller', and due to Pearce's early death, he had experienced 'a much larger share of their friendship than [he] could otherwise have expected'.[31] The root of this friendship lay in the time that Sutcliff and Anderson spent together in the Sutcliffs' home after dinner, when Sutcliff's conversation and anecdotes about his friends and acquaintances used to, in Anderson's words, 'delightfully ... beguile the evening'.[32] As has been true in every age, a friendship can only flourish when this essential prerequisite for its existence — time spent together — is present.[33]

By the time that Anderson came to leave Olney at the end of October, he had come to the decision, with the advice of Fuller and presumably Sutcliff, to return to a pastorate in Scotland. His constitution was simply not strong enough for him to go to India. Before he returned to Scotland, however, he spent a full academic year of study at Bristol.

He saw Sutcliff again in March of the following year, 1806, when William Robinson was set apart for service in India. The service was held on 12 March in New Road Chapel, Oxford, where James Hinton was the pastor. Sutcliff had a similar role in the service as at the commissioning of Rowe, Moore, Mardon and Biss. He gave a brief introductory discourse as to the meaning of what they were about, he received a short account of the theological convictions of Robinson and the other missionary being sent out with him, James Chater (d. 1829), as well as their reasons for going overseas, and he led in prayer as hands were laid on them. Ryland then addressed the two men from Acts 26:17-18, which records the commission given to Paul by the risen Christ to open the eyes of the Gentiles and 'turn them from darkness to light, and from the power of Satan unto God'. Following Ryland's address there was a sermon by Fuller, based on 2 Chronicles 20:20. The service concluded with J. Webster Morris praying. In the evening there was another service at which Sutcliff preached. The following month Robinson and Chater sailed for India.[34]

Anderson left Bristol in mid-June, spent a couple of weeks in London, then headed north to Scotland. On the way he stopped at Olney to visit Sutcliff. After his arrival in London he had written to Sutcliff to tell him that he hoped to be in Olney for Sunday, 6 July.[35] He left London on the Saturday and arrived in Olney the same day at four p.m. Sutcliff had asked him to preach the following day at all three services, which he did gladly. In his diary he noted that Sutcliff now had six students studying with him: Thomas Coles, John Smith, John (?) George, David Davies, George Dobney and John Richards.[36] None of these men went on to become missionaries, and it is evident that from 1806 onwards Sutcliff also began to train men for pastoral ministry in Great Britain. He had already had one such individual back in 1800, William Brown (1768-1818) from Isleham, Cambridgeshire, who had studied with Sutcliff for about eighteen months and in 1803 became the pastor of the Baptist church in Keysoe, Bedfordshire.[37] Then there was Anderson himself, though he had come to Sutcliff expecting to go to India. In fact, after 1806 most of the men whom Sutcliff trained went into pastorates in Britain.[38]

Anderson reached Edinburgh on 18 August. His subsequent ministry there, and indeed throughout the whole of Scotland, was of immense importance. In addition to the church that he gathered together in Edinburgh, which is now known as Charlotte Chapel and which eventually grew until there were 500 hearers at an average service, he initiated the Edinburgh Gaelic School Society (1810), played an important part in the founding of the Edinburgh Bible

Society in 1809 and was involved in a host of other voluntary societies. Moreover, for many years he would spend his summers in the Highlands on extensive preaching tours, and eventually formed an itinerant preaching society aimed specifically at reaching its inhabitants with the gospel and in such a way that their distinct Celtic culture survived.[39]

His close friendship with Fuller and Sutcliff also led to the opening of a correspondence with the Serampore Trio. This in turn opened the way for face-to-face meetings between Anderson and Ward in 1820, and Anderson and Marshman in 1826-1827, and the establishment of a firm friendship between Anderson and the missionaries at Serampore. This friendship would be of great significance when Fuller and Sutcliff had passed from the scene and tensions developed to the point where there was a rupture between the missionaries at Serampore and the Baptist Missionary Society in 1828. Anderson was to play a similar role with the Serampore Mission to the one Fuller had undertaken for so many years with regard to the nascent Baptist Missionary Society.[40] Especially important was Anderson's realization that at the heart of the Baptist Missionary Society in its early years had been a 'spirit of strong personal attachment between its leading individuals in England and those in India, and that this spirit was vital to the success of any entire missionary enterprise'.[41] This conviction undoubtedly had some of its roots in the time that Anderson had spent with Sutcliff. For there in Olney he had seen what he later described as 'the very strong affection which existed between ... Sutcliff and Fuller,' two of the key figures in the Society.[42]

## John Webster Morris

One name that has come up a number of times already in this story of Sutcliff's life is that of John Webster Morris, and since he was very close at one time to not only Sutcliff, but also Fuller and Ryland, something should be said about him.[43] Morris began his Christian life as a member of the Baptist cause in Worstead, Norfolk. Its pastor, Edward Trivett (1712-1792), had a thriving ministry over the space of forty years, baptizing some 390 and seeing eleven members of the church, including Morris, called into pastoral ministry. Morris had been trained as a printer, but around the age of twenty he began to manifest gifts that led the Worstead Church on 13 August 1784 to call him as a preacher of the gospel. The following year he settled at Clipston, where he would pastor the Baptist church till 1803.

During these years Morris was at the side of Sutcliff, Fuller, Ryland and Carey as they were led step by step to form the Baptist Missionary Society. He shared their vision and entered fully into all of the key decisions that were made. In the minds of many at the time, his name was integrally linked with theirs. In a letter that Carey wrote to Morris late in 1797, he told the Clipston pastor: 'Next to seeing your face, a letter from you is one of my greatest gratifications. I see the handwriting, and read the heart of my friend; nor can the distance of one fourth of the globe prevent a union of hearts.' And Ward, just prior to his first meeting with Carey after he had landed in India in 1799 noted, 'I felt very unusual sensations as I drew near to the house [i.e. Carey's house]. So near to brother Carey, after a voyage of 16,000 miles, and a tedious passage up the river...! What an interesting situation. If Fuller, or Morris, or Ryland, or Sutcliff had been here! How would they have felt!'[44]

In the late 1790s Fuller observed in a letter to Joseph Kinghorn, the minister of St Mary's Baptist Church in Norwich, that he and his friends had found 'a foreign mission to resemble a good foreign trade; it increaseth riches at home'. We have seen that this was true of Sutcliff's congregation, which experienced slow but steady growth throughout the last decade of the eighteenth century and the first of the following century. More generally we get a glimpse of what was happening from some remarks made by Fuller in a letter to John Saffery. Writing in mid-1798, Fuller told Saffery: 'Many of our places of worship are too small. Some whole villages nearly are crowding to hear the gospel.'[45] Now Fuller's observation to Kinghorn was especially true of the Clipston congregation. In 1792 Morris and the leaders of the church had noted in their annual letter to the Northamptonshire Association that Sutcliff's reprint of Jonathan Edwards' *Humble Attempt* had been a tremendous encouragement to them in the whole matter of praying for revival. It gave them hope, they said, that 'The day is not far distant when God shall build up Zion and appear in his glory.'[46] A foretaste of that day was granted a few years later as Morris and the leaders in the church became increasingly burdened for the unconverted in their village and surrounding district.

The congregation decided to set aside 25 February 1795 in particular for fasting and prayer for revival in their locality. Soon after a wave of revival swept through the village. The size of the weekly congregation dramatically increased and it was with difficulty that space could be found in the meeting-house to accommodate all who wanted to come and worship. Five years later, in the final year of the century, there was another profound movement of the Spirit. A young man named John Gulliver (1778-1832) was checked in a career of spiritual indifference and apathy by his mother's death and subsequently converted. Unable to contain the fire that now burnt in his heart, he began to share his faith with his friends and neighbours. Throughout the village young people's prayer meetings were started, some as early as four o'clock in the morning.[47] When Morris wrote to Sutcliff at the end of May that year, he stated that 'Near 30 young people have been awakened within a week or two. Scarce a day passes but some are, or appear to be, converted to God!' A month later Morris told Sutcliff that the ardour of his congregation had not diminished one whit and there were now some fifty individuals, the majority of them between the ages of ten and twenty, seeking to find peace with God.[48]

In the middle of this revival at Clipston, Sutcliff drew up a circular letter for the Northamptonshire Association, meeting in Nottingham that year from 3-5 June. The letter dealt with the 'qualifications necessary to an admission into a Christian church'. It is evident from the beginning of the letter that Sutcliff is not dealing with a merely theoretical issue. The churches in the association were definitely receiving an influx of new members, which Sutcliff described as 'a pleasing business'. Hopeful that this influx might be the sign of 'still greater blessings in reserve', Sutcliff earnestly recommended 'a spirit of extraordinary prayer, both to the churches and to individuals, and this not only at our monthly prayer-meetings, but on other occasions. The Lord has promised to take away the heart of stone and to give a heart of flesh (see Ezekiel 36:2ff), but for this he hath said he will be "inquired of by the house of Israel to do it for them" (Ezekiel 36:37).'[49] Sutcliff's use here of Ezekiel 36:37 to emphasize the importance of pleading with God to pour out his Holy Spirit in revival recalls the Prayer Call of 1784, where this same text was used to encourage corporate prayer.

At the beginning of August, Sutcliff received a letter from Thomas King, one of the deacons at Cannon Street Baptist Church in Birmingham, in which King rejoiced in what he had heard about the Clipston revival. 'God grant,' he prayed, that 'it may go from church to church until it gets to every heart.'[50] King's prayer was granted, but not exactly in the way that either he or Sutcliff expected. According to the London Baptist minister John Rippon, in 1794 there were 326 Calvinistic Baptist churches in England and fifty-six in Wales, more than double the number which were in existence forty years previously.[51] In 1798, when Rippon drew up another list, there were 361 churches in England and eighty-four in Wales. Commenting on these statistics, Rippon stated, 'It is said, that more of our meeting-houses have been enlarged within the last five years, and more built within the last fifteen, than had been built and enlarged for thirty years before.'[52] This comment was no exaggeration. While there was steady growth throughout the last forty years or so of the eighteenth century, in the final decade of that century the denomination saw a rapid expansion that continued unabated into the early decades of the following century.[53] In other words, while Sutcliff and men like Thomas King were looking for Spirit-imparted revival to take place in the sudden conversion of significant numbers of individuals, as had happened on both sides of the Atlantic in the mid-eighteenth century, and as was happening at Clipston in 1800, the Spirit of God was at work in their midst, converting the lost in a quieter and less dramatic way.

During his time at Clipston Morris helped to support himself through a printing-press that he opened. Soon he was printing the circular letters of the Northamptonshire Association and the *Periodical Accounts* of the Baptist Missionary Society, as well as sermons and tracts by his friends. A few weeks before the revival at Clipston he told Sutcliff that he was thinking of starting a journal, of which he would be the editor, proprietor and printer! To ensure that it would sell, he was hoping to enlist Fuller's talents as a regular contributor to the journal. By this time, Fuller was increasingly known and respected in British evangelical circles as a leading theologian. But, Morris told Sutcliff, he had one main difficulty, namely, securing Fuller's agreement to contribute to the new venture. As he saw it, there were two main hurdles to overcome in getting Fuller to agree to support his venture. First, Fuller regularly wrote for *The Evangelical Magazine*, an inter-denominational periodical that had been established in 1793 and was the most widely circulated journal of its kind in England. Fuller not only wrote for this journal, but his name regularly appeared on its front cover as one of its main supporters. Second, Fuller 'has as much on his hands as he can well get through with'. Nevertheless, Morris was sure that if Sutcliff agreed to support his venture, 'Brother Fuller will follow of course.'[54] This remark by Morris says much about the way that Fuller relied on Sutcliff's advice.

Sutcliff cautioned Morris about getting himself in 'pecuniary difficulties' that could arise if the magazine failed to sell. Morris assured his friend that if he sold 300 copies per month he would be able to break even. In fact, he was optimistic that the magazine could earn him £100 a year.[55] As for a title, Morris came up with *The Biblical Magazine*. He had considered *The Baptist Magazine*, but the younger Robert Hall and John Ryland objected to this title 'as a sectarian appellation'.[56] The following year *The Biblical Magazine* was launched. In its first year of publication it appeared bi-monthly; in 1802 Morris began to issue it every month. Along with sermons, essays and notes on biblical and theological subjects, there was a good sprinkling of anecdotes, news items, obituaries and poetry. In 1804 it merged with the *Theological Magazine and Review*, a Congregationalist journal established in 1801, to become the *Theological and Biblical Magazine*.[57]

Sutcliff appears to have been able to persuade Fuller to contribute a few fugitive pieces to Morris's publication, and he himself was recruited as a contributor and editor. With his problem with his right hand, both of these tasks proved to be difficult indeed for the Olney pastor. On occasion he got his students to help him, but if they were all occupied, he had no alternative but to do the best he could.[58] Among the pieces that he did contribute to Morris's periodical was a translation of *The Epistle to Diognetus,* a second-century apology for the Christian faith which contains a number of sublime passages. With its strong Pauline overtones, it had a favoured place in the hearts of eighteenth- and nineteenth-century evangelicals. In common with the patristic scholarship of the day, Sutcliff wrongly believed that this epistle came from the hand of Justin Martyr (*c.* 100 - *c.* 165). Neither its author nor its exact provenance is known.[59]

The growth in the Clipston congregation — now averaging 700-800 a service — meant that the meeting-house needed to be enlarged. Therefore, in August 1802 Morris had an architect from Coventry come and inspect the Clipston meeting-house to see if an extension was feasible. Instead, the architect suggested that the meeting-house be torn down and a new one erected. The congregation were not prepared to countenance such a step, and Morris felt he had no alternative but to leave.[60] Sutcliff advised him to think it over and not to act rashly. Morris consequently delayed tendering his resignation, but he told Sutcliff that there was no way he would preach in the meeting-house another summer. The close quarters of the meeting-house made it quite uncomfortable in warm weather, and Morris felt that his health was not good enough to preach in such a suffocating environment. That October, when two persons fainted in the gallery during a service and several others had to go and stand at the door for air, Morris determined that he would leave unless a new meeting-house was built.[61] The congregation stood their ground and insisted on building an extension onto the existing meeting-house. Much to his own regret and that of his congregation Morris resigned in March 1803 and went to Dunstable in Bedfordshire. Fuller, in particular, had tried to dissuade him from leaving, but with no success. Morris had only been gone a few months when the congregation came to the realization that their former pastor had been right, and they had to tear down the old meeting-house and erect a new one![62]

Morris was at Dunstable for six years. For him, it proved to be a place of both bane and blessing In the autumn of 1805 his wife was taken seriously ill and within a couple of weeks was dead. Her death on Wednesday, 18 September, was preceded by violent convulsions. Morris told Sutcliff, 'She died not only like a saint, but like a martyr!' Thomas Blundel preached her funeral sermon that Sunday, while Christopher Anderson supplied for Blundel at Luton.[63] The following year Morris told Sutcliff that he would like to get married again, but he had no opportunities of meeting a suitable partner. Did Sutcliff know of anyone who might be right for him? If he did, Morris wrote, 'Do have the goodness to give me a line in confidence; I should be unspeakably obliged.' By 1808 Morris had found a second wife. Whether Sutcliff had played matchmaker, though, we do not know![64]

Then there were numerous opportunities for evangelism in the countryside surrounding Dunstable. 'Doors are open all around us [for] preaching,' he told Sutcliff in November 1806, 'and we have nobody to do it.' One village where there was a tremendous response to the gospel was Hockliffe, four miles north-west of Dunstable. A barn, which had been purchased and renovated for congregational worship and preaching, had been opened the previous summer, and for the next few years it was 'much crowded'. Although it was a fair distance from Olney, a number of Sutcliff's students regularly walked the twenty miles or so to preach there.[65] For these students it was, as Morris remarked on one occasion to Sutcliff, 'an instance of self-denial that few would undertake but for the love of Jesus'.[66]

Suddenly, though, in the first quarter of 1809, all of Morris's hopes and projects were dashed to the ground as he had to declare bankruptcy. Sutcliff had been right to caution him about getting involved in printing a magazine. He had lost a considerable amount of money in it, especially after its merger with the Congregationalist *Theological Magazine and Review.* He had also lost money on an edition of Samuel Hopkins' *Memoirs of Miss Susanna Anthony,* for which Sutcliff, along with Fuller and Ryland, had written a preface in 1802. Ever the optimist, Morris told Sutcliff that these memoirs of a member of Hopkins' Rhode Island congregation would sell in time. As the book became more scarce it would become more valuable. A letter of Fuller to Ward that July gives us some of the details of Morris's failure. He had invested close to £1,000 into his printing business, while telling his friends that he was getting back £300 to £400 a year. But the truth of the matter was that his profits were nowhere near his expenditures and he was digging himself deeper and deeper into debt. 'Poor Morris!,' Fuller remarked, 'I am grieved for him; but he is ruined. His pride and extravagance since he has been at Dunstable is beyond anything.'[67]

When Fuller said that Morris was ruined, he was not only thinking of his financial situation, but also of his status as a minister of the gospel. True to their Reformed heritage, the eighteenth-century Calvinistic Baptists were firmly convinced that one of the marks of a genuine church is that it upholds regular and orderly discipline. And among the offences they regarded as meriting the disciplinary action of the church was bankruptcy. In their thinking, insolvency was a breach of the apostle Paul's explicit command to 'Owe no man anything' (Romans 13:8) and was evidence that business had not been conducted with due regard for others or for one's Christian witness in the world. While the Baptist community recognized that there were some instances of bankruptcy where the person concerned was not to blame, such instances were considered rare. 'Not one instance out of ten, or perhaps twenty ... can be entirely exonerated from blame and criminality,' wrote the Welsh Baptist Micah Thomas (1778-1853) in 1821.[68]

With regard to discipline, Philip Doddridge, although a Congregationalist, spoke for the Baptists too when he wrote on behalf of his own congregation in 1741: 'We do hereby declare that if any person in stated communion with us shall become a bankrupt, or as it is commonly expressed fail in the world, he must expect to be cut off from our body, unless he do within two months give to the church by the elders in word or writing, such an account of his affairs as shall convince us that his fall was owing not to his own sin or folly but to the afflicting hand of God upon him. In which case, far from adding affliction to the afflicted, we hope that as God shall enable us we shall be ready to vindicate, comfort and assist him as his friends and brethren in Christ.'[69]

Disgraced, Morris had to leave his charge at Dunstable and he never again pastored a church for any length of time. Although his own folly and extravagance had ruined him he was not willing to take responsibility for his failure. At the time of his bankruptcy, he did ask Sutcliff to pity his misfortune and forgive his errors.[70] But as time went on he became impenitent. He blamed his failure on others and refused to confess that he was at fault. Fuller had an opportunity to meet with him in December 1811. He also sent a note to him, asking him if he was willing to confess his sin and the dishonour that he had brought upon God's name. If so, Fuller, who knew himself also to be a sinner 'deeply indebted to mercy', would have no hesitation in embracing him and 'the days of past friendship and affection' would be revived. Morris, however, proudly refused to acknowledge his sin and the ties between him and Fuller, Sutcliff and Ryland were severed.[71] What Fuller, and Sutcliff for that matter, considered reprehensible in Morris's conduct was obviously not the bankruptcy so much as the impenitence. The end of their friendship with Morris could only have caused Sutcliff much sadness, but it would also have prompted reflection on his own need for God's grace to keep him from falling.

## A response to the teaching of Paine

Some indication of the respect that Sutcliff had come to enjoy among his fellow Baptists may be seen in the fact that in the dozen years from 1797 to 1808, the Olney pastor was asked to preach at the annual assembly of the Northamptonshire Association on five different occasions and to draw up its circular letter four times. Only Andrew Fuller played a more prominent role, preaching at no less than ten of the annual assemblies during these years and drawing up the circular letter on four distinct occasions.

The circular letter that Sutcliff wrote in 1797 was entitled *The Divinity of the Christian Religion Considered and Proved* and was aimed at displaying the divinely inspired nature of the Scriptures. A few years prior to its appearance, Thomas Paine (1737-1809) had published *The Age of Reason* (1794, 1795). Paine was a warm advocate and brilliant popularizer of a variety of radical causes: the American and French Revolutions, the abolition of slavery, and Deism. Paine had been raised a Quaker, but by the time that he came to write *The Age of Reason* his faith had been reduced to belief in 'one God and no more' and a hope for 'happiness beyond this life'. He refused to accept the authority of any credal document, indeed anything beyond his own reason. 'My mind,' he said at one point in *The Age of Reason*, 'is my own church.'[72]

With such views it is not surprising that Paine adamantly opposed the idea of special revelation. Due to the fact that human language is regularly in a state of flux and because of the variety of problems presented by translation from one language into another, Paine asserted that special revelation in a written form was simply impossible. Yet he was confident that God had revealed himself and that this divine revelation could be found in nature. In essence, creation was his Bible. All 'other Bibles and Testaments' were thus branded as 'forgeries'. In the created realm he read, in God's very own handwriting, 'the certainty of his existence and the immutability of his power'. All that can be known about God must therefore be obtained through the exercise of human reason in the examination of God's handiwork.[73] Bolstering Paine's confidence in human reason was the world-view of Newtonian science, which, with its emphasis on rational enquiry, lay at the heart of eighteenth-century intellectual life.

Paine's broadside against the scriptural foundations of Christianity did not go unanswered. There were some thirty rejoinders, including Andrew Fuller's *The Gospel Its Own Witness* (1799), that saw the light of day before 1800.[74] Fuller's first response had come at the 1796 annual assembly of the Northamptonshire Association when he preached on Hebrews 6:12-14. Not afraid to wrestle with theological issues in the pulpit, Fuller declared near the end of his sermon: 'The present age seems to be an age of trial. Not only is the gospel corrupted by those who bear the Christian name, but, of late, you well know, it has been openly assailed. The most direct and daring opposition has been made to the very name of Christianity. I am not going to alarm you with any idea that the church is in danger; no, my brethren, the church of which we, I trust, are members, and of which Christ, and Christ alone, is the head, is not in danger; it is built upon a rock, and the gates of hell shall not prevail against it.... Nevertheless, it becomes us to feel for the souls of men, especially for the rising generation; and to warn even good men that they be not unarmed in the evil day.'[75]

Many who heard Fuller that day would have had little difficulty in identifying the perpetrator and nature of this open assault on the Christian faith: Paine and his *Age of Reason*. Though Fuller had no fears for the ultimate safety of the church, he was concerned about the impact of Paine's book on men and women of his day, and especially for the young, 'the rising generation'. It is hardly fortuitous that the very next year, when Sutcliff was asked to draw up the circular letter for the association, he focused his readers' thoughts on the divine nature of God's Word. Since somewhere between 1,500 and 2,000 copies of this letter were printed and distributed far and wide throughout the churches of the association, it is obvious that Fuller and Sutcliff were seeking to repel Paine's attack against Christianity on the very field of battle which the latter had chosen, namely, the mind of the common man and woman.

Sutcliff argued first for the possibility of divine revelation, and then gave five reasons why he believed the Scriptures were such a revelation: the character of the writers of Scripture — they 'appear to be fair, open, ingenuous, and honest men'; the conformity of the contents of God's Word with the nature and attributes of God — the Scriptures are 'worthy of God'; the way in which the Scriptures meet the deepest needs of human beings; the peculiar care with which God has favoured the Bible over the centuries — especially, Sutcliff emphasized, 'at the Reformation', when 'God, as it were, raised it from the dead'; and the various miracles attested in the Scriptures. 'Surely,' Sutcliff wrote, 'none can reject Christianity, attended with such proofs, so plain, so full, so numerous.' Those who did, he could only conclude, did so out of either 'culpable inattention' or 'the most criminal aversion'.[76] If Sutcliff's reasoning appears somewhat facile, the nature of his audience must be borne in mind. He was not seeking to convince theologians, but to provide the ordinary believers in the churches of the association with some protection against the missiles being hurled at them by popularizing Deists like Paine.

## Principles of church fellowship

The three other circular letters that Sutcliff wrote for the Northamptonshire Association in these years dealt with issues relating to the nature of the church and its ordinances: *Qualifications for Church Fellowship* (1800), *The Ordinance of the Lord's Supper considered* (1803), and *On obedience to Positive Institutions* (1808). A close examination of the first two of these letters will reveal some of the ways in which Sutcliff was seeking to preserve his Calvinistic Baptist heritage in a changing environment and in the process modifying it.

At the beginning of *Qualifications for Church Fellowship* Sutcliff noted what we have already observed earlier in this chapter: like their sister churches in the rest of the nation, the Baptist churches in the Northamptonshire Association on the whole were experiencing steady growth. This receiving of new members, Sutcliff remarked, was indeed 'a pleasing business', but one that required 'caution, lest you be crowded with characters, who, instead of being a blessing among you, will be the bane of your societies' and 'tenderness, lest contrary to our Lord's example you break the bruised reed, or discourage the weaker part of his sincere disciples'.

Caution especially was needed, for, as the Olney pastor went on to note, 'many, once large and flourishing churches' were in ruins because of 'a want of due attention to the character of such as they admitted into their communion'. The Holy Spirit was grieved and he withdrew 'his divine influences from [their] sacred ordinances'.[77] Sutcliff did not specify the particular churches he had in mind. Most likely it was those Nonconformist congregations which, during the course of the eighteenth century, had succumbed to either Arianism or Socinianism.

Who, then, should be received into the membership of a local church? Although Sutcliff tackled this question from both the vantage-point of the prospective member and that of the congregation, the essence of his response in both cases was the classical

Nonconformist answer: visible saints. For Sutcliff, as for his seventeenth- and eighteenth-century forebears, religion was a matter of private conscience rather than public order and the church a fellowship of believers rather than an army of conscripted men and women.[78] In Sutcliff's words, 'A Christian society ... is styled "a spiritual house, a holy priesthood," "a holy temple," "a habitation for God, through the Spirit" (1 Peter 2:5; Ephesians 2:21-22)... Those who are proper characters to be received into communion with a Christian church should be spiritual men ... men disposed to seek the good of the interest of Christ in general and of that society to which they unite in particular, men devoted to God, men who hold fast the form of sound words, and who in their spirit and walk, adorn the doctrine of God our Saviour.'[79]

Or, as he put it more plainly at the ordination of Thomas Morgan (1776-1857) as pastor of Cannon Street Baptist Church in 1802, 'Men are not born Christians. They are made such by the Holy Spirit. They are not members of a Christian church by natural birth, but become such by their own act and deed.'[80]

Alongside this perspective on the nature of the local church as a gathering of visible saints, Sutcliff's theological forebears had also defined the local church in terms of the signs identified by the Calvinist tradition as being indicative of a genuine church of Christ. In the traditional Calvinist understanding, the church is present where the Word of God is faithfully preached, the sacraments of baptism and the Lord's Supper administered and discipline upheld. Thus the earliest Calvinistic Baptist book exclusively focused on church government, *The Glory of a True Church and its Discipline display'd* (1697) by Benjamin Keach, maintained that a true church of Christ is composed of 'converted persons', is a community where 'the Word of God and sacraments are duly administered, according to Christ's institution', and which has 'regular and orderly discipline'.[81]

Sutcliff did not deny the validity of this approach to the nature of the church. But, as Philip G. A. Griffin-Allwood, a Canadian Baptist historian, has pointed out with regard to Andrew Fuller's theology of the church, it was the proclamation of the Word of God which took precedence in Sutcliff's understanding of the church's nature.[82] This fact is clearly seen in the way that Sutcliff outlines what he regards as the purposes for which local churches exist. When Sutcliff listed these purposes in *Qualifications for Church*

*Fellowship*, he stated that local churches have been brought into being for two principal reasons: the edification of believers and 'the promotion of the cause of Christ at large'. Again, in his address at Thomas Morgan's ordination, he specifically mentioned three reasons: 'the honour of Christ, the advancement of his cause, and their [i.e. the members of the church] own profit'.[83] Given his remarks in *Jealousy for the Lord of Hosts,* at which we have looked in chapter 10, 'the promotion of the cause of Christ at large' and 'the advancement of his [i.e. Christ's] cause' can only mean uninhibited evangelism at home and abroad. A statement of Sutcliff's good friend Andrew Fuller well encapsulated the Olney Baptist's thinking in this regard: 'The true churches of Jesus Christ travail in birth for the salvation of men. They are the armies of the Lamb, the grand object of whose existence is to extend the Redeemer's kingdom.'[84]

Then it is not surprising that *Qualifications for Church Fellowship,* written as it was by a convinced Baptist, emphasized that believer's baptism is a sign of the 'declared willingness' of a local church 'to yield obedience to all the commandents of Jesus Christ'. As Sutcliff went on to elaborate, 'He with whom we have to do is a Prince as well as a Saviour; and that profession cannot claim to be treated as sincere which does not bow with unlimited subjection to his authority. Christ hath all power in heaven and earth, and has declared the terms of his discipleship to be "that we deny ourselves, take up the cross, and follow him" (cf. Luke 9:23). He hath also required those who repent of their sins to be baptized in his name... If any man hesitate to comply with what the Lord hath manifestly required, whatever may be thought of his piety in other respects, we cannot consistently treat him as a member of the visible church of Christ, as herein in a great degree consists the visibility of Christianity.'[85]

The other ordinance of Calvinistic Baptist church life, the Lord's Supper, received a scant, though illuminating, mention near the end of the letter. In the midst of a series of exhortations, Sutcliff admonished his readers: 'Be regular in taking your seat at the table of the Lord.'[86] When Sutcliff came to treat the subject of the Lord's Supper more fully in 1803, he emphasized in no uncertain terms that failure to partake regularly of the supper with one's church grieved the Spirit.[87]

At first glance, Sutcliff's commitment to congregational church govermnment and his firm insistence on believer's baptism and regular participation at the Lord's Supper seem to form 'an unbroken continuum' with the views of such Baptist predecessors as John Gill and Benjamin Wallin, for whom preservation of these distinctives was a prerequisite for revival.[88] Upon closer examination, however, there have been significant shifts in values. Sutcliff's interest in preserving Baptist distinctives is more than matched by his passion for revival and evangelism. *Qualifications for Church Fellowship* opened, in fact, with a brief communication regarding revivals then going on in the United States, followed by a prayer that God, 'with whom is the residue of the Spirit, [may] extend these showers of blessings to our churches,' and an observation that this already seemed to be happening. 'By the letters from the churches,' Sutcliff noted, 'we are not without hope that some drops have already begun to fall upon us, and which we are willing to hope may be an earnest of still greater blessings in reserve. To this end, we earnestly recommend a spirit of extraordinary prayer, both to the churches and to individuals; and this not only at our monthly prayer-meetings, but on other occasions.'[89]

Moreover, Sutcliff's commitment to Baptist distinctives was mollified by his evangelical catholicity and his deep appreciation for evangelical paeodobaptist pastors and communities, a fact that has been noted earlier in this biography and which marked his entire life. Evidence that can be cited in this regard not only includes his friendship with John Newton, but also his even closer friendship with some of Newton's successors, in particular Christopher Stephenson;[90] an appreciative visit which he and Fuller made to see the aged Anglican evangelical John Berridge during the winter of 1790-1791 and which Sutcliff later described in glowing terms in the interdenominational *Evangelical Magazine;*[91] and statements such as the following which Sutcliff made publicly at the ordination of Thomas Morgan: 'Cheerfully we own that the Established Church is honoured with a noble list of worthies. Their names we love. Their memories we revere... Numbers in that connexion are zealous for truth and are patterns of holiness. For their usefulness we pray; and in their success, in turning sinners from darkness to light, we rejoice.'[92] This respect for Anglican preachers and evangelists stands in marked contrast to the attitude of Baptists earlier in the century, for whom the established church was but a step on the road to Roman Catholicism.[93]

A striking illustration of Sutcliff's view of other denominational bodies may also be found in the preface that he, along with Ryland and Fuller, wrote for the English publication of the memoirs of the Congregationalist Susanna Anthony in 1802. Speaking of her view of baptism, which differed from their own, Sutcliff and his two friends noted that 'considerable variety' could often be found between eminent believers. The reasons for such variety were not only to be found in 'the diversity of constitution and religious advantages', but even in 'God's different manner of working upon different persons'. One lesson that the three friends drew from this fact was 'not to set up the form and order of the experience of any one as a model by which to judge concerning those of others'. And, they continued, 'While we perceive not only varieties, but contrarieties in the views and feelings even of eminent Christians, the former are but as the various features, and the latter as the accidental spots, in the human countenance. The great and essential principles of Christianity are found in every Christian, no less than the distinguishing properties of humanity are found in every man.'[94]

Sutcliff, Ryland and Fuller here revealed themselves to be true heirs of the Evangelical Revival, which was centred upon 'the great and essential principles' of the Christian faith, their vigorous propagation and the bonds of fellowship that these principles established between all genuine believers. Obviously, as has been shown, Sutcliff's Baptist convictions were not thereby nullified;[95] but their priority for his own life and ministry were not what such convictions had been for many earlier eighteenth-century Baptists.

## Views on the Lord's Supper

Prior to the 1770s the communion table in the vast majority of eighteenth-century Calvinistic Baptist churches remained closed to those who had not experienced believer's baptism. During that decade, however, there appeared a tract, written by Daniel Turner (1710-1798) and John Collett Ryland, defending the position of open communion. As British Baptist historian Robert W. Oliver has noted, it is hardly fortuitous that such a piece appeared at the very time when the Evangelical Revival was beginning to make an impact on Calvinistic Baptist life and thought. Friendships had been, or were beginning to be, formed across denominational lines, and men and women were being forced to reconsider the issue of the basis of fellowship at the Lord's Table, an issue that had lain quiescent in English Calvinistic Baptist circles since the previous century.[96]

Sutcliff numbered both open and closed communionists among his closest friends. John Ryland, Jr, following in his father's footsteps, was strongly committed to the position of open communion. William Carey also favoured the open communion position. Andrew Fuller, on the other hand, was a firm advocate for closed communion.[97] Where did Sutcliff stand on this issue? Nothing is said about the issue in the covenant of the Olney church, nor does Sutcliff mention it in *The Ordinance of the Lord's Supper considered.* The omission of any reference to it in this may well have been out of a desire not to raise what could be an extremely divisive issue.

Proof as to where Sutcliff stood can be found, however, in the diary of the Olney schoolmaster Samuel Teedon. Although Teedon was a member of the Anglican church, he also used to frequent the Baptist meeting-house. On 6 November 1791, he recorded in his diary that had he received in the Baptist church what he called, in his Anglican nomenclature, the 'sacrament'. The following month he noted that he 'received the Holy Sacrament twice', at the parish church and 'in the evening at Mr Sutcliff's'.[98] Since Teedon knew Sutcliff fairly well and since the issue of open and closed communion was not a minor one in Baptist circles in the late eighteenth century, Teedon must have known where Sutcliff stood on this matter. These diary entries therefore indicate that Sutcliff probably adhered to a policy of open communion, in which all believers, regardless of whether or not they were baptized as believers, were welcome to the Lord's Table.

It should be noted that membership in the Olney church, as some of the texts cited above clearly indicate, was restricted to baptized believers. Given Sutcliff's evangelical catholicity, his position is not at all surprising. What is noteworthy is that Andrew Fuller, his closest friend, was of a different opinion regarding this issue, yet it obviously made no material difference in their friendship.[99]

Now, with regard to the nature of the Lord's Supper, Sutcliff unequivocally advocated a memorialist view of the table and in so doing helped to further a profound re-evaluation of the nature of the Lord's Supper that was taking place in his day. Ernest A. Payne has maintained that from the beginnings of the Baptist testimony in the seventeenth century, there has never been unanimity with respect to the nature of the Lord's Supper and that no one perspective can justly claim to have been the dominant tradition.[100] If this statement has in view the entire history of Baptist witness in all of its breadth and depth, it may be regarded as roughly accurate. However, as soon as specific periods and eras are examined, the evidence demands that it be seriously qualified. Michael J. Walker has shown, for instance, that when it comes to nineteenth-century English Baptist history, Zwinglianism, or the memorialist position, emerges as 'the chief contender for a blanket description of Baptist attitudes to the Lord's Supper'.[101] In the previous century, the prevalent view, at least for the first seven decades, appears to have been that associated with the name of Calvin. In this perspective on the nature of the Lord's Supper, when the elements of bread and wine are eaten and drunk by one who has faith, he or she receives what they symbolize, namely Christ. This reception is accomplished by the Holy Spirit, who acts as a kind of link or bridge between believers and the ascended Christ. Christ is received by believers in the supper, 'not because Christ inheres the elements, but because the Holy Spirit binds believers' to him. Without faith, only the bare elements are received.[102] Two eighteenth-century Calvinistic Baptist reflections on the Lord's Supper reveal that Calvin's approach to the supper was preserved by his Baptist heirs as late as the early 1770s.

A lucid Calvinistic perspective on the supper is found in *Thoughts on the Lord's Supper, Relating to the Nature, Subjects, and right Partaking of this Solemn Ordinance* (1748) by Anne Dutton (1692-1765). A High Calvinist and prolific author, Dutton corresponded with many of the leading evangelical figures of the eighteenth century — Philip Doddridge, Howel Harris, George Whitefield, John Wesley — encouraging them, giving them advice, even chiding them. On one occasion Whitefield confessed that 'Her conversation is as weighty as her letters.' And Harris once wrote to her that he was convinced that 'Our Lord has entrusted you with a talent of writing for him.'[103] Now Dutton devoted the first section of her sixty-page treatise on the Lord's Supper to outlining its nature. In this section Dutton argued that the Supper is, among other things, a 'communication'. 'As our Lord is spiritually present in his own ordinance,' she wrote, 'so he therein and thereby doth actually communicate, or give himself, his body broken, and his blood shed, with all the benefits of his death, to the worthy receivers.'[104] Here Dutton was affirming that Christ is indeed present at the celebration of his supper and makes it a means of grace for those who partake of it with faith. Following Calvin, whether knowingly or unknowingly, she argued that the Lord's Supper is definitely a means of spiritual nourishment and that at the table believers, by the Spirit, do meet with Christ.

A second witness to this perspective on the Lord's Table comes from the diary of Isaac Staveley, a young clerk and a member of Eagle Street Baptist Church, London during the latter years of the pastorate of Andrew Gifford. Written daily from 24 February 1771 to 22 September of that year, the diary opens a window upon 'the interests, way of life, thoughts and activities which we may suppose to have applied to a considerable number of Baptists during the later part of the 18th century'.[105] The centre of Staveley's life was the Baptist fellowship to which he belonged and his chief delight the sermons of Gifford and visiting ministers, of which he wrote extensive summaries in his diary. Participation in the Lord's Supper was also an important event for Staveley. After the evening sermon on 3 March, the young clerk recorded that he and his fellow Baptists 'came around the table of our dear dying Lord to feast on the sacrifice of his offered body, show his death afresh, to claim and recognise our interest therein, to feast on the sacrifice of his offered body as happy members of the same family of faith and love'.[106]

Staveley probably was not aware of the fact that the phrase 'to feast on the sacrifice of his offered body', which he used twice in this short extract, had its roots in the soil of Calvin's theology of the Lord's Supper. In his *magnum opus*, the *Institutes of the Christian Religion*, the Genevan Reformer had written that the Lord's Supper confirms 'for us the fact that the Lord's body was once for all so sacrificed for us that we may now feed upon it, and by feeding feel in ourselves the working of that unique sacrifice'.[107] Such language, both that of Staveley and that of Calvin, is foreign to a mind-set that regards the Lord's Table merely as a memorial.

The view that the Lord's Supper is primarily or simply a memorial began to become widespread in Baptist circles during the last quarter of the eighteenth century. Abraham Booth, the influential London Baptist leader, stated in 1778 that the Lord's Supper was designed to be 'a memorial of *God's love to us* and of Immanuel's *death for us*'.[108]

Twenty or so years later, Sutcliff's mentor and friend, John Fawcett, declared in his spiritual classic, *Christ Precious to those that Believe* (1799), that the 'Lord's Table ... is wisely and graciously designed to revive in our minds the remembrance of him who gave his life a ransom for our souls. This institution is happily contrived to represent, in a lively and striking manner, the love, the sufferings, and the death of our blessed Redeemer, together with the benefits which we derive from them. When we unite in this solemnity, all the springs of pious affection should be let loose, while we contemplate the dying agonies of the Prince of Peace. We should feel the sweet meltings of godly sorrow, and the warmest exertions of gratitude, love and joy.'[109] Like this text from his mentor, Sutcliff's letter on the Lord's Supper abounded in memorialist language and the Calvinist tradition hardly made a showing.

Sutcliff took for his guiding verse throughout this letter the statement of Christ in Luke 22:19: 'This do in remembrance of me.' Seen through the lens of this text, the Lord's Supper 'is a standing memorial of Christ. When you see the table spread and are about to partake of the bread and wine, think you hear Christ saying, "Remember me." Remember who he is… Again: Remember what he has done… Once more: Remember where he is, and what he is doing.'[110]

The fact that Christ instructed us to remember him, Sutcliff continued, clearly 'implies his absence'. Moreover, if a friend, who has gone away, left us with a small present prior to his departure and asked us to 'keep it as a memorial of his friendship', then, even if the present has 'little intrinsic worth, we set a high value on it, for his sake'. Gazing upon this present aids in the 'recollection of our absent friend'. So it is with the ordinance of the Lord's Supper. It is designed 'to draw our attention to, and assist our meditations upon an unseen Jesus'.[111]

This emphasis upon Christ's absence, and thus upon the supper as a place primarily for meditation and remembrance, dominated Sutcliff's thinking about the Lord's Table. In the catechism that he wrote and had published in 1783, the Lord's Supper was said to be 'a solemn eating of bread, and drinking of wine, in commemoration of the death of Christ'.[112] And in a later circular letter which he drew up in 1808, *On obedience to Positive Insitutions,* he unequivocally stated that baptism and the Lord's Supper are 'memorials of the absent Saviour'. In baptism, 'We behold Jesus dying for our offences, and rising again for our justification,' and in the supper 'We see his body broken, and his blood shed for the remision of sins.'[113]

Towards the end of *The Ordinance of the Lord's Supper considered* Sutcliff also emphasized that remembrance of what Christ has done for the believer should lead him or her to a renewed commitment to the Saviour: 'To him who gave his life a ransom, it becomes you to devote your lives. Bought with a price, remember you are not your own. Resolve therefore in the strength of divine grace, to glorify God in your body and in your spirit, which are God's. Each time you approach this sacred ordinance consecrate yourselves anew to the service, honour and glory of the blessed Jesus.'[114]

The Lord's Table is thus a place of reconsecration. Finally, Sutcliff stressed that participation in the supper is a matter of obedience to the command of Christ; it is an open avowal of one's 'subjection to him as a Sovereign'. As such he warned his readers: 'Never treat the positive institutions of the Redeemer as matters of indifferency.'[115] But, as Walker has cogently shown with respect to the memorialist position in the later decades of the nineteenth century, such a position was generally accompanied by some degree of ambivalence with regard to the importance of the table for the believer's Christian experience. Thus, although Sutcliff sought to guard against indifference about the supper, his perspective on the nature of the table would, in time, help to foster such an attitude.

For only two brief moments does an inkling of the Calvinistic perspective on the supper shine through in this strongly memorialist interpretation of the table. Near the beginning of the tract, it is stated that Christ 'still often visits in a spiritual manner his saints in attending divine ordinances'.[116] This statement reveals an awareness that the Lord's Supper is more than simply a memorial, but it remains undeveloped. Then, in a section of the tract which deals with those who, for no apparent reason, occasionally absented themselves from the celebration of the supper, Sutcliff asked a pointed question: 'Is not this the way to grieve the holy Spirit by which "you are sealed unto the day of redemption" (Eph 4:30)? That Spirit whose delight it is on one hand, to glorify Jesus; and on the other, to see him glorified by you.'[117] It may be the case that here Sutcliff simply had in view the fact that failure to be present at the table constitutes an act of disobedience, and it is for this reason alone that the Spirit is grieved. On the other hand, does this question betray a belief that the supper is a means by which the Spirit provides God's people with spiritual nourishment?

An earlier statement that Sutcliff had made in his sermon

*Jealousy for the Lord of Hosts illustrated* does seem to indicate that Sutcliff had not totally ruled out as inadmissible a Calvinistic view of the Lord's Supper. Speaking of the Spirit as 'the grand promise of the New Testament', he affirmed that his 'influences are the soul, the great animating soul of all religion. These withheld, divine ordinances are empty cisterns and spiritual graces are withering flowers.'[118] Without the Spirit the ordinances of baptism and the Lord's Supper are devoid of any spiritual value for those who receive them. With him present, though, they become vehicles of blessing.

Apart from these spare hints of the richer, Calvinistic view of the Lord's Table, however, Sutcliff's tract on the supper marked a definite setting aside of this view in favour of the leaner memorialist perspective. And it presaged what would come to be the majority view among English Baptists in the nineteenth century.

Walker has noted that nineteenth-century Baptists became enamoured of the memorialist position in reaction to the emergence in the 1830s of Tractarianism in the Church of England, a movement that was open to Roman Catholic theology and piety, and the revival of English Roman Catholicism.[119] When Sutcliff wrote his letter on the Lord's Table, however, neither of these events was so much as on the horizon. Why then did he embrace the memorialist position? Payne has suggested that eighteenth-century rationalism, with its 'suspicion of the mysterious and inexplicable', may have been a major factor in the advance of memorialist views among the Calvinistic Baptists.[120] It is indeed fascinating to observe that Joseph Priestley (1733-1804), the leading Unitarian author of the era, can speak of the Lord's Supper in terms identical to those of Sutcliff. The supper, he maintained, was instituted by Christ 'in commemoration of his death'. It is intended to serve as 'a memorial' of Christ's death and as a means whereby Christians make a public declaration of their allegiance.[121]

As has been shown, however, Sutcliff was part of a major rethinking of Baptist teaching on the church. For him, the keynote of the local church's nature was the proclamation of the Word of God. In his thinking, it was the preaching of the Word that enabled the kingdom of God to move forward and to occupy the realms of darkness and convert them into strongholds of light. Such an evangelistic focus, though, tended to downplay the importance of the Lord's Supper, an ordinance expressly designed for believers.

The memorialist perspective fitted well with a growing ambivalence regarding the table.

Sutcliff was privileged to have played a key role in the movement of the Spirit that transformed an inward-looking, insular denomination primarily concerned with the preservation of its ecclesial experience and heritage into a body of churches that was outward-looking with hands outstretched to evangelical believers in other denominations and vitally concerned about the advance of Christ's kingdom throughout the earth. It was a movement in which much was gained, but also something lost. Sutcliff's theology of the Lord's Supper was indeed a poor alternative to the rich perspective of his Baptist forebears, who had come to the table believing that there God would give them something deeply satisfying and precious.

## Views on the atonement

*The Ordinance of the Lord's Supper considered* is also significant in one other important respect: it contains the clearest evidence of Sutcliff's commitment to the governmental theory of the atonement. First propounded by the Dutch jurist and theologian Hugo Grotius, this perspective on the death of Christ had received a warm welcome in New England among the theological heirs of Jonathan Edwards.[122] Although Jonathan Edwards himself published nothing that promoted the governmental view, his private notebooks reveal that he was probably moving in that direction. Moreover, he did not hesitate to write a preface for *True Religion Delineated* (1750) by Joseph Bellamy, in which Bellamy blazed the trail that contemporary and later New Divinity thinkers like Samuel Hopkins, John Smalley, Stephen West (1735-1819) and Jonathan Edwards, Jr (1745-1801) would take with regard to the atonement.

In the thinking of these authors, sin is primarily the flouting of God's moral rule as the Governor of the universe. Therefore, in order to maintain the honour of his government, God has to punish sin. However, because God is also a God of benevolence and mercy, he finds a way whereby sin might be punished and the honour and majesty of his government upheld: Christ lays down his life, displaying God's holy aversion to sin and his unalterable determination to punish it.

During the mid-1790s, there is good evidence that Sutcliff and his immediate circle of friends were busy reading the New Divinity writers on the atonement. Writing to Ryland on 21 April 1794, for instance, Fuller thanked his friend for sending him a copy of *'Dr Edwards on Free Grace and Atonement'*. He had read it 'with great pleasure. I suppose I read it sometime ago; but I never relished it so well before.' The following January, Fuller informed Sutcliff that he had just received a package of pamphlets from the younger Edwards. Among them was Stephen West's *The Scripture Doctrine of the Atonement Proposed to Careful Examination* (1785), a book that helped to make popular the governmental theory of the atonement among certain sectors of New England Calvinism. So precious did Fuller regard this item by West, that he told Sutcliff: 'I w[oul]d not take 1/1 [a guinea]' for it.'[123]

From the mid-1790s on, the three friends regularly used governmental language to describe the atonement. For instance, in a sermon that he preached in 1796 before the Northamptonshire Baptist Association, Fuller emphasized that the death of Christ should be viewed from the vantage-point of 'the moral government of God — as a glorious expedient to secure its honours'. Six years later, in *The Calvinistic and Socinian Systems Examined and Compared*, Fuller enunciated a view of the atonement that is unmistakably governmental. 'The incapacity of God to show mercy without an atonement,' he declared, 'is no other than that of a righteous governor, who, whatever good-will he may bear to an offender, cannot admit the thought of passing by the offence, without some public expression of his displeasure against it; that, while mercy triumphs, it may not be at the expense of law and equity, and of the general good.'[124]

In similar fashion, Sutcliff could assert in his tract on the Lord's Supper that Christ's death 'has vindicated the moral government of Jehovah, and demonstrated the awful desert of the sinner. Thus he has opened a way for the honourable exercise of divine mercy, and God is just, while he is the justifier of him who believeth in Jesus. At the same time, while the atonement of Christ exhibits the strongest possible evidence of the divine hatred to sin on the one hand, and demonstrates on the other, the righteous nature of the sinner's condemnation had it taken place, it proves in the most convincing manner, that his salvation must be an act of mercy, and illustrates most gloriously the freeness of that grace that shines in the pardon of iniquity.'[125]

Although Sutcliff and his friends appreciated much of the thinking of the New England theologians about the atonement, they did not restrict themselves to merely repeating what these authors wrote. For instance, they continued to use other models to discuss the death of Christ, especially that which described Christ's death as a penal, substitutionary sacrifice. As Fuller asserted in 1802, 'We believe that Christ, in laying down his life for us, actually *died as our substitute*; endured the curse of the Divine law, that we might escape it; was delivered for our offences, that we might be delivered from the wrath to come; and all this while we were yet enemies.' Similarly, Sutcliff could joyfully proclaim that Christ 'died for our offences' and 'gave his life a ransom for many'.[126] In other words, they genuinely sought to live by the advice that Fuller gave to Isaac Mann (1785-1831), when the latter asked him some questions about the extent of the atonement: 'Read the Bible not with a system before your eyes, but as a little child with humility and prayer.'[127]

## Sutcliff is much in demand

Not only was Sutcliff's wisdom and Christian maturity as a writer in much demand by the association, but there were numerous requests made upon his time to speak at ordinations and the opening of Baptist meeting-houses, as well as to give his support to small, out-of-the-way village causes.

In April 1809, for instance, the Hackleton Congregationalists, with whom Carey had been associated in his earliest years as a believer, asked Sutcliff to come on Monday, 17 April and baptize eighteen new converts. The Hackleton church was obviously in transition and fast becoming a Baptist congregation. Sutcliff gladly came and after giving a short address to those who had come to watch, he baptized the new believers in a nearby brook with 'the greatest solemnity and deliberation'. By the time that he came to baptize the final individual, Lucy Timms, Sutcliff was visibly exhausted. She came down into the water and clutching his arm remarked with concern, 'Sir, you must be very tired.' 'Yes,' Sutcliff replied, 'but I could baptize one more,' and he proceeded to baptize her. That evening at seven o'clock Sutcliff preached in the Hackleton meeting-house from Matthew 28:18-20, a very appropriate text for the day.[128]

In private, Sutcliff was frequently consulted for his advice and counsel. For instance, when his old friend Thomas Purdy was dying in 1802 and was unable to continue his ministry at Chipping Norton, one of the leaders in the church, Thomas Parsons, wrote to Sutcliff seeking his advice about a new pastor.[129]

Not all the enquiries he received, though, were so straightforward as this one. During the course of 1803 and 1804, Sutcliff received a couple of letters from a man named J. Marriott (d.1812), a member of the Baptist work at Ampthill, where Andrew Fuller's father-in-law, William Coles, was now the pastor. This may well be the same man who was one of Sutcliff's High Calvinist critics in the early years of his ministry at Olney. The church had a great opportunity for growth, but there was a major hindrance, one of the deacons by the name of Whitbread. According to Marriott, Whitbread, who was married, had been having an ongoing affair with another woman, and was making 'religion stink' in the village. Coles refused to believe Marriott or any of the other eyewitnesses to this affair, and when Marriott persisted in making his accusations about Whitbread, Coles had him 'cut off' from the church. But, Marriott told Sutcliff in September 1804, if he left, half of the members of the church had threatened to leave with him.[130] How Sutcliff advised Marriott we do not know, but it was obviously a very tricky situation, since the pastor of the Ampthill church was his best friend's father-in-law. From Marriott's later correspondence with Sutcliff, it appears that he did leave the church. However, at the time of Marriott's death in 1812 from an accidental fall, he was living once again in the Ampthill area.[131] Coles had retired in 1806, and Marriott may well have decided to return.

Fuller also regularly plied Sutcliff with questions and queries. F. A. Cox noted that Fuller was accustomed to say that whenever he received some mail from the missionaries in India that confused him by the variety of its contents, he would ride over to Olney, lay it before Sutcliff, 'who would unravel and explain all with perfect ease, determining what it would be best to suppress and what to publish [in the *Periodical Accounts*]'. In April 1808, for instance, Fuller received a large quantity of letters from India. Before he answered them he wanted Sutcliff to read them over with him, which he estimated would take five to six hours! One of them in particular contained what he described to Sutcliff as an 'urgent and most delicate case'. 'I must have your advice' about it, he told him. Sutcliff, as Fuller later said at the time of his friend's funeral, 'excelled in practical judgement'. He would take his time in considering matters that were laid before him, and only after he had ruminated on all the issues at stake would he give his answer. If he saw others hastily pressing for a decision, he would genially tell them, 'Let us consult the town-clerk of Ephesus, and do nothing rashly.'[132] This was, of course, an allusion to the words of the city clerk of Ephesus in Acts 19:35-36, who brought calm to the Ephesian mob when it seemed bent on riot and bloodshed.

A good example of the way that Fuller relied on Sutcliff's advice is afforded by the decision of William Nichols (1762-1835) to accept the pastorate of the Baptist cause in Collingham, Nottinghamshire. Sutcliff had a long-standing interest in this work, since he had known the previous pastor, William Shaw, for over thirty years. Shaw, who had been at Collingham since 1777, had died towards the end of 1803. Now Nichols made a good living as a commercial traveller for a hosiery firm and acceptance of the Collingham pastorate would mean that he would have to give up this lucrative career. He was also an active deacon at Friar Lane Baptist Church in Nottingham and had been engaged in preaching with some success in a number of the villages surrounding the town.

Nichols had sought Fuller's advice in late 1806 as to whether or not he should respond positively to the call that the Collingham church had extended to him. Fuller immediately went over to consult with Sutcliff. In their discussion two concerns surfaced.

First, would Nichols be willing to give up his trade? Although both Fuller and Sutcliff wanted to see the Collingham pastorate filled, neither of them was about to try to persuade Nichols to give up his career. If Nichols made this decision, 'It must be a freewill offering of [his] own to God.' Yet, as they discussed it, they were both agreed that if Nichols did indeed give up the advantages that his career held out for him, he would not lose in the end, even though he would probably have to wait till the Lord's coming to receive his reward.

Then, as to his involvement in the Nottingham work, Fuller and Sutcliff were hopeful that the believers there would be willing to part with Nichols for the further advance of the kingdom of God.

On the basis of this judicious advice that came from both Fuller and Sutcliff, Nichols made the decision to go to Collingham. When Sutcliff was informed of Nichols' acquiescence to the Collingham call, he was convinced that God would honour this costly sacrifice made for Christ's sake.[133]

## The Bedfordshire Union of Christians

In a recent article on the historical background of the Baptist Missionary Society, William H. Brackney, the principal of McMaster Divinity College in Hamilton, Ontario, has argued that Sutcliff was a firm proponent of the necessity and efficacy of voluntary religious associations that were focused on achieving specific goals.[134] Clear evidence of this assertion may be found not only in Sutcliff's active participation in the Baptist Missionary Society, but also in his staunch support of an organization known as the Bedfordshire Union of Christians.[135]

Since the time of John Bunyan, Bedfordshire and two of its adjacent counties, Buckinghamshire and Hertfordshire, had seen a number of instances where Baptists and paedobaptist Congregationalists had worked together in common causes. There were a number of mixed Baptist-paedobaptist congregations in these counties, including Bunyan Meeting in Bedford and the work at Hitchin, over which Sutcliff's friend John Geard was the pastor. Moreover, from the beginning of his ministry at Olney, Sutcliff had striven to build close ties with fellow evangelicals in Olney, which included the Congregationalists in the town. It was in what had thus been an especially fruitful area for co-operation between Baptists and paedobaptists that Samuel Greatheed, the pastor of the Congregationalist work in Woburn, invited neighbouring ministers to a meeting at Ampthill on 24 August 1797 to discuss the formation of a society that would bear witness to their unity in Christ and forward the evangelization of their part of the country.

Among those who attended this first meeting were William Coles, Fuller's father-in-law, Thomas Hillyard, the minister of the Congregationalist church in Olney, and William Payne, the Baptist pastor of the cause at Gamlingay, Cambridgeshire. There was enthusiastic support for Greatheed's idea and a second meeting was planned for the following month on 26 September. It was hoped that there would be a large attendance at this meeting. Unfortunately, a major storm accompanied by devastating floods hit the British Isles that week. Roads were flooded and impassable, and many were drowned in the neighbourhood of Olney and Newport Pagnell.

A further meeting was consequently scheduled for 31 October at which time the Union of Bedfordshire Christians was formally inaugurated after Greatheed had preached a stirring message from Psalm 133:1. In this sermon Greatheed maintained that one of the main objectives of the new society was to bring the light of the gospel into the 'dark and depraved' areas of Bedfordshire and its adjoining counties — Northamptonshire, Huntingdonshire, Cambridgeshire, Hertfordshire and Buckinghamshire — by 'preaching, exhorting, reading, conversion and prayer'. Greatheed, however, emphasized that the 'primary design' of the society was 'to restore the universal Church of Christ to some measure of its primitive harmony and unity; and thereby to remedy the positive and obvious evils, which have been produced by discord among Christians.'[136]

It would seem that Greatheed idealistically looked forward to a day, prior to the millennium, when there would indeed be an organic reunion of the church. Such a reunion was an ultimate goal for Greatheed, though, and not something to be immediately implemented. As he said in the same sermon, 'We aim at union, not uniformity; we wish to excite your zeal, not to alter your opinions; we long to promote your love to all fellow Christians, not to lessen your attachment to those with whom you are immediately connected.'[137]

Sutcliff was not at the inaugural meeting of this society. He first attended a meeting of the society on 17 November 1797 at the Congregationalist meeting-house in Olney. He applied for membership in the union at that time and soon became 'its leading and perhaps most active supporter'.[138] The union had been divided into five districts, of which Olney fell in the north-western section. Between his joining the society in 1797 and his death seventeen years later there were very few of the regular meetings of this section of the union that Sutcliff did not attend, and a good number of them were actually held in his church in Olney. On two occasions he was asked to preach at the anniversary meeting of the union, when all of the various districts met together for worship and celebration. The first was in April 1799, when he preached on John 3:30. Though the weather was inclement, it was a very well-attended meeting. It is interesting to note that a Methodist minister by the name of Woolmer closed the meeting in prayer.[139] In 1806 Sutcliff again addressed the union, when he spoke on Matthew 6:10.

Despite the fact that Sutcliff was such an active participant in this society, it is doubtful whether he shared Greatheed's idealism about an organic reunion of the church. Nevertheless, he certainly entered heartily into the subsidiary aim of the union, namely, the evangelization of the 'dark and depraved' areas around Olney. Even before he had joined the union, he and Thomas Hillyard had been engaged in preaching in the villages in the Olney neighbourhood.[140] Since the formation of the Baptist Missionary Society in 1792 and then, three years later, that of the interdenominational London Missionary Society, there had been a great concern awakened amongst the evangelicals in Olney about the state of the unconverted who lived in the villages around them. Hillyard, who was an especially able evangelist, began to go out in May 1796, preaching in the open air in the village streets. On one occasion five to six hundred gathered to hear him proclaim the good news of salvation in Christ.

The following summer, Hillyard repeated this method of evangelism with Sutcliff joining him. Before they went they had a prayer meeting, at which they particularly prayed that 'God would open the hearts and the houses of some people in the villages to have the gospel preached among them'. Despite some initial opposition, homes were opened in three villages, where every Sunday evening, a number of the young men from the three churches in Olney — the Baptist, the Congregationalist and the Anglican — would go and lead in worship. Sermons would be read, especially those that were 'plain, practical, awakening sermons, which hold out human depravity and misery by the fall, and salvation by Christ'.

Sutcliff had thus already come to a firm conviction regarding the need to evangelize the villages around Olney before he joined the union. For him, participation in the union solidified his resolve to engage in evangelism with fellow evangelicals. By early 1798 the joint evangelistic efforts under the auspices of the union had resulted in houses being opened in Lavendon and Grendon for prayer meetings and regular meetings for worship and preaching established in four other villages: Emberton, Clifton Reynes, Denton (in Northamptonshire) and Newton Blossomville.[141]

In the last-named village a noteworthy event took place during the summer of 1799. Hillyard, who was the preacher that evening, was standing in front of a wall. On the other side of the wall was the garden belonging to the home of the Anglican minister, who at that time was a man by the name of Hurst. Hillyard was thus well within earshot of anyone who was in the garden. As it happened, Hurst's five unmarried daughters were sitting there, and as they heard the glorious truth of the gospel proclaimed their hearts were opened and all five were converted. Their father was nonplussed for a while, till he could not but acknowledge the change that had taken place in his daughters. Of the five, two eventually joined the Congregationalist church in Olney, and one the Baptist. Needless to say, the father had to put up with much ribbing and rebuke from fellow Anglican clerics for allowing three of his daughters to associate with Dissenters![142]

It was jokingly said in Olney that many of those who were awakened and converted under the preaching of Hillyard eventually ended up at the Baptist meeting-house.[143] If this was true, it certainly caused no resentment on the part of Hillyard. Nor is there any indication at all that Sutcliff ever purposely engaged in what has come to be called 'sheep-stealing'. However, the baptizing of new converts by Sutcliff in the Ouse would invariably attract a large crowd. When, for example, Sutcliff baptized the eight young women in October 1806, after which Christopher Anderson had preached in the meeting-house, around 700 people were present for the baptism. The public immersion of the believers would undoubtedly impress upon the minds of some of the onlookers who were not Baptists their need to be baptized.[144] There was no explicit design to win other evangelicals as adherents of the Baptist cause, but that is what often happened.

Indeed, in the final years of Sutcliff's life this charge of sheep-stealing was increasingly raised against the Baptists throughout England. In the wake of these charges, which were aired in the widely read, inter-denominational journal, *The Evangelical Magazine,* came a hardening of denominational boundaries as the Baptists started their own monthly journal in 1809, *The Baptist Magazine,* and sought to create a nationwide union of Calvinistic Baptist congregations in 1812-1813. Sutcliff would be involved in both of these ventures, but he could hardly have approved of the marked decline in evangelical co-operation that accompanied them, for that was something to which he had been committed for most of his life.[145]

# 13.
# Final years

> *'How great a matter is Christian perseverance, to hold out to the end, and be saved! I have sometimes wondered at the grace in that astonishing gradation, Jude 24. What "him" must that be that is able to keep me from falling and to present me — to present me faultless — faultless before the presence of his glory — and that with joy — yea, with exceeding joy!'*
>
> (Andrew Fuller).

On the first day of June 1810, Sutcliff sat down to write a reply to a letter that he had just received from Christopher Anderson. It had been some time since he had heard from his former student, now a close friend. As he told Anderson, he had been upset and had even repined at hearing 'nothing from Christopher'. The previous week he had dined with a mutual friend in Wellingborough, who had naturally asked him for news of Anderson. Sutcliff was mortified to have to tell him that he had no news. But Anderson's letter had made matters right.

Of news at Olney, Sutcliff had little to tell. The following Friday, 8 June, he hoped to baptize four new believers. Two of them, Elizabeth Felts of Filgrave and Elizabeth Hawkins of Clifton Reynes had, it would appear, been reached with the gospel through the village preaching that Sutcliff was still active in promoting. But, with a holy dissatisfaction, he told Anderson, 'I long to see the work progress.' Then he added, 'Often think my time is near a close. The thought is solemn. It might be more alarming. Jude 21, "Looking," etc. is my text.'[1]

## A busy schedule

Yet for a man who thought his life was rapidly drawing to a close, Sutcliff was extraordinarily busy. In addition to his ministry at Olney that month, Sutcliff was involved in two ordinations, preached at the opening of a new meeting-house and was one of the preachers at the annual assembly of the Northamptonshire Association.

On Wednesday, 20 June, he was at College Lane in Northampton for the ordination of Thomas Blundell, Jr (1786-1861), the eldest son of his friend by the same name, though apparently the son chose to spell his surname with an extra '1' at the end. After an opening prayer, Sutcliff gave a clear and succint statement of the principles of Dissent, thus reminding Blundell and his hearers of the heritage that was theirs as Baptists, a heritage they were to treasure and to hand on. This pointing out of the reasons why the Baptists dissented from the worship and polity of the Church of England was regularly done at ordinations so that those entering upon the Baptist ministry might demonstrate some knowledge of their heritage.[2] Sutcliff then asked various questions of Blundell, seeking to elicit the reasons why he believed that he was called to pastoral ministry. Sermons by Fuller and Ryland followed Blundell's being set apart by the laying on of hands.[3]

It would have grieved Sutcliff to see what the younger Blundell later did with the heritage that had been entrusted to him. In 1824 he resigned from his charge in Northampton, and after a brief but disastrous spell as a teacher, left the Baptists altogether and joined the established church in the early 1830s. As an Anglican curate in Wiltshire, Blundell wrote a defence of his actions in a tract that he entitled *Conformity Vindicated* (1835).

The day following Blundell's ordination Sutcliff, Fuller and Ryland rode over to Kislingbury, a small village just to the west of Northampton, where they were all involved in a second ordination, that of one of Ryland's former students at Bristol by the name of Adams. On this occasion, Fuller asked the questions of the ordinand, and Ryland and Sutcliff preached, the latter reminding the people of their responsibilities under their new pastor. Speaking from Psalm 122:6, Sutcliff would have stressed that it was vital that they be a praying congregation and a people who loved one another.[4] The following week, on Friday 29 June, Sutcliff was preaching in

Nottinghamshire at the opening of a new meeting-house in the village of Sutton on Trent. As a veteran promoter of village preaching, it must have gladdened Sutcliff's heart to see the way the gospel had taken root in this small village in a brief eighteen months.[5]

Now, prior to all of this activity Sutcliff had preached in the evening of Wednesday, 13 June at the annual meeting of the Northamptonshire Association, which was held in Luton. The assembly that year was a very painful experience. Shortly before the association met, it had been discovered that the pastor of the Luton church, Thomas Blundel, Sr — one of the founders of the Baptist Missionary Society, a friend of Sutcliff, and a man whose sermons Fuller once described as 'admirable'[6] — was guilty of adultery. The church, though stunned, proceeded to remove him from the office of pastor and excommunicated him. Fuller, never one to mince words when it came to sin, preached in the morning of 13 June on 2 Corinthians 13:5, a solemn call to self-examination: 'Examine yourselves, whether ye be in the faith.' Sutcliff, who also had to act as the moderator of the assembly that year, spoke from Romans 13:11, a text that introduces a summons to spiritual vigilance and sobriety.

Not surprisingly, when the ministers assembled on the Thursday morning to select a topic for the following year's circular letter, as well as to share their spiritual experiences of the previous year, they chose the theme of walking with God. John Jarman (d.1830), the minister of Friar Lane Baptist Church in Nottingham, was asked to write this letter. When he did so, he made a clear reference to Blundel's fall, though without specifically naming him. 'We have seen,' he wrote, some of God's 'standard bearers ... led captive by Satan in the chains of their own lusts'. Men, by whose talents they had been instructed and edified, had 'wrought such folly in Israel, as to fill the hearts of the friends of God with anguish, and afford matter for profane triumph to his enemies'.[7] Jarman may also have had in mind Morris's bankruptcy, which had occurred only two years before.

The fall of Blundel, Sr must have cast a shadow over his son's ordination, which took place only a week after the assembly of the association. The younger Blundell had wanted his father to preach on that occasion. That was, of course, impossible and Fuller preached in his stead. Unlike Morris, though, Blundel repented of his wrongdoing. Fuller met him a couple of years later in London, when Blundel 'wept bitterly and confessed his sin'. Fuller encouraged him to write a letter to the Luton congregation, in which he admitted that it had been right for them to exclude him for what he had done. 'I have wept and still weep that I should have given the occasion,' he said. He had no hopes of ever pastoring again, but he longed for their forgiveness.[8] Over the next eight years Blundel rebuilt his life, and in 1820 he was called to pastor Keighley Baptist Church in Yorkshire, a young work that had been started in 1812. It was William Steadman, the friend of Fuller and Sutcliff, who recommended that the Keighley work consider calling Blundel. He laboured here faithfully for four years, dying of a stroke in 1824.[9]

## The importance of the Spirit's work in evangelism

Now the circular letter that was issued at the 1810 assembly in Luton was written by Fuller. It was a masterly presentation of the vital importance of relying upon the Holy Spirit in the work of evangelism.[10] Fuller took it for granted that a desire to see the advance of the gospel lay at the heart of his readers' thinking and experience. Though he and his readers were Baptists, he stressed that the aim of their lives was not to convert others to their distinctive opinions as Baptists, but to advance the growth of Christ's kingdom: 'We may be of what is called a sect, but we must not be of a sectarian spirit, seeking only the promotion of a party. The true churches of Jesus Christ travail in birth for the salvation of men. They are the armies of the Lamb, the grand object of whose existence is to extend the Redeemer's kingdom.'[11]

Vital to this work of evangelism, be it at home or abroad, Fuller continued, was a conscious and deliberate reliance on the aid of the Spirit. Yes, there were High Calvinists who abused this doctrine and made the necessity of the Spirit's work in converting sinners an excuse for their own lackadaisical attitude towards evangelism. 'God can convert sinners,' they say, 'without any exertions or contributions of ours.' Yes, he can, responded the Kettering pastor, and he will; but those who continue to think thus will see their churches come to nought and ruin![12]

Yet even those who were evangelical Calvinists enjoyed much less of the Spirit's help than might be expected. The reason for this, Fuller asserted, was that they failed to appreciate their desperate need of the Spirit. Thus they neglected regular prayer for his empowerment and the cultivation of an attitude of dependence upon him. To rectify this situation Fuller took his readers on a whirlwind tour of the Scriptures, in which he demonstrated, from both the Old and New Testaments, that behind the success of God's cause in every age there has been the person and power of the Holy Spirit. For instance, at the time of the return of Israel from the Babylonian captivity when the temple of God had yet to be fully rebuilt, the prophet Zechariah clearly indicated that the work of rebuilding would have no hope of success but for the Spirit's empowering presence (Zechariah 4:6). Again, during the era in which the New Testament was written the gospel made its conquests through the Spirit's power and that alone. To prove his point Fuller produced a cluster of texts from the New Testament: Acts 11:21; 2 Corinthians 2:14; Acts 16:14; 2 Corinthians 10:4. Two outstanding examples of the Spirit's free and unhampered power were Corinth, that 'sink of debauchery', but a place where God had 'much people' (Acts 18:10), and Jerusalem, where the Lord Jesus was rejected and crucified, but where many later bowed to Christ 'at the pouring out of his Spirit'.[13]

The practical implications of what Fuller was saying he now spelled out in one succint paragraph: 'If all our help be in God,' as Fuller had sought to show, then 'To him it becomes us to look for success.' And that looking to God takes place in the sphere of prayer, both corporate and private. After all, 'It was from a prayer meeting, held in an upper room, that the first Christians descended, and commenced that notable attack on Satan's kingdom in which three thousand fell before them.' And Fuller continued, thinking now of more recent events, 'It was in prayer that the late undertakings for spreading the gospel among the heathen originated.'[14]

Reinforcing these illustrations of the vital necessity of prayer for the Spirit's aid were the promises of Scripture. We are living, Fuller reminded his readers, in a period that the New Testament styles 'the ministration of the Spirit' (2 Corinthians 3:8). The period following Pentecost is described in this way, Fuller averred, because it is an age for which are reserved 'the richest effusions of the Holy Spirit'. By gathering in 'great accessions to the church from among the Gentiles', these effusions will bring great glory to Christ. Thus to pray for the Spirit's outpouring and help at such a time is to ask God to accomplish that on which he has set his heart from all eternity and in which he supremely delights, namely, the glorification of his beloved Son.[15]

## Concern for the future of the work

To the older men and women who could recall the issuing of the Prayer Call of 1784 and the founding of the Baptist Missionary Society eight years later, Fuller's train of thought and argumentation here would not have been new. The 'theology of radical dependence on the Spirit' that lies at the heart of this circular letter and which informed the thinking and spirituality of Fuller, Sutcliff and their friends, was something that they had witnessed on many occasions — in their prayer meetings and in sermons and tracts emanating from this circle of men.

But Fuller, Sutcliff and Ryland were all conscious that their lives were drawing to a close and that they needed to pass on to the next generation the heart of their spiritual experience and convictions. In 1806, for instance, Carey had written to Sutcliff and asked him whether or not more ministers ought to be brought onto the committee of the society: 'I see that the whole rests on a few: brother Fuller, yourself, Dr Ryland, and one or two more. Were you to die, who would be found that would take equal interest in the active parts of the work?' Similarly, in a letter that Ryland received from Marshman in the same year and which he copied for Sutcliff's perusal, Marshman asked, 'If brethren Fuller, Sutcliff, Morris, and yourself were removed, who would there be to step forward and carry on the work? ... I think it can never be managed better than you manage it, but none of you are immortal, and some of you not young.'[16]

That very winter Sutcliff contracted typhus fever and was 'brought to the brink of the grave', as the annual letter that the Olney church sent to the association put it. When the missionaries in Serampore heard of his illness, Ward told Sutcliff in a letter that he wrote early in 1808, 'I seem to tremble for the ark, while I am anxiously looking at the health of two or three among you.'[17] Such reminders of mortality made it vital that the vision that had motivated Fuller, Sutcliff, Ryland and the circle around them should not be lost, but transmitted to the new generation that would fill their places after their deaths.

## Sutcliff and Ryland visit Scotland

In 1811 it was Fuller that was ill. He came down with a fever in April which hung on till October. It robbed him of his sleep and rendered him so weak that he was unable to preach for three months.[18] That summer he had hoped to visit northern England and Scotland on behalf of the Baptist Missionary Society, but he was far too ill to manage the entire trip. In the final week of May he wrote to Sutcliff and asked him if he would be willing to go to Scotland, either by himself or with Ryland, and he would take care of northern England. Sutcliff subsequently met with Fuller on 1 June to discuss what would be entailed in a trip to Scotland. Meanwhile Fuller had written to Ryland, and encouraged him to travel with Sutcliff.[19] Both friends agreed to go and made plans to leave soon after the association meetings which were held in Oakham from 4 to 6 June.

The two men spent most of that month and the first couple of weeks of the following month in Scotland. Among the Baptist churches that they visited were ones in Edinburgh — that of Archibald McLean, the Scotch Baptist — Dunfermline, Glasgow, Greenock and Kilwinning. They were also well received in a number of Presbyterian congregations known to history as the Burghers, whose roots went back to a secession from the Church of Scotland in 1733. Anderson joined them for some of their journey and Sutcliff would have been glad of the time together to deepen their friendship.[20]

One unique opportunity that they had in presenting the need of the mission was to a society of Christian female servants located in Aberdeen. This society had been formed with the intention of supporting the translation of the Scriptures. Each of its members gave a penny a week towards that end. It met at least four times a year, at which time a minister of the gospel would be asked to attend to 'give necessary information and advice, as well as open and close ... in prayer'. Both Sutcliff and Ryland were invited to attend the summer quarterly meeting. After prayer together and their sharing of the needs of the Missionary Society, the secretary of the society presented them with a donation of twenty pounds and one shilling for the translation of the Scriptures by the Serampore missionaries into some of the languages and dialects of India.[21]

The two English Baptists were deeply impressed by this society of Christian women. Nine years earlier, in the preface that they had written for the memoirs of Susanna Anthony, Sutcliff and Ryland had noted that 'great eminency in godliness' is often found 'in the common walks of life' and that there is 'no station so humble as to incapacitate us for glorifying [Christ's] name'.[22] The truth of what they had written on that occasion came home to them afresh as they met with these Christian servants and saw them give of the little that they had.

By the end of their trip Sutcliff and Ryland had collected about £1,400, roughly two-thirds of what Fuller would normally receive in donations from a trip to Scotland.[23] More importantly, the personal contacts that they had made had helped to garner prayer support for the society. Both men were deeply grateful for, and long remembered, the many kindnesses that they were shown from various Christians with whom they had stayed.[24]

## Requests for help in finding pastors

The autumn of 1811 saw Sutcliff as busy as ever. In late November, for instance, he preached on Titus 2:13 at a ministerial meeting of the Northamptonshire Association that took place in Kettering.[25] Earlier in the month he had travelled over to King's Lynn in Norfolk for the ordination of Thomas Welsh (1787-1862), one of his students of whom he thought very highly.

Sutcliff had received a letter the previous year from one of the leaders among the King's Lynn Baptists, a man named Thomas Torr. Torr had asked him if there was a young man at his seminary of 'genuine piety, evangelical sentiments, with decent abilities' whom he could recommend to fill the pastoral office in their church. The church, he informed Sutcliff, had recently erected a new meeting-house that could seat 400 people. The congregation was obviously looking for a man whose preaching could fill the new building. Torr may well have been given Sutcliff's name by one of the former pastors of the King's Lynn church, William Richards (1749-1818), who had known Sutcliff at Bristol.[26] Sutcliff recommended Welsh and was thus naturally asked to preach as Welsh assumed the pastorate of the Baptist work in this Norfolk town.[27]

Ordinations are generally events pregnant with promise. Presumably that of Welsh was no different in this respect. By February 1813, however, scarcely sixteen months after his installation as pastor, Welsh was having to leave King's Lynn. One of the members of the congregation told Sutcliff that Welsh was not a good preacher: 'He cannot compel people to come and take pews.' The principal men of the congregation, this individual went on to say, have 'an insatiable thirst for a large congregation', and because Welsh could not provide this, he had to go. Fuller had heard a similar report about Welsh's preaching when he was in Norfolk collecting for the Baptist Missionary Society. 'His preaching seemed flat,' he had been told. Yet the congregation 'spoke of him with much esteem as to his Christian character'.[28]

Sutcliff or Fuller must have informed Ryland of Welsh's dilemma, for on the recommendation of Ryland, the Baptist church in Newbury, Berkshire, asked Welsh to preach for them and eventually called him as their pastor. The previous pastor of the Newbury work, a church that had its roots in the 1650s, had been John Perry (1759-1812), a man who had spent himself in village evangelism. Welsh's ministry extended to 1839 and under his leadership the church experienced a steady increase in members — 178 in twenty-five years — and preaching centres were established in a number of surrounding villages, places like Longlane, Newtown and Headley. It appears that the King's Lynn Baptists had simply not given Welsh enough time to mature as a preacher. Sutcliff, though, knew from his own personal experience that good preaching does not happen overnight. Sutcliff did not live to see the fruit of Welsh's ministry at Newbury, but, as that ministry proved, the Olney pastor had had good reason to think highly of him. Welsh must also have thought highly of his former tutor, for he named his son John Sutcliff Welsh.[29]

The letter from Torr seeking a pastor for the King's Lynn congregation was typical of many such requests that Sutcliff received during his final years.[30] One that would certainly have stirred up old memories came from Joseph Kinghorn, the Norwich Baptist. Writing the month before Sutcliff travelled over to King's Lynn for Welsh's ordination, Kinghorn solicited Sutcliff's help in finding a pastor for the Baptist church in Worstead — the Norfolk congregation from which J. Webster Morris had gone into the ministry. The church was evidently flourishing. There were, Kinghorn told Sutcliff, around 150 members, and as many as 400 regular adherents. 'It opens a field of very extensive utility,' Kinghorn told Sutcliff, 'and I should be glad to see it well occupied.' What

Kinghorn did not tell Sutcliff was that Morris was helping in the leadership of the church till it found a pastor. Sutcliff would not have been impressed.[31]

## A call for a new union of churches

The year 1812 marked the twentieth anniversary of the Baptist Missionary Society. Fuller had been persuaded by Joseph Ivimey, the pastor of Eagle Street Baptist Church in London, to hold special services in the metropolis for the occasion. The previous year Ivimey had written an article entitled 'Union essential to Prosperity' which appeared in *The Baptist Magazine*.[32] In this brief article, that occupied just four pages of the monthly serial, Ivimey noted that the early nineteenth century was a time when there was 'a greater degree of union manifested amongst Christians than at any former period'. This unity had come about largely through the establishment of various interdenominational Bible, tract and missionary societies. The Baptist Missionary Society, which had 'paramount claims to the attention' of Baptists, was a good example in this regard. In focusing the attention of Baptists on a single object, the evangelization of Asia, it had done more towards creating a sense of unity among the Baptists than any explicit plan for union.

Yet Ivimey was convinced that not all of the resources of the Baptist churches were being tapped in promoting this evangelistic enterprise. He therefore suggested that there be held an annual assembly, either in London or one of the other larger cities in England, to which 'the ministers and messengers from the neighbouring churches, and ... two deputies from every [Baptist] association' would be invited. An update on the progress of the work in India could be presented at such a meeting, as well as information about itinerant preaching in the British Isles, sermons could be preached and a collection made. Ivimey was certain that by such means 'a spirit of zeal and benevolence would be thus diffused through all our churches'. The article concluded with a suggestion that such a meeting be held in the summer of 1812.

When Ivimey first approached Fuller with this idea, it met with a cool reception. Fuller, as British historian Brian Stanley has recently pointed out, was wary about forging strong links between the Missionary Society and London. He had deep reservations about the theology of some of the London Baptists.[33] London, after all, had been the home of Gill and Brine for many years, and the influence of their teaching was still felt, even though they had both been dead for more than four decades. Moreover, though neither of them was a doctrinal antinomian, many of those who wore their High Calvinist mantle were champions of antinomianism. Fuller, writing in 1804 to Ward, told him that 'Nowhere does antinomianism grow more strongly than in London.'[34]

Fuller also had a strong dislike of the pomp and show that seemed to infect evangelical organizations that were based in the capital. In Fuller's mind, to quote Stanley, 'To go down the road of public meetings, presided over by wealthy notables and full of "speechifying", would be a dangerous concession to worldliness.'[35]

Furthermore, Fuller was rightly fearful that if the society established its base of operations in London, the day-to-day management of the society, which he undertook with the vital help of Sutcliff, would be wrested from him by the London churches and the running of the society fall into the hands of men who had no personal acquaintance with Carey. As Fuller once remarked regarding the origins of the society, he and his friends were like men 'deliberating about the importance of penetrating into a deep mine, which had never before been explored. We had no one to guide us; and, while we were thus deliberating, Carey, as it were, said, "Well, I will go down if *you* will hold the rope." But, before he went down, he, as it seemed to me, took an oath from each of us at the mouth of the pit to this effect, that while we lived *we* should *never* let go the rope.' Then Fuller added, 'There was great responsibility attached to us who began the business.' Fuller had no innate love of power, but he was convinced that this personal commitment to Carey to stand by him through thick and thin would be imperilled if he gave up the personal administration of the society. Similarly, Sutcliff emphasized that neither he nor Fuller nor Ryland considered themselves to be the 'legislators' or power-brokers of the society. They were simply 'co-workers' with their brethren in India, raising funds for the Serampore mission and finding further labourers for that field of missionary advance. As he frankly told one London Baptist who was badgering him to move the society to London, if the society's committee ever began to 'legislate for India', he fully expected that the Serampore Trio 'would issue a declaration of independence' and he would 'not be sorry if they did'.[36] Nevertheless, though Fuller received Ivimey's suggestion 'very coldly', he did tell him, 'I will, however, consult brother Sutcliff about it, and will let you know our opinion on the subject.'[37]

No record of that discussion between Sutcliff and Fuller appears to exist. The result we know: both Fuller and Sutcliff gave their hearty support to Ivimey's suggestion. What changed Fuller's mind? Sutcliff's love of true evangelical unity may have been a factor. Another factor might have been the recognition on the part of both of them that the society did need to secure a more solid base of support among the London churches, something that Marshman had actually suggested to them back in 1806.[38]

Whatever the exact reasons, on Wednesday, 24 June, the Baptist Missionary Society held two services, one in the morning and one in the evening, at the Dutch Church, known as the Austin Friars, just off Old Broad Street. This church, which had been built in 1354 and had once belonged to the Augustinian Friars prior to the Reformation, had been given by Edward VI to a congregation of religious refugees from the Netherlands in 1660. Sutcliff, Fuller and Ryland had all travelled up to London for the services. Fuller preached at the morning service from Romans 1:14-17 after Sutcliff had led the congregation in prayer. Fuller, as the secretary of the society, then gave a report on the state of the mission. In the evening, it was John Saffery of Salisbury who led in prayer and Ryland who preached. After Ryland's message Fuller again gave a report on the mission.

Ryland's sermon was drawn from Isaiah 9:7. In the course of it he prompted the congregation to reflect on what God had done through one man's life, that of William Carey. Ryland confessed that when he baptized Carey in 1783, he thought little of what God would do with this man's life: a key figure in the founding of the Missionary Society, a translator of the Scriptures into a number of Indian languages and dialects, and since 1801 a professor of oriental literature at the College of Fort William in Calcutta. Yet, Ryland, like Carey, Fuller and Sutcliff, was well aware that 'No man should glory in men.' For behind all of Carey's accomplishments was the zeal of God, the Lord of hosts. It was he that had done all that had been wrought. And it was he, Ryland confidently proclaimed, who 'must perform all that is achieved in the future', when ultimately the entire earth would be filled with his glory, 'all nations submitting to his government, all the tribes of mankind rejoicing in his salvation'.[39]

Near the close of this sermon Ryland mentioned that one of Carey's sons gave his missionary father great heartache, for he was as yet unconverted. Jabez Carey (1793-1862) was the one of whom he was speaking. The father had long prayed for Jabez to turn to Christ, and had asked his closest friends in England to join him in prayer for his son's conversion. Pausing after this mention of Jabez, Ryland then added with tears freely flowing down his cheeks: 'Brethren, let us send up a united, universal and fervent prayer to God, in solemn silence, for the conversion of Jabez Carey.' In the words of F. A. Cox, this appeal for prayer was like 'a sudden clap of thunder, and the pause afterwards as intensely solemn as silence and prayer could make it'. For at least two minutes silence pervaded the entire church as close to two thousand people bowed in prayer. The next packet of mail from India brought news of Jabez's putting his trust in Christ that very summer.[40]

The day following these meetings there was an early morning gathering at John Rippon's church in Southwark, where it was agreed that 'a more general union of the Particular (or Calvinistic) Baptist churches in the United Kingdom' would indeed be desirable and that plans be made to have the inaugural meetings of this union the following year in June 1813. Eight further resolutions were passed at that time, among them a request that Sutcliff and Robert Hall, Jr preach at the annual meeting of the society the following year on 26 June. Sixty pastors endorsed the plans for this union, among whom were most of the leading Baptist ministers of the day.[41] Incidentally, it says much for Sutcliff's gifts as a preacher that he was asked to be one of the two speakers the following year at the annual meeting of the society and that the other man who was asked, the younger Hall, was 'the most powerful of early nineteenth-century English preachers'.[42]

## The Serampore fire and its results

When Sutcliff and his friends met in London for these two historic days, they knew nothing of a disastrous fire that had gutted the printing office of the Serampore mission on 11 March. The entire building, an immense amount of English paper, irreplaceable manuscripts on which the Serampore missionaries had laboured for years — all gone in a few hours.

News of the fire, the damage of which was later estimated at £9,000-£10,000, only reached England in early September. On 9 September Ryland received a lengthy letter from Marshman describing the fire. Sutcliff probably heard the following week. Ever interested in books, he was especially concerned about the loss of Carey's manuscripts. He asked one of Carey's nephews, Jesse Hobson, if he had any idea as to how many of Carey's manuscripts had perished in the fire, but Hobson knew little more than Sutcliff himself. Fuller, who was in Norfolk, did not hear of the fire until 18 September. As he told Sutcliff, he was convinced that the loss would ultimately issue in good. At best, he confided to his friend, it would reveal to what extent the English Baptists were committed to the mission in India.[43]

That depth of commitment was soon manifest as donations, from both Baptists and other British evangelicals, poured in to replace what had been lost. Within two months well over £10,000 had been received. In Olney, Sutcliff himself gave £6, as did his sister-in-law, Sarah. From Thomas Osborn, who had requested the Olney Baptists to select another deacon in his place three years previously as he had lost his eyesight,[44] came £4, from William Wilson, Sutcliff's right-hand man, £1, and from the Anglican minister, Christopher Stephenson, £5. Martha Wallis, in whose home the society had been formed, gave £20. Ryland collected £10 from the celebrated evangelical politician William Wilberforce. The Baptist church in Hebden Bridge, where Sutcliff's old mentor, John Fawcett, was still the pastor, gave over £16. Sutton in the Elms in Leicestershire, one of the founding churches of the Northamptonshire Association and where one of Sutcliff's former students by the name of Burdett was pastoring, gave £33, an immense amount for a small, rural congregation.[45]

Mary Drewery, the recent biographer of Carey, has pointed out that the economic climate of Britain during the period when these gifts were flooding in was hardly one that was conducive to such giving. Great Britain was still at war with Napoleon, and by 1812 many of the nation's industries were at a standstill. In the West Riding of Yorkshire there was a severe crisis in the wool trade. And in Leicestershire the hosiery industry was hard hit. No longer able to trade with countries on the European continent, this particular industry had looked to America for a new market. But this collapsed when war broke out with the United States in the summer of 1812.

There were poor harvests in that year and the previous year, and numerous soup kitchens had to be established throughout the British Isles for the relief of the poor. Yet it was in such a time of economic distress that the society was able to raise over £10,000 in two months!

The raising of money to replace the losses caused by the Serampore fire had the unforeseen effect of making the mission known throughout the length and breadth of Great Britain. There were loud and persistent calls for a painting of Carey, which eventually issued in one being done by the portrait artist Robert Home (1762-1834). In the midst of this fame and adulation, Fuller sounded a well-needed warning. 'The fire,' he wrote to Ward on 7 January 1813, 'has given your undertaking a celebrity which nothing else, it seems, could; a celebrity which makes me tremble.' He went on: 'The public is now giving us their praises. Eight hundred guineas have been offered for Dr Carey's likeness! If we inhale this incense, will not the Lord be offended and withdraw his blessing, and then where are we? Ought we not to tremble? ... When the people ascribed "ten thousands to David," it wrought envy in Saul, and proved a source of long and sore affliction. If some new trials were to follow, I should not be surprised; but, if we be kept humble and near to God, we have nothing to fear.'[46] Fuller's prognostication of 'some new trials' proved to be truer than he could have imagined.

## Problems with the East India Company

From the very beginning of the mission in India, its political status was an extremely tenuous one. Up till 1858, British possessions and interests in India were run by the East India Company. The executive body of the company in England was the Court of Directors, which consisted of twenty-four men. After the passage of the India Bill in 1784, the directors retained their control over the commercial affairs of the company, but in political matters were subject to a Board of Control that was appointed by the British government. Unofficially, the majority of the members of the company were strongly opposed to missions. They argued that overt evangelization of the Indian people might well provoke them into revolt, which would of course hurt the company's financial interests. Thus, all missionaries who sought to work within the company's territories in India required a licence to do so. Moreover, since the directors of the company were drawn from the ranks of the political and religious establishment, most of them regarded missionaries who were Dissenters with considerable disdain and suspicion. It should be noted, however, that there were some directors in the company, like Charles Grant, who were evangelicals and thus supportive of the cause of missions. Due to this general attitude of the East India Company, evangelical Dissenters who went out to India prior to 1813 thus made no attempt to apply for a licence, since they reasonably assumed that they would not be granted one. Nevertheless, officials of the company in Bengal were generally willing to turn a blind eye to the presence of the Baptist missionaries associated with the Serampore mission, especially after Carey's appointment in 1801 to the faculty of the company's College of Fort William.[47] Serampore itself, it should be noted, was not under the jurisdiction of the East India Company, since it was one of two colonies the Danish had established in India for trading purposes, the other being Tanquebar in the south.

This semi-benevolent attitude of company officials in India towards unlicensed missionaries began to alter in 1811, after a bill was introduced into the British House of Lords by Viscount Sidmouth (1767-1844), which sought to curb the growth of evangelical Dissent by placing definite restrictions on those who could qualify as Dissenting preachers. Deeply concerned about the quality of men who, in significant numbers, were becoming preachers in the ranks of a revived Dissent, Sidmouth's bill was designed to put serious limits on the opportunities available for 'cobblers, tailors, pig-drovers, and chimney-sweepers,' to use Sidmouth's words, to become preachers. The bill failed to gain even a second reading, but it had helped to harden the attitude of the East India Company towards Dissenting missionaries who lacked a permit to reside in India. On 6 March 1813 William Johns and John Lawson (1787-1825), two Baptist missionaries who had recently arrived in India without permits, were ordered to leave the country. After much protest by the Serampore Trio, Lawson, who was an engraver and who had studied with Sutcliff, was allowed to stay. Johns, though, was deported, further appeals availing nothing.

The East India Company's charter came up for renewal in 1813 and, as Fuller told Ward on 7 January of that year, 'We are all on the alert to besiege the government and perhaps Parliament for a clause in favour of missions, or for liberty to send missionaries, and security when arrived.'[48] Fuller, Sutcliff and their friends were determined to take the offensive and to campaign for a clause in the renewed charter that would give legal toleration for missionaries already working in the company's territories and permission to send out more missionaries as they were required. Five days later Fuller wrote to Sutcliff and told him that either he or Sutcliff would have to go up to London to speak with 'the ministers and other members of Parliament about the charter business'. He would be ready to go, if his health were better. He feared catching a cold from the damp weather. Then he added, 'Perhaps I must go, and if you or [James] Hinton be wanted, I must write.'[49]

As it turned out, Fuller felt well enough to travel up to London in early February and spend two weeks there.[50] Fuller perceived that the situation was a serious one, and that the discussion regarding the company's charter could easily go against the Baptists. He urged Sutcliff to join him in London in early March for a meeting with Robert Hobart, Earl of Buckinghamshire (1760-1816), who was the president of the East India Company's Board of Control. On Wednesday, 3 March, Fuller and Sutcliff — with Joseph Ivimey and William Burls, a deacon of Carter Lane Baptist Church in London and later the treasurer of the Baptist Union — met with the earl. He was very cordial to the four Baptists, and Fuller later wrote that week to Ward to tell him, 'I do not suspect but that you will be tolerated *as you have been*, but whether any more I cannot tell.' Fuller had even had an interview with the prime minister, Robert Banks Jenkinson, Earl of Liverpool (1770-1828), who was just at the beginning of a distinguished fifteen-year premiership. Lord Liverpool had promised Fuller that the Board of Control would give his request serious consideration. But Fuller and Sutcliff were cautious, knowing full well the strength and influence of those opposed to granting the Dissenters freedom to evangelize India. As William Wilberforce commented at the time, 'The opinions of nine-tenths, or at least of a vast majority of the House of Commons would be against any motion which the friends of religion might make' with regard to the admission of missionaries to the Indian subcontinent. Thus, despite their cordial interview with the Earl of Buckinghamshire and the promise made by Lord Liverpool, the conclusion to which Fuller and Sutcliff eventually came was that they had to prepare for petitioning Parliament.'[51]

The debate on the charter of the East India Company opened in the House of Commons on 22 March. Fuller and Sutcliff were in London again shortly after the opening of the discussion and had another opportunity to visit Lord Buckinghamshire. Fuller told the earl that 'The wish of the Baptist Society was that they might obtain, by a legal enactment, the protection of the Society's British property and liberty to send out our missionaries in the Company's ships.' Lord Buckinghamshire pointed out some difficulties that he saw with the granting of such a freedom, to which Fuller replied, 'We had hoped, my lord, his Majesty's government would have assisted us, but if they refuse to do so we must petition Parliament on the subject; and there are thousands who will sign our petitions.' Stung by Fuller's reply, Lord Buckinghamshire indignantly turned on him and said, 'If you will you must, and those who will sign your petition know nothing at all of the subject.' At this point Sutcliff spoke up. 'Not so, my lord,' he said, 'they will be persons who have been reading on the subject for twenty years.'[52] As was evident in the previous year's response to the losses sustained in the Serampore fire, the regular publication of the *Periodical Accounts* of the mission had helped to create an informed awareness of, and support for, the missionary endeavour in India.

After their return from London, Fuller told Sutcliff that they would have to put their strategy with regard to petitions into full operation. On Monday, 29 March, Fuller wrote to Sutcliff, 'Things are at such a crisis with us about petitioning Parliament that we must hold a meeting for consultation at Northampton tomorrow. I have sent to Mr Hall of Leicester pressing him to meet us by Tuesday dinner, and should greatly wish your company at the same time... I have thought of two kinds of petitions: first, one from societies... Every society must frame a petition for itself... Second, one from places, which may suit all the cities and towns nearly in the kingdom.'[53]

Sutcliff set out for Northampton the following day, and met Fuller and Hall at an inn called the Saracen's Head at half-past one. After dinner there, they went over to the College Lane church and discussed their strategy. They were, of course, not the only ones involved in organizing petitions. Petitions were also written by supporters of the interdenominational London Missionary Society, which had been founded in 1795 and at that time was known simply as 'The Missionary Society', and the Anglican-based Church

Missionary Society, founded in 1799. Wilberforce in particular threw himself into the struggle with the same energy that he had devoted to the abolition of the slave-trade. Now that the slave-trade had been abolished, he considered the exclusion of missionaries from India to be 'by far the greatest of our national sins'. During the spring of 1813 encouraging men and women to write petitions occupied most of his time, but he regarded it as 'the greatest object which men ever pursued'.[54]

Fuller and Sutcliff wholeheartedly agreed. Fuller spent the greater part of that spring in London. Sutcliff did not spend nearly as much time as Fuller in the capital, but he was there again in the first week of April, when he attended a public meeting of supporters of the society on 6 April in the New London Tavern. This tavern, which was well known for its dinners, had a spacious room on its upper floor that could easily accommodate well over 350 and was frequently used by religious and benevolent societies. Sutcliff opened the meeting in prayer and, along with Ryland, Fuller and the others who began the Baptist Missionary Society, received the thanks of those present for having initiated this missionary organization. A petition was drawn up to be sent to Parliament, and approval given to a circular letter that was to be mailed to all of the Baptist pastors in Great Britain. The latter earnestly entreated these ministers to petition Parliament with 'one heart and one soul' to grant legal toleration for the missionaries in India and permission to send out others.[55]

All of this time spent in London, however, carried with it a price, especially for Fuller. Writing to Christopher Anderson on 14 June, Fuller told him that he had never known 'such a year of toil before as this has hitherto been'. He was worn out. There was, in addition to his pastoral labours and work as secretary of the society, 'this petitioning, writing to and waiting on the Members of Parliament, which have required three or four journeys to London'. His congregation in Kettering was suffering as a result. 'In watching the India vineyard, my friends often tell me I neglect my own; and I cannot disprove the charge,' he told Anderson.[56]

Parliament was inundated with petitions, bearing half a million signatures supporting the evangelization of India.[57] And on the day that it came to a vote on the issue, 22 June, Wilberforce spoke for three hours in the House of Commons. His health was not good — he had chest problems and in previous months had developed a curvature of the spine — but his speech that day is considered one of his finest. He described the moral degradation of many of the natives of India and their abominable religious beliefs, and then pronounced the cure: Christianity. 'I should deem it almost morally impossible,' he declared, 'that there could be any country in the state in which India is proved ... now to be, which would not be likely to find Christianity the most powerful of all expedients for improving its morals, and promoting alike its temporal and eternal welfare.' The speech ended with praise of the selfless dedication of Carey and the other missionaries who were labouring in India to secure these ends. In Wilberforce's eyes, the Serampore mission was nothing less than 'one of the chief glories of our country'.[58]

The petitions and Wilberforce's speech carried the day, as the motion to admit missionaries to India was approved by eighty-nine votes to thirty-six. The changes to the charter did not include all that Fuller and Sutcliff would have liked to have seen. For instance, the requirement that all missionaries going to India must have a licence to reside there was left in force and the East India Company continued to have some degree of control over missionary activity. Nevertheless, the revised charter clearly granted freedom to the missionaries in India to itinerate and to preach in public, and cleared the way for a steady stream of missionaries to go to India and to labour there.[59]

Fuller and Sutcliff, it will be recalled, had been very anxious that the missionaries that were sent out to India and to Sierra Leone should avoid meddling in politics and be extremely discreet in the airing of their political views. Their own extensive involvement in the political realm during 1813 was not a violation of this conviction. What was at stake during the debates in Parliament that year was the very freedom to preach the gospel in India.

Moreover, both men were quite prepared to countenance disobedience to the government over this issue. As Fuller had said in 1800, 'In sending out missionaries we should certainly be glad of the concurrence of the governing powers; yet if it be not to be obtained we think ourselves warranted by the Scripture to go without it. Jesus said to the primitive ministers, "Go, preach the gospel to every creature" (Mark 16:15). He did not direct them to ask leave of any prince or government, but to go, and if persecuted in one city to flee to another.'[60]

Similarly, Sutcliff could say around the same time that a local church 'disclaims all dependence on the magistrate as magistrate, and totally denies his authority to legislate within her walls'.[61] The spreading of the gospel to the nations of the world was a command that Christ had laid upon local churches, and obedience to his legislation had a higher claim upon the consciences of Fuller and Sutcliff than obedience to the state. The mettle and spirit that they showed in the debates surrounding the renewal of the East India Company's charter flowed from such convictions as well as from their Calvinistic Baptist heritage.

## Sutcliff on reading the Word of God

Two weeks prior to the vote on the renewal of the East India Company's charter, Sutcliff had attended the annual meeting of the Northamptonshire Association in Kettering. The Olney pastor had been asked to prepare the circular letter that year on the topic of reading the Word of God. In it Sutcliff encouraged his readers to peruse the Scriptures 'with a sacred awe', because they were 'the voice of Him who gave us our existence'. They should thus be studied with gratitude. Deprived of this book, he and his readers would have been in 'dark despair, without a ray of hope', much like many of those in India. Nevertheless, Sutcliff was confident that 'The Word of the Lord, which has begun to run and to be glorified in Bengal (cf. 2 Thessalonians 3:1), shall prevail,' and 'those who sit in the region of darkness, and the valley of the shadow of death, shall see the light of life.' He also urged his readers to read this book with faith in its divine origin, for such faith would issue in a heart that is attentive to all that God has revealed in his Word. Finally, Sutcliff emphasized that the reading of the Scriptures must be accompanied by fervent prayer for the illumination of the Spirit, since only he can give 'a sacred relish' for God's truth.

This circular letter was to be the last of Sutcliff's published works. Though easy to read, it bears ample witness to what had been at the heart of his life and of his ministry at Olney: the receptive and retentive listening to the Scriptures, 'a book of 'divine origin ... high authority ... unrivalled excellency'.[62]

Despite a very busy schedule and what he described as a 'paralytic attack' the previous November, Sutcliff's health at this time appears to have been good. Yet, as he wrote to Anderson on

Saturday, 19 June, he was aware more than ever that he and his wife were 'both going down the declivity of life'. His 'motto', as he had told his Scottish friend three years before, was Jude 21: 'Looking for the mercy of our Lord Jesus Christ.' 'Free, sovereign grace,' he went on to emphasize, 'is all my hope, my only boast.'[63]

## The formation of the Baptist Union

The following Monday Sutcliff travelled up to London for the annual meeting of the Baptist Missionary Society and the inauguration of the Baptist Union. At six o'clock on the evening of Wednesday, 23 June, Sutcliff preached from Galatians 4:4 to a crowded meeting in the Jews' Chapel, Spitalfields. This chapel had originally served a French Huguenot congregation during the time that Spitalfields was a leading centre of settlement for Huguenot refugees fleeing France after the revocation of the Edict of Nantes in 1685. In 1809 the chapel was purchased by the London Society for the Propagation of the Gospel among the Jews for evangelistic outreach to the Jewish population of London. According to one later report, Sutcliff's sermon was 'an energetic and judicious discourse'.[64]

Early the next morning Sutcliff attended the inaugural meeting of the Baptist Union in the vestry of Carter Lane Baptist Church, Southwark, not far from the southern end of the old London Bridge. John Rippon, the pastor of this church and an old friend of Sutcliff, had come to be widely respected as one of the leading figures of the Baptist denomination in the metropolis. However, it is noteworthy that Rippon did not generally take the lead in the initiation of new enterprises. When he was once asked why this was so, he is said to have replied, 'Why, I see the Dover coach go by my house every morning, and I notice that the leaders get most lashed'![65] Nevertheless, it was beneath the three-quarter painting of Rippon's predecessor, John Gill, which hung on one of the walls of the vestry, that Rippon chaired the inaugural meeting of the union.

The initial constitution of the union included a brief statement of faith that set forth the main doctrines of Calvinism. It would have been very familiar to Sutcliff, since it was almost identical to that which the Northamptonshire Association affirmed as its basis of union. The last but one item of the constitution would also have been quite significant for Sutcliff. It was recommended to all of the churches of the new union that on the first Monday evening of every month they observe 'the monthly prayer meeting for the spread of the gospel that has for many years been observed in most of the churches'. This was, of course, a reference to the Prayer Call of 1784. Sutcliff would have been the first to acknowledge that all that had been accomplished for God among the Calvinistic Baptists in the years since this momentuous call to prayer was rooted in that event. As F. A. Cox later bore witness on the occasion of the fiftieth anniversary of the founding of the Baptist Missionary Society, 'Copious showers of blessing from on high [had] been poured forth upon the churches' as a result of the decision taken in 1784 to pray regularly for revival. The linking of the Baptist Union to this prayer movement must have been very gratifying to Sutcliff and to his mind would have held out promise for the future of the union. The next twenty years, however, were rocky ones for the nascent organization. As Ernest Payne has remarked, it was mainly the energy and conviction of Joseph Ivimey that prevented the union from disintegrating or petering out during these years.[66]

## Eustace Carey is sent out to India

The first Baptist missionary to take advantage of the revised charter of the East India Company was Eustace Carey, the nephew of William Carey. Like his uncle, Eustace was born in Paulerspury and, also like his uncle, he had studied with Sutcliff. He came to Olney in the autumn of 1809, where he stayed till early 1812. He then went to Bristol for a period of training at the academy.[67]

When Fuller first requested a permit for Eustace Carey to go to India, the Directors of the East India Company quibbled with the wording of the request. As Fuller informed Sutcliff in a letter that he wrote to him on 15 November the directors supposed 'we wanted him to go out to assist his uncle in the *printing office*; to which they have an objection!' Fuller had rephrased the request and explicitly told the directors that the society wanted a permit for young Carey to go out *'as a missionary'*. As he went on to tell Sutcliff, 'I think they are galled with the rope wherewith the petitions and government have tied their hands, and do not like to grant a *favour,* before they are obliged to it, and yet do not know what to object.'[68]

The society's request was soon accepted and at the end of December Fuller could tell Sutcliff that passage for Eustace Carey and his new wife, the former Esther Fosbrook of Leicester, had been booked on an East India Company vessel that was sailing for India in February of the following year. Fuller further informed his friend that the young Carey's commissioning was set for January in Northampton and that he had asked Robert Hall, Jr to preach on the occasion.[69]

The setting apart of young Carey took place on 19 January in the College Lane Church, John Ryland's previous pastoral charge. After the service had been opened with the singing of a hymn, Thomas Blundell, Jr, who was the pastor of the church, led in prayer. Fuller then briefly explained to the congregation that their meeting together was primarily designed to commend Carey 'to God by prayer and the laying on of hands'. The latter, Fuller was careful to point out, was 'not to impart authority' to Carey, but to express their 'cordial approbation of him and union with him' in his going out to India. Young Carey then shared with the congregation what had led him to take this step in his life. After Carey's testimony, Sutcliff came forward, laid his hands on Carey, along with the other ministers present, and led the congregation in prayer for the young man.[70] Robert Hall then went to the pulpit and gave what he called 'a few hints of advice' to Carey. It was a stirring address that drew attention to the important qualifications requisite of a missionary.

In words that would have pleased Sutcliff as he listened, Hall told Carey and the rest of his hearers that 'An effusion of the Spirit of prayer on the Church of Christ is a surer pledge of success in the establishment of missions than the most splendid exhibitions of talent.'

Sutcliff would also have concurred when Hall stressed the importance of a missionary's cultivating an 'unshaken persuasion of the promises of God respecting the triumph and enlargement of his kingdom': 'It is impossible that the mind of a missionary should be too much impressed with the beauty, glory, and grandeur of the kingdom of Christ as it is unfolded in the oracles of the Old and New Testaments; or with the certainty of the final accomplishment of these oracles, founded on the faithfulness and omnipotence of their author. To those parts of Scripture his attention should be especially directed in which the Holy Spirit employs and exhausts, so to speak, the whole force and splendour of inspiration in depicting the future reign of the Messiah, together with that astonishing spectacle of dignity, purity, and peace which his Church will exhibit when, "having the glory of God" (Revelation 21:11), her bounds shall be commensurate with those of the habitable globe, when every object on which the eye shall rest will remind the spectator of the commencement of a new age, in which the tabernacle of God is with men and he dwells among them.'[71]

As Hall reminded Carey, there would be deep discouragements in store for him in India, where Satan maintained 'an almost undisputed empire' through the tyranny of idolatry. Only a vigorous faith in the promises of God 'respecting the future renovation of mankind' would be able to support him during these times of discouragement and give him an unshakeable 'perseverance and resolution'. This hope in the glorious future of Christ's kingdom, Hall further noted, was intimately linked to the conviction that nothing less than the almighty power of God could scale 'the formidable bulwarks of idolatry' and 'the seemingly invincible rampart of prejudice and superstition', and so establish the rule of his Son. Sutcliff's similar optimism regarding the ultimately irresistible advance of Christ's kingdom has already been noted in chapter 8. In fact, Hall himself observed in a brief character sketch that he wrote of Sutcliff soon after the latter's death that 'the future glory of the kingdom of Christ and the best means of promoting it' were among Sutcliff's 'favourite topics' of discussion and prayer.[72] Sutcliff must therefore have heard Hall's emphasis in this regard with especial delight.

In his closing remarks, Hall reminded Carey of the peculiar joy that Christians have in being members of the body of Christ: 'You are now about to be removed from us, who, it is probable, shall see your face no more; but you will not be removed from the communion of saints, which no seas can divide, no distance impair, in which we shall often meet at a throne of grace, whence fervent prayers will ascend to the Father of mercies that he may keep you under his holy protection and cause the richest of his blessings to descend "on the head of him who was separate from his brethren" (Genesis 49:26).'[73]

As it turned out, Hall almost certainly did see Carey again, for in 1826 the latter left Bengal for good due to ill health and returned to England. There was one present that day, though, to whom Hall's words did apply, albeit unintentionally — John Sutcliff. Eustace Carey's ministry was just beginning, but that of Sutcliff was fast drawing to a close. Within six weeks of Eustace Carey's commissioning Sutcliff's pulpit ministry had come to an end and he found himself facing death.

# 14.
# 'The fathers are dying'

*'As sinners never think they have sin enough till it brings them to hell, so saints never think they have grace enough till it brings them to heaven'* (Matthew Henry).

On 27 February1814 Sutcliff preached what proved to be his last sermon. It was taken from Job 42:5-6: 'I have heard of thee by the hearing of the ear: but now mine eye seeth thee. Wherefore I abhor myself, and repent in dust and ashes.'[1] A few days later, while on a trip to London, Sutcliff was stricken with what appears to have been a heart attack. Fuller, in his funeral sermon for his friend, tells us that on the night of 3 March, Sutcliff 'was seized ... with a violent pain across his breast and arms, attended with great difficulty of breathing'.[2]

Dr David Bartlett, a medical doctor who is currently serving as an elder in the Sutcliff Church, believes that Sutcliff either suffered a heart attack or a severe episode of angina pectoris. The description of a 'violent pain across his breast and arms', Bartlett notes, fits with the diagnosis of heart pain, but the associated difficulty in breathing is not that common in a heart attack and virtually unknown in episodes of angina. On balance, however, he believes that Sutcliff did indeed experience a heart attack and that it was accompanied by sufficient damage to cause acute heart failure. With his heart unable to generate sufficient pressure to pump the blood around his body, there would have been blood congestion in his veins and backward pressure in his capillaries. The latter in turn would have caused more fluid than normal to be forced into the tissues at various places in his body, including the lungs. The build-up of fluid in his lungs would obviously occasion the difficulty in breathing.[3]

Sutcliff was kept ten days in London, and then over the course of two days taken home to Olney. Fuller received word about his friend's condition on 24 March and immediately wrote to Ryland, 'I have just received an alarming letter from Olney, and must go, if possible, to see our dear brother tomorrow... They fear he has water in his chest; he cannot lie down, for want of breath, but sits, night after night, in a large chair. Well, the government is on *His* shoulders... God grant we may finish our course with joy.'[4]

It would appear that subsequent to his heart attack Sutcliff experienced what is a common symptom in heart failure, namely, considerable shortness of breath or orthopnea, caused by the collection of fluid in his lungs.[5]

On Fuller's first visit to Sutcliff, the Olney pastor told his friend that he expected to recover, but if not, he was prepared for death, since he was at peace with God. As Sutcliff had told his brother Daniel in a letter that he wrote around the time of Fuller's first visit, 'All is in the hands of a wise and gracious God. We are the Lord's servants, and he has a right to dispose of us as he pleases, and to lay us aside at any time.'[6] Fuller had hoped to visit Sutcliff again in the first week of May, but an urgent matter had compelled him to travel over to Norwich that week. When he returned home there was a letter awaiting him from one of Sutcliff's students, Lee Compere, informing him that Sutcliff was 'far from recovery'. Fuller wrote to Sutcliff on 8 May to tell him that he was hopeful that he would be able to find time to see Sutcliff the following week on Tuesday, 16 May. The day before this visit Fuller wrote to Carey to let him know that their mutual friend was 'in imminent danger from a dropsy', i.e. a generalized edema, and was not expected to live.[7]

## Sutcliff's last days

A week or so after Fuller had visited Sutcliff, the latter's younger brother, Daniel, arrived from Yorkshire. It was not the first time that Daniel had been to Olney. There had been a few visits over the years. Moreover, the two brothers, who had been the best of friends since their childhood days, had also kept in touch regularly. Daniel was like his brother in many ways: cautious, gentle in temperament, somewhat reserved but taking 'great pleasure in the company of his friends', deeply interested in the advance of Christ's kingdom at home or abroad, and enamoured of books.[8]

Now, for eighteenth-century evangelicalism, the death-bed of a believer was a particularly important occasion. In Sutcliff's own words, it was a place to bear a 'witness for God: a witness to the importance, the supports, the comforts of religion'. At the funeral of Joshua Symonds in November 1788, Sutcliff had also noted that the death of believers with their faith intact did 'credit to their holy profession'. In other words, the triumphant death of a believer set a seal upon the testimony of his or her life.[9] In a recent study of the accounts of the deaths of believers in eighteenth- and nineteenth-century evangelicalism, Henry D. Rack, a noted historian of early Methodism, has further observed that attending the deaths of evangelical Calvinists there was often 'a heightened stress on human helplessness and total dependence on grace'. This was in definite contrast to the Arminian Methodists, who placed a greater emphasis on feelings of rapture and joy.[10]

When Sutcliff was asked by his brother about his feelings, for instance, he said that he was calm and happy, but did not have strong consolations. He was assured of his salvation because he knew that he had come to Christ and felt a 'union of heart with him, his people, and his cause'. He was quite conscious, though, of his need for sovereign grace. When a certain individual who came to visit him spoke about all that Sutcliff had done in furthering the cause of Christ, the latter replied with some emotion, 'I look upon it all as nothing; I must enter heaven on the same footing as the converted thief, and shall be glad to take a seat by his side.' A similar note was struck during a conversation with a member of his congregation, who may have been William Wilson, the Olney deacon. 'Do your utmost for the cause of Christ,' Sutcliff said to him. 'I have done a little, and am ashamed that I have done no more. I have such views of its importance, that, had I ability, I would spread the gospel through the world.'[11]

As Sutcliff and his brother chatted during these last days of his life, the dying man emphasized that 'His views of divine things were far more vivid and impressive than they had been before.' He had a greater sense of human depravity and 'the exceeding sinfulness of sin'. He was thus more than ever cognizant of the responsibility laid upon those who were called to the ministry of preaching and teaching God's Word. A number of times he said in his brother's hearing, 'Ministers will never do much good till they begin to *pull sinners out of the fire*!' If only he could preach again, he told Daniel,

'I should say things which I never said before: but God has no need of me; he can raise up men to say them better than I could say them.'[12]

On 5 June, Sutcliff asked one of his students to write a letter for him to Fuller. After recording some of the expenses relating to his students, for which reimbursement was to be made by the society, Sutcliff extended his 'most affectionate love to brother Fuller'. The student then went on to state on Sutcliff's behalf that as to 'the state of his health, he can say nothing more encouraging. He hopes,' the student concluded, 'for the prayers of his Christian friends.'[13]

Fuller visited Sutcliff again around 10 June. Of his friend's condition he informed Ryland on 11 June: 'Brother Sutcliff gets no better. I fear there is little or no hope of him.'[14] A night or so later, Sutcliff thought he would not live till the morning. His wife, brother and sister-in-law were roused, as well as the six students who were studying in Sutcliff's academy. When his wife reached his side, he was feeling somewhat better, but still he said to her, 'My love, I commit you to Jesus; our separation will not be long, and I think I shall often be about you. Read much in the Psalms of David, and be much in prayer. I wish I had spent more time in prayer.'[15]

The last time that Fuller saw him alive was the following week — Sunday, 19 June. Fuller was on his way to London for the annual meeting of the Missionary Society. It must have been a solemn occasion as the two friends said goodbye. When Fuller was about to leave, expecting to see his friend's face no more in this world, he said to him, 'I wish you, my dear brother, an abundant entrance into the everlasting kingdom of our Lord Jesus Christ!' Sutcliff hesitated before replying, not out of doubts about his salvation, but because he honestly questioned whether the term 'abundant' could be rightly applied to him. 'That is more than I expect,' he eventually responded. 'I think I understand the connexion and import of those words — "Add to your faith virtue ... give diligence to make your calling and election sure ... for so an entrance shall be ministered unto you *abundantly*" (2 Peter 1:5,10,11). I think the idea is that of a ship coming into harbour with a fair gale and a full tide. If I may but reach the heavenly shore, though it be on a board or broken piece of the ship, I shall be satisfied.'[16]

It was a pensive Fuller who rode to London later that day. His long, intimate friendship with Sutcliff, which God had cemented together through their shared theological convictions and co-operation in the work of the ministry and the Missionary Society, made him feel as if he were about to lose a very close member of his immediate family.[17] One can only imagine that he wept as he rode along. His conviction that Sutcliff was about to enter into the presence of the Lord Jesus would not have meant that he shed no tears for his own personal loss.

Around three o'clock in the morning of 22 June, Sutcliff awoke, conscious that the end was very near. Now among those present in his house on that day was Thomas Welsh, whose induction as pastor of the Newbury church in Berkshire Sutcliff had attended the previous October. In fact, the last entry that Sutcliff made in the Olney Church Book in his own handwriting was on 10 October 1813 and was a record of having signed a letter of dismissal for Welsh's wife, the former Mary Weldone, to the Newbury church. She had come into membership of the Olney church on 23 February 1804 and had met Welsh during his time as one of Sutcliff's students.[18] Out of his deep love for Sutcliff, Welsh had ridden from Newbury especially to be with his former tutor in his last days. Calling Welsh to his side, Sutcliff took hold of his hand and exhorted him: 'Preach as you will wish you had when you come to die. It is one thing to preach, and another to do it as a dying man. I am glad you are settled where you are. I think you may say, I dwell among my own people. I am glad we ever knew one another. Spiritual unions are sweet. I have fled to Jesus; to his cross I am united. The Lord bless you, and make you a blessing!'[19]

That afternoon, about five o'clock, a noticeable change took place in Sutcliff's condition — he began to vomit some blood. 'It is all over,' he said, 'this cannot be borne long.' Welsh, who was standing by his side, asked him, 'You are prepared for the issue?' to which Sutcliff replied, 'I think I am, I do not feel my mind shaken; go and pray for me.' As Welsh went and prayed, Sutcliff's life ebbed away. About half an hour before he drew his last breath, he said, using the words of the martyr Stephen and the psalmist, 'Lord Jesus, receive my spirit. It is come ... perhaps a few minutes more ... heart and flesh fail... God.' The last of these words come from Psalm 73:26: 'My flesh and my heart faileth: but God is the strength of my heart and my portion for ever.' Sutcliff appears to have been going to say the second clause of this verse, but his strength was failing fast.

As we have already seen, a few days earlier he had encouraged his wife to read much in the Psalms. Like many in the history of the church, Sutcliff had obviously found in the Psalms an invaluable tool in prayer. Yet Sutcliff did manage to summon one last reserve of strength and with decided emphasis he spoke what proved to be his final words: 'That God is the *strength* of his people is an idea that I never saw before *as I now see it.*' [20]

## The funeral sermon

During Sutcliff's illness, his pulpit had been supplied by his students, but understandably it was his old friend, Andrew Fuller, whom he asked to preach his funeral sermon. The text from which he requested Fuller to preach was Jude 20-21. As we have seen, it was a text on which he had long dwelt. Since Fuller was away in London at the time of Sutcliff's death, the funeral had to be delayed till the following Tuesday, 28 June. Fuller arrived home that weekend, preached and administered the Lord's Supper at Kettering on 26 June, and had the Monday to compose his funeral sermon for Sutcliff.

The weather that Tuesday was hot and sultry, but it did not hinder upwards of fifteen or sixteen hundred people from attending the funeral.[21] Baptists from churches throughout the Northamptonshire Association, as well as numerous individuals from other denominations, came to pay their last respects.[22] The Anglican rector of Olney, Christopher Stephenson, and his curate, Henry Gauntlett, were among the pallbearers, as was the minister of the Congregationalist church in Olney, Thomas Hillyard. When Fuller discovered that the majority of the people were unable to find a seat in the meeting-house and consequently had to stand outside in the graveyard, he decided to preach in the open air. The windows of the meeting-house were thus opened so that those within could hear his sermon.[23]

According to Fuller, Sutcliff saw in Jude 20-21, especially the concluding clause of verse 21, a concise expression of his 'last sentiments and his future prospects', that is, those theological principles that he had spent his life teaching and of which he was firmly persuaded, and the hope that had undergirded him as he faced eternity. After briefly setting this text in its historical context, the Kettering pastor went on to note that this text also contained four principles essential to 'true evangelical religion'.

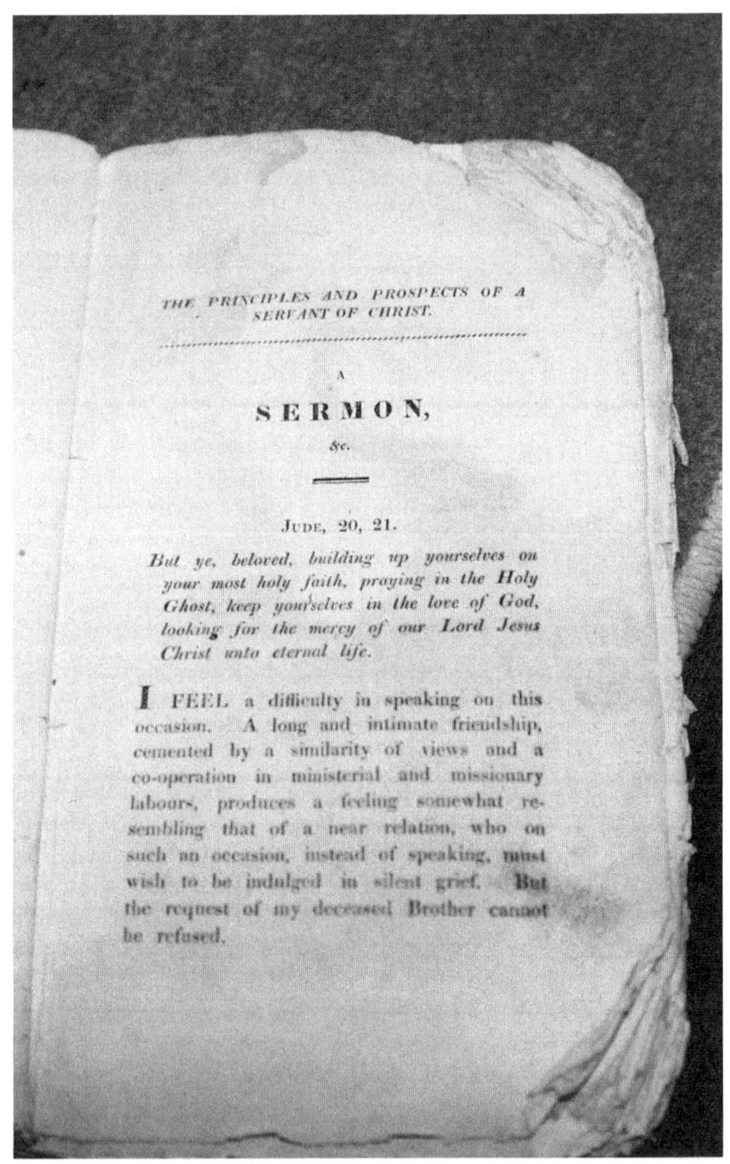
THE PRINCIPLES AND PROSPECTS OF A SERVANT OF CHRIST.

A

SERMON,

&c.

JUDE, 20, 21.

*But ye, beloved, building up yourselves on your most holy faith, praying in the Holy Ghost, keep yourselves in the love of God, looking for the mercy of our Lord Jesus Christ unto eternal life.*

I FEEL a difficulty in speaking on this occasion. A long and intimate friendship, cemented by a similarity of views and a co-operation in ministerial and missionary labours, produces a feeling somewhat resembling that of a near relation, who on such an occasion, instead of speaking, must wish to be indulged in silent grief. But the request of my deceased Brother cannot be refused.

Opening page of the published version of Fuller's funeral sermon for John Sutcliff.
*(Reproduced by courtesy of Sutcliff Baptist Church, Olney.)*

First, *true evangelical religion was founded on the 'death and resurrection of Christ'*. The Scriptures, Fuller asserted, give but one answer to the question, 'What must I do to be saved?' 'Believe on the Lord Jesus Christ, and thou shalt be saved' (Acts 16:31). To build one's religion on anything else — human reason, good deeds, 'impressions' that one is a 'favourite of God', a faith that fails to issue in a life of holiness — was to ensure the ultimate ruin of one's life.[24]

Then Fuller emphasized that *the faith which is founded on Christ's death and resurrection grows by 'praying in the Holy Spirit'* (Jude 20). Without the Holy Spirit, there can be no true prayer. And without such prayer, there can be 'no intercourse with God'. This truth had long been affirmed by Calvinistic Baptist spirituality. John Bunyan, for instance, in one of his earliest writings, *I will pray with the Spirit* (1662), had stated emphatically: 'When the Spirit gets into the heart, then there is prayer indeed, and not till then.'[25] Yet the Spirit's work, Fuller went on, is not something 'of which we are always sensible'. Prayer should not be neglected because one is 'unconscious of being under divine influence'. In actual fact, it is 'in prayer that the Spirit of God ordinarily assists us'.[26]

At the heart of this discussion about the importance of prayer for 'true evangelical religion' was a statement that Sutcliff had uttered a number of times during his final illness: 'I wish I had prayed more.' He had uttered this weighty saying, as we have seen, to his wife about ten days before his death. He had also said it to Fuller on the latter's last visit. At first Fuller found this statement rather puzzling, coming as it did from a man who had been at the heart of a prayer movement that had been essential to the revitalization of the Baptist denomination. While riding up to London on 19 June he had ruminated on this statement and eventually came up with the following interpretation and application, which he told to Joseph Ivimey in the metropolis: 'I do not suppose that brother Sutcliff meant that he wished he had prayed more frequently, but more *spiritually*. I wish I had prayed more for the influences of the Holy Spirit, I might have enjoyed more of the power of vital godliness. I wish I had prayed more for the assistance of the Holy Spirit, in studying and preaching my sermons; I might have seen more of the blessing of God attending my ministry. I wish I had prayed more for the outpouring of the Holy Spirit to attend the labours of our friends in India; I might have witnessed more of the effects of their efforts in the conversion of the heathen.'[27]

Whether or not Fuller correctly interpreted Sutcliff's statement, his application certainly resonated with themes dear to Sutcliff's heart: personal renewal, the revival of the church and Spirit-empowered witness. In his sermon for Sutcliff Fuller did not exactly reproduce what he had told Ivimey, but the substance of these remarks was incorporated into the sermon. He mentioned how his deceased friend's 'weighty saying' was equally applicable to himself, for he wished that he had prayed more for the 'success of the gospel', 'the salvation of those about' him, his own soul and indeed all of his 'undertakings'.[28]

Third, *evangelical religion is marked by love to God,* a love that loves him for who he is as well as for what he has done for sinners. Fuller spent some time elaborating on this aspect of 'true religion', since it had been central to Sutcliff's ministry. He reminded his audience that Sutcliff 'dwelt much in his preaching on the glory of the divine character and government as displayed in the law and the gospel' and he recalled Sutcliff's 'firm persuasion that all religious affections which disregarded this were spurious and would prove of no account at the great day'. He thought this way, Fuller asserted, because he was convinced that 'God must be loved *as* God, or he is loved not at all.'

This particular way of expressing these convictions had its roots in the theology of Jonathan Edwards. For example, in his classical study of spiritual experience, *The Religious Affections* (1746), Edwards had argued at length that a love of God which entailed no love for God as he is in himself and no relish for the beauty of God was really self-love, for God was simply being loved for what he did for the individual concerned.[29]

Fourth, Fuller spoke of what had been a major emphasis of evangelical Christianity ever since the Reformation: *the believer's acceptance with God is based solely on the work of Christ.* Fuller, who had known Sutcliff for thirty-eight years, had no doubt that his friend had been 'a just and holy man', whose lifestyle was characterized by 'good works'. Nevertheless, Fuller asserted, Sutcliff's 'dependence for acceptance with God was not on them. He looked for eternal life through "the mercy of our Lord Jesus Christ"'(Jude 21).' The best of Christian men and women, Fuller continued, 'have always been the most sensible of their own unworthiness,' and their

Sutcliff's tomb
(The inscription on the end of the tomb facing the camera is in memory of his wife, Jane, who is buried with him.)

Close-up of the inscription on the tomb

need for Christ's righteousness to cover their many imperfections. Not only had this been prominent in Sutcliff's thinking, but it had also loomed large in his preaching and teaching. 'He preached the doctrine of sovereign grace in such a manner as to *warn* every man against trusting to his own righteousness, and *teach* every man in what way he must be saved, if saved at all, as well as to lead those who have believed in Jesus to ascribe it to the grace of God that they were what they were.'[30]

The final section of Fuller's sermon was centred on the 'future prospects' that awaited all who built their lives on these four principles: 'an immediate reception into the presence of Christ' after death, the resurrection of the body, mercy as well as rewards on the Day of Judgement, eternal communion with God.

Having dealt with the text, Fuller could have ended the sermon at this point. Certain, however, that Sutcliff would have approved, Fuller brought the sermon to a close on an evangelistic note. The death of a pastor is ever a serious event, he told his audience, targeting the Olney Baptists in particular. Sutcliff had gone to give an account of his ministry among them. Some who had sat under that ministry would be a source of great joy to him, for they would be found 'to have received the love of the truth'. But others, Fuller feared, 'will be found to have sat under his ministry in vain'. Yet it was not too late for even these to profit by Sutcliff's ministry. Though he was dead, his life still bore witness to the grace and mercy of God in Christ, as Fuller had sought to show in his sermon. For those who embraced the principles that Sutcliff had made his own, 'Death ... is not death, but the introduction to everlasting life.' On the other hand, those who believe not the Son 'will never see life', Fuller solemnly asserted, for the 'wrath of God abideth' on them.[31]

## Fuller's failing health and a memoir of Sutcliff

When Fuller preached this sermon for his deceased friend, he was not at all a well man. One of the Kettering deacons who attended the funeral, George Wallis, the nephew of Beeby and Martha Wallis, noted in his diary that he had been 'much affected' at the loss of Sutcliff and 'at the thought of our aged ministers leaving us, which, if I live, must be the case also of *him* who so faithfully, so ably improved the words chosen by the deceased'.[32] Fuller was not unaware of his failing health, but he was determined to labour as long as he could, even though he sensed that his work, like Sutcliff's, was nearing its completion. Soon after Sutcliff's funeral, he set off for the north of England on behalf of the Missionary Society. That summer there were numerous requests to have Sutcliff's funeral sermon published and to include with it a memoir of the Olney pastor, but Fuller had hardly a spare moment. When he wrote on 4 August to let Carey, Marshman and Ward know of Sutcliff's death, he told them, 'If I could get time I would print the sermon and add something of a memoir.'[33]

Unable to find the time to draw up both a memoir and a sketch of Sutcliff's character, Fuller asked Robert Hall to help him by doing the latter. Hall initially agreed, but eventually wrote to Fuller in September to tell him that he had not been able to succeed to his own satisfaction: 'I have made several efforts, and have sketched, as well as I could, the outlines of what I conceive to be his character; but have failed in producing such a portrait as appears to me fit for the public eye.' Hall then added, 'I am perfectly convinced that your intimacy with him, and your powers of discrimination, will enable you to present to posterity a much juster and more impressive idea of him than I can.'[34]

Hall did draw up a sketch of about 700 words, which has been utilized a number of times already in the course of this biography, but it remained unpublished till after Hall's death in 1831. He noted that Sutcliff's character was especially marked by 'a sweet humility' and suffused with 'a savour of experimental piety'. Gentle and kind, he was always sensitive to the feelings of others. Moreover, Hall noted: 'Few men took a deeper interest than our deceased brother in the general state of the church and the propagation of the gospel abroad. The future glory of the kingdom of God and the best means of promoting it were his favourite topics, and usurped a large part of his thoughts and his prayers; nor was he ever more in his element than when he was exerting his powers in devising plans for its extension.'[35]

Fuller finally found the time to prepare Sutcliff's funeral sermon and a brief memoir for the press during September and early October. This was mainly due to the fact that on Sunday, 4 September, he had had 'a very serious attack of an inflammation of the liver' that compelled him to rest at home till the middle of October. Able to preach only twice during this period, he had taken up his pen, written out his sermon and drawn up a memoir of Sutcliff. Entitled *The Principles and Prospects of a Servant of Christ,* it was published during the last week of October.[36]

At the end of the memoir was a sketch of Sutcliff's character, in which Fuller readily admitted that 'Sutcliff's talents were less splendid than useful.' What was quite striking, though, was the way that he excelled in practical judgement and sage counsel. Indeed, Fuller had been of the opinion for quite a while that 'Abraham Booth was the first counsellor and John Sutcliff the second' of their denomination. Benevolent to an extraordinary degree, Sutcliff was patient and mild with his congregation, his colleagues and his students, and always gentle in his reproofs. Never hasty in making friends, he rarely had reason to repent of his friendships. Thus he 'seldom lost his friends', but, Fuller wrote with evident emotion, 'His friends have lost him!'[37]

The day before Fuller had fallen ill from his liver complaint, Jane Sutcliff had died. Barely eleven weeks had elapsed since her husband's death. Since there is no indication at all that she was sick during her husband's final illness, it may well be the case, as Kenneth Howard believed, that her death was precipitated by her deep grief at her husband's passing. Since Fuller was too ill to preach her funeral sermon, John Geard, Sutcliff's old friend from his Bristol days, spoke at her funeral from Romans 5:2. Fuller, later reflecting on Jane's death, stated: 'Death has swept away almost all my old friends; and I seem to stand expecting to be called for soon. It matters not when, so that we may be found in Christ.'[38]

## Controversy at Olney after Sutcliff's death

After Sutcliff's death, the Olney church was well supplied by a number of men till James Simmonds was eventually called as pastor in 1818. Among these preachers were William Yates (d.1845), who went out to India as a missionary in 1815, and Solomon Young (d.1826), who later became a tutor at Stepney Academy, a Baptist seminary in London, with both of whom the church was deeply impressed.

Following these two men was William Hawkins, a former member of Joseph Kinghorn's congregation in Norwich and a graduate of Edinburgh University. Hawkins came to Olney in

Sutcliff Baptist Church, Olney, as it appeared in the nineteenth century
(showing Sutcliff's tomb)
(Reproduced by courtesy of Sutcliff Baptist Church, Olney.)

The church, as it appears today.
(Inscriptions in the brickwork show that parts of the building date back to before Sutcliff's time.)

January 1815 on the recommendation of Fuller, who had received a letter about him from Kinghorn.[39] Hawkins was expected to follow what had obviously been Sutcliff's preaching regimen: once during the week as well as three times on a Sunday, in the morning, the afternoon and the evening. The largest congregation was that at the Sunday afternoon service, when there were between five and six hundred.[40]

By early April, though, Hawkins' preaching had caused considerable unrest in the congregation. As he told Kinghorn in a letter that he wrote on 4 April, there were a number in the church who were quite displeased with his preaching: 'These are they who worshipped Mr Sutcliff and they object to me that I do not preach about the *Law*, only about the *Gospe*l, and because I cannot enter into the absurd scheme of disinterested love and all the dogmas of the American school. Mr Sutcliff was a great admirer of the Transatlantic divinity and drank deep into their theory. He was also very diligent in circulating their writings among his people and now the happy fruits begin to show themselves.'[41]

Hawkins' criticism here is generally directed against Sutcliff's commitment to the theology of Jonathan Edwards and that of his New England heirs, in particular, Joseph Bellamy and Samuel Hopkins. In mentioning what he calls the 'absurd scheme of disinterested love', Hawkins has in mind the emphasis in the writings of Edwards and his followers on the fact that regeneration changes the heart's affections from a self-directed focus to one in which God and holiness are loved for their own sakes. As we have seen from Fuller's funeral sermon for Sutcliff, the latter also upheld this conviction. However, it should be noted that Hopkins developed this view of regeneration in a surprising direction. He argued that God was to be loved entirely for his own sake with *absolutely* no consideration of what one might receive from him. In other words, genuine regeneration entailed a willingness to be damned if God so willed it.[42] This was a clear departure from the thought of his mentor, Edwards, for whom 'Love to God ... will make a man forever unwilling ... to be deprived of that part of his happiness which he has in God's being blessed and glorified.'[43] Moreover, Fuller had made it clear in his sermon at Sutcliff's funeral that the Olney pastor had no 'notion of loving God for his own excellency as should render us indifferent to our own salvation'.[44] Fuller, as we have seen, had also mentioned that Sutcliff had no hesitation in preaching the law in order to set forth 'the glory of the divine character and government', but there is no evidence that he did so at the expense of the gospel.

In a letter that Hawkins wrote to Kinghorn two weeks later, his criticism was even more biting: 'Mr Sutcliff . . . laboured to inculcate all the subtleties of the Amercian school. He pointed out at great length the metaphysical distinction between moral and natural inability — dwelt much upon the Law of God as a transcript of the divine character as lovely, beautiful etc., etc., whereas Christ and his cross were but subordinate topics. . . When persons under serious convictions went to Mr Sutcliff to enquire of him about the way of salvation, the first question he put always was, "What do you think of the *Law* and of *God* as a lawgiver — is he not *lovely, beautiful* in this character? Have you read Bellamy and Hopkins and the rest? I'll lend you them." Not a word of encouragement or comfort to poor, cast-down, despairing sinners. This, of course, kept people back and I suppose for the last ten years not about a dozen people have been added to the church.'[45]

What Hawkins says in this text about the way that Sutcliff dealt with unbelievers under conviction has obviously come from someone within the Olney congregation who was disgruntled with either Sutcliff himself or his theology. Hawkins' assertion in this regard flies in the face of everything that others said about his character — his concern for others' feelings, his gentleness and kindness — and his evangelistic passion. Moreover, contrary to Hawkins' estimate of the numbers who had been added to the church since 1805, the actual figure of new members between 1805 and Sutcliff's death in 1814 was forty-three. That Sutcliff drew a distinction between moral and natural inability and preached on the law as a revelation of God's character and beauty is, as we have seen, true, but Hawkins is patently in the wrong when he states that 'Christ and his cross' thereby became 'subordinate topics' for Sutcliff. Fuller, who had known Sutcliff for practically the entire time that he was at Olney and had heard him preach dozens of times, stated that his friend had long taught the death of Christ for sinners as the only way of salvation and their only comfort in the face of death.[46]

Hawkins claimed that when he first came to Olney he had resolved not to 'combat' the views of Sutcliff and that he had endeavoured during his time in the town to stick to this resolution. Yet at some point he must have made his disagreement with Sutcliff patent from the pulpit of the Baptist meeting-house. For as Ryland commented in a letter to John Saffery, Hawkins had 'sadly ... divided' the congregation before he left Olney on 24 April and had 'saucily ... expressed himself about brother Sutcliff and American divinity'.[47] Hawkins also had opportunity to speak at the Congregationalist meeting-house as well as in the parish church, in both of which he seems to have sought further support in his quarrel with Sutcliff's theology, so that by the time that he left Olney the entire town was in an uproar.[48]

Understandably, both Fuller and Ryland were deeply disturbed by this turn of events. Hawkins' criticism of Sutcliff's theology was at the same time a criticism of their theological views. By this time, though, Fuller was a dying man. In the last letter that he ever sent to Ryland, which he dictated on 28 April, only nine days before his death, he gave his answer to Hawkins and those who agreed with him: 'We have some, who have been giving out of late, that "If Sutcliff and some others had preached more of Christ, and less of Jonathan Edwards, they would have been more useful." If those who talk thus, preached Christ half as much as Jonathan Edwards did, and were half as useful as he was, their usefulness would be double what it is. It is very singular that the Mission to the east should have originated with men of these principles; and without pretending to be a prophet, I may say, if ever it falls into the hands of men who talk in this strain, it will soon come to nothing.'[49]

In other words, to take Edwards as a theological mentor was to learn from a man whose writings were supremely Christ-centred, focused on the work of his cross and the glory of his person. Moreover, Fuller rightly felt that the rectitude of Sutcliff's principles lay in their tangible fruit, namely the Baptist Missionary Society. Edwards' theology had been vital to the involvement of Sutcliff, not to mention Fuller and Ryland, in this missionary endeavour.

Eight days' after Fuller's death on 7 May, Ryland preached his friend's funeral sermon. In it he made a point of quoting Fuller's last letter to him in its entirety, and thus made public the Kettering Baptist's refutation of Hawkins' charges. When Ryland eventually published this funeral sermon, he added a postscript, in which he sought to provide a clear explanation of the important distinction between 'those religious affections, which are founded on the transcendently excellent and amiable nature of divine things as they are in themselves, and those which are primarily founded on a conceived relation to self-interest'. His two closest friends were gone, and the responsibility of defending their shared theological convictions — convictions by which they had lived and laboured together, and which had been given shape and substance by the writings of Edwards — now wholly devolved upon him. Near the conclusion of the postscript Ryland thus wrote, 'If I knew I should be with Sutcliff and Fuller tomorrow, instead of regretting that I had endeavoured to promote that religion delineated by Jonathan Edwards in his treatise on *Religious Affections* and in his *Life of David Brainerd,* I would recommend his writings, and Dr Bellamy's ... with the last effort I could make to guide a pen.'[50]

## Tribute to an enduring friendship

Ryland, as it turned out, lived for another ten years. As the principal of the Bristol Academy he exercised an immense influence on the Baptist denomination, as many of the men whom he trained during these years went on to become Baptist pastors and missionaries, and entered their ministries imbued with Ryland's evangelical Calvinism and commitment to revival. When he died in 1825, Robert Hall was asked to preach his funeral sermon. In the memoir of Ryland that accompanied this sermon when it was published, Hall recalled the 'intimate friendship which subsisted between that lovely triumvirate, Fuller, Ryland, and Sutcliff, which never suffered a moment's interruption or abatement', and which was bound together by their 'common attachment' to the Baptist Missionary Society. 'Of congenial sentiments and taste, though of very different temperament and character, there was scarce a thought which they did not communicate to each other, while they united all their energies in supporting the same cause.' Founded on the same religious principles, theirs was a friendship which was 'destined to survive when the heavens are no more, and to spring fresh from the ashes of the universe'.[51]

In the years immediately following, this friendship between Sutcliff, Fuller and Ryland was often recollected with fondness by those who had known the three men. Carey, reflecting on their friendship in 1827, spoke of the 'full and free communion of soul' that characterized the relationship of Fuller, Sutcliff, Ryland and himself.[52] Eventually, though, that generation passed on to its reward — Carey, the last of the friends, died in 1834 — and Sutcliff especially became all but forgotten, apart from scant mention in connection with the story of William Carey. Like his silhouette, long believed to be the only extant portrayal of his facial features, he became something of a shadowy figure in late eighteenth-century Baptist history.

Hopefully, this story of his life has shown that he deserves greater recognition and has given substance to remarks such as the following, made by Christopher Anderson soon after he learned of Sutcliff's death: 'In him, I saw bright lines of resemblance to our Lord and Master, such as are seldom, very seldom to be met with in poor mortals. Such amiableness of manners, so much of the meekness and gentleness of Christ, united with sound judgment and warm affection, we seldom or never see united to such a degree as they were in him.'[53]

# Appendix I:
# The published works of John Sutcliff[1]

*A View of the Doctrine of Divine Providence.* Northampton: T. Dicey, 1779.

'Preface' to Joseph Bellamy, *Sermons upon the following Subjects, viz. the Divinity of Jesus Christ, the Millennium, the Wisdom of God in the Permission of Sin.* 1758 ed.; repr. Northampton: Thomas Dicey and Co., 1783, pp.iii-iv.

*The First Principles of the Oracles of God, represented in a Plain and Familiar Catechism, for the Use of Children.* Northampton: 1784.[2]

*The Authority and Sanctification of the Lord's Day, Explained and Enforced.* N.p.: 1786.

'Preface' to Jonathan Edwards, *An Humble Attempt to Promote Explicit Agreement and Visible Union of God's People in Extraordinary Prayer for the Revival of Religion and the Advancement of Christ's Kingdom on Earth, pursuant to Scripture Promises and Prophecies concerning the Last Time.* 1747 ed.; repr. Northampton: T. Dicey and Co., 1789, pp.iii-vi.

'The Address immediately preceding the Interment' in John Ryland, Jr, *Christ, the great Source of the Believer's Consolation; and the grand Subject of the Gospel Ministry. A Sermon, Occasioned by the Death of the Rev. Joshua Symonds.* London: (1789), pp.37-41.[3]

'Appendix. A brief narrative of the first rise of the Church assembling at the Old Meeting, in Mill-Lane, Bedford: with a short account of their pastors, until the present time, and various other particulars, chiefly extracted from their church-book' in John Ryland, Jr, *Christ, the great Source of the Believer's Consolation; and the grand Subject of the Gospel Ministry. A Sermon, Occasioned by the Death of the Rev. Joshua Symonds.* London: (1789), pp.42-60.[4]

*Jealousy for the Lord of Hosts illustrated.* London: W. Button, 1791.

'An Interview with the Late Mr Berridge', *The Evangelical Magazine,* 2 (1794), pp.73-6.

'Obituary: Character and Death of Mrs Andrews', *The Evangelical Magazine,* 3 (1795), pp.291-3.
*The Divinity of the Christian Religion Considered and Proved.* Northampton: T. Dicey and Co., 1797.
*Qualifications for Church Fellowship.* Clipston: J. W. Morris, 1800.
'Dissertation on Man', *The Biblical Magazine,* 1 (1801), pp.169-71.[5]
'Reflections on the Approaching Harvest', *The Biblical Magazine,* 2 (1802), pp.293-5.
'Justin's Epistle to Diognetus', *The Biblical Magazine,* 2 (1802), pp.41-8.
'To the Christian Females of Great Britain' in John Sutcliff, John Ryland, Jr and Andrew Fuller, eds, *Memoirs of Miss Susanna Anthony.* Clipston: J. W. Morris, 1802, pp.i-viii.
'Introductory Discourse' in John Ryland, Jr and Andrew Fuller, *The Difficulties of the Christian Ministry, and the Means of surmounting them; with the Obedience of Churches to their Pastors explained and enforced.* Birmingham: J. Belcher, 1802, pp.1-8.
*The Ordinance of the Lord's Supper considered.* Dunstable: J. W. Morris, 1803.
*On obedience to Positive Institutions.* Dunstable: J. W. Morris, 1808.
*On Reading the Word of God.* Kettering: J. G. Fuller, 1813.

# Appendix II: Jealousy for the Lord of hosts illustrated

*'I have been very jealous for the Lord God of hosts'* (1 Kings 19:10).

The infinitely great and glorious Jehovah, in every period of time, has had some among the sons of men to appear on his behalf and oppose the spirit and conduct of a revolted world. Divine wisdom and goodness have been greatly displayed by properly qualifying such persons for the stations they were to occupy. In the front of this army of witnesses for God, Elijah stands distinguished above numbers. He lived in a period of great degeneracy. Corruption of manners awfully prevailed, even among the people of Israel. Ahab, a wicked, an idolatrous king, sat on the throne. Idolatry, practised and patronized by the court, spread like a torrent through the land. In opposition to the overwhelming flood, Elijah appeared to stand alone. But boldness undaunted and firmness immovable seem, in general, to have been eminent features in his character. True, in the beginning of this chapter, we have one instance of cowardice left on record. Terrified by the daring threats of the bloody Jezebel, he fled for his life. This step, it should seem, he took without a divine warrant. For it he was called to account. The Lord said unto him, 'What dost thou here, Elijah?' (1 Kings 19:9). What are the greatest and best of men when left unto themselves? By their conduct, let us take warning. Pertinent is the petition of the psalmist, 'Hold thou me up, and I shall be safe' (Psalm 119:117), necessary the caution of the apostle, 'Let him that thinketh he standeth take heed lest he fall' (1 Corinthians 10:12).

Our text, you observe, is part of the reply made by the prophet in his own defence. In it, perhaps, something may be censured. His answer seems to indicate a degree of impatience under his trials and murmuring that his endeavours to promote the cause of God were unsuccessful. Unsuccessfulness in our ministerial work is indeed a heavy trial. It damps our ardour, dispirits our souls and weakens our hands in the work of God. To publish our report from sabbath to sabbath, from year to year, and yet to be compelled to return lamenting, 'Who hath believed our report, and to whom is the arm of the Lord revealed?' (Isaiah 53:1) is distressing. Yet we must not murmur. Fidelity and zeal, prayer and watchfulness are our incumbent duties. Should we apparently labour in vain and spend our strength for nought, surely our judgement is with the Lord and our work with our God.

But though we conjecture that in the language and spirit of Elijah something may be censured, we assert there is much that ought to be commended. The temper he describes exceedingly becomes all who sustain a public character in the cause of Christ. Yet let none imagine it should only be found in men immediately employed in sacred office; it enters deep into and is ingrafted in the very soul of true Christianity. It is an essential part of that 'holiness, without which no man shall see the Lord' (Hebrews 12:14).

In handling this subject, let us explain what we mean by jealousy for God, add a few general observations, and point out some of the methods in which it will be discovered.

I. Our subject must be explained, the meaning of the term 'jealousy' ascertained. It is introduced in the sacred Scriptures in various connections and does not always convey the same determinate idea. To be jealous *for* and *of* an object are exceedingly distinct. Jealousy *of* a person implies a suspicion of his fidelity, a suspicion that his character and conduct are not in reality what we expected or wished. But jealousy *for* God implies no unworthy suspicion of, but on the contrary, the highest degree of confidence in and esteem of him.

Jealousy *for* an object implies love to and tender concern for it, and includes a suspicion of some mischievous design formed against it. Thus Paul, in his second epistle to the church at Corinth, writes, 'I am jealous over [or upon account of] you with godly jealousy' (2 Corinthians 11:2). And why? What was it that kindled jealousy in the bosom of the apostle over these Corinthian converts? He was alarmed lest, as the serpent deceived Eve by his subtlety, so their minds should be corrupted from simplicity towards Christ (see 2 Corinthians 11:3); he suspected they were in danger. He thought he perceived mischief hatching. Satan was their inveterate and politic foe. Well aware of his traitorous designs against these Christian converts, whose spiritual interests were so dear to his heart, Paul trembled lest he should gain an advantage over them. He was jealous over them with a godly jealousy.

When the prophet uttered the language of our text, he seems to have had his eye principally upon the divine honour and interest in the world. Hence he adds, 'The children of Israel have forsaken thy covenant, thrown down thine altars, and slain thy prophets with the sword; and I, ... I only, am left; and they seek my life, to take it away' (1 Kings 19:10). He saw God's name awfully profaned and his cause greatly reduced. Israel had acted in an unfaithful manner towards the Lord of hosts and an unrighteous part towards his servants. Elijah saw idolatry spread, where formerly the pure worship of God had prevailed. The light of divine truth which had shone so beautifully in this benighted world appeared as if just about to be extinguished. This he knew would be the joy of the heathen, the triumph of hell. Alarming thought! This touched his feelings, roused his fears, thrilled through all the powers of his soul, kindled every spark of holy love into a flame of sacred zeal, made him all eye, all ear, all attention to objects so dear to his inmost soul. 'I have been very jealous for the Lord God of hosts' (1 Kings 19:10).

Surely the existence of this disposition is essential to the Christian character. It shone conspicuously in the conduct of an incarnate Jesus. Christianity consists in conformity to him as our great pattern. 'He that saith he abideth in him ought himself also so to walk, even as he walked' (1 John 2:6). Jealousy is the companion of love. Rather, it is the exercise of love in a particular mode. And however warm our professions, however splendid in the eyes of men our actions, an inspired apostle has declared in the most positive terms that without love, we are nothing (see 1 Corinthians 13:2). You who wear the name of Christians, have you Christian hearts? Where is your jealousy for Christ? The dignity of his character is condemned; the efficacy of his atoning sacrifice is ridiculed. Is not the former the object in which you glory? Is not the latter the foundation on which you build your hope? An attempt — though blessed be God it is in vain — yet an attempt to degrade the one and demolish the other must operate like an electric shock through all your souls. Instantly you will exclaim like men amazed, 'If the foundations be destroyed, what can the righteous do?' (Psalm 11:3).

II. Having thus explained what we understand by jealousy for God, we now add a few general observations upon the subject.

1. Jealousy for God will be regulated by *an implicit regard to the Word of God.* The inspired volume is the divine directory, the infallible guide, to which 'you do well to take heed, as to a light that shineth in a dark place' (2 Peter 1:19). This is the code of royal laws, the book of unalterable statutes in the kingdom of Christ. Influenced by jealousy for God, you will consider Jesus as a teacher sent from above, you will sit at his feet and receive the law from his mouth. The Bible you will consider as the word of Christ; attachment to him, as the prophet, the great prophet of your profession, the founder and lawgiver of your holy religion, will engage you to hear him in all things. To the Bible you will adhere as the sacred *chest*, containing the oracles of God, attending to which you may separate truth from error and so receive the former as the most salutary food, but reject

the latter as the most deadly poison; as the *measuring reed* by which everything in the house and worship of God is to be exactly adjusted, that so Zion's fair building may rise according to the pattern seen in the mount (see Exodus 25:40), while all the goings- out and comings-in of her highly favoured inhabitants are divinely approved; as the *test* by which every part of your experience is to be examined, that so the pure gold and the worthless dross may be distinguished; and as the unerring *rule* by which your conduct, as it respects God, your neighbour and yourselves, in things civil or sacred, may be regulated, that so a conscience void of offence towards God and man may be in some happy degree enjoyed.

This divine directory, this infallible guide, is *complete;* it stands in no need of any addition. To introduce articles of faith, or modes of worship, unauthorized by the sacred Word is one character of the son of perdition and one branch of the mystery of iniquity. Human innovations in matters of religion have kindled the fire of divine jealousy, the flames of which have burst forth and consumed the ringleaders of such impious deeds. Witness the awful case of Nadab and Abihu. This event was designed to inculcate upon the minds of spectators and of succeeding generations to the close of time an implicit attention, in all matters of religion, to God's revealed will.

As this divine rule has no defect, so it contains nothing superfluous or improper. Undoubtedly some things here enjoined, comparatively viewed, are of greater importance than others; yet, nothing that bears the stamp of royal authority, no edict that is issued out under the broad seal of Jehovah, should ever be considered as a trifling article or represented as a matter of indifference. While the weightier matters of the law, judgement, mercy and faith are regarded according to their native importance, even paying tithe of mint, anise and cummin, so long as God enjoined them, must not be omitted. If, when some articles of faith, some modes of worship are represented as 'indifferent', no more is intended than that comparatively viewed they are *not of equal importance with some others in certain cases,* the fact will be allowed. But if this phrase means that such doctrines or parts of worship are of *no importance*, that the former may be believed or disbelieved, the latter practised or neglected, without any offence in the sight of God, this is denied. Neutrality in religion is by Christ himself eternally excluded: 'He that is not with me is against me; and he that gathereth not with me scattereth abroad' (Matthew 12:30).

2. This holy jealousy is accompanied with a spirit of universal benevolence. Here love to God is always attended with the same towards our neighbour. Descending angels celebrated with rapturous songs the goodwill of heaven towards men. Saints feel a similar temper, and so far as this divine principle prevails, they exemplify it in all their actions. 'He that is joined unto the Lord is one spirit' with him (1 Corinthians 6:17). Inspired,

brethren, with this benevolent disposition, you will readily deny yourselves for a neighbour's good and so copy his example who 'pleased not himself' (Romans 15:3); but, although he was rich, became poor, that we through his poverty might be made rich (see 2 Corinthians 8:9). You will tenderly sympathize with the afflicted and according to your ability, as occasion may require, manifest the compassionate heart, employ the consoling tongue and stretch out the relieving hand. Cordially you will rejoice in the prosperity of a friend, nor envy his lot, though more favoured than your own. Earnestly will you pray for the welfare of an enemy, nor meanly insult, though he may fall. In a word, cheerfully you will assist in promoting where you can the temporal, but especially the eternal interests of those around you. And as the temporal concerns of men, contrasted with those that are eternal, are infinitely lighter than a feather weighed in one scale against the ponderous globe we inhabit in the other, so your attention will be principally engaged by what relates to their immortal felicity. This will exercise your warmest feelings and alternately excite your most painful fears or most pleasing hopes.

Nor will this benevolent temper merely regard such as are of your own society or those enclosed in the small circle of your personal acquaintance. The heart of a true Christian exhibits a fair commentary on the second table of the moral law. The question was once proposed, 'Who is my neighbour?' (Luke 10:29). By your neighbour, brethren, you do not simply mean the man who lives at the next door; you mean a fellow creature, a member of the human race, let him be found wherever he may. Let him be an ignorant negro, dwelling in the unexplored regions of Africa, or an untutored savage, wandering in the inhospitable forests of America, he is your fellow creature, he is your neighbour, he is your brother.[1] He has a soul, a soul that will exist for ever, a soul that has interests equally important with those of your own. And though the ability of your hand may be very limited, not so that of your heart. This possesses a power that approaches to a kind of infinity. Who can fix the bounds of those benevolent wishes that such a heart can breathe? It is enlarged, it expands, it heaves, it swells, it grows warmer and warmer. It can embrace a globe. It can stretch its arms like seas and grasp in all the habitable shores. And what is its language? What are the sentiments it utters? Listen, listen to the enchanting sound: 'Let the earth be filled with the knowledge of the glory of the Lord, as the waters cover the sea' (cf. Habbakuk 2:14).

What a contrast is this to that fire of hell, to that spirit inhaled from beneath, which has brought thousands to die in forms the most painful and ignominious! Yet such characters have existed, who have committed the bodies of their fellow creatures to the flames and consigned their souls to eternal burnings, all under a pretence of zeal for God. Infinitely more amiable and becoming the spirit of Christianity was their conduct who submitted with patience to the cruel stroke, who never returned reviling for reviling, but contrariwise blessing for cursing. Such resemble Stephen, who closed his life praying for his murderers; they resemble Jesus, who employed some of his last moments, when enduring the agonies of death, in interceding for his crucifiers.

3. It includes in it a reigning, a superlative regard to the interest of Christ. He has a kingdom in this world. True believers are members of it, subjects of Jesus as King in Zion. These are loyal subjects. They have the interest of their prince and the prosperity of his kingdom at heart. Like the psalmist, they will be ready to say, 'If I forget thee, O Jerusalem, let my right hand forget her cunning. If I do not remember thee, let my tongue cleave to the roof of my mouth; if I prefer not Jerusalem above my chief joy' (Psalm 137:5-6).

This regard for the interest of Christ must be a reigning, superlative one. It must have the ascendancy in the heart. Jesus admits of no rival in the breasts of his subjects. A union between God and Mammon, between Christ and the world, has often (but always in vain) been attempted. It stands enacted as an eternal law through his dominions that unless a man hate 'his father, and mother, and wife, and children, and brethren, and sisters, yea, and his own life also, he cannot be his disciple' (cf. Luke 14:26). The import of this language seems to be that if the possession of any one enjoyment, even life itself, shall become inconsistent with loyalty and fidelity to Jesus, even that must be sacrificed as a proof of the reality of our attachment to him.

Now while this temper is evidently essential to the Christian character, it is equally so to a holy jealousy for God's honour. Those who are jealous for the Lord of hosts will feel a tender concern for his interest and watch with keen attention every effort to injure his cause. Devoted to the service of the Redeemer, they will habitually study how they may promote the prosperity of his kingdom.

III. This leads us, in the third place, to point out some of the methods in which this temper will discover itself.

1. It will be seen in *a serious attention to the interests of personal Christianity.* Jealousy for God will be attended with jealousy over yourselves. You will seriously endeavour to prove all things that you may hold fast that, and only that, which is good (see 1 Thessalonians 5:21). You will examine *the reality of your religion.* You will be ready to ask yourselves, 'While I have a name to live, am I not dead? Am I a possessor of a new heart? Am I born again? Am I translated from under the power of darkness into the kingdom of God's dear Son? (see Colossians 1:13). Do I positively bear those good fruits without which, like an unprofitable tree, I must be hewn down and cast into the fire? Are my evidences of personal

Christianity carefully collected from and compared with the Scriptures? Have I the authority of God to rank myself among the number of his children?'

Farther, you will examine *the purity of your religion;* 'tis an unhappiness when wood, hay and stubble are mingled with gold, silver and precious stones (see 1 Corinthians 3:12). Convinced of this, you will look to the purity of your faith. Viewing the pernicious effects of error, you will enquire, 'Are my ideas of truth conformable to those exhibited in the sacred volume? Do I in no instance receive for doctrines the commandments of men? Did I take up my religious creed as I received a name from my ancestors, or did I search the Scriptures, determined to buy the truth whatever it cost me and never to sell it, whatever price any might offer for it? Have I adopted no mistakes which ought to be renounced? Are there no farther views than what I have already attained, which ought to be embraced? Let me search the Scriptures, knowing 'they are profitable for doctrine, for reproof, for correction and instruction in righteousness', in order, that like the 'man of God' I may 'be perfect, thoroughly furnished unto every good work' (cf. 2 Timothy 3:16, 17).'

You will look, brethren, to *the purity of your experience.* Deeply sensible of the danger of corrupt mixtures, the danger of pride and self-seeking being the real principles that influence your conduct, instead of a single eye to the divine honour, you will look well to yourselves. You will carefully inspect your hearts and examine with severity the springs of action that lie hid from every human eye. You will put the query home: 'Is love, genuine love to God, an ingredient in my religion? Is the true beauty of his character the ground of my esteem, or do I only love him from some mean and selfish consideration? Do I love him for what he is in himself, as infinitely amiable in every discovery of his moral character, or only because I look upon him as my friend and consider myself as interested in his favour?' Brethren, beware of self-love under the disguise of professed love to God. 'If ye love them that love you, what reward have ye? Do not even the publicans the same?' (Mattthew 5:46).

You will look into *the purity of your worship.* With profound reverence you will regard the divine precept: 'What thing soever I command you, observe to do it: thou shalt not add thereto, nor diminish from it' (Deuteronomy 12:32). With sacred awe you will consider how God has manifested on various occasions his most tremendous jealousy over positive institutions and punished in the most alarming manner deviations from his revealed will; deviations which in themselves appeared very small, but which acquired a magnitude beyond all conception, because they were departures from the express injunctions of the Most High. Affectionately desirous of approving yourselves as obedient children, whose fear towards God is not taught by the precept of men, you will ask your consciences, 'What authority have I for the manner in which I worship God and observe his ordinances? Do I copy the example of the adorable Jesus, or have I in any instance departed from that blessed pattern? Have I studied with impartiality the instructions he has given me in his divine Word, or am I governed by the opinion and practice of those around me?' You should remember, brethren, that everything in religion is personal; that your conscience is accountable to no master but Christ; that nothing can be performed in faith, but what he has enjoined; and that nothing will be accepted by him, but what he has commanded.

You will look also to *the purity of your walk.* This is an article of the utmost consequence. It will be your concern to be 'blameless and harmless, the sons of God without rebuke, in the midst of a crooked and perverse [generation], among whom ye shine as lights in the world; holding forth the word of life' (Philippians 2:15-16). Here the credit of your profession is deeply interested. Convinced of this you will conscientiously regard the principles of justice and equity in all your civil affairs. You will attentively adhere to the golden rule: 'All things whatsoever ye would that men should do to you, do ye even so to them' (Mattthew 7:12). In a word, clearly convinced of the imperfection of your knowledge of yourselves and fully satisfied that in many cases you are improper judges of your own actions, yet beholding the equity and discerning the goodness of every divine requirement, you will be ready to say, 'Search me O God, and know my heart: try me, and know my thoughts; and see if there be any wicked way in me, and lead me in the way everlasting' (Psalm 139:23-24).

2. It will be seen in *fervent prayer for the outpouring of the divine Spirit.* This is the grand promise of the New Testament, as the coming of Christ was of the Old. His influences are the soul, the great animating soul, of all religion. These withheld, divine ordinances are empty cisterns and spiritual graces are withering flowers. These suspended, the greatest human abilities labour in vain and the noblest efforts fail of success.

Look into the New Testament. There you find a Paul 'brought up ... at the feet of Gamaliel' (Acts 22:3); an Apollos who possessed in an eminent degree the powers of oratory; a Peter whose heart burned with the zeal of a seraph and a John whose soul was animated in every power by the Spirit of his divine master. Yet hear one of them, in the name of all the rest, when giving account of their labours saying, 'Neither is he that planteth anything, neither he that watereth, but God that giveth the increase' (1 Corinthians 3:7).

Your observation and experience will perfectly harmonize with these sentiments. Anxious to see the advancement of the Redeemer's kingdom, you will give vent to your fervent desires by warm addresses at a throne of grace. When you hear the solemn charge, originally addressed more immediately to those who minister in sanctuary services, 'Ye that make mention of the Lord, keep not silence, and give him no rest, till he establish, and till he make Jerusalem a praise in the earth' (Isaiah 62:6-7), you will be ready to envy their employ, to wish for a kind of partnership in the business, and each say, 'For Zion's sake will I not hold my peace, and for Jerusalem's sake I will not rest, until the righteousness thereof go forth as brightness, and the salvation thereof as a lamp that burneth' (Isaiah 62:1).

Some who move in the lower orders of life, who find it difficult sometimes to provide things honest in the sight of all men, are often ready to say, 'What can I do? I am so poor in the world I can do nothing, or I gladly would.' If you mean as you say, if you are thoroughly honest and do not secretly please yourselves with the thought that your circumstances are such that nothing can be expected from you, if you have really a mind to work, here is employ. You have as free access to the throne of grace as any. If you can *do* nothing for Zion, you may *speak* to the King on her behalf. In this way you may as effectually serve the interests of Christ by your prayers, as the rich with their purses. Take the hint. Go home. Put it into practice as an evidence of the truth of what you profess.

3. It will be seen in *a diligent endeavour to promote the cause of Christ in the world* — a cause divinely excellent; a cause which should warm the hearts and influence the conduct of the Redeemer's followers. An attention to this is immediately, yet not merely, the work of ministers. While these take the lead, they ought to be seconded and supported by the vigorous efforts of all the friends of truth and holiness. Animated by the principle in our text, such will be ready to say to their ministers, as the men of Israel said to Ezra, when an important affair was to be undertaken, 'Arise, for this matter belongeth unto thee: we also will be with thee: be of good courage, and do it' (Ezra 10:4).

Having your souls enlivened by this disposition, you will each study your station and what can be done in it. You have each a place to occupy, a post to maintain. Fill up the place, make good the post where you are stationed. For instance, you who are heads of families, great is the truth reposed in your hands. Your children, your servants, claim your attention. Their health, their temporal concerns, lie near your hearts. The feelings of humanity, the dictates of natural affection, lead you thus far. But you profess to be Christians. And if your hearts are influenced by the principles of Christianity, your practice will correspond with your profession. So doing you will pay a due regard to the eternal interests of your domestics. The example of Abraham, approved by heaven, and recorded in the page of sacred history, will be admired and imitated. 'I know,' saith Jehovah, 'that he will command his children and his household after him, and they shall keep the way of the Lord, to do justice and judgement' (Genesis 18:19).

Were we to take a view of the numerous orders in human society and the distinct obligations of each in a religious view, we should carry the subject beyond the limits now assigned. Suffice it to remark that every one has a proper line in which he should walk and some peculiar privilege which should be improved. The part which every individual acts is of importance, as the smallest wheel, the minutest pin in a watch, is of consequence to the regular movement of the whole machine. Even you that are servants are repeatedly exhorted so to act that you 'may adorn the doctrine of God our Saviour in all things' (Titus 2:10).

James addressed his epistle to those that were 'scattered abroad' (James 1:1). This is the common lot of God's people. Certainly it is to answer some wise end in the general plan of divine providence. Nor is it perhaps hard to determine what this may be. Are they not the salt of the earth? (see Matthew 5:13). It is not proper that the salt should lie all in one heap. It should be scattered abroad. Are they not the light of the world? (see Matthew 5:14). These taken collectively should, like the sun, endeavour to enlighten the whole earth. As all the rays, however, that each can emit are limited in their extent, let them be dispersed that thus the whole globe may be illuminated. Are they not witnesses for God? It is necessary they be distributed upon every hill and every mountain, in order that their sound may go into all the earth and their words unto the ends of the world (see Psalm 19:4).

Brethren, is it not to the last degree desirable that these characters should be illustrated, that these ends should be accomplished? Nothing, nothing will prompt you on so to act like the divine passion, the celestial fire, that burned in the bosom and blazed in the life of Elijah.

It is time to finish. A few minutes and I have done. How would such a temper tend to promote your own comfort, make happy all the friends of God around you, and promote the interests of religion! Yes, brethren, this divine temper would eminently tend to promote your own comfort. It will inspire your minds with a holy cheerfulness amidst all your labours and toils. Numerous discouragements that now damp your spirits would never be felt. Activity and pleasure would here be found united. The lukewarm professor may drag on, but like Pharaoh's chariots when the wheels were off, it will be heavily; while the vigorous, the active follower of Jesus mounts upon the wings of eagles and, as he ascends, sings the songs of seraphs. It will tend to make happy all the friends of God around you. These beholding your heavenly ardour will be filled with holy joy. Rejoicing to see you come up 'to the help of the Lord against the mighty' (Judges 5:23), they will cheerfully give you the 'right hand of fellowship' (Galatians 2:9). These, like Barnabas, will be glad, when they thus see the grace of God (see Acts 11:23). Devils may hate, wicked men may laugh, formal professors may persecute, but these will open their arms, open their hearts to embrace you. In a word, this will tend to promote the interests of religion in the world. The cause of Christ will prosper; he must increase; his kingdom shall come. But, though he is indebted to none, he kindly condescends to employ his people in accomplishing these glorious purposes. What love, what zeal, what activity become you when thus employed! Animated with jealousy for the Lord God of hosts, you will be 'like the sun, when he goeth forth in his strength' (Judges 5:31) or 'like an army terrible with banners' (Song of Songs 6:4,10). Under the divine smile, Satan will fall before you like lightning from heaven (see Luke 10:18), his power be broken, his policy confounded; while the empire of Jesus shall advance, his kingdom arise and the crown flourish upon his head. 'Therefore, my beloved brethren, be ye steadfast, unmoveable, always abounding in the work of the Lord, forasmuch as ye know that your labour is not in vain in the Lord' (1 Corinthians 15:58).

# Notes

**Introduction**

1. The best of these biographies are: Eustace Carey, *Memoir of William Carey, D.D.* (London: Jackson and Walford, 1836); George Smith, *The Life of William Carey, D.D., Shoemaker and Missionary* (London: John Murray, 1885); S. Pearce Carey, *William Carey* (London: Hodder and Stoughton, 1923), recently reprinted as S. Pearce Carey, *William Carey,* ed. Peter Masters (London: Wakeman Trust, 1993); F. Deaville Walker, *William Carey. Missionary Pioneer and Statesman* (1925 ed.; repr. Chicago: Moody Press, n.d.); Mary Drewery, *William Carey: A Biography* (1978 ed.; repr. Grand Rapids: Zondervan Publishing House, 1979); Timothy George, *Faithful Witness: The Life and Mission of William Carey* (Birmingham, Alabama: New Hope, 1991).
2. Cited by Hugh Anderson, *The Life and Letters of Christopher Anderson* (Edinburgh: William P. Kennedy, 1854), p.379.
3. J. W. Morris, *Memoirs of the Life and Death of the Rev. Andrew Fuller* (London: 1816), p.101.
4. John Taylor, comp., *Biographical and Literary Notices of William Carey, D. D.* (Northampton: The Dryden Press, Taylor & Son/London: Alexander & Shepheard, 1886), p.27.
5. Not long after Fuller's death, two important biographies appeared: that by his close friend and colleague, John Ryland, Jr, *The Work of Faith, the Labour of Love, and the Patience of Hope, illustrated; in the Life and Death of the Reverend Andrew Fuller* (London: Button & Son 1816), with a second edition being published in 1818; and that by John Webster Morris, *Memoirs of the Life and Death of the Rev. Andrew Fuller* (1816). Later in the century, Fuller's son, Andrew Gunton Fuller, wrote a winsome memoir of his father, *Andrew Fuller* (London: Hodder and Stoughton, 1882). The only full-length biography of Fuller in this century has been Gilbert Laws, *Andrew Fuller: Pastor, Theologian, Ropeholder* (London: Carey Press, 1942).

6. For Pearce, there has been Fuller's labour of love, *Memoirs of the Rev. Samuel Pearce, M.A.* in *The Complete Works of the Rev. Andrew Fuller,* ed. Andrew Gunton Fuller and revised Joseph Belcher (1845 ed.; repr. Harrisonburg, Virginia: Sprinkle Publications, 1988), vol. III, pp.367-446; and S. Pearce Carey, *Samuel Pearce, M.A., The Baptist Brainerd* (London: The Carey Press, n.d.).

Ryland's life and ministry have been outlined by J. E. Ryland, 'Memoir' in *Pastoral Memorials: Selected from the Manuscripts of the late Revd John Ryland, D. D.* (London: B. J. Holdsworth, 1826), vol. I, pp.1-59; and James Culross, *The Three Rylands: A Hundred Years of Various Christian Service* (London: Elliot Stock, 1897), pp.67-91.

A good overview of the lives of Marshman and Ward is that of John Clark Marshman, *The Life and Times of Carey, Marshman, and Ward* (London: Longman, Brown, Green, Longmans, & Roberts, 1859), 2 vols.

7. There is an early biographical sketch by Fuller attached to his funeral sermon for Sutcliff: *The Principles and Prospects of a Servant of Christ* in *The Complete Works of the Rev. Andrew Fuller,* vol. I, pp.342-56. This same sketch appeared in *The Baptist Magazine,* 7 (1815), pp.45-53.

The most substantial piece on Sutcliff that has been published is Thomas Wright, *The Town of Cowper* (London: Sampson Low, Marston, Searle, & Rivington, 1886), pp.150-67. Unfortunately, 'Wright does not enjoy an impec-cable reputation as a historian' (Kenneth W. H. Howard, Letter to Michael A. G. Haykin, 7 August 1987).

In unpublished material there is Maurice F. Hewett, 'Sutcliff: The Meeting and the Man' (Unpublished typescript, Bristol Baptist College Library, n.d.), pp.44-112. Page references to this work are from a copy made by Kenneth W. H. Howard in 1951 and which is now in my possession. According to Howard, Hewett was 'a very careful historian', but 'He was certainly not a sharer of Sutcliff's "Edwardsean Calvinism"' (Letter to Michael A. G. Haykin, 7 August 1987).

Howard, who was pastor of Sutcliff Baptist Church in Olney from 1949 to 1954, collected a great deal of material on Sutcliff, both primary and secondary sources, in the hopes of writing his biography. However, the only piece which he published is a small, though fine, biographical sketch: 'John Sutcliff of Olney', *The Baptist Quarterly,* 14 (1951-1952), pp.304-9. Howard also wrote an unpublished manuscript: 'John Sutcliff—and the Home of His Married Years' (typescript, 5 pages, 19 August 1952). Extracts from this paper appeared in the *Baptist Times*, 98, No. 5084 (21 August 1952), pp.3,5.

8. A. Christopher Smith, 'The Legacy of William Carey', *International Bulletin of Missionary Research,* 16, No.1 (January 1992), p.2.

9. 'The Address immediately preceding the Interment' in John Ryland, Jr, *Christ, the great Source of the Believer's Consolation; and the grand Subject of the Gospel Ministry. A Sermon, Occasioned by the Death of the Rev. Joshua Symonds* (London: 1789), p.40.

10. Cited by Ian Sellers, 'Other Times, Other Ministries: John Fawcett and Alexander McLaren', *The Baptist Quarterly,* 32 (1986-1987), p.185.
11. 'Jonathan Edwards and the Crucial Importance of Revival' in D. Martyn Lloyd-Jones, *The Puritans: Their Origins and Successors* (Edinburgh: The Banner of Truth Trust, 1987), p.361.

**Chapter 1: God's preparation for a great work**
1. Benjamin Wallin, *The Joyful Sacrifice of a Prosperous Nation* (London: 1760), p.26.
2. Benjamin Keach, *The Gospel Minister's Maintenance Vindicated* (London: 1689), p.102.
3. For a good overview of the life and ministry of Gill, see Timothy George, 'John Gill' in Timothy George and David S. Dockery, eds, *Baptist Theologians* (Nashville, Tennessee: Broadman Press, 1990), pp.77-101. On Brine's life and theology, see Peter Toon, *The Emergence of Hyper-Calvinism in English Nonconformity 1689-1765* (London: The Olive Tree, 1967), pp.100-139.
4. Ryland, *Life and Death of the Rev. Andrew Fuller* (1816 ed.), pp.5-8. Cf. the similar remarks in Benjamin Godwin, *Memoirs of Richard Morris* (2nd. ed.; London: Cox and Son, 1819), p.56: 'At the same time [i.e. the 1780s], among Calvinistic Dissenters there was an extreme jealousy of orthodoxy; so that any modification of the views of Dr Gill, who was then considered almost oracular, or any deviation from the usual terms in which those doctrines were expressed, which he so firmly maintained, and so ably advocated, was considered as a certain mark of heterodoxy.'
5. J. M. Cramp, *Baptist History* (Toronto: H. Lloyd, Baptist Bookroom, 1871), pp.443,435-6.
6. Thomas J. Nettles, *By His Grace and for His Glory. A Historical, Theological, and Practical Study of the Doctrines of Grace in Baptist Life* (Grand Rapids: Baker Book House, 1986), pp.73-107.
7. Peter Naylor, *Picking Up a Pin for the Lord: English Particular Baptists from 1688 to the Early Nineteenth Century* (London: Grace Publications Trust, 1992), pp.187-91.
8. John Gill, *The Cause of God and Truth* (London: W. H. Collingridge, 1855), pp.166-7; *Faith in God, and his Word, the Establishment and Prosperity of his People* (5th. ed.; London: 1793), pp.31-3.
9. Ryland, *Life and Death of the Rev. Andrew Fuller* (1818 ed.), p.11. On Eve, see Kenneth A. C. Parsons, ed., *The Church Book of the Independent Church (Now Pound Lane Baptist), Isleham 1693-1805* (Cambridge: Cambridge Antiquarian Records Society, 1984), p.255.
10. Abel Jones Parry, *History of the Cloughfold Baptist Church, From 1675 to 1875* (Manchester: John Heywood, n.d.), pp.121-2.
11. Susannah Spurgeon and J. W. Harrald, eds., *C. H. Spurgeon's Autobiography* (London: Passmore and Alabaster, 1899),vol. I, p.310.
12. John Gill, *An Exposition of the Old Testament* (London: Mathews and Leigh, 1810), vol. IV, p.662. With regard to the legal and social situation

of the Baptists during this period, see Russell E. Richey, 'Effects of Toleration on Eighteenth-Century Dissent', *The Journal of Religious History,* 8 (1974-1975), pp.350-63.

13. Cited by Geoffrey F. Nuttall, *Howel Harris 1714-1773: The Last Enthusiast* (Cardiff: University of Wales Press, 1965), p.46.

14. W. R. Ward, 'Pastoral Office and the General Priesthood in the Great Awakening' in W. J. Sheils and Diana Wood, eds, *The Ministry: Clerical and Lay* (Oxford: Basil Blackwell for the Ecclesiastical History Society, 1989), p.322.

15. For further details, see W. E. Blomfield, 'Yorkshire Baptist Churches in the 17th and 18th Centuries' in *The Baptists of Yorkshire* (2nd. ed.; Bradford/London; Wm Byles & Sons Ltd./London: Kingsgate Press, 1912), pp.73-88; Ian Sellers, ed., *Our Heritage. The Baptists of Yorkshire, Lancashire and Cheshire* (Leeds: The Yorkshire Baptist Association/The Lancashire and Cheshire Baptist Association, 1987), pp.10-11; B. A. Ramsbottom, *The Puritan Samson. The Life of David Crosley 1669-1744* (Harpenden, Hertfordshire: Gospel Standard Trust Publications, 1991).

16. James E. Bradley, 'Religion and Reform at the Polls: Nonconformity in Cambridge Politics, 1774-1784', *The Journal of British Studies,* 23, No.2 (Spring 1984), pp.59-61. For further details of Robinson's life and ministry, see Graham W. Hughes, *With Freedom Fired. The Story of Robert Robinson, Cambridge Nonconformist* (London: Carey Kingsgate Press, 1955); L. G. Champion, 'Robert Robinson: A Pastor In Cambridge', *The Baptist Quarterly,* 31 (1985-1986), pp.241-6; Len Addicott, 'Introduction' to L. Addicott, L. G. Champion and K. A. C. Parsons, *Church Book: St Andrew's Street Baptist Church, Cambridge 1720-1832* (London: Baptist Historical Society, 1991), pp.viii-xviii.

17. Raymond Brown, *The English Baptists of the Eighteenth Century* (London: The Baptist Historical Society, 1986), pp.80-81. Eifion Evans notes that Gifford was among the subscribers to a 1774 edition of sermons by the Welsh Calvinistic Methodist Daniel Rowland (1711-1790) — see E. Evans, *Daniel Rowland and the Great Evangelical Awakening in Wales* (Edinburgh: The Banner of Truth Trust, 1985), pp.345-6. For further details of Gifford's life, see L. G. Champion, *Farthing Rushlight. The Story of Andrew Gifford 1700-1784* (London: The Carey Kingsgate Press, 1961).

18. Michael R. Watts, *The Dissenters* (Oxford: Clarendon Press, 1978), p.389.

19. Murdina D. MacDonald, 'London Calvinistic Baptists 1689-1727: tensions within a Dissenting community under Toleration' (Unpublished D. Phil. Thesis, Regent's Park College, Oxford University, 1982), pp.50-66.

20. Sellers, ed., *Our Heritage,* p.13.

21. Ryland, *Life and Death of the Rev. Andrew Fuller* (1818 ed.), p.39.

22. Andrew Fuller, 'The Nature and Importance of Walking by Faith', *Works,* vol. I, p.117, note.

23. *The Second London Confession of Faith,* 26.7 in William L. Lumpkin, *Baptist Confessions of Faith* (rev. ed.; Valley Forge: Judson Press, 1969), p.287.
24. D. W. Lovegrove, *Established Church, Sectarian People. Itineracy and the transformation of English Dissent, 1780-1830* (Cambridge: Cambridge University Press, 1988), p.7.
25. Cited by Joseph Ivimey, *A History of the English Baptists* (London: B. J. Holdsworth, 1823), vol. III, p.277.
26. Benjamin Wallin, *The Christian Life, In Divers of its Branches, Described and Recommended* (London: Aaron Ward, 1746) vol. II, p.ix. See also his *A Humble Address to the Churches of Christ* (London: J. Ward, 1750), p.1 ; *The Christian Salutation* (London: 1766), p.iv; *The Scripture-Doctrine of Christ's Sonship* (London: 1771), pp.v-vi. On the state of Wallin's own congregation at Maze Pond, see R. Philip Roberts, *Continuity and Change. London Calvinistic Baptists and The Evangelical Revival 1760-1820* (Wheaton, Illinois: Richard Owen Roberts, Publishers, 1989), p.71.
27. W. T. Whitley, 'The Baptist Interest under George I', *Transactions of the Baptist Historical Society, 2 (1910-1911),* pp.95-109. See also the meticulous analysis of the Evans list and other relevant sources by Watts (*Dissenters,* pp.267-71,491-510), who concurs with Whitley's estimate.
28. Arthur S. Langley, 'Baptist Ministers in England about 1750 A.D.', *Transactions of the Baptist Historical Society,* 6 (1918-1919), pp.138-57. See also Alan D. Gilbert, *Religion and Society in Industrial England. Church, Chapel and Social Change, 1740-1914* (London/New York: Longman Group Ltd, 1976), pp.35,37.
29. Cited by Morris, *Memoirs of the Life and Death of the Rev. Andrew Fuller,* p.267.
30. B. Wallin, *The Folly of Neglecting Divine Institutions* (London: 1758), pp.iv,v. In a letter written in 1773 to the American Baptist James Manning (1738-1791), Wallin takes note of what he regards as the two leading threats to the Calvinistic Baptist cause. The one is the growth of anti-trinitarian sentiment. 'The other is a popular ignorance of the authority of Christ, in particular church fellowship, which some are bold enough to put on the footing of prudence and convenience among the disciples of Jesus. The one strikes at the doctrine, the other at the discipline of the gospel' (Cited by Reuben Aldridge Gould, *Life, Times, and Correspondence of James Manning* (Boston: Gould and Lincoln, 1864), p.213). See the excellent remarks on this way of thinking by Geoffrey F. Nuttall, 'Methodism and the Older Dissent: Some Perspectives', *The Journal of the United Reformed Church History Society,* 2 (1978-1982), p.272; Roberts, *Continuity and Change,* pp.55-85.
31. Cited by Evans, *Daniel Rowland,* p.243.
32. For Calvinistic Baptist perspectives on the revival, see A. C. Underwood, *A History of the English Baptists* (London: The Carey

Kingsgate Press Ltd, 1947), pp.159-60; Olin C. Robison, 'The Particular Baptists in England, 1760-1820' (Unpublished D. Phil. thesis, Regent's Park College, Oxford University, 1963), pp.141-54. See also the remarks of Nuttall, 'Methodism and the Older Dissent', pp.272-4.

33. Cited by Dafydd Densil James Morgan, 'The Development of the Baptist Movement in Wales between 1714 and 1815 with particular reference to the Evangelical Revival' (Unpublished D.Phil. thesis, Regent's Park College, University of Oxford, 1986), p.39.

34. *Ibid.*, pp.39-40.

35. Watts, *Dissenters,* pp.329-30; Naylor, *Picking Up a Pin for the Lord,* p.54.

36. Cited by Robison, 'Particular Baptists', pp.142-3.

37. *Charles Welsey. A Reader,* ed. John R. Tyson (New York/Oxford: Oxford University Press, 1989), p.418 (entry for 18 October 1756).

38. J. Turner, Letter to John Sutcliff, 13 January 1776 (Sutcliff Papers, Angus Library, Regent's Park College, Oxford University).

39. Ivimey, *History of the English Baptists,* vol. III, p.280.

40. John Locke, *An Essay concerning Human Understanding* 4.19.5,7, ed. Peter H. Nidditch (1975 ed.; repr. Oxford: Clarendon Press, 1984), p.699.

41. S. Johnson, *A Dictionary of the English Language* (London: 1755), entry for 'Enthusiasm'.

42. 'Walking with God' in *Select Sermons of George Whitefield* (London: The Banner of Truth Trust, 1958), p.104.

43. *The Correspondence and Diary of Philip Doddridge, D.D.,* ed. John Doddridge Humphreys (London: Henry Colburn and Richard Bentley, 1830), vol. III, p.381.

44. *The Journal of the Rev. John Wesley, A.M.,* ed. Nehemiah Curnock (1911 ed.; repr. London: The Epworth Press, 1960), vol. II, pp.256-7, n.1.

45. G Whitefield, *Sermons on Important Subjects* (London: Thomas Tegg, 1833), p.432.

46. J. D. Walsh, 'Elie Halévy and the Birth of Methodism', *Transactions of the Royal Historical Society,* 5th. Series, 25 (1975), p.16.

47. Cited by Susie I. Tucker, *Enthusiasm. A Study in Semantic Change* (Cambridge: University Press, 1972), p.34. For the details of the Bell affair, see L. Tyerman, *The Life and Times of the Rev. John Wesley, M.A., founder of the Methodists* (5th. ed.; London: Hodder and Stoughton, 1880), vol. II, pp.433-44,460-62; Henry D. Rack, *Reasonable Enthusiast. John Wesley and the Rise of Methodism* (London: Epworth Press, 1989), pp.338-41.

48. Whitefield, 'Indwelling of the Spirit', *Sermons on Important Subjects,* p. 433.

49. Cited by R. Tudur Jones, 'The Evangelical Revival in Wales: A Study in Spirituality' in James P. Mackey, ed., *An Introduction to Celtic Christianity* (Edinburgh: T & T Clark, 1989), pp.251-2. For a more extensive discussion of these phenomena, see Michael A. G. Haykin, *Revivals and*

*Signs and Wonders: Some Evangelical Perspectives from the Eighteenth Century* (Richmond Hill, Ontario: Canadian Christian Publications, 1994).
50. John Brine, *A Treatise on Various Subjects,* revised J. A. Jones (4th. ed.; London: James Paul, 1851), pp.64-5 (see also pp.138-40).
51. John Gill, *A Complete Body of Doctrinal and Practical Divinity* (1839 ed.; repr. Paris, Arkansas: The Baptist Standard Bearer, Inc., 1989), p.781. For this reference, I am indebted to Roberts, *Continuity and Change,* p.80.
52. Morgan, 'Baptist Movement in Wales between 1714 and 1815', p.127.
53. Cited by Henry Spyvee, *Colchester Baptist Church — The First 300 Years, 1689-1989* (Colchester: Colchester Baptist Church, 1989), p.30.
54. H. B. Case, *The History of the Baptist Church in Tiverton 1607-1907* (London: Baptist Union Publication Department/Tiverton, Devon: Gregory & Son, Palmerston Press, 1907), p.37.
55. Cited by Charles B. Jewson, 'St Mary's, Norwich', *The Baptist Quarterly,* 10 (1940-1941), p.283.
56. *The Works of the Reverend George Whitefield, M. A.* (London: Edward and Charles Dilly, 1771), vol. III, pp.10-11. For the use of Whitefield's *Works* I am indebted to Leigh B. Powell.

**Chapter 2: Early years in West Yorkshire**
1. Daniel Defoe, *A Tour Thro' the Whole Island of Great Britain* (London: Peter Davies, 1927), vol. II, p.597.
2. *Ibid.,* pp. 599-600.
3. *Ibid.,* p.600.
4. *Ibid.,* p.602.
5. For a discussion of this supremacy, see especially R. G. Wilson, 'The Supremacy of the Yorkshire Cloth Industry in the Eighteenth Century' in N. B. Harte and K. G. Ponting, eds, *Textile History and Economic History. Essays in Honour of Miss Julia de Lacy Mann* (Manchester: Manchester University Press, 1973), pp.225-46.
6. Frank Baker, *William Grimshaw 1708-1763* (London: Epworth Press, 1963), pp.28-9.
7. Isaac Mann, *Memoirs of the Late Rev. Wm Crabtree* (London: Button and Son, 1815), pp.49-50; Sellers, ed., *Our Heritage,* p.16.
8. Fuller, *Principles and Prospects of a Servant of Christ, Works,* vol. I, p.349; John Fawcett, Jr, *An Account of the Life, Ministry, and Writings of the Late Rev. John Fawcett, D.D.* (London: Baldwin, Cradock, and Joy/ Halifax: P.K. Holden, 1818), pp.161-2; John Fawcett, Jr, 'Memoir of Mr Daniel Sutcliff', *The Baptist Magazine,* 15 (1823), p.89.
9. Neither Fuller nor Fawcett mentions the names of Sutcliff's parents. However, a letter from them to John, which the latter received on 7 March 1773, contains their names: Daniel and Hannah Sutcliff — Letter to John Sutcliff (Sutcliff Papers). The name of John's father also appears on the 'Members' List' of Wainsgate Baptist Church, Yorkshire.

10. Fuller, *Principles and Prospects of a Servant of Christ, Works,* vol. I, p.349. See also Fawcett, 'Memoir of Mr Daniel Sutcliff', p.89.
11. Daniel and Hannah Sutcliff, Letter to John Sutcliff, received on 7 March 1773 (Sutcliff Papers).
12. 'Members' List', Wainsgate Baptist Church.
13. Fuller, *Principles and Prospects of a Servant of Christ, Works,* vol. I, pp.352-3.
14. Fawcett, *Life, Ministry, and Writings of the Late Rev. John Fawcett,* p.162.
15. Sellers, ed., *Our Heritage,* pp.10-12; W. E. Blomfield, 'Yorkshire Baptist Churches in the 17th and 18th Centuries' in *The Baptists of Yorkshire,* pp.77-86. On Richard Thomas, see F. G. Hastings, 'Richard Thomas of Harley Wood', *The Baptist Quarterly,* 6 (1932-1933), pp.86-8.
16. Fawcett, *Life, Ministry, and Writings of the Late Rev. John Fawcett,* p.162.
17. The definitive life of Grimshaw is Frank Baker's *William Grimshaw.* The following account of his life and ministry is chiefly drawn from this book.
18. *The Doctrine of Justification by Faith* in *The Works of John Owen,* ed. William H. Goold (1850-1853 ed.; repr. Edinburgh: The Banner of Truth Trust, 1965), vol. V, p.3.
19. *Ibid.* (*Works,* vol. V, pp.9, 17).
20. Baker, *William Grimshaw,* p.46.
21. *Ibid.,* p.65.
22. Mann, *Memoirs of the Late Rev. Wm Crabtree,* p.16.
23. Baker, *William Grimshaw,* p.243.
24. Fawcett, *Life, Ministry, and Writings of the Late Rev. John Fawcett,* pp.15-17.
25. Baker, *William Grimshaw,* p.271.
26. Fawcett, *Life, Ministry, and Writings of the Late Rev. John Fawcett,* p.107.
27. Sellers, 'Other Times, Other Ministries' p.183; Fawcett, *Life, Ministry, and Writings of the Late Rev. John Fawcett,* pp.15,107.
28. Fawcett, *Life, Ministry, and Writings of the Late Rev. John Fawcett,* p.108.
29. *Ibid.,* pp.173-5.
30. *Ibid.,* p.162.
31. Fuller, *Principles and Prospects of a Servant of Christ, Works,* vol. I, p.350.
32. Fuller wrongly assumes that Sutcliff became a member of the Baptist cause in the heart of Hebden Bridge *(Ibid.)*
33. 'Members' List', Wainsgate Baptist Church.
34. Fawcett, *Life, Ministry, and Writings of the Late Rev. John Fawcett,* p.162. On Dan Taylor, see especially Frank Beckwith, 'Dan Taylor (1738-1816) and Yorkshire Baptist Life', *The Baptist Quarterly,* 9 (1938-1939), pp.297-306.

35. Cited by Blomfield, 'Yorkshire Baptist Churches', p.105.
36. Brown, *English Baptists of the Eighteenth Century,* p.82.
37. Fawcett, *Life, Ministry, and Writings of the Late Rev. John Fawcett,* p.162.
38. *Ibid.*
39. William Thomas, Letter to John Sutcliff, 27 March 1773 (Fawcett, *Life, Ministry, and Writings of the Late Rev. John Fawcett,* p.179). Fawcett spells Thomas's name as 'Tommas'.
40. William Thomas, Letter to John Sutcliff, 8 September 1770 (Sutcliff Papers).
41. Fawcett, Letter to John Sutcliff, 9 February 1771 (American Baptist Historical Society Archives, Rochester, New York). Fawcett reproduces a letter from his father to Sutcliff under this date (*Life, Ministry, and Writings of the Late Rev. John Fawcett,* p.163) which is very similar but not identical to that in the American Baptist Historical Society Archives.
42. Sutcliff, Letter to John Fawcett, 13 April 1771 (Fawcett, *Life, Ministry, and Writings of the Late Rev. John Fawcett,* pp.163-4). This is the earliest extant piece of correspondence from the pen of Sutcliff.
43. Fawcett, *Life, Ministry, and Writings of the Late Rev. John Fawcett,* p.164.
44. *Ibid.,* p.165.
45. *Ibid.,* p.296.

**Chapter 3: Bristol, 'The metropolis of the West'**
1. Defoe, *A Tour Thro' the Whole Island of Great Britain,* vol. II, p.435.
2. Anon., *A Complete History of Somerset* (1742, cited by Peter T. Marcy, 'Eighteenth Century Views of Bristol and Bristolians' in Patrick McGrath, ed., *Bristol in the Eighteenth Century* (Newton Abbott, Devon: David & Charles, 1972), p.27).
3. Cited by W. E. Minchinton, 'Bristol — Metropolis of the West in the Eighteenth Century', *Transactions of the Royal Historical Society,* 5th Series, 4 (1954), p.86.
4. Defoe, *A Tour Thro' the Whole Island of Great Britain,* vol. II, p.437.
5. Ralph H. Brentnall, 'Bristol's Architecture, Past and Present' in C. M. MacInnes and W. F. Whittard, eds, *Bristol and Its Adjoining Counties* (Bristol: British Association for the Advancement of Science, 1955), p.262.
6. John Rippon, 'A Brief Essay Towards An History of the Baptist Academy at Bristol', *The Baptist Annual Register* (London: 1794-1797), 2:421.
7. *Ibid.,* p.430.
8. On these first three principals, see Norman S. Moon, *Education for Ministry: Bristol Baptist College 1679-1979* (Bristol: Bristol Baptist College, 1979), pp.3-26; Roger Hayden, 'Evangelical Calvinism among eighteenth-century British Baptists with particular reference to Bernard

Foskett, Hugh and Caleb Evans and the Bristol Baptist Academy, 1690-1791' (Unpublished Ph.D. thesis, University of Keele, 1991).
9. Rippon, 'Brief Essay', *Baptist Annual Register,* 2:436.
10. *Ibid.* See also Hayden 'Evangelical Calvinism', pp.191,200.
11. Rippon, 'Brief Essay', *Baptist Annual Register,* 2:435-6.
12. Cited by Norman S. Moon, 'Caleb Evans, Founder of the Bristol Education Society', *The Baptist Quarterly,* 24 (1971-1972), p.176.
13. Rippon, 'Brief Essay', *Baptist Annual Register,* 2:435.
14. *Ibid.,* p.441.
15. *Ibid.,* p.442.
16. K. R. Manley, 'The Making of an Evangelical Baptist Leader: John Rippon's early years, 1751-1773', *The Baptist Quarterly,* 26 (1975-1976), p.262.
17. Hugh Evans, *The Able Minister* (Bristol: 1773), p.43.
18. *Ibid.,* p.12; Caleb Evans, *The Kingdom of God* (Bristol: 1775), pp.22-3.
19. Postscript to John Sutcliff, Letter to the Tutors and Gentlemen of the Bristol Education Society, 21 May 1774 (NLW Ms 1207D, The Isaac Mann Collection, The National Library of Wales).
20. *The Baptist Annual Register* (London: 1791-1793), 1:253-6.
21. Fuller, *Principles and Prospects of a Servant of Christ, Works,* vol. I, p.350.
22. Hayden, 'Evangelical Calvinism', pp.vi-vii.
23. On the influence of Edwards, see especially E. A. Payne, 'The Evangelical Revival and the Beginning of the Modern Missionary Movement', *Congregational Quarterly,* 21 (1943), pp.223-36; Robison, 'Particular Baptists', pp.162-70; Watts, *Dissenters,* pp.456-61. For Sutcliff and like-minded Baptists, Edwards became a 'kind of *pastor pastorum*' (Hayden, 'Evangelical Calvinism', p.354).
24. Lovegrove, *Established Church, Sectarian People,* pp.68-9,78-9.
25. C. Evans, *Advice to Students Having in View Christian Ministry* (Bristol: 1770), pp.3-4.
26. John Sutcliff, 'The Importance of Secret Prayer', *The Baptist Magazine,* 8 (1816), p.149.
27. C. Evans, *A Charge and Sermon; Delivered at the Ordination of the Rev. Thomas Dunscombe* (Bristol: 1773), p.7.
28. *Ibid.,* pp.5-6.
29 Geard, Letter to John Sutcliff, 9 August 1773 (Sutcliff Papers).
30. Hayden, 'Evangelical Calvinism', p.346.
31. *Ibid.*
32. Marjorie E. Reeves, 'Protestant Nonconformity' in R. B. Pugh and Elizabeth Crittall, eds, *A History of Wiltshire* (London: Oxford University Press for the Institute of Historical Research, 1956), vol. III, p.126.
33. Ivimey, *History of the English Baptists,* vol. II, p.587.
34. William Sutcliff, Letter to John Sutcliff, 1 October 1773 (Sutcliff Papers).

35. Thomas Purdy, Letter to John Sutcliff, 9 June 1775 (Sutcliff Papers).
36. William Sutcliff, Letter to John Sutcliff, 21 July 1779 (Sutcliff Papers).
37. H. Evans, Letter to John Fawcett, 4 June 1773 (Fawcett, *Life, Ministry, and Writings of the Late Rev. John Fawcett,* pp.165-6).
38. William Crook, Letter to John Sutcliff, 17 October 1774 (Sutcliff Papers).
39. Letter to John Sutcliff, received 4 October 1772 (Sutcliff Papers).
40. Geard, Letter to John Sutcliff, 5 July 1773 (JRL English Mss 369-71, John Rylands University Library, University of Manchester).
41. Thomas Purdy, Letter to John Sutcliff, 8 September 1774 (Sutcliff Papers).
42. Andrew Fuller, Letter to William Carey, 7 June 1799 (Letters of Andrew Fuller, typescript transcript, Angus Library, Regent's Park College).
43. Cooper, Letter to John Sutcliff, 1 July 1775 (Sutcliff Papers)
44. 'A Manuscript of the Revd J. Sutcliff of Olney', p.21 (Bristol Baptist College, Bristol). This manuscript, roughly a foot in length and four inches wide, consists of a number of pages that are sewn together on which there are sermon notes, highly abridged reflections on points of doctrine, an outline for a systematic theology and pithy sayings. The pages are only numbered on one side.
45. Cooper, Letter to John Sutcliff, 2 January 1776 (Sutcliff Papers).
46. Purdy, Letter to John Sutcliff, received 24 July 1772 (Sutcliff Papers).
47. Sutcliff, Letter to John Fawcett, 4 November 1773 (Fawcett, *Life, Ministry, and Writings of the Late Rev. John Fawcett,* p.167).
48. Daniel and Hannah Sutcliff, Letter to John Sutcliff, received 7 March 1773 (Sutcliff Papers).
49. Fawcett, Letter to John Sutcliff, 20 March 1773 (*Original Letters of the Revd Dr Fawcett, Rev. Andw Fuller, Mr J. W. Morris, & Revd Dr Ryland, 1773-1813,* BMS Archives, Angus Library, Regent's Park College).
50. P. E. Razzell, *The Conquest of Smallpox: The Impact of Innoculation on Smallpox Mortality in Eighteenth Century Britain* (Firle, Sussex: Caliban Books, 1977).
51. Fawcett, Letter to John Sutcliff, 29 May 1773 (JRL English Mss 369-71).
52. Fawcett, *Life, Ministry, and Writings of the Late Rev. John Fawcett,* p.181.
53. J. Ryland, 'Autograph Reminiscences' (Bristol Baptist College, Bristol), p.47.
54. Letter to John Sutcliff, 26 August 1773 (Sutcliff Papers).
55. John Barker, *Shrewsbury Free Churches* (Shrewsbury: Brown and Brinnand, Ltd, 1912?), p.25; M. M. T., *From Dun's Shut to Claremont Street 1620-1970. A Brief Survey of Baptist Work and Witness in Shrewsbury During Three and a Half Centuries* (Shrewsbury, 1970), p.7; Thomas Phillips, Letter to John Sutcliff, 20 October 1773 (Sutcliff Papers).

56. Thomas Phillips, Letter to John Sutcliff, 21 December 1773 (Sutcliff Papers). See also Thomas Phillips, Letter to John Sutcliff, 26 February 1774 (Sutcliff Papers), in which Pyne and his friends are described as 'really separatists'.
57. Fawcett, Letter to John Sutcliff, 20 November 1773 (*Original Letters ... 1773-1813,* BMS Archives).
58. Fawcett, *Life, Ministry, and Writings of the Late Rev. John Fawcett,* pp.184-5.
59. Phillips, Letter to John Sutcliff, 26 February 1774 (Sutcliff Papers).
60. Phillips, Letter to John Sutcliff, 19 April 1774 (Sutcliff Papers).
61. Sutcliff, Letter to the Tutors and Gentlemen of the Bristol Education Society, 21 May 1774 (NLW Ms 1207D).

**Chapter 4: Sutcliff's friends: John Ryland, Jr**
1. For information on Ryland's family and ancestors, see his 'Autograph Reminiscences' ; William Newman, *Rylandiana: Reminiscences relating to the Rev. John Ryland, A. M. of Northampton* (London: George Wightman, 1835); James Culross, *The Three Rylands: A Hundred Years of Various Christian Service* (London: Elliot Stock, 1897).
2. Ryland, 'Autograph Reminiscences', p.6.
3. Newman, *Rylandiana,* p.1.
4. Josiah Bull, *John Newton of Olney and St Mary Woolnoth. An Autobiography and Narrative* (London: The Religious Tract Society, 1868), p.205.
5. Ryland, 'Autograph Reminiscences', p.10. On Beddome, see 'Memoir' in *Sermons printed from the manuscripts of the late Rev. Benjamin Beddome* (London: William Ball, 1835), pp.ix-xxviii.
6. Thomas Brooks, *Pictures of the Past: The History of the Baptist Church, Bourton-on-the-Water* (London: Judd & Glass, 1861); Hayden, 'Evangelical Calvinism', p.143.
7. Robert W. Oliver, *Baptists in Bradford on Avon. The History of the Old Baptist Church, Bradford on Avon 1689-1989* (Bradford on Avon: 1989), pp.7-8.
8. 'Obituary for 1793: The Rev. John Reynolds, A. M.', *Baptist Annual Register,* 2:42.
9. John C. Ryland, Diary, (p.5), entry for 3 April 1745 (Angus Library, Regent's Park College).
10. J. C. Ryland, *A Body of Divinity in Miniature* (London: 1790), p.93.
11. Newman, *Rylandiana,* p.50.
12. *Ibid.,* pp.10-11.
13. *The Autobiography of William Jay,* eds George Redford and John Angell James (1854 ed.; repr. Edinburgh: The Banner of Truth Trust, 1974), p.294.
14. B. R. White, 'Open and Closed Membership among English and Welsh Baptists', *The Baptist Quarterly,* 24 (1971-1972), p.332.

15. D. W. Bebbington, *Evangelicalism in Modern Britain* (London: Unwin Hyman, 1989), p.36.
16. *History of College Street Chapel, Northampton* (Northampton: Taylor & Son, The Dryden Press, 1893), pp.36-40; Ernest A. Payne, *College Street Church, Northampton 1697-1947* (London: The Kingsgate Press, 1947), p.19.
17. *History of College Street Chapel,* p.39.
18. Nuttall, *Howel Harris,* pp.31-2, 75, n.99; 'Extracts from the Diary of the Late Rev. Dr Ryland', *The Baptist Magazine,* 53 (1861), p.279.
19. For his friendship with Toplady, see *The Complete Works of Augustus M. Toplady* (London: J. Cornish and Sons, 1869), pp.601,856,866; George Lawton, *Within the Rock of Ages: The Life and Work of Augustus Montague Toplady* (Cambridge: James Clarke & Co., 1983), pp. 78,89,171; for his friendship with Newton, see Bull, *John Newton* ; for his friendship with Rowland Hill, see Michael A. G. Haykin, 'Rowland Hill: Some Anecdotes', *The Banner of Truth,* 317 (February 1990), pp.19-20.
20. *Autobiography of William Jay,* eds Redford and James, p. 293.
21. 'The Experience of John Ryland', *The Baptist Quarterly,* 4 (1928-1929), pp.17-26.
22. Ryland, 'Autograph Reminsicences', pp.34-35,36,38,39.
23. *Ibid.,* p.31.
24. 'Introduction' to *Letters of John Newton* (Edinburgh: The Banner of Truth Trust, 1960), p.8.
25. *Out of the Depths. The Autobiography of John Newton* (New Canaan, Connecticut: Keats Publishing, Inc., 1981), p.65.
26. Cited by Bernard Martin, 'Some Dissenting Friends of John Newton', *The Congregational Quarterly,* 29 (1951) p.144.
27. On Newton's relationship with Baptists, see R. W. Thomson, 'John Newton and His Baptist Friends', *The Baptist Quarterly,* 9 (1938-1939), pp.368-71; Martin, 'Some Dissenting Friends of John Newton', pp.134-44,236-45; Geoffrey F. Nuttall, 'Baptists and Independents in Olney to the Time of John Newton', *The Baptist Quarterly,* 30 (1983-1984), pp.31-6; Michael A. G. Haykin, 'Anglican and Baptist: A View from the 18th Century', *Prolegomena,* 2, No. 1 (Spring 1990), pp.21-28; Douglas Bruce Hindmarsh, ' "I am a Sort of Middle Man": John Newton and the English Evangelical Tradition Between the Conversions of Wesley and Wilberforce' (Unpublished D.Phil. Thesis, Oxford University, 1993), pp.78-9, 147-74.
28. Bull, *John Newton,* p.138.
29. Ryland, 'Autograph Reminsicences', p.31.
30. 'Remarks on *The Quarterly Review,* for April 1824, Relative to the Memoirs of Scott and Newton' in *Pastoral Memorials,* vol. II, p.346.
31. John Newton, Letters to John Ryland, Jr (Bristol Baptist College, Bristol).
32. Grant Gordon, of Ontario Theological Seminary, Willowdale, Ontario, is preparing a critical edition of these letters.

33. Ryland, *Serious Remarks on the Different Representations of Evangelical Doctrine* (Bristol: J. G. Fuller, 1818), 2:8.
34. 'A Confession of Faith delivered by John Ryland junr of Northampton' (Bristol Baptist College, Bristol), p.13.
35. Ryland, *Serious Remarks,* 2:7-11; Ryland, *Life and Death of the Rev. Andrew Fuller* (1818 ed.), p.6, note.
36. Lumpkin, *Baptist Confessions of Faith,* p.266.
37. Cited by Curt D. Daniel, 'Hyper-Calvinism and John Gill' (Unpublished Ph. D. thesis, University of Edinburgh, 1983), p.308.
38. John Newton, Letter to John Ryland, 17 October 1771 ('Omicron to Dr. R.j.', Bristol Baptist College, Bristol). This letter is only extant in a copy that Ryland made of the original and then inserted in this notebook. For further discussion of the letter, see Hindmarsh, '"Sort of Middle Man"', pp.155-6.
39. John Newton, *Cardiphonia; or, The Utterance of the Heart* (London: T. Nelson and Sons, 1857), p.361.
40. For a very helpful discussion of these matters, see John von Rohr, *The Covenant of Grace in Puritan Thought* (Atlanta, Georgia: Scholars Press, 1986), pp.116-17.
41. Newton, Letter to John Ryland, 16 January 1772 (*Cardiphonia,* pp.361-3).
42. See further Hindmarsh, ' "Sort of Middle Man"', pp.155-61.
43. Cited by Edwin Sidney, *The Life of the Rev. Rowland Hill, A. M.* (3rd. ed.; London: Baldwin & Cradock, 1835), p.87.
44. *Ibid.,* p.87.
45. Ryland, Letter to John Sutcliff, 26 August 1774 (American Baptist Historical Society Archives).
46. Ryland, Letter to John Sutcliff, 26 August 1774 (American Baptist Historical Society Archives); Sidney, *Rowland Hill,* p.121.
47. Ryland, Letter to John Sutcliff, 26 August 1774 (American Baptist Historical Society Archives).
48. Roberts, *Continuity and Change,* p.81.
49. Ryland, Letter to John Sutcliff, 26 August 1774 (American Baptist Historical Society Archives).
50. John Ryland, *Seasonable Hints to a bereaved Church; And The Blessedness of the Dead, who die in the Lord* (Northampton: T. Dicey and Co., 1783), p.57. The copy of this sermon that was consulted was a microfilm copy of an original in the Angus Library, Regent's Park College.
51. Ryland, Letter to John Williams, 28 August 1807 (American Baptist Historical Society Archives.
52. Ryland, Letter to John Sutcliff, 26 January 1775 (JRL English Mss 369-71).

**Chapter 5: Shrewsbury and Birmingham**

1. Purdy, Letter to John Sutcliff, 22 September 1774 (Sutcliff Papers).
2. Purdy, Letter to John Sutcliff, 12 July 1774 (Sutcliff Papers).

3. Purdy, Letter to John Sutcliff, 22 September 1774 (Sutcliff Papers).
4. Turner, Letter to John Sutcliff, 28 September 1774 (Sutcliff Papers).
5. Turner, Letter to John Sutcliff, 12 November 1774 (Sutcliff Papers).
6. Purdy, Letter to John Sutcliff, 17 November 1774 (Sutcliff Papers).
7. Mary Andrews, Letter to John Sutcliff, 3 November 1774 (Sutcliff Papers).
8. Ryland, Letter to John Sutcliff, 12 November 1774 (JRL English Mss 369-71).
9. Purdy, Letter to John Sutcliff, 17 November 1774 (Sutcliff Papers).
10. Hewett, 'Sutcliff: The Meeting and the Man', pp.54-5.
11. M. M. T., *From Dun's Shut to Claremont Street 1620-1970,* p.7.
12. *Ibid.,* p.8.
13. Peggy Skrymsher, Letter to John Sutcliff, 10 January 1775 (Sutcliff Papers).
14. John Cooper, Letter to John Sutcliff, 23 January 1775 (Sutcliff Papers). Cooper is quoting from a letter that he received from Sutcliff.
15. Fawcett, *Life, Ministry, and Writings of the Late Rev. John Fawcett,* p.204.
16. Conrad Gill, *History of Birmingham* (London: Oxford University Press, 1952), vol. I, p.99.
17. *Ibid.,* vol. I, p.127.
18. Arthur S. Langley, *Birmingham Baptists Past and Present* (London: The Kingsgate Press, 1939), p.32.
19. *Ibid.*.
20. Robert K. Dent, *Old and New Birmingham: A History of the Town and Its People* (Repr. : EP Publishing Ltd, 1972), vol. I, p.174.
21. James Turner, Letter to Richard Smith, 14 June 1755 (NLW Ms 1207D).
22. James Hargreaves, *The Life and Memoir of the Late Rev. John Hirst* (Rochdale: Joseph Littlewood, 1816), p.345.
23. Turner, Letters to John Sutcliff, 8 April 1777 and 13 January 1776 (Sutcliff Papers); James Turner, *Christ the only Foundation* (Coventry: 1774), p.33.
24. Turner, Letter to John Sutcliff, 28 September 1774 (Sutcliff Papers).
25. Turner, Letter to John Sutcliff, 8 April 1777 (Sutcliff Papers).
26. *Ibid.*
27. Turner, Letter to John Sutcliff, 23 October 1776 (Sutcliff Papers).
28. Turner, Letter to John Sutcliff, 1 April 1779 (Sutcliff Papers).
29. Hugh Evans, Letter to John Sutcliff, 28 February 1775 (JRL English Mss 369-71). See also Thomas Purdy, Letter to John Sutcliff, 8 July 1775 (Sutcliff Papers).
30. Geard, Letter to John Sutcliff, 2 May 1775 (Sutcliff Papers).
31. William Wilkins, Letter to John Sutcliff, 31 March 1775 (Sutcliff Papers).
32. Fawcett, Letter to John Sutcliff, 10 April 1775 (JRL English Mss 369-71].

33. Purdy, Letter to John Sutcliff, 11 April 1775 (Sutcliff Papers).
34. This is the view of Hayden, 'Evangelical Calvinism', p.196.
35. Purdy, Letter to John Sutcliff, 9 June 1775 (Sutcliff Papers).
36. Evans, Letter to John Sutcliff, 30 June 1775 (JRL English Mss 369-71).
37. Jonathan Edwards, *A Treatise on Religious Affections,* ed. John E. Smith (New Haven: Yale University Press, 1959), p.451. See also the comments of Bebbington, *Evangelicalism in Modern Britain,* pp.57-8.

**Chapter 6: Olney**

1. For details regarding the town of Olney I am especially indebted to Thomas Wright, *The Life of William Cowper* (London: T. Fisher Unwin, 1892), pp.163-7; Gordon Osborn, *Cowper Country. An introduction to the town of Olney and the immediate neighbourhood* (Olney, Buckinghamshire: A. G. H. Osborn, 1976); Donald E. Demaray, *The Innovation of John Newton (1725-1807). Synergism of Word and Music in Eighteenth Century Evangelism* (Lewiston/Queenston: The Edwin Mellen Press, 1988), pp.123-4; C. J. Knight, *Olney Town Guide* (Olney, Buckinghamshire: C. J. Knight, 1989).
2. William Cowper, Letter to William Unwin, 18 November 1782; Cowper, Letter to Mrs Newton, 23 November 1782 in *The Letters and Prose Writings of William Cowper,* eds James King and Charles Ryskamp (Oxford: Clarendon Press, 1981), vol. II, pp. 91,93.
3. Cited by Demaray, *Innovation of John Newton,* p.314, n.10.
4. Helpful in understanding the social and economic realities faced by the working class in eighteenth-century England is Robert W. Malcolmson, *Life and Labour in England 1700-1780* (London: Hutchinson & Co., 1981).
5. Cited by Maurice F. Hewett, 'John Gibbs, 1627-1699', *The Baptist Quarterly,* 3 (1926-1927), p.319. On Gibbs, see also Richard L. Greaves, 'The Organizational Response of Nonconformity to Repression and Indulgence: The Case of Bedfordshire', *Church History,* 44 (1975), pp.481-2. For the details of the early history of the Baptist cause in Olney down to the time of Sutcliff, I am indebted to Hewett, 'John Gibbs'; Hewett, 'Sutcliff: The Meeting and the Man', pp.10-43; Geoffrey F. Nuttall, 'Baptists and Independents in Olney to the Time of John Newton', *The Baptist Quarterly,* 30 (1983-1984), pp.26-37; P. B. Gravett, *Over Three Hundred Years of God's Grace — A Short History of Sutcliff Baptist Church* (Olney, 1987).
6. Hewett, 'John Gibbs', p.319.
7. On Davis, see Hewett, 'Sutcliff: The Meeting and the Man', pp.25-8; Geoffrey F. Nuttall, 'Northamptonshire and *The Modern Question*: A Turning-Point in Eighteenth-Century Dissent', *Journal of Theological Studies,* N. S., 16 (1965), pp.104-8; Watts, *Dissenters,* pp.292-6,324; Michael Plant, 'Richard Davis of Rothwell', *The Banner of Truth,* 29 (May 1988), pp.26-30.

8. For further information on Maurice, see Hewett, 'Sutcliff: The Meeting and the Man', pp.27-30; Nuttall, 'Northamptonshire and *The Modern Question*', pp.108-11.
9. Hewett, 'Sutcliff: The Meeting and the Man', p.36; Nuttall, 'Baptists and Independents in Olney', pp.30-31. Gravett (*Sutcliff Baptist Church,* p.10) follows the view of Hewett about 'Mr Rogers'.
10. For further information on Walker, see Hewett, 'Sutcliff: The Meeting and the Man', pp.38-43; Nuttall, 'Baptists and Independents in Olney', pp.31,34-5.
11. Hewett, 'Sutcliff: The Meeting and the Man', p.38.
12. *Ibid.*
13. *Ibid.,* p.39. This covenant is written in the second extant minute book of Sutcliff Baptist Church, which includes the minutes from 20 December 1752 to 3 May 1767 (Olney Church Book II, Sutcliff Baptist Church, Olney). The entire covenant, including its preamble, has been printed in *The Strict Baptist Historical Society Bulletin,* 10 (1973). Gravett has also included the covenant and a brief summary of the preamble in his *Sutcliff Baptist Church,* pp.23-5.
14. Charles W. Deweese, *Baptist Church Covenants* (Nashville: Broadman Press, 1990), pp.26-7. This book is an excellent introduction to the use of covenants in Baptist churches, especially those churches in the English-speaking world on both sides of the Atlantic.
15. The unrevised version of Article XIII may be found in Gravett, *Sutcliff Baptist Church,* p.25. The *Strict Baptist Historical Society Bulletin* only contains the revised article.
16. Watts, *Dissenters,* p.320.
17. 'On Women Speaking in the Church', *The Baptist Magazine,* 7 (1815), pp.150-52; S., 'On Women Speaking in the Church', *The Baptist Magazine,* 7 (1815), pp.236-7; J[ames] L[ister], 'On the Silence of Women in the Churches', *The Baptist Magazine,* 7 (1815), pp.415-18.
18. Wright, *The Town of Cowper,* pp.136-7. For a photograph of this interior as it looked in the nineteenth century, see Christopher Stell, *An Inventory of Nonconformist Chapels and Meeting-houses in Central England* (London: HMSO, 1986), p.23. Also see p.109.
19. Cited Nuttall, 'Baptists and Independents in Olney', p.31.
20. *Ibid.,* p.32.
21. *Ibid.,* p.33.
22. Lumpkin, *Baptist Confessions of Faith,* pp.168-9.
23. One exception is the Western Association, comprising Gloucestershire, Wiltshire, Somerset, Devon and Cornwall, which remained a vibrant association for most of the years after its inception in the seventeenth century.
24. For the early history of the association, see especially T. S. H. Elwyn, *The Northamptonshire Baptist Association* (London: Carey Kingsgate Press Ltd, 1964), pp.11-35.
25. For a copy of the letter, see *ibid.,* pp.12-13.

26. Cowper, Letter to Mrs Madan, 18 June 1768, (*Letters and Prose Writings,* vol. I, p.197).
27. Walker, 'The Epistle to the Church at Olney' (Sutcliff Baptist Church, Olney).
28. Caleb Evans, Letter to John Sutcliff, 23 October 1775 (JRL English Mss 369-71). See also J. Alsop, Letter to John Sutcliff, 21 August 1775 (Sutcliff Papers).
29. On Mary Andrews, see John Sutcliff, 'Character and Death of Mrs Andrews', *The Evangelical Magazine,* 3 (1795), pp.291-3; Hewett, 'Sutcliff: The Meeting and the Man', p.55.
30. Fuller, *Principles and Prospects of a Servant of Christ, Works,* vol. I, p.354.
31. Fawcett, *Life, Ministry, and Writings of the Late Rev. John Fawcett,* p.212.
32. Turner, Letter to John Sutcliff, 7 December 1775 (Sutcliff Papers).
33. Fawcett, *Life, Ministry, and Writings of the Late Rev. John Fawcett,* pp.213-14.
34. *Ibid.,* pp.214-15.
35. *Ibid.,* p.215.
36. Olney Church Book III, entry for 26 November 1775 (Sutcliff Baptist Church, Olney).
37. John Newton, Diary (1773-1805), entry for 6 August 1776 (Princeton University Library)
38. Diary (1776), entry for 7 August 1776 ('Extracts from the Manuscript Diaries of the Rev. Joshua Symonds, pastor of the Bunyan Meeting, Bedford 1766-88,' transcribed H. G. Tibbutt, The Cowper and Newton Museum, Olney).
39. Newton, Diary (1773-1805), entry for 7 August 1776.
40. Neither the Olney Church Book minutes nor the diaries of John Newton or Joshua Symonds mention the laying on of hands, but it was customary at this point in the ordination service of eighteenth-century Dissenting ministers. See Philip Doddridge's remarks regarding ordination procedures among Dissenters earlier in the century: 'An Appendix, Relating to the usual methods of Ordination among the Protestant Dissenters' in *The Miscellaneous Works of Philip Doddridge* (London: William Ball, 1839), p.884). For another example of the laying on of hands at a Calvinistic Baptist ordination, see Ivimey, *History of the English Baptists,* vol. IV, p.593, where Ivimey recounts the ordination of Samuel Medley (1738-1799) on 13 July 1768 at Watford in Hertfordshire.
41. See Doddridge, 'Ordination among the Protestant Dissenters' (*Miscellaneous Works,* p.885).
42. Newton, Diary (1773-1805), entry for 7 August 1776.
43. Hewett, 'Sutcliff: The Meeting and the Man', pp.36-7.
44. Newton, Diary (1773-1805), entries for 27 June 1775 and 7 August 1776.
45. Olney Church Book III, entry for 7 August 1776.

46. Turner, Letter to John Sutcliff, 28 August 1776 (Sutcliff Papers).
47. Olney Church Book III, entry for January 1776.
48. Joshua Llewellyn, Letter to John Sutcliff, 12 June 1777 (Sutcliff Papers). See also James Turner, Letter to John Sutcliff, 9 September 1778 (Sutcliff Papers).
49. Hewett, 'Sutcliff: The Meeting and the Man', p.58.
50. Olney Church Book III, entry for 6 August 1777; Newton, Diary (1773-1805), entry for 6 August 1777.
51. Newton, Diary (1773-1805), entries for 2 January 1776 and 3 January 1778.
52. Symonds, Diary (1776), entry for 28-30 May1776.
53. Newton, Diary (1773-1805), entry for 29 May 1776.
54. Symonds, Diary (1776), entry for 28-30 May 1776.
55. Diary (1773-1805), entry for 29 and 30 May 1776.
56. John Rippon, *Baptist Annual Register* (London: 1793), 1:226-7.
57. Ivimey, *History of the English Baptists,*, IV, pp.603-4.
58. Robert Hall Warren, *The Hall Family* (Bristol: J. W. Arrowsmith, 1910), p.17.
59. Robert Hall, *The Doctrine of the Trinity Stated* (2nd. ed.; Coventry: J.W. Piercey, 1776), p.2.
60. *Ibid.,* p.4.
61. *Ibid.,* pp.20-23.
62. *Ibid.,* p.32.
63. Laws, *Andrew Fuller,* p.127.
64. Fawcett, Letter to John Sutcliff, 6 April 1779 (*Original Letters ... 1773-1813,* BMS Archives).
65. See Joseph Jenkins, Letter to John Sutcliff, 19 March 1777 (JRL English Mss 369-71); Peggy Skrymsher, Letter to John Sutcliff, 20 July 1777 (Sutcliff Papers); James Turner, Letter to John Sutcliff, 13 August 1777 (Sutcliff Papers); Joshua Llewellyn, Letter to John Sutcliff, 12 June 1777 (Sutcliff Papers); John Gill, Jr, Letter to John Sutcliff, 3 April 1778 (Sutcliff Papers).
66. Thomas Purdy, Letter to John Sutcliff, 6 August 1778 (Sutcliff Papers); James Turner, Letter to John Sutcliff, 9 September 1778 (Sutcliff Papers); Caleb Evans, Letter to John Sutcliff, 16 January 1779 (NLW Ms 1207D).
67. Arnold A. Dallimore, *George Whitefield. The Life and Times of the Great Evangelist of the Eighteenth-Century Revival* (Westchester, Illinois: Cornerstone Books, 1980), vol. II, p.505.
68. Turner, Letter to John Sutcliff, 1 April 1779 (Sutcliff Papers).
69. John Sutcliff, *A View of the Doctrine of Divine Providence* (Northampton: T. Dicey, 1779), p.2.
70. *Ibid.,* pp.3-5.
71. *Ibid.,* p.8.
72. L. G. Champion, 'Evangelical Calvinism and the Structures of Baptist Church Life', *The Baptist Quarterly,* 28 (1979-1980), p.199.

73. Sutcliff, *Divine Providence,* pp.5-7.
74. *Ibid.*, pp.5-6.
75. *Ibid.*, pp.11,13.

**Chapter 7: Sutcliff's friends: Andrew Fuller**

1. The best account of Fuller's ancestors remains that of John Ryland, Jr in the *Life and Death of the Rev. Andrew Fuller* (1818 ed., pp.8-10). The story of his childhood, his conversion and his early Christian experience was recounted by Fuller in a series of letters that he wrote between the late 1790s and 1815. Ryland quotes them at length (*Life and Death of the Rev. Andrew Fuller*, pp.11-40) and they form the basis of the following narrative of Fuller's early years. Unless otherwise indicated, all of the quotations dealing with this period of Fuller's life are taken from this section of Ryland's biography, the 1818 edition.
2. Andrew Fuller, *Strictures on Sandemanianism, in Twelve Letters to a Friend, Works,* vol.II, p.563; E. F. Clipsham, 'Andrew Fuller and Fullerism: A Study in Evangelical Calvinism', *The Baptist Quarterly,* 20 (1963-1964), p.103.
3. Fuller, *Strictures on Sandemanianism, Works,* vol. II, p.564.
4. Clipsham, 'Andrew Fuller and Fullerism', p.107.
5. For Fuller's Christology, see Michael A. G. Haykin, 'A Socinian and Calvinist Compared: Joseph Priestley and Andrew Fuller on the Propriety of Prayer to Christ', *Nederlands Archief voor Kerkgeschiedenis/Dutch Review of Church History,* 73 (1993), pp.178-98.
6. For further discussion of these Christological debates, see Peter Toon, 'The Growth of a Supralapsarian Christology', *The Evangelical Quarterly,* 39 (1967), pp.23-9. I am indebted to Robert W. Oliver for this reference.
7. Ryland, *Life and Death of the Rev. Andrew Fuller,* p. 6, note.
8. Morris, *Memoirs of the Life and Death of the Rev. Andrew Fuller,* p.28.
9. Turner, Letter to John Sutcliff, 9 September 1778 (Sutcliff Papers).
10. F. A. Cox, *History of the Baptist Missionary Society, from 1792 to 1842* (London: T. Ward & Co./G. & J. Dyer, 1842), vol. I, pp.261-2; Morris, *Memoirs of the Life and Death of the Rev. Andrew Fuller,* p.476.
11. Turner, Letter to John Sutcliff, 6 January 1779 (Sutcliff Papers). See also the remarks of Hayden, 'Evangelical Calvinism,' pp.218-19.
12. Turner, Letter to John Sutcliff, 24 November 1779 (Sutcliff Papers).
13. J. E. Hale, *Cannon Street Baptist Church, Birmingham. Its History from 1737 to 1880* (London: Elliot Stock/Birmingham: Hudson & Son, 1880), p.9.
14. Ryland, *Life and Death of the Rev. Andrew Fuller,* p.43.
15. *Ibid.*, p.129.
16. Fuller, Letter to John Sutcliff, 28 January 1781 (Letters of Andrew Fuller).
17. A. G. Fuller, 'Memoir of the Rev. Andrew Fuller' in *The Principal*

*Works and Remains of the Rev. Andrew Fuller* (London: Henry G. Bohn, 1852), p.32, note. Cf. Fuller, *Andrew Fuller,* p.168.
18. Morris, *Memoirs of the Life and Death of the Rev. Andrew Fuller,* p.270.
19. Fuller, *Works,* vol. II, p.342. The edition reprinted in this collection of Fuller's works is the second edition. Unless otherwise indicated, references will be to this edition. Extremely helpful in tracing the differences between the two editions is Robert W. Oliver, 'The Emergence of a Strict and Particular Baptist Community among the English Calvinistic Baptists 1770-1850' (Unpublished Ph.D. thesis, London Bible College, 1986), pp.82-7.
20. Fuller, *Works,* vol. II, p.334.
21. *Ibid.,* vol. II, p.343. Incidentally, it was this psalm and the way it is used in the book of Acts that was one of the means whereby Fuller began to seriously question the High Calvinist system (*ibid.,* vol. II, pp.328-9).
22. *Ibid.,* vol. II, p.345.
23. *Ibid.*
24. *Ibid.,* vol. II, p.346.
25. *Ibid.*
26. *Ibid.,* vol. II, p. 353.
27. *Ibid.,* vol. II, p. 357.
28. *Ibid.,* vol. II, pp.358-60.
29. *Ibid.,* vol. II, pp.376-9.
30. *Ibid.,* vol. II, p.380.
31. James E. Tull, *Shapers of Baptist Thought* (1972 ed.; repr. Macon, Georgia: Mercer University Press, 1984), p.90.
32. L. Berkhof, *Systematic Theology* (4th. ed.; Grand Rapids: Wm. B. Eerdmans Publ. Co., 1949), pp.247-8.
33. Fuller, *Dialogues and Letters Between Crispus and Gaius, Works,* vol. II, pp.675,663,658). See also the discussion of Fuller's views in this regard by Nettles, *By His Grace and for His Glory,* pp.111-15.
34. Naylor, *Picking Up a Pin for the Lord,* p.148.
35. Berkhof, *Systematic Theology,* p.248.
36. Fuller, *Works,* vol. II, pp. 383-6.
37. Fuller, Letter to John Sutcliff, 27 September 1782 (Letters of Andrew Fuller).
38. In the century before that of Fuller, this was especially a problem for Richard Baxter — see Iain Murray, 'Richard Baxter — "The Reluctant Puritan"?' in *Advancing in Adversity* (London: The Westminster Conference, 1991), pp.12-13.
39. Fuller, 'Memoir of the Rev. Andrew Fuller', p.32.
40. 'Breviates' in Sutcliff, *Divine Providence,* p.14.
41. *Help to Zion's Travellers* in Charles G. Sommers, William R. Williams and Levi L. Hill, eds, *The Baptist Library* (New York: Lewis Colby & Co., 1846), vol. III, p.87.

42. Ryland, *Life and Death of the Rev. Andrew Fuller,* pp.130-31. On the Diceys, see Victor E. Neuberg, 'The Diceys and the Chapbook Trade', *The Library,* Fifth Series, 24 (1969), pp.219-31.
43. *Colchester Baptist Church — The First 300 Years, 1689-1989,* p.31. For Spyvee's account of Steevens' ministry, see *ibid.,* pp.31-9.
44. Steevens, Letter to John Sutcliff, 10 November 1785 (JRL English Mss 369-71).
45. For details, see Oliver, 'Strict and Particular Baptist Community', pp.87-95.
46. *Ibid.,* p.95.
47. The Minute Book of Fuller Baptist Church, Kettering, entries for 17 August 1785, 6 November 1785, 22 December 1785 and 26 February 1796 (Fuller Baptist Church, Kettering, Northamptonshire).
48. Fuller, Letter to John Sutcliff, 13 March 1781 (Letters of Andrew Fuller).
49. Fuller, Letter to John Sutcliff, February 1780 (?) (American Baptist Historical Society Archives).
50. Olney Church Book III, entry for 10 September 1780.
51. *Ibid.,* entry for 7 December 1780.
52. See chapter 5.
53. Fuller, Letter to John Sutcliff, 28 January 1781 (Letters of Andrew Fuller).
54. Fuller, *Principles and Prospects of a Servant of Christ, Works,* vol. I, p.350.
55. Letter from Olney Baptist Church to the Northamptonshire Baptist Association, 1781 (Northamptonshire Baptist Association: Ms Letters from the Churches, vol. I, Northamptonshire Record Office, Northampton).
56. Cited by Ford K. Brown, *Fathers of the Victorians* (New York: Cambridge University Press, 1961), p.505.
57. Underwood, *History of the English Baptists,* p.166.

**Chapter 8: The Prayer Call of 1784**
1. The last edition of the catechism was printed in 1820.
2. Fuller, *Principles and Prospects of a Servant of Christ, Works,* vol. I, p.350, note.
3. John Sutcliff, *The Authority and Sanctification of the Lord's Day, Explained and Enforced* (n.p.: 1786), p.10, note.
4. 'Breviates' in Sutcliff, *Divine Providence,* p.14.
5. Fuller, Letter to John Sutcliff, 8 April 1778 (Sutcliff Papers).
6. Fuller, Letter to John Sutcliff, 28 January 1781 (Letters of Andrew Fuller).
7. Fuller, *Principles and Prospects of a Servant of Christ, Works,* vol. I, p.350.
8. *Ibid.* The phrase 'optimistic eschatology' is that of E. F. Clipsham in 'Andrew Fuller and Fullerism', p.113.

9. Cited by C. C. Goen, 'Jonathan Edwards: A New Departure in Eschatology', *Church History,* 28 (1959), pp.28-9. For a brief overview of Edwards' eschatological perspective, see Iain H. Murray, *Jonathan Edwards. A New Biography* (Edinburgh: The Banner of Truth Trust, 1987), pp.296-9.
10. George, *Faithful Witness,* pp.51-2.
11. John Sutcliff, *The Divinity of the Christian Religion Considered and Proved* (Northampton: T. Dicey and Co., 1797), pp.8-9.
12. *Ibid.,* p.11.
13. John Sutcliff, *Jealousy for the Lord of Hosts illustrated* (London: W. Button, 1791), p.16.
14. John Sutcliff, *On Reading the Word of God* (Kettering: J. G. Fuller, 1813), pp.4,8.
15. Sutcliff, *Jealousy for the Lord of Hosts,* p.12.
16. Sutcliff, 'Importance of Secret Prayer', pp.149-50. The mini-biography of Hooker may be found in Cotton Mather, *Magnalia Christi Americana: or, The Ecclesiastical History of New England* (Hartford: Silas Andrus, 1820), vol. I, pp.302-19.
17. Sutcliff, *Divine Providence,* p.4.
18. Ryland, *Life and Death of the Rev. Andrew Fuller* (1818 ed.), p.69.
19. Fuller, *Works,* vol. I, p.131.
20. 'Extracts from the Diary of the Late Rev. Dr Ryland', pp.282-3. The date of this entry in Ryland's diary is 17 March 1790.
21. J. A. De Jong, *As the Waters Cover the Sea. Millennial Expectations in the Rise of Anglo-American Missions 1640-1810* (Kampen, The Netherlands: J. H. Kok N.V., 1970), p.166.
22. For an extant piece of Erskine's correspondence with Sutcliff, see his Letter to John Sutcliff, 14 October 1799 (The Isaac Mann Collection, The James Marshall and Marie-Louise Osborn Collection, Yale University Library, New Haven).
23. Michael J. Crawford, *Seasons of Grace. Colonial New England's Revival Tradition in Its British Context* (New York: Oxford University Press, 1991), pp.41-2; William Romaine, 'An Earnest Invitation to the Friends of the Established Church', *The Whole Works of the Late Reverend William Romaine, A. M.* (Edinburgh: T. Nelson, 1840), pp.864-71.
24. Jonathan Edwards, *Humble Attempt,* ed. Stephen J. Stein in *The Works of Jonathan Edwards* (New Haven/London: Yale University Press, 1977), vol. V, p.321. See also the fine studies of the origins of the concert of prayer by Arthur Fawcett, *The Cambuslang Revival. The Scottish Evangelical Revival of the Eighteenth Century* (London: The Banner of Truth Trust, 1971), pp.223-7; Edward Charles Lyrene, Jr, 'The Role of Prayer in American Revival Movements, 1740-1860' (Unpublished Ph.D. thesis, Southern Baptist Theological Seminary, 1985), pp.34-48.
25. Edwards, *Humble Attempt, Works,* vol. V, p.317. For an excellent analysis of the *Humble Attempt,* see Lyrene, 'Role of Prayer', pp.57-78.

26. Edwards, *Humble Attempt, Works,* vol. V, p.320.
27. *Ibid.,* p.341.
28. *Ibid.,* p.344.
29. *Ibid.,* pp.347-8.
30. *Ibid.,* p.356.
31. *Ibid.,* pp.357-9.
32. *Ibid.,* p.359.
33. *Ibid.,* p.362.
34. *Ibid.,* p.363.
35. Crawford, *Seasons of Grace,* p.231.
36. Harry S. Stout, *The New England Soul. Preaching and Religious Culture in Colonial New England* (New York/Oxford: Oxford University Press, 1986), p.136.
37. Edwards, *Humble Attempt, Works,* vol. V, p.365.
38. *Ibid.,* p.366.
39. Alan Heimert, *Religion and the American Mind: From the Great Awakening to the Revolution* (Cambridge, Massachusetts: Harvard University Press, 1966), p.336.
40. *Ibid.,* p.336.
41. Murray, *Jonathan Edwards,* p.299.
42. Ryland, *Life and Death of the Rev. Andrew Fuller* (1818 ed.), p.96.
43. Fuller, *Nature and Importance of Walking by Faith, Works,* vol.I, p.117, note.
44. *Ibid.,* p.131.
45. 'Minutes' in John Ryland, Jr, *The Nature, Evidences, and Advantages, of Humility* (n.p.: 1784), p.12.
46. *Ibid.,* p.12.
47. Sutcliff, *Jealousy for the Lord of Hosts,* p.12.
48. Edwards, *Humble Attempt, Works,* vol.V, p.348.
49. John H. Gerstner, *Jonathan Edwards: A Mini-Theology* (Wheaton, Illinois: Tyndale House Publishers, Inc., 1987), p.96.
50. Cited by Stephen J. Stein, 'The Quest for the Spiritual Sense: The Biblical Hermeneutics of Jonathan Edwards', *The Harvard Theological Review,* 70 (1977), p.108.
51. 'Preface' to Jonathan Edwards, *An Humble Attempt to Promote Explicit Agreement and Visible Union of God's People in Extraordinary Prayer, For the Revival of Religion and the Advancement of Christ's Kingdom on Earth, pursuant to Scripture-Promises and Prophecies concerning the Last Time* (1748 ed.; repr. Northampton: T. Dicey and Co., 1789), pp.iv-v.
52. Olney Church Book III, entry for 29 June 1784.
53. Ryland, *Life and Death of the Rev. Andrew Fuller* (1818 ed.) pp.97,98,103.
54. *Ibid.,* p.107.
55. Andrew Fuller, *An Enquiry into the Causes of Declension in Religion, With the Means of Revival* (n.p.: 1785), p.8.

56. Thomas Blundel, 'The River of Life Impeded' in his *Sermons on Various Subjects* (London: J. Burditt, 1806), p.183.
57. Sutcliff, *Authority and Sanctification of the Lord's Day*, pp.1-2.
58. Crawford, *Seasons of Grace*, p.229.
59. Sutcliff, *Authority and Sanctification of the Lord's Day*, p.2.
60. Cited by Jonathan Edwards Ryland, 'Memoir of Dr Ryland' in *Pastoral Memorials: Selected from the Manuscripts of the Late Revd. John Ryland, D.D. of Bristol* (London: 1826), vol. I, p.17.
61. 'Pastoral Cautions: An Address to the Late Mr Thomas Hopkins', *The Works of Abraham Booth* (London: 1813),vol. III, p.178.
62. Sutcliff, 'Preface' to Edwards' *Humble Attempt*, pp.iv,v-vi.
63. E. A. Payne, *The Prayer Call Re-Sounded* (London: The Baptist Union of Great Britain and Ireland, 1962), p.5.

**Chapter 9: Sutcliff's friends: William Carey**

1. Letter from Olney Baptist Church to the Northamptonshire Baptist Association, 1784.
2. Sutcliff, *Jealousy for the Lord of Hosts*, p.2.
3. Letter from Olney Baptist Church to the Northamptonshire Baptist Association, 1785.
4. Letter from Olney Baptist Church to the Northamptonshire Baptist Association, 1788.
5. Wright, *Life of William Cowper*, p.289.
6. C. B. Lewis, 'John Sutcliff', *The Baptist Magazine*, 67 (1875), p.454, note.
7. There has been a long-standing tradition that the only extant likeness of Sutcliff's facial features is a silhouette. This silhouette first appeared with the memoir of Sutcliff that was printed in *The Baptist Magazine* shortly after his death: Andrew Fuller, 'A Memoir of the Rev. John Sutcliff, of Olney, Bucks', *The Baptist Magazine*, 7 (1815), pp.45-53. By the time that the centenary of Sutcliff's death came to be remembered in 1914 it was a firm tradition that the only known portrait of Sutcliff was this silhouette (see *Sutcliff Centenary*, Northampton: Bonaventure Press, 1914, p.8). For another copy of this silhouette, see John T. Godfrey and James Ward, *The History of Friar Lane Baptist Church, Nottingham* (Nottingham: Henry B. Saxton/London: Simpkin, Marshall, Hamilton, Kent & Co., Ltd., 1903), p.225. Yet, Kenneth W. H. Howard has identified a likeness of Sutcliff in a composite portrait of Baptist ministers ranging from the seventeenth to the mid-nineteenth centuries (Kenneth W. H. Howard, Letter to Michael A. G. Haykin, 28 August 1987). This composite collection may be found in *The Transactions of the Baptist Historical Society*, 1 (1908-1909). Both the silhouette and the portrait appear in this book (see frontispiece and page 52).
8. Lewis, 'John Sutcliff', p.454, note; Carey, *William Carey*, ed. Masters, p.111.

9. William Cowper, Letter to John Newton, 9 April 1780 (Cowper, *Letters and Prose Writings,* vol. I, pp.330-31).
10. William Cowper, Letter to John Newton, 16 April 1780 (Cowper, *Letters and Prose Writings,* vol.I, p.333).
11. 'Extracts from the Diary of the Late Rev. Dr. Ryland', p.282. The entry is for 28 May 1788.
12. John Robinson, *Memoirs of the Rev. W. Robinson, Baptist Missionary* (Benares: 1858), p.13; Robert Hall, Jr, 'Character of the Rev. John Sutcliff' in T*he Works of the Rev. Robert Hall, A.M.,* ed. Olinthus Gregory and Joseph Belcher (New York: Harper & Brothers, 1854), vol. II, p.388.
13. Olney Church Book III, entries for 11 May 1786, 14 July 1786 and 2 November 1786. After Sutcliff's death, Wilson was described in the church minutes as a 'valuable deacon' (Hewett, 'Sutcliff: The Meeting and the Man', p.64).
14. Olney Church Book III, entry for 23 December 1784.
15. William Cowper, Letter to John Newton, 14 December 1784 (Cowper, *Letters and Prose Writings,* vol. II, pp.314-15).
16. Olney Church Book III, entries for 10 March 1799 and 29 April 1792.
17. Olney Church Book III, entry for 20 January 1785.
18. William Cowper, Letter to John Newton, 19 February 1785 (Cowper, *Letters and Prose Writings,* vol. II, p.328).
19. William Hawkins, Letter to Joseph Kinghorn, 17 April 1815 (Ms 4281, T143, Norfolk Record Office, Norwich).
20. Drewery, *William Carey,* p.10.
21. Carey, *Memoir of William Carey,* p.7.
22. *Ibid.,* p.25.
23. Carey, *William Carey,* ed. Masters, p.413.
24. *Ibid.,* pp.xiv-xv.
25. T. Scott, *The Force of Truth* (Edinburgh: The Banner of Truth Trust, 1984), p.85.
26. Carey, *William Carey,* ed. Masters, p.25.
27. Newton, *Out of the Depths,* p.68.
28. Carey, *Memoir of William Carey,* p.12.
29. *Ibid.,* p.12. For an excellent discussion of the legal ramifications of Carey's dishonesty, see Drewery, *William Carey,* pp.16-18.
30. Carey, *Memoir of William Carey,* p.14.
31. G.B., Letter to John Sutcliff, 7 July 1775 (Sutcliff Papers).
32. Hewett, 'Sutcliff: The Meeting and the Man', pp.74-7; Cowper, Letter to John Newton, 8 February 1783 (Cowper, *Letters and Prose Writings,* vol. II, pp. 105-6).
33. Carey, *Memoir of William Carey,* pp.12-13.
34. James R. Beck, *Dorothy Carey. The Tragic and Untold Story of Mrs William Carey* (Grand Rapids: Baker Book House, 1992).
35. Carey, *William Carey,* ed. Masters, p.33.
36. See chapter 4, section on the revival at Shepshed.

37. Morris, *Memoirs of the Life and Death of the Rev. Andrew Fuller*, pp.66-8.
38. Carey, *Memoir of William Carey*, pp.15-16.
39. *Ibid.*, p.16.
40. *Ibid.*, pp.16-17.
41. Ryland, 'The Zeal of the Lord of Hosts' in *Missionary Sermons. A Selection from the Discourses delivered on behalf of the Baptist Missionary Society on various occasions* (London: The Carey Press, 1924), p.25.
42. Iain Murray, 'Divine Providence and Captain Cook', *The Banner of Truth*, 274 (July 1986), p.7.
43. Carey, *Memoir of William Carey*, p.18.
44. Wiliam Carey, *An Enquiry into the Obligations of Christians, to use Means for the Conversion of the Heathens* (1792 ed.; repr. Didcot, Oxfordshire: The Baptist Missionary Society, 1991), pp.40-41.
45. Carey, *Memoir of William Carey*, p.33. On Mary Carey, see Joan N. Harding, 'Mary Carey' in A. S. Clement, ed., *Great Baptist Women* (London: The Carey Kingsgate Press, Ltd., 1955), pp.47-55; Carey, *William Carey*, ed. Masters, pp.36-8.
46. Carey, *Memoir of William Carey*, p.17.
47. Olney Church Book III, entries for 17 June and 14 July 1785.
48. Carey, *William Carey*, ed. Masters, p.43.
49. Olney Church Book III, entry for 17 July 1785.
50. 'The Venerable John Stanger of Bessels Green', *The Baptist Quarterly*, 27 (1977-1978), p.301.
51. John Taylor, comp., *Biographical and Literary Notices of William Carey, D.D.* (Northampton: The Dryden Press, Taylor & Son/London: Alexander & Shepheard, 1886), p.36.
52. Olney Church Book III, entry for 16 June 1786.
53. Carey, *Memoir of William Carey*, p.17; 'Extracts from the Diary of the Late Rev. Dr Ryland', p.281. The entry from Ryland's diary is for 21 September 1786.
54. Olney Church Book III, entries for 16 June and 10 August 1786.
55. 'Extracts from the Diary of the Late Rev. Dr Ryland', p.281. The entry is for 1 August 1787.
56. On John Stanger, see Payne, 'Venerable John Stanger of Bessels Green', pp.300-320.
57. Carey, *Memoir of William Carey*, p.68. At this point Eustace Carey is citing an unpublished item from the hand of Andrew Fuller entitled 'An attempt at a memoir of brother Carey'.
58. *Ibid.*, p.68.
59. *Ibid.*, p.46; Ivimey, *History of the English Baptists*, vol. IV, p.438, note.
60. Hewett, 'Sutcliff: The Meeting and the Man', p.75; George, *Faithful Witness*, p.24.
61. Ryland, *Life and Death of the Rev. Andrew Fuller* (1818 ed.), pp.148-9, note.

62. Carey, *Memoir of William Carey,* p.69.
63. J. B. Middlebrook, *William Carey* (London: The Carey Kingsgate Press Ltd, 1961), p.19.
64. John Owen, *The True Nature of a Gospel Church and its Government, The Works of John Owen,* ed. William H. Goold (1850-1853 ed.; repr. Edinburgh: The Banner of Truth Trust, 1968), vol. XVI, p.93.
65. Carey, *Enquiry,* pp.35-6.
66. *Ibid.,* pp.40-41.
67. Ernest A. Payne, 'Introduction' to Carey, *Enquiry,* pp.20-21.
68. Carey, *Enquiry,* p.88.
69. *Ibid.,* p.103.
70. Andrew F. Walls, 'Missionary Societies and the Fortunate Subversion of the Church', *The Evangelical Quarterly,* 60 (1988), p.144; Carey, *Enquiry,* p.104.
71. Carey, *Enquiry,* p.108.
72. Walls, 'Missionary Societies', p.146.
73. Carey, *Memoir of William Carey,* p.47; Carey, *William Carey,* ed. Masters, p.58.
74. Carey, *Memoir of William Carey,* pp.47-8.
75. *Ibid.,* p.69.
76. Morris, *Memoirs of the Life and Death of the Rev. Andrew Fuller,* pp. 96-7; Culross, *The Three Rylands,* p.61.
77. Carey, *Memoir of William Carey,* pp.53-4.
78. Marshman, *The Life and Times of Carey, Marshman, and Ward,* vol. I, p.10.
79. Ryland, *Life and Death of the Rev. Andrew Fuller* (1818 ed.), p.112, note; Ryland, 'Autograph Reminiscences', p.11.
80. Ryland, *Life and Death of the Rev. Andrew Fuller* (1818 ed.), pp.111-12 and note.
81. Cited in *Periodical Accounts of the Serampore Mission, N. S.,* I (1834), pp. 638-9. For another perspective on the elder Ryland, see Iain H. Murray, 'William Carey: Climbing the Rainbow', *The Banner of Truth,* 349 (October 1992), pp.20-21.
82. Cited by J. E. Ryland, 'Memoir' in *Pastoral Memorials,* vol. I, p.17, note.
83. Cox, *History of the Baptist Missionary Society,* vol. I, pp.7-8.
84. Ryland, *Life and Death of the Rev. Andrew Fuller* (1818 ed.), p.148.
85. Carey, *Memoir of William Carey,* p.623.

**Chapter 10: The Baptist Missionary Society**

1. Carey, *Enquiry,* p.105.
2. Gill, *Exposition of the New Testament*, vol. III, p.710.
3. Watts, *Dissenters,* pp.482-5; Norman S. Moon, 'Baptists and the Clarendon Code' in Norman S. Moon and Ernest A. Payne, *Baptists and 1662* (London: The Carey Kingsgate Press Ltd., 1962), p.31.

4. Robison, 'Particular Baptists', pp.420-21.
5. Olney Church Book III, entry for 22 September 1790. This entry occurs out of order, several pages after those for 1790.
6. Hewett, 'Sutcliff: The Meeting and the Man' p.93; Robison, 'Particular Baptists', p.425.
7. 'New Road Baptist Church. Episodes in its history' (Photocopied typescript, n.d.), pp.4-5; Robison, 'Particular Baptists', pp.425-6.
8. Letter from Olney Baptist Church to the Northamptonshire Baptist Association, 1790.
9. Hewett, 'Sutcliff: The Meeting and the Man', p.108.
10. Brian A. Packer, *Planted By Vidler. Northiam Unitarian Chapel: A History* (Tenterden, Kent: Brian A. Packer, 1988), pp.1-8. Between 1795 and 1800 Fuller wrote a series of letters defending the orthodox view of eternal punishment against Vidler's opinions. See Fuller, *Letters to Mr Vidler, on the Doctrine of Universal Salvation, Works,* vol. II, pp.292-327.
11. 'Breviates' in John Gill, Jr, *On Christian Patience* in John Rippon, ed., *The Baptist Annual Register* (London: 1791-1793), vol. I, pp.35-6.
12. See Thomas Stutterd, Letters to John Sutcliff, 12 March 1788, 18 May 1789, 20 May 1790 and 25 August 1790 (Hewett, 'Sutcliff: The Meeting and the Man', pp.101-4). Thomas Stutterd was a valued member of Salendine Nook Baptist Church on the outskirts of Huddersfield. This church had been planted in 1731 by members of the Rodhill End congregation, the church that Sutcliff had attended with his parents as a youngster and which was about eleven miles north-west of Salendine Nook across the moors. Stutterd's business frequently took him to the midlands, where he often exercised his preaching gifts. A number of midlands churches — for instance, that at Cote, where Thomas Dunscombe was the pastor, and that at Bugbrooke, Northamptonshire — looked upon Stutterd's occasional visits as red-letter days. While there is no record of Stutterd ever having preached for Sutcliff at Olney, there is every likelihood that he did, for he would visit Olney when he was travelling in the midlands.

For more information on Stutterd, see Percy Stock, *Foundations* (Halifax: Edward Mortimer Ltd, 1933); Ernest A. Payne and James R. C. Perkin, *Such Is Our Story. A brief History of Bugbrooke Baptist Church 1805-1955* (London: The Carey Kingsgate Press Ltd, 1955), pp.20-21. I am indebted to Dr Perkin for a gift of this history of the Bugbrooke congregation.
13. Thomas Langdon, Letter to John Sutcliff, 17 June 1790 (JRL English Mss 369-71).
14. While we do not have direct evidence that Sutcliff attended Pearce's ordination, there is every probability that he did. Fifteen years earlier he had served and worshipped at Cannon Street for six months and still had friends, like Robert Mozeley, a deacon, in the congregation (see Robert Mozeley, Letter to John Sutcliff, March 1778 in the Sutcliff Papers). Moreover, in a letter that Andrew Fuller wrote to Sutcliff only a week or

so before Pearce's ordination, he said that he hoped to see Sutcliff at Birmingham (Fuller, Letter to John Sutcliff, 10 August 1790, JRL English Mss 369-71).
15. Ryland, *Life and Death of the Rev. Andrew Fuller* (1818 ed.), p.143.
16. *Autobiography of the Rev. William Jay*, pp.374-5.
17. For Pearce's life, see especially Fuller, *Memoirs of the Rev. Samuel Pearce, M.A., Works*, vol. III, pp. 367-446; Carey, *Samuel Pearce*.
18. On Taylor, see James Hargreaves, *The Life and Memoir of the Late Rev. John Hirst* (Rochdale: Joseph Littlewood, 1816), pp.134-46.
19. John Sutcliff, Letter to John Hirst, 9 July 1788 (Hargreaves, *Life and Memoir of the Rev. John Hirst*, pp.142-5). Hargreaves wrongly gives Sutcliff's Christian name as 'Joseph' (*ibid.*, p.145).
20. Carey, *Samuel Pearce*, pp.93-4.
21. Arthur S. Langley, *Birmingham Baptists Past and Present* (London: The Kingsgate Press, 1939), p.32.
22. This phrase is actually used of Pearce by Fuller (*Memoirs of the Rev. Samuel Pearce, Works*, vol. III, p.372), but it is equally applicable to Sutcliff.
23. Fuller, Letter to John Sutcliff, 13 April 1791 (Letters of Andrew Fuller).
24. For Ryland's opinion of Hall, see his *The Indwelling and Righteousness of Christ no Security against Corporeal Death, but the Source of Spiritual and Eternal Life* (London: W. Button & Son, 1815), p.37. For the details of the funeral, see J. W. Morris, 'Memoir of the Rev. Robert Hall' in *The Complete Works of the Late Rev. Robert Hall*, ed. J. W. Morris (London: W. Simpkin and R. Marshall, 1828), p.36; John Ryland, Jr, *Salvation finished, as to its Impetration, At the Death of Christ; And with respect to its Application, At the Death of the Christian* (London: 1791), p.83.
25. Robert Hall, Sr, Letter to John Sutcliff, 10 March 1786 (NLW Ms 1207D).
26. On these meetings, see especially Reginald H. Spooner, 'Northamptonshire Ministers' Meetings, 1770-1816' *Baptist History and Heritage*, 11 (1976), pp.84-93.
27. Robert Hall, Jr, 'Character of the Rev. John Sutcliff', *Works of the Rev. Robert Hall, A.M.*, vol. II, p.389.
28. For the entire sermon, see Appendix II.
29. Fuller, Letter to John Sutcliff, 13 March 1781 (Letters of Andrew Fuller).
30. Sutcliff, *Jealousy for the Lord of Hosts*, p.3. For further discussion of this sermon, see Michael A. G. Haykin, '"A Habitation of God, through the Spirit": John Sutcliff (1752-1814) and the revitalization of the Calvinistic Baptists in the late eighteenth century', *The Baptist Quarterly*, 34 (1991-1992), pp.311-13.
31. Sutcliff, *Jealousy for the Lord of Hosts*, pp.5-9.

32. *Ibid.*, p.8.
33. *Ibid.*, p.12.
34. *Ibid.*, pp.14-15.
35. *Ibid.*, pp.15,16.
36. See chapter 3, section on Sutcliff's studies at the Bristol Academy, and especially chapter 8.
37. Cited by Martin Hood Wilkin, *Joseph Kinghorn, of Norwich* (Norwich: Fletcher and Alexander/London: Arthur Hall & Co., 1855), p.183.
38. Sutcliff, 'Preface' to Joseph Bellamy, *Sermons upon the following Subjects, viz. The Divinity of Jesus Christ, The Millennium, The Wisdom of God in the Permission of Sin* (1758 ed.; repr. Northampton: Thomas Dicey and Co., 1783), p.iii.
39. Sutcliff, *Authority and Sanctification of the Lord's Day*, p.3; *Divine Providence*, pp.5-7. See also *The First Principles of the Oracles of God, represented in a Plain and Familiar Catechism, For the Use of Children*, revised Joseph Belcher (1784 ed.; repr. Whitchurch, Shropshire: R. B. Jones, 1820), p.3.
40. Sutcliff, *Jealousy for the Lord of Hosts*, p.10.
41. On the topic of 'disinterested love' in the writings of Edwards and the New Divinity, see especially Joseph A. Conforti, 'Samuel Hopkins and the New Divinity: Theology, Ethics, and Social Reform in Eighteenth-Century New England', *The William and Mary Quarterly*, 34 (1977), pp.572-89; Stephen Post, 'Disinterested Benevolence: An American Debate over the Nature of Christian Love', *The Journal of Religious Ethics*, 14 (1986), pp.356-67; William Breitenbach, 'Piety and Moralism: Edwards and the New Divinity' in Nathan O. Hatch and Harry S. Stout, eds, *Jonathan Edwards and the American Experience* (New York/Oxford: Oxford University Press, 1988), pp.183-4,191-2.
42. In the three-volume edition of Fuller's collected *Works*, it has been retitled *Instances, Evil, and Tendency of Delay, in the Concerns of Religion* (*Works*, vol. I, pp.145-51).
43. *Ibid.*, p.146.
44. *Ibid.*, p.147.
45. See Fuller's remarks on the Reformation in his *The Calvinistic and Socinian Systems Examined and Compared, as to their Moral Tendency*, *Works*, vol. II, p.121.
46. Fuller, *Instances, Evil, and Tendency of Delay, Works*, vol. I, pp.147,148.
47. Michael J. Walker, *Baptists at the Table. The Theology of the Lord's Supper amongst English Baptists in the Nineteenth Century* (Didcot, Oxfordshire: The Baptist Historical Society, 1992), p.7.
48. Morris, *Memoirs of the Life and Death of the Rev. Andrew Fuller*, p.98; Ryland, *Life and Death of the Rev. Andrew Fuller* (1818 ed.), p.149.
49. Carey, *Memoir of William Carey*, pp.73-4.
50. Morris, *Memoirs of the Life and Death of the Rev. Andrew Fuller*, p.99.

51. Benjamin Beddome, Letter to Andrew Fuller, 2 October 1793 (East India Correspondence 1807-1813, BMS Archives).
52. Carey, *William Carey,* ed. Masters, p.63.
53. Carey, *Memoir of William Carey,* p.74.
54. Carey, *William Carey,* ed. Masters, p. 64.
55. Sellers, ed., *Our Heritage,* p.21; Fuller, *Memoirs of the Rev. Samuel Pearce, Works,* vol. III, p.378, note.
56. Thomas Steadman, *Memoir of the Rev. William Steadman* (London: Thomas Ward and Co., 1838), p.90.
57. Carey, *William Carey,* ed. Masters, p.73; Olney Church Book III, entry for 27 May 1792.
58. Carey, *William Carey,* ed. Masters, p.74; Sidney F. Clark, 'Nottingham Baptist Beginnings', *The Baptist Quarterly,* 17 (1957-1958), p.165.
59. Ryland, *Godly Zeal, Described and Recommended* (Nottingham: 1792), pp.1-2.
60. *The Poems of William Cowper,* eds John D. Baird and Charles Ryskamp (Oxford: Clarendon Press, 1980), vol. I, p.166; Murray, 'William Carey: Climbing the Rainbow', p.17.
61. Cited by A. Christopher Smith, 'The Spirit and Letter of Carey's Catalytic Watchword. A Study in the Transmission of Baptist Tradition', *The Baptist Quarterly,* 33 (1989-1990), p.227.
62. *Ibid.,* pp.226-37.
63. Ryland, *Life and Death of the Rev. Andrew Fuller* (1818 ed.), p.150.
64. Carey, *William Carey,* ed. Masters, p.77.
65. Hewett, 'Sutcliff: The Meeting and the Man', p.93.
66. Marshman, *Life and Times of Carey, Marshman, and Ward,* vol. I, p.15. The phrase 'catalytic moment' is from George, *Faithful Witness,* p.33. For the resol-ution, see the 'Breviates' in Ryland, *Godly Zeal,* p.16.
67. William Cowper, Letter to William Hayley, 2 October 1792 (Cowper, *Letters and Prose Writings,* vol. IV, p.205).
68. Fuller, Letter to John Ryland, 9 July 1792 (Ryland, *Life and Death of the Rev. Andrew Fuller,* 1818 ed., p.286); Fuller, Letter to Stephen Gardiner, 25 August 1792 (Ryland, *Life and Death of the Rev. Andrew Fuller,* 1818 ed., pp.286-91).
69. Carey, *Samuel Pearce,* p.134; Carey, *William Carey,* ed. Masters, p.84.
70. Ayer's name is sometimes spelled 'Eayres' or 'Ayres'.
71. The description of Hogg as 'distinguished-looking' is taken from E. A. Payne, *The First Generation. Early Leaders of the Baptist Missionary Society in England and India* (London: Carey Press, 1937), p.13.
72. 'Abraham Greenwood, 1749-1827', *The Baptist Quarterly,* 2 (1924-1925), p.88.
73. *Ibid.,* p.89.
74. James Culross and John Taylor, *Founders and Pioneers of Modern Missions* (Northampton: Taylor & Son, The Dryden Press/London: A. H. Stockwell & Co., 1899), pp.15-16.

75. 'Memoir of the Late Rev. John Ayer', *The Baptist Magazine,* 14 (1822), pp.177-80.
76. For Heighton, see W. G., 'Memoir of the Late Rev. W. Heighton, of Road, Northamptonshire', *The Baptist Magazine,* 20 (1828), pp.441-6; Payne, *First Generation,* pp.12-13; E. A. Payne, *Roade Baptist Church 1688-1938. The Story of a Northamptonshire Church During Two and a half Centuries* (London: Wyman & Sons, Ltd., 1938), pp.12-17.
77. For Blundel, see *Nonconformity in Northamptonshire* (Northampton: Taylor & Son, The Dryden Press, 1892), I, No. XXI; Payne, *First Generation,* pp.13-14; J. S. Fisher, *People of the Meeting House: Tales of a Church in Luton* (Luton: *c.* 1975), pp.32-4.
78. For Timms, see *Nonconformity in Northamptonshire,* I, No.XI.
79. Cited by Roger Hayden, 'Kettering 1792 and Philadelphia, 1814: The Influence of English Baptists upon the Formation of American Baptist Foreign Missions 1790-1814 (2)', *The Baptist Quarterly,* 21 (1965-1966), p.65. For Staughton, see especially S. W. Lynd, *Memoir of the Rev. William Staughton* (Boston: Lincoln, Edmands, & Co., 1834); Roger Hayden, 'William Staughton: Baptist Educator and Missionary Advocate', *Foundations,* 10 (1967), pp.19-35.
80. For the amount that each gave and what that amount meant to each of them, see Carey, *William Carey,* ed. Masters, pp. 85-7.
81. Morris, *Memoirs of the Life and Death of the Rev. Andrew Fuller,* p.49.
82. 'Preface' to the *Periodical Accounts Relative to the Baptist Missionary Society* (Clipstone: J.W. Morris, 1801), vol. II, p.iii.
83. Carey, *Samuel Pearce,* pp.139-40.
84. The definitive life of Thomas is still C. B. Lewis's exhaustive *The Life of John Thomas* (London: Macmillan and Co., 1873). For a brief synopsis of Thomas's personality, see Beck, *Dorothy Carey,* pp.68-9. The quote from Carey is from a letter that he wrote on 17 June 1796 (Lewis, *John Thomas,* p.157, note).
85. The Accounts of the Particular Baptist Society for Propagating the Gospel amongst the Heathen, Minute Book for 2 October 1792 - 7 May 1799, entry for 13 November 1792 (BMS Archives).
86. 'Andrew Fuller and the Baptist Mission', *Foundations,* 10 (1967), p.10.
87. Lewis, *John Thomas,* pp.222-3.
88. Fuller, Letter to John Sutcliff, 2 January 1793 (Letters of Andrew Fuller).
89. Fuller, Letter to John Ryland, 16 January 1793 (Ryland, *Life and Death of the Rev. Andrew Fuller,* 1816 ed., p.362). In the second edition, Ryland changed 'a very troublesome boil' to 'indisposition' (Ryland, *Life and Death of the Rev. Andrew Fuller,* 1818 ed., p.151).
90. For a full discussion of Ryland's call to Broadmead, see Grant Gordon, 'The Call of Dr John Ryland Jr', *The Baptist Quarterly,* 34 (1992), pp.214-27.
91. Fuller, Letter to John Ryland, 16 January 1793 (Ryland, *Life and Death of the Rev. Andrew Fuller,* 1818 ed., p.151).

92. *Ibid.*, pp.151-2.
93. Beck, *Dorothy Carey,* p.70.
94. *Ibid.*, pp.71-6.
95. Carey, *William Carey,* ed. Masters, p.102.
96. Carey, *Memoir of Wiliam Carey,* pp.76-7.
97. See the discussion of these alternatives by Beck, *Dorothy Carey,* pp.76-8.
98. Fuller, Letter to John Fawcett (Fawcett, *Life, Ministry, and Writings of the late Rev. John Fawcett,* p.297). For a description of the effects of this stroke, see Letter to John Sutcliff, 6 February 1793 (Letters of Andrew Fuller).
99. Fuller, Letter to Thomas Steevens (Lewis, *John Thomas,* p.226).
100. Wilkin, *Joseph Kinghorn of Norwich,* p.218.
101. Benjamin Beddome, Letter to Andrew Fuller, 2 October 1793 (East India Correspondence ).
102. Fuller, Letter to Thomas Steevens, 26 March 1793 (Cited by Doyle L. Young, 'The Place of Andrew Fuller in the Developing Modern Missions Movement', Unpublished Ph.D. Thesis, Southwestern Baptist Theological Seminary, 1981, p.200).
103. This may be readily seen by consulting the subscription lists contained in the *Periodical Accounts* issued by the Baptist Missionary Society during the first dozen years of the nineteenth century.
104. Fuller, Letter to John Sutcliff, 15 March 1793 (Letters of Andrew Fuller).
105. Fuller, *The Nature and Encouragements of the Missionary Work, Works,* vol. I, pp.510-12; Fuller, Letter to John Fawcett, 12 April 1793 (Cited by Young, 'Andrew Fuller', p.203).
106. Carey, Letter to John Sutcliff, 27 November - 29 December 1800 (BMS Archives).
107. *The Diary of Samuel Teedon,* ed. Thomas Wright (1902), p.75. This remark is made in the entry for 27 September 1793. See also *ibid.*, pp.10, 24, the entries for 30 December 1791 and 14 May 1792.
108. *Ibid.*, p.54, entry for 26 March 1793.
109. Carey, Letter to Andrew Fuller, 21 May 1793 (Carey, *Memoir of William Carey,* pp.88-9). For an account of these events, see Lewis, *John Thomas,* pp.234-8; Drewery, *William Carey,* pp.48-9.
110. Carey, *Memoir of Wiliam Carey,* pp.93-5.
111. Carey, Letter to John Sutcliff, 24 May 1793 (BMS Archives).
112. Fuller, Letter to John Saffery, 30 May 1793 (Young, 'Andrew Fuller', p.202).

**Chapter 11: 'He gave some to be pastors and teachers'**

1. Carey, Letter to John Sutcliff, 3 January 1794 (Carey, *Memoir of William Carey,* p.135).
2. *Missionary Correspondence: containing Extracts of Letters from the late Mr Samuel Pearce, to the Missionaries in India, Between the Years*

*1794, and 1798; and from Mr John Thomas, from 1798, to 1800* (London: T. Gardiner and Son, 1814), pp.1-7.
3. Cox, *History of the Baptist Missionary Society,* vol. I, pp.51-2.
4. *Ibid.,* pp. 52-3.
5. Carey, *Samuel Pearce,* p.104.
6. Fawcett, Letter to John Sutcliff, 13 December 1779 (*Original Letters ... 1773-1813,* BMS Archives).
7. Fuller, Letter to John Sutcliff, 16 September 1794 (Letters of Andrew Fuller).
8. Fuller, Letter to John Sutcliff, 19 November 1794 (Letters of Andrew Fuller); Morris, Letter to John Sutcliff, 8 November 1794 (*Original Letters ... 1773-1813,* BMS Archives); Fuller, Letter to John Sutcliff, 22 January 1795 (Letters of Andrew Fuller).
9. John Sutcliff, 'Character and Death of Mrs Andrews', *The Evangelical Magazine,* 3 (1795), p.292; Fuller, Letter to John Sutcliff, 13 February 1795 (Letters of Andrew Fuller).
10. Sutcliff, 'Character and Death of Mrs Andrews', pp.292-3; Samuel Greatheed, Letter to John Sutcliff, 14 March 1795 (JRL English Mss 369-71).
11. William Bull, Letter to John Sutcliff, 13 March 1795 (JRL English Mss 369-71); Samuel Greatheed, Letter to John Sutcliff, 14 March 1795 (JRL English Mss 369-71).
12. Sutcliff, Letter to Thomas Stutterd, 1 March 1794 (in Hewett, 'Sutcliff: The Meeting and the Man', p.105).
13. Fuller, Letter to John Sutcliff, 13 March 1795 (Letters of Andrew Fuller).
14. Clipsham, 'Andrew Fuller and the Baptist Mission', p.8.
15. Sutcliff, Letter to Andrew Fuller, 30 April 1795 (Andrew Fuller's Correspondence 1793-1815, BMS Archives).
16. For the letter in which Carey informed them of his decision, see Carey, *Memoir of Wiliam Carey,* pp.189-92.
17. The Accounts of the Particular Baptist Society for Propagating the Gospel amongst the Heathen, Minute Book for 2 October 1792 - 7 May 1799, entry for 7 April 1795 (BMS Archives).
18. Lewis, *The Life of John Thomas,* p.282.
19. Carey, *William Carey,* ed. Master, p.402. Carey devotes an entire chapter to Carey's love of gardening (see *ibid.,* pp.396-413). See also William Carey, Letters to John Sutcliff, 10 October 1798, 1 January 1806 and 4 May 1808 (BMS Archives).
20. Sutcliff, Letter to Andrew Fuller, 14 April 1795 (Andrew Fuller's Correspondence 1793-1815). See also Pearce, Letter to William Carey, 26 September 1798 (*Missionary Correspondence,* p.70).
21. The Accounts of the Particular Baptist Society for Propagating the Gospel amongst the Heathen, entry for 12 November 1793.
22. For further information on George, see the excellent biography by Grant Gordon, *From Slavery to Freedom. The Life of David George,*

*Pioneer Black Baptist Minister* (Hantsport, Nova Scotia: Lancelot Press, 1992).

23. *Periodical Accounts Relative to the Baptist Missionary Society,* vol. I, p.99. On Grigg, see Howard Grimshaw Hartzell, 'Jacob Grigg — Missionary and Minister', *The Chronicle,* 6 (1943), pp.83-90,130-43; Kenneth E. Hyde, 'The Union Church of Launceston, Cornwall. III. Jacob Grigg', *The Baptist Quarterly,* 14 (1951-1952), pp.203-12; Stiv Jakobsson, *Am I Not A Man and A Brother? British Missions and the Abolition of the Slave Trade and Slavery in West Africa and the West Indies 1786-1838* (Uppsala: Gleerup, 1972), pp.84-100; Basil Amey, 'Baptist Missionary Society Radicals', *The Baptist Quarterly,* 26 (1975-1976), pp.363-76; Gordon, *From Slavery to Freedom,* pp.132-41.

24. Fuller, Letter to John Sutcliff, 30 August 1795 (BMS Archives) — this letter is written on a copy of a letter from Carey dated 18 March 1795; Olney Church Book III, entry for 30 October 1795.

25. Fuller, Letter to John Sutcliff, 3 October 1796 (Letters of Andrew Fuller). Sutcliff had written to Grigg at least twice prior to this point: see Jacob Grigg, Letter to John Sutcliff, 25 April 1796 (NLW Ms 1207D).

26. Fuller, Letter to William Carey, 11 October 1796 (Gordon, *From Slavery to Freedom,* p.140).

27. *Ibid.*

28. Amey, 'Baptist Missionary Society Radicals', p.365.

29. Marshman, *Life and Times of Carey, Marshman, and Ward,* vol. I, p.75.

30. Fuller, Letter to John Sutcliff, 26 January 1796 (Letters of Andrew Fuller).

31. Morris, Letter to Andrew Fuller (Amey, 'Baptist Missionary Society Radicals', p.370).

32. The Accounts of the Particular Baptist Society for Propagating the Gospel amongst the Heathen, entry for 2 February 1796.

33. Fuller, Letter to John Fountain, 25 March 1796 (Amey, 'Baptist Missionary Society Radicals', p.367).

34. Fuller, Letter to John Sutcliff, 18 February 1799 (Letters of Andrew Fuller); Amey, 'Baptist Missionary Society Radicals', p.370.

35. Fuller, Letter to John Sutcliff, 26 April 1799, Letter to William Carey, 18 April 1799 (Letters of Andrew Fuller). For Fuller's attitude towards political involvement, see also Jakobsson, *Am I Not A Man and A Brother?,* pp.100-104; Michael A. G. Haykin, '"Resisting Evil": Civil Retaliation, Non-resistance and the Interpretation of Matthew 5:39a among Eighteenth-Century Calvinistic Baptists,' in Daniel G. Lundy, ed., *The Ethics of Jesus. The Believer as Salt and Light* (Toronto: Gospel Witness Publications, 1994) pp.100-105.

36. Fountain, Letter to John Sutcliff, 16 September 1799 (BMS Archives).

37. Fountain, Letter to Andrew Fuller (Carey, *Memoir of William Carey,* p.359).

38. John Rippon, Letter to John Sutcliff, December 1793 (Ms. II.a.18.148,

Congregational Library Ms. Collection, Dr Williams's Library, London); Ryland, Letter to John Sutcliff, 28 January 1795 (The James Marshall and Marie-Louise Osborn Collection, Yale University Library); 'List of persons intered [sic] in the burying ground belonging to the Baptist Church at Olney, Bucks', Olney Church Book I; Letters from Olney Baptist Church to the Northamptonshire Baptist Association.

39. Carey, *Memoir of Wiliam Carey,* p.380.

40. Letter from Olney Baptist Church to the Northamptonshire Baptist Association, 1801.

41. Hewett, 'Sutcliff: The Meeting and the Man', p.87; Howard, 'John Sutcliff', pp.ii-iii. A shortened version of the latter appeared as 'John Sutcliff and Olney', *Baptist Times,* 98, No. 5084 (21 August 1952), pp.3,5.

42. Fuller, *Principles and Prospects of a Servant of Christ, Works,* vol. I, p.351.

43. Howard, 'John Sutcliff', p.iii; Fuller, *Principles and Prospects of a Servant of Christ, Works,* vol. I, p.352. On Sutcliff's belief regarding the knowledge that glorified believers have of what is transpiring on earth, see Ivimey, *History of the English Baptists,* vol. IV, p.441, note. Ivimey further remarks that this 'is a most impressive sentiment, especially to those who have recently been deprived of endeared friends; but that it is fully sustained by scripture I am not perfectly satisfied'.

44. Hewett, 'Sutcliff: The Meeting and the Man', p.87.

45. Howard, 'John Sutcliff', p. iii. Hewett ('Sutcliff: The Meeting and the Man', p.87) wrongly states that 21 High Street had previously belonged to the Johnston family.

46. Fuller, *Principles and Prospects of a Servant of Christ, Works,* vol. I, p.355.

47. Hewett, 'Sutcliff: The Meeting and the Man', p.87.

48. Fuller, *Principles and Prospects of a Servant of Christ, Works,* vol. I, p.353.

49. Cited by Roger Thomas, 'Philip Doddridge and Liberalism in Religion' in Geoffrey F. Nuttall, ed., *Philip Doddridge, 1702-1751. His Contribution to English Religion* (London: Independent Press Ltd., 1951), pp.136-7. For the attitude of one of Sutcliff's good friends, Ryland, to theological education, see Michael A. G. Haykin, 'John Ryland, Jr (1753-1825) and Theological Education', *Nederlands Archief voor Kerkgeschiedenis/ Dutch Review of Church History,* 70 (1990), pp.173-91.

50. For Brunsdon, see his Letter to John Sutcliff, 30 July 1800 (BMS Archives); *Periodical Accounts,* vol. I, p.500; for Chamberlain, see William Yates, *Memoirs of Mr John Chamberlain, Late Missionary in India* (Calcutta: The Baptist Mission Press, 1824).

51. See Yates, *John Chamberlain,* pp.18,24,27.

52. *Ibid.,* pp.23,25-26,34.

53. Brunsdon, Letter to John Sutcliff, 30 July 1800 (BMS Archives).

54. The Accounts of the Particular Baptist Society for Propagating the Gospel amongst the Heathen, entry for 20 November 1798.

55. A. Christopher Smith, 'British Recruits for Serampore, 1800-1825', *The Baptist Review of Theology,* 2, No. 2 (Fall 1992), pp.11-12; Fuller, Letter to John Sutcliff, 18 February 1799 (Letters of Andrew Fuller).
56. Daniel Brunsdon, Letter to John Ryland, 26 February 1799 (BMS Archives); Fuller, Letter to John Sutcliff, 3 April 1799 (Letters of Andrew Fuller); Yates, *John Chamberlain,* p.27.
57. A Christopher Smith, 'The Legacy of William Carey', *International Bulletin of Missionary Research,* 16, No.1 (January 1992), p.2.
58. A. Christopher Smith, 'William Ward, Radical Reform, and Missions in the 1790s', *American Baptist Quarterly,* 10 (1991), p.218. The following account of Ward's career prior to his going to India in 1799 is drawn from this superb study of Ward's early years.
59. Fuller, Letter to William Carey, 18 April 1799 (Letters of Andrew Fuller); Ward, Letter to William Carey, October 1798 (Carey, *William Carey,* ed. Masters, p.172).
60. Fuller, Letter to John Sutcliff, 18 February 1799 (Letters of Andrew Fuller).
61. For Marshman's life prior to his going to India, see especially Marshman, *Life and Times of Carey Marshman and Ward,* vol. I, pp.99-108, from which the following account of this period of his life is primarily drawn. Two other biographical sketches are: Benjamin Davies, 'Joshua Marshman, D.D. Late Missionary in Bengal, East Indies', *The Canada Baptist Magazine, and Missionary Register,* 2, No. 1 (June, 1838), pp.1-6; Thomas Hamilton, 'Marshman, Joshua (1768-1837)', *The Dictionary of National Biography* (1893 ed.; repr. London: Oxford University Press, 1963-1964), vol. XII, pp.1140-41.
62. For Grant's career prior to his conversion, see *Periodical Accounts,* vol. I, pp.500-503.
63. Fuller, Letter to John Sutcliff, 18 February 1799 (Letters of Andrew Fuller).
64. Fuller, Letters to John Sutcliff, 3 April 1799 and 26 April 1799 (Letters of Andrew Fuller).
65. *Periodical Accounts,* vol. I, pp.509-10.
66. Edwards, *Religious Affections,*p.339.
67. *Periodical Accounts,* vol. I, pp.510-11.
68. *Ibid.,* vol I, pp.512-17.
69. Pearce, Letter to William Carey, March 1799 *(Missionary Correspondence,* pp.71-5; Fuller, Letter to John Sutcliff, 23 February 1799 (Letters of Andrew Fuller); Fuller, *Memoirs of the Rev. Samuel Pearce, Works,* vol. III, pp.409-14.
70. Fuller, *Memoirs of the Rev. Samuel Pearce, Works,* vol. III, p.417.
71. *Periodical Accounts,* vol. I, p.520.
72. Carey, *Samuel Pearce,* pp.204-5. See also the Accounts of the Particular Baptist Society for Propagating the Gospel amongst the Heathen, entry for 7 May 1799.
73. *Periodical Accounts,* vol. I, pp.520-21; Christopher Anderson, *The*

*Christian Spirit which is essential to the triumph of the Kingdom of God* (London: 1824), p.26.
74. This figure may be found in the financial accounts at the back of the Accounts of the Particular Baptist Society for Propagating the Gospel amongst the Heathen.
75. Fuller, Letter to John Sutcliff, 1 September 1801 (Letters of Andrew Fuller).
76. Fuller, Letter to John Sutcliff, 3 July 1799 (Letters of Andrew Fuller); Pearce, Letter to John Ryland, 20 July 1799 (Fuller, *Memoirs of the Rev. Samuel Pearce, Works,* vol. III, p.426).
77. Morris, *Memoirs of the Life and Death of the Rev. Andrew Fuller,* p.182.
78. Fuller, *Memoirs of the Rev. Samuel Pearce, Works,* vol. III, pp.429-37.
79. Brian Stanley, *The History of the Baptist Missionary Society 1792-1992* (Edinburgh: T & T Clark, 1992), p.20.
80. Ryland, *Life and Death of the Rev. Andrew Fuller* (1818 ed.), pp.164-5.
81. For a clear presentation of Scotch Baptist origins, see especially D. B. Murray, 'The Seventeenth and Eighteenth Centuries' in D.W. Bebbington, ed., *The Baptists in Scotland* (Glasgow: The Baptist Union of Scotland, 1988), pp.9-25.
82. The description of Glas's view of faith is that of Murray, 'Seventeenth and Eighteenth Centuries', p.15.
83. Ryland, *Life and Death of the Rev. Andrew Fuller* (1818 ed.), p.170.
84. For the Haldanes and their influence on Baptist life in Scotland, see especially D. E. Meek and D. B. Murray, 'The Early Nineteenth Century' in Bebbington, ed., *Baptists in Scotland,* pp.26-47.
85. *Ibid.,* p.31.
86. Ryland, *Life and Death of the Rev. Andrew Fuller* (1818 ed.), p.169.
87. *Ibid.,* p.170.
88. Fuller, *Andrew Fuller,* p.114.
89. Carey, *Samuel Pearce,* p.216.
90. For an account of these visits, see Fuller, *Andrew Fuller,* pp.112-17; Dudley Reeves, 'Andrew Fuller in Scotland', *The Banner of Truth,* 106-7 (July/August 1972), pp.33-40.
91. William Button, Letter to John Sutcliff, 5 July 1805 (Sutcliff Papers).
92. Ryland, Letter to John Saffery, 22 October 1799 (Reeves Collection 8/32, Angus Library, Regent's Park College).
93. For these figures, see Letters from Olney Baptist Church to the Northamptonshire Baptist Association, 1790-1808.
94. Brunsdon, Letter to John Ryland, 26 February 1799 (BMS Archives).
95. Olney Church Book III, entry for 21 March 1799; Hannah Smith, Letter to John Sutcliff (Yates, *John Chamberlain,* pp.93,95).

**Chapter 12: Other friends, other ministries**

1. The title of this chapter is indebted to that of an article by Ian Sellers, 'Other Times, Other Ministries: John Fawcett and Alexander McLaren', *The Baptist Quarterly,* 32 (1986-1987), pp.181-98.

2. *Periodical Accounts,* vol. II, pp.107,109. For an account of Brunsdon's death, see *ibid.,* vol. II, pp.195-200.
3. Carey, Letter to John Sutcliff, September 1811 (cited *Periodical Accounts,* vol. IV, p.353).
4. Sutcliff *et al.,* Letter to Krishna Pal *et al.*, 19 August 1801 (BMS Archives).
5. Carey, Letter to John Sutcliff, February 1801 (*Periodical Accounts,* vol. II, p.150).
6. S. Neill, *A History of Christianity in India 1707-1858* (Cambridge: Cambridge University Press, 1985), p.191.
7. *Ibid.,* p.194; Smith, 'British Recruits for Serampore', pp.11-12; Ward, Letter to John Chamberlain, 17 May 1807 (NLW Ms. 1207D); Fuller, Letter to William Carey, 15 May 1809 (Letters of Andrew Fuller).
8. Yates, *John Chamberlain,* p.149; Chamberlain, Letter to John Sutcliff, 27 November 1805 (NLW Ms. 1207D); Chamberlain, Letter to John Sutcliff, 29 June 1807 - 6 August 1807 (BMS Archives).
9. Ryland, Letter to William Christian, 10 December 1803 (Hewett, 'Sutcliff: The Meeting and the Man', p.89); Fuller, Letter to John Sutcliff, 4 November 1803 (Letters of Andrew Fuller); Hannah Biss, Letter to Jane Sutcliff, 5 July 1808 (BMS Archives).
10. Richard Mardon, Letter to John Ryland, 11 February 1803 (BMS Archives); William Moore, Letter to John Sutcliff, 17 September 1805 (BMS Archives).
11. Cox, *History of the Baptist Missionary Society,* vol. I, p.265, note.
12. Fuller, Letters to John Sutcliff, 11 November 1803 and 22 November 1803 (Letters of Andrew Fuller).
13. For Ann Coles, see Ryland, *Life and Death of the Rev. Andrew Fuller* (1818 ed.), pp.293-5.
14. Fuller, Letter to John Sutcliff, 11 November 1803 (Letters of Andrew Fuller).
15. Smith, 'British Recruits for Serampore', p.10.
16. For Robinson's life and ministry, see John Robinson, *Memoirs of the Rev. W. Robinson, Baptist Missionary* (Benares: Medical Hall Press, 1858). This is a rare book, not mentioned in Edward C. Starr, *A Baptist Bibliography.* For access to it, I am indebted to Mrs Marjorie Tirrell, of Sutcliff Baptist Church, Olney. Mrs Tirrell is descended from William Robinson's sister, Elizabeth. The details about Robinson's early career which follow are drawn from the first two chapters of this memoir. For a more recent account of his life and ministry, see Ernest A. Payne, *South-East from Serampore. More Chapters in the Story of the Baptist Missionary Society* (London: The Carey Press, 1945), pp.7-14, 24-56.
17. Joseph Conforti, 'Jonathan Edwards's Most Popular Work: "The Life of David Brainerd" and Nineteenth-Century Evangelical Culture', *Church History,* 54 (1985), pp.188-201.
18. *Ibid.,* p.193. See also Hayden, 'Evangelical Calvinism', p.344.

19. Olney Church Book III, entries for 23 February and 22 March 1804 ; Robinson, *Memoirs of the Rev. W. Robinson,* pp.17-18.
20. William Robinson, Letter to John Sutcliff, 18 March 1807 (BMS Archives).
21. Robinson, *Memoirs of the Rev. W. Robinson,* pp.18-19.
22. William Robinson, Letter to John Sutcliff, 18 March 1807 (BMS Archives).
23. This point is made by Tom Nettles, 'Training Men for the Ministry' in Roger O. Beardmore, ed., *Shepherding God's Flock. Essays on Leadership in the Local Church* (Harrisonburg, Virginia: Sprinkle Publications, 1988), p.239.
24. For Anderson, see especially Anderson, *Life and Letters of Christopher Anderson*; Derek B. Murray, 'Christopher Anderson and Scotland' in Donald E. Meek, ed., *A Mind for Mission. Essays in Appreciation of The Rev. Christopher Anderson (1782-1852)* (Edinburgh: The Scottish Baptist History Project, 1992), pp.3-7. The following sketch of Anderson's early years is drawn from these two works.
25. Fuller, Letter to Christopher Anderson, 16 March 1805 (BMS Archives).
26. Anderson, *Life and Letters of Christopher Anderson,* pp.33-6.
27. *Ibid.,* p.42.
28. Olney Church Book III, entries for 5 September - 4 October, 1805. Sadly, Martha Boon, later Martha Roberts, was disfellowshipped on 4 February 1808 for fornication (see Olney Church Book III, entries for 14 August 1807 and 4 February 1808).
29. Anderson, *Life and Letters of Christopher Anderson,* p.43.
30. Joshua Rowe, Letter to John Sutcliff, 14 November 1806 (BMS Archives); Fuller, Letter to John Sutcliff, 4 January 1808 (The James Marshall and Marie-Louise Osborn Collection, Yale University Library).
31. Anderson, Letter to William Carey, 14 February 1822 (Anderson, *Life and Letters of Christopher Anderson,* p.258).
32. Anderson, *Life and Letters of Christopher Anderson,* p.234, note; Hugh Anderson, *A Discourse occasioned by the Death of the Rev. William Carey, D.D.* (2nd. ed.; London: 1835), p.31, note.
33. Gilbert Meilaender, *Friendship. A Study in Theological Ethics* (Notre Dame/ London: University of Notre Dame Press, 1981), pp.1-2.
34. Robinson, *Memoirs of the Rev. W. Robinson,* pp.21-3.
35. Anderson, Letter to John Sutcliff, 19 June 1806 (JRL English Mss 369-71).
36. Anderson, *Life and Letters of Christopher Anderson,* p.59. Hewett ('Sutcliff: The Meeting and the Man', p.91) thought that Davies was either Philip Davies or an R. Davies. For the identification of Davies as David Davies, see David Davies, Letter to John Sutcliff, 21 May 1808 (Sutcliff Papers).
37. H. G. Tibbutt, *Keysoe Brook End and Keysoe Row Baptist Churches* (Keysoe and Keysoe Row: Keysoe Brook End and Keysoe Row Baptist

Churches, 1959), pp.14-15; Parsons, ed., *Church Book of the Independent Church Isleham*, p.251.

38. For a list of these students, see Maurice F. Hewett, 'Sutcliff's Academy at Olney', *The Baptist Quarterly*, 4 (1928-1929), pp.276-9. That this (unsigned) article was written by Hewett may be seen by comparing it with his list and discussion of Sutcliff's students in 'Sutcliff: The Meeting and the Man', pp.89-93.

39. D. E. Meek and D. B. Murray, 'The Early Nineteenth Century' in Bebbington, ed., *The Baptists in Scotland*, pp.34-5; Murray, 'Christopher Anderson and Scotland', pp.6-7; Donald E. Meek, 'Christopher Anderson, The Scottish Highlands and Ireland' in Meek, ed., *A Mind for Mission*, pp.17-24.

40. A. Christopher Smith, 'Christopher Anderson and "The Serampore Fraternity"' in Meek, ed., *A Mind for Mission*, pp.25-37.

41. See Anderson, *The Christian Spirit which is essential*, pp.22-3.

42. *Ibid.*, p.25.

43. For Morris's early years, especially helpful is Ernest A. Payne and A. Rattray Allan, *Clipston Baptist Church. The Record of One Hundred and Fifty Years' Witness* (Northampton: 1932), pp.8-9. See also William Perkins, 'Morris, John Webster', *The Dictionary of National Biography*, vol. XIII, p.998.

44. Carey, Letter to John Webster Morris, 5 December 1797 (*Periodical Accounts*, vol. I, p.380); William Ward, Diary, entry for 1 December 1799 (BMS Archives).

45. Wilkin, *Joseph Kinghorn of Norwich*, pp.283-4; Fuller, Letter to John Saffery, 11 May 1798 (Letters of Andrew Fuller).

46. Letter from Clipston Baptist Church to the Northamptonshire Baptist Associ-ation, 1792.

47. Payne and Allan, *Clipston Baptist Church*, p.11; *The Baptist Magazine*, 24 (1832), p.73 (the obituary of John Gulliver).

48. Morris, Letters to John Sutcliff, 30 May 1800 and 30 June 1800 (*Original Letters ... 1773-1813*, BMS Archives). See also Fuller, Letter to John Saffery, 3 July 1800 (Letters of Andrew Fuller).

49. John Sutcliff, *Qualifications for Church Fellowship* (Clipston: J. W. Morris, 1800), pp.1-2.

50. Thomas King, Letter to John Sutcliff, 31 July 1800 (Sutcliff Papers). See also Fuller, Letter to William Carey, 24 September 1800 (Letters of Andrew Fuller).

51. *Baptist Annual Register*, 2:16,23. For the number of Baptist churches in existence in England and Wales in the early and mid-eighteenth century, see the statistics given in chapter 1.

52. *Baptist Annual Register* 3:40,42.

53. Lovegrove, *Established Church, Sectarian People*, p.38.

54. Morris, Letter to John Sutcliff, 17 March 1800 (*Original Letters ... 1773-1813*, BMS Archives).

55. Morris, Letter to John Sutcliff, 30 June 1800 (*Original Letters ... 1773-1813,* BMS Archives).
56. Morris, Letter to John Sutcliff, 19 November 1800 (*Original Letters ... 1773*-1813, BMS Archives). What was later known as *The Baptist Magazine* began in 1809 and had no immediate connection with Morris.
57. Rosemary Taylor, 'English Baptist Periodicals, 1790-1865', *The Baptist Quarterly,* 27 (1977-1978), pp.55-6.
58. Morris, Letters to John Sutcliff, 1 May 1801, 6 January 1802, 28 May 1802, 31 January 1803, 3 May 1806 (*Original Letters ... 1773-1813,* BMS Archives).
59. 'Justin's Epistle to Diognetus', *The Biblical Magazine,* 2 (1802), pp.41-8. Also see Morris, Letter to John Sutcliff, 6 January 1802 (*Original Letters ... 1773-1813,* BMS Archives). For another translation of the Epistle to Diognetus by a Baptist author, see that by James Lister in *The Baptist Magazine,* 30 (1838), pp.413-15.
60. Morris, Letter to John Sutcliff, 16 September 1802 (*Original Letters ... 1773-1813,* BMS Archives).
61. Morris, Letter to John Sutcliff, 30 September 1802 and Letter to Sutcliff received 27 October 1802 (*Original Letters ... 1773-1813,* BMS Archives).
62. Morris, Letters to John Sutcliff, 31 January 1803 and 11 June 1803 (*Original Letters ... 1773-1813,* BMS Archives); Fuller, Letter to William Carey, 28 February 1803 (Letters of Andrew Fuller).
63. Morris, Letters to John Sutcliff, 17 September 1805 and 18 September 1805 (*Original Letters ... 1773-1813,* BMS Archives).
64. Morris, Letters to John Sutcliff, 29 December 1806 and 30 March 1808 (*Original Letters ... 1773-1813,* BMS Archives).
65. Morris, Letters to John Sutcliff, 6 November 1806, 29 December 1806, 13 March 1807, 11 October 1807 and 9 April 1808 (*Original Letters ... 1773-1813,* BMS Archives). For an account of the opening of the place of worship at Hockliffe, see *The Theological and Biblical Magazine,* 6 (1806), p.258.
66. Morris, Letter to John Sutcliff, 6 November 1806 (*Original Letters ... 1773-1813,* BMS Archives).
67. Morris, Letter to John Sutcliff, March 1809 (*Original Letters ... 1773-1813,* BMS Archives); Fuller, Letter to William Ward, 16 July 1809 (Letters of Andrew Fuller).
68. Micah Thomas, 'Bankruptcy', *The Baptist Magazine,* 14 (1822), p.96.
69. Cited by Malcolm Deacon, *Philip Doddridge of Northampton 1702-1751* (Northampton: Northamptonshire Libraries, 1980), pp.83-4.
70. Morris, Letter to John Sutcliff, March 1809 (*Original Letters ... 1773-1813,* BMS Archives)
71. Fuller, Letter to John Sutcliff, 17 December 1811 (Letters of Andrew Fuller); Fuller, Letter to Christopher Anderson, 4 December 1811 (Anderson, *Life and Letters of Christopher Anderson,* pp.193-4); Fuller, Letter to Christopher Anderson, 31 December 1811 (*ibid.,* pp.195-6).

72. Thomas Paine, *The Age of Reason*, introd. Philip S. Foner (Secaucus, New Jersey: Citadel Press, Inc., 1974), p.50.
73. *Ibid.*, pp.63,68,70,185,187-8,190.
74. For Fuller's response to Paine, see Michael A. G. Haykin, '"The Oracles of God": Andrew Fuller and the Scriptures', *Churchman*, 103 (1989), pp.60-76.
75. Fuller, *The Nature and Importance of an Intimate Knowledge of Divine Truth', Works*, vol. I, p.172.
76. Sutcliff, *Divinity of the Christian Religion*, pp.3-7.
77. Sutcliff, *Qualifications for Church Fellowship*, pp.2-3.
78. Watts, *Dissenters*, p.34.
79. Sutcliff, *Qualifications for Church Fellowship*, pp.4,6.
80. 'Introductory Discourse' in John Sutcliff, John Ryland and Andrew Fuller, *The Difficulties of the Christian Ministry, and the Means of surmounting them; with the Obedience of Churches to their Pastors explained and enforced* (Birmingham: 1802), p.3.
81. Cited by James Barry Vaughn, 'Public Worship and Practical Theology in the Work of Benjamin Keach (1640-1704)' (Unpublished Ph.D. thesis, University of St Andrews, 1989), pp.326-7. See also the texts cited in this regard by Philip George Allister Griffin-Allwood, 'The Canadianization of Baptists: From Denominations to Denomination, 1760-1912' (Unpublished Ph.D. thesis, Southern Baptist Theological Seminary, 1986), pp.30-33.
82. Griffin-Allwood, 'Canadianization of Baptists', pp.33-4.
83. Sutcliff, *Qualifications for Church Fellowship*, p.3; Sutcliff, 'Introductory Discourse', p.3.
84. Andrew Fuller, *The Promise of the Spirit, the Grand Encouragement in Promoting the Gospel, Works*, vol. III, p.359, italics added.
85. Sutcliff, *Qualifications for Church Fellowship*, pp.7,8-9.
86. *Ibid.*, p.11.
87. John Sutcliff, *The Ordinance of the Lord's Supper considered* (Dunstable: 1803), p.6.
88. The phrase 'an unbroken continuum' is taken from Roberts, *Continuity and Change*, p.250.
89. Sutcliff, *Qualifications for Church Fellowship*, p.2.
90. Hewett, 'Sutcliff: The Meeting and the Man' , p.94; Howard, 'John Sutcliff', p.ii.
91. 'An Interview with the Late Mr Berridge', *The Evangelical Magazine*, 2 (1794), pp.73-6. See also Ryland, *Life and Death of the Reverend Andrew Fuller*, p.225; Michael A. G. Haykin, 'John Sutcliff's Testimony to John Berridge', *The Banner of Truth*, 309 (June 1989), pp.13-18,32.
92. Sutcliff, 'Introductory Discourse', p. 5.
93. Roberts, *Continuity and Change*, p.81.
94. *Memoirs of Miss Susanna Anthony* (Clipston: J. W. Morris, 1802), pp.vi-viii.
95. The continuing strength of Sutcliff's Baptist convictions is amply

illustrated by a story conveyed to Thomas Wright by a woman who had known Sutcliff and had attended his funeral. According to this woman, 'One Independent minister of high standing came from Newport [this was probably William Bull], five miles distant, on purpose to consult him. Having given his opinion with customary freedom and kindness, to the great satisfaction and pleasure of the visitor, Mr Sutcliff went to the door with him, and opened it; thereupon the latter, taking his hand, shook it heartily, and said, "I do love you, brother John, but should love you much better if you were not a Baptist." Mr Sutcliff cleared his throat and replied very deliberately and quietly, "Should you not love Jesus Christ much better if He were not a Baptist? Good morning, sir," and shut the door to' (Wright, *Town of Cowper,* pp.166-7).

96. Oliver, 'Strict and Particular Baptist Community', pp.40-41. For an examin-ation of the arguments of Turner and Ryland in favour of open communion, see *ibid.,* pp.42-50. It was Abraham Booth who eventually answered Turner and Ryland with his *Apology for the Baptists* (1778), which was the standard defence of closed communion for many years. See *ibid.,* pp.60-69.

97. On the correspondence between Carey and Fuller over this issue, see E. Daniel Potts, ' "I throw away the guns to preserve the ship". A Note on the Serampore Trio', *The Baptist Quarterly,* 20 (1963-1964), pp.115-17.

98. *Diary of Samuel Teedon,* pp.4 (entry for 6 November 1791), 7 (entry for 4 December 1791).

99. For further discussion, see Michael A. G. Haykin, 'On Friendship,' *Refor-mation Today,* 140 (July-Aug. 1994), pp.26-30.

100. E. A. Payne, *The Fellowship of Believers. Baptist Thought and Practice Yesterday and Today* (2nd. ed.; London: Carey Kingsgate Press, Ltd., 1952), p.61.

101. Walker, *Baptists at the Table,* p.3.

102. Victor A. Shepherd, *The Nature and Function of Faith in the Theology of John Calvin* (Macon, Georgia: Mercer University Press, 1983), p.220. Other helpful studies on Calvin's theology of the Lord's Supper include B.A. Gerrish, 'The Lord's Supper in the Reformed Confessions', *Theology Today,* 13 (1966-1967), pp.224-43; John D. Nicholls, '"Union with Christ": John Calvin on the Lord's Supper' in *Union and Communion, 1529-1979* (London: The Westminster Conference, 1979), pp.35-54; John Yates, 'Rôle of the Holy Spirit in the Lord's Supper', *Churchman,* 105 (1991), pp.355-6.

103. Cited by Stephen J. Stein, 'A Note on Anne Dutton, Eighteenth-Century Evangelical', *Church History,* 44 (1975), pp.488,489. Stein's article is the best recent study of Dutton. For two earlier studies which fail to do her justice, see J. C. Whitebrook, 'The Life and Works of Mrs Ann Dutton', *Transactions of the Baptist Historical Society,* 7 (1921), pp.129-46; H. Wheeler Robinson, *The Life and Faith of the Baptists* (London: The Kingsgate Press, 1946), pp.50-56.

104. A. Dutton, *Thoughts on the Lord's Supper, Relating to the Nature, Subjects, and right Partaking of this Solemn Ordinance* (London: 1748), p.4.
105. L. G. Champion, 'Baptist Church Life in London, 1771', *The Baptist Quarterly,* 18 (1959-1960), p.300.
106. *Ibid.,* pp.301-2.
107. John Calvin, *Institutes of the Christian Religion* 4.17.1, trans. Ford Lewis Battles in John T. McNeill, ed., *Calvin: Institutes of the Christian Religion* (Philadelphia: The Westminster Press, 1960), 2:1361. I am indebted for this reference to Walker, *Baptists at the Table,* p.9.
108. Payne, *Fellowship of Believers,* p.65.
109. John Fawcett, *Christ Precious to Those That Believe* (4th. ed.; 1839 ed.; repr. Minneapolis, Minnesota: Klock & Klock Christian Publ., 1979), pp.230-31.
110. Sutcliff, *Ordinance of the Lord's Supper,* pp.2,3.
111. *Ibid.,* pp.3-4.
112. John Sutcliff, *The First Principles of the Oracles of God,* revised Joseph Belcher (Whitchurch, Shropshire: 1820), p.14.
113. John Sutcliff, *On obedience to Positive Institutions* (n.p.: 1808), p.6.
114. Sutcliff, *Ordinance of the Lord's Supper,* p.7. When Susannah Stow, a member of the Baptist congregation in Olney, was seeking to join Cannon Street Baptist Church in Birmingham, she wrote to Sutcliff seeking a letter of dismission. In the course of her letter, she told Sutcliff that what she missed about worshipping in Olney were Sutcliff's 'very affectionate addresses ... particularly at the Table of the Lord to recollect the solemn vows we had made that we would be the Lord's'. 'They are so deep in my memory,' she added, 'I shall never forget them' (Letter to John Sutcliff, 3 March 1800, Sutcliff Papers).
115. Sutcliff, *Ordinance of the Lord's Supper,* p.9.
116. *Ibid.,* p.2.
117. *Ibid.,* p.6. See also Sutcliff, *Obedience to Positive Institutions,* pp.8 9.
118. Sutcliff, *Jealousy for the Lord of Hosts,* p.12.
119. Walker, *Baptists at the Table,* pp.84-120.
120. Payne, *Fellowship of Believers,* pp.64-5.
121. J. Priestley, *Institutes of Natural and Revealed Religion,* in *The Theological and Miscellaneous Works of Joseph Priestley,* ed. J. T. Rutt (New York: Klaus Reprint Co., 1972), vol. II, pp.336-7.
122. For the thought of these theologians about the atonement, see especially Dorus Paul Rudisill, *The Doctrine of the Atonement in Jonathan Edwards and His Successors* (New York: Poseidon Books, Inc., 1971); Allen C. Guelzo, 'Jonathan Edwards and the New Divinity: Change and Continuity in New England Calvinism, 1758-1858' in Charles G. Dennison and Richard C. Gamble, eds, *Pressing Toward the Mark. Essays Commemorating Fifty Years of the Orthodox Presby-terian Church* (Philadelphia: The Committee for the Historian of the Orthodox

PresbyterianChurch, 1986), pp.160-62; A. C. Guelzo, *Edwards on the Will. A Century of American Theological Debate* (Middletown, Connecticut: Wesleyan University Press, 1989), pp.129-35.

123. Fuller, Letter to John Ryland, 21 April 1794 (Ryland, *Life and Death of the Rev. Andrew Fuller,* 1818 ed., p.226); Fuller, Letter to John Sutcliff, 22 January 1795 (Letters of Andrew Fuller).

124. Fuller, *Calvinistic and Socinian Systems Examined and Compared, Works,* vol. II, pp.154-5. A little later he wrote, 'God ... in the punishment of sin, is not to be considered as acting in a merely private capacity, but as the universal moral Governor' (*ibid.,* p.157).

125. Sutcliff, *Ordinance of the Lord's Supper,* p.3.

126. Fuller, *Six Letters to Dr Ryland Respecting the Controversy with the Rev. A. Booth, Works,* vol. II, p.706; Sutcliff, *Ordinance of the Lord's Supper,* p.3. See also Fuller, *The Future Perfection of the Church*: 'We, as transgressors, being justly exposed to eternal death, must have borne our iniquity, had he not offered himself as a substitute in our place, life for life' (*Works,* vol. I, p.250); Fuller, *The Believer's Review of his State*: 'Either Christ must be the sacrifice, or we must die in our sins and perish' (*Works,* vol. I, p.303).

127. Fuller, Letter to Isaac Mann, 2 September 1806 (Letters of Andrew Fuller).

128. Dorothy Tippleston, *William Carey and Hackleton Baptist Church* (Northampton: 1955), pp.12-13; Church Book of Hackleton Baptist Church, Northamptonshire, entry for 17 April 1809. On four subsequent occasions, Sutcliff came and baptized believers at Hackleton: entries for 31 July 1809; 16 August 1810; 30 September 1811; 22 April 1813.

129. Thomas Parsons, Letter to John Sutcliff, 7 February 1802 (Sutcliff Papers); F. H. Rollinson, 'Chipping Norton Baptist Church, 1694-1944', *The Baptist Quarterly,* 11 (1942-1945), pp. 283-4.

130. J. Marriott, Letters to John Sutcliff, 8 January 1803 and 6 September 1804 (Sutcliff Papers).

131. Marriott, Letters to John Sutcliff, 17 and 26 July 1806, 14 September 1806 (Sutcliff Papers); M. Clark, Letter to John Sutcliff, 9 June 1812 (Sutcliff Papers).

132. Cox, *History of the Baptist Missionary Society,* p.262; Fuller, Letter to John Sutcliff, 18 April 1808 (Letters of Andrew Fuller); Fuller, *Principles and Prospects of a Servant of Christ, Works,* vol. I, pp.353-4.

133. James Edwards, 'Memoir of the Late Rev. William Nichols, of Collingham', *The Baptist Magazine,* 29 (1837), 1-5; John T. Godfrey and James Ward, *The History of Friar Lane Baptist Church, Nottingham* (Nottingham: Henry B. Saxton/London: Simpkin, Marshall, Hamilton, Kent & Co., Ltd.: 1903), pp.36-7 and 36, note 2.

134. W. H. Brackney, 'The Baptist Missionary Society in Proper Context. Some Reflections on the Larger Voluntary Religious Tradition', *The Baptist Quarterly,* 34 (1991-1992), p.368.

135. For this union, see John Brown and David Prothero, *The History of the Bedfordshire Union of Christians* (London: Independent Press Ltd., 1946); Roger H. Martin, 'English Particular Baptists and Interdenominational Cooperation', *Foundations,* 22 (1979), pp.236-7.
136. S. Greatheed, *General Union Recommended to Real Christians* (London: 1798), p.xvii.
137. *Ibid.,* p.ix. For a discussion of Greatheed's idealism in this regard, see Roger H. Martin, *Evangelicals United: Ecumenical Stirrings in Pre-Victorian Britain, 1795-1830* (Metuchen, New Jersey/London: The Scarecrow Press, Inc., 1983), pp.30-32.
138. Minutes of the Bedfordshire Union of Christians, entry for 17 November 1797 (Ms Z 206/1, Bedfordshire County Record Office, Bedford); Martin, 'English Particular Baptists', p.237.
139. *The Evangelical Magazine,* 7 (1799), pp.215-16.
140. See Samuel Greatheed, '[Letter] to the Editor', *The Evangelical Magazine,* 5 (1797), pp.276-9. I wish to thank D. Bruce Hindmarsh for drawing my attention to this valuable letter.
141. Minutes of the Bedfordshire Union of Christians, entries for 21 February 1798 and 26 November 1799.
142. 'A short account of the Independent Church at Olney, Bucks, from the period when the late Revd Thomas Hillyard commenced his labours amongst them' (Olney Congregational Church Book, Olney, Buckinghamshire). On Hillyard, see also H. G. Tibbutt, *Bunyan Meeting, Bedford 1650-1950* (Bedford: The Trustees of Bunyan Meeting, 1950), pp.42-52.
143. 'Short account of the Independent Church at Olney.'
144. Robison, 'Particular Baptists', p.295.
145. Martin, 'English Particular Baptists', pp.239-43.

**Chapter 13: Final years**
1. Anderson, *Life and Letters of Christopher Anderson,* p.192; Olney Church Book III, entries for 6 May, 27 May, 3 June and 8 June 1810.
2. See the remarks of Joseph Kinghorn in a letter that he wrote to William Newman (1773-1835) in 1811 (Wilkin, *Joseph Kinghorn of Norwich,* p.336).
3. *The Baptist Magazine,* 2 (1810), pp.492-3.
4. *Ibid.,* p.493.
5. *Ibid.,* p.492.
6. Fuller, Letter to William Carey, 24 September 1800 (Letters of Andrew Fuller).
7. J. Jarman, *The Nature and Importance of walking with God* (Nottingham: R. Dowson, 1811), pp.7-8.
8. Fuller, Letter to William Ward, 4 February 1812 (Letters of Andrew Fuller). It is from this letter that we learn the nature of Blundel's sin.
9. 'Brief History of the Baptist Church, Keighley, Yorkshire', *The Baptist Magazine,* 27 (1835), pp.192-3; Joseph Rhodes, *A Century of Keighley Baptist History, 1810-1910* (Keighley: 1910), pp.16-18.

10. Fuller, *The Promise of the Spirit, Works,* vol. III, pp.359-63. It was the perusal of this small, but powerful tract that first introduced me to the rich, spiritual legacy to be found in the writings of Fuller, Sutcliff and their friends.
11. *Ibid.,* p.359.
12. *Ibid.,* p.360.
13. *Ibid.,* pp.360-62.
14. *Ibid.,* p.362.
15. *Ibid.,* p.362.
16. Carey, Letter to John Sutcliff, 22 August 1805 (BMS Archives); Ryland, Letter to John Sutcliff, 21 September 1805 (*Original Letters ... 1773-1813,* BMS Archives). For further discussion of Marshman's letter to Ryland, see Stanley, *History of the Baptist Missionary Society,* p.27.
17. Fuller, Letter to John Ryland, 1 March 1807 (Ryland, *Life and Death of the Rev. Andrew Fuller,* 1818 ed., p.249); Letter from Olney Baptist Church to the Northamptonshire Baptist Association, 1807 (Sutcliff Papers); Ward, Letter to John Sutcliff, 14 January 1808 (BMS Archives).
18. Fuller, Letter to John Sutcliff, received 29 May 1811 (Letters of Andrew Fuller); Fuller, Letter to William Ward, 7 October 1811 (Letters of Andrew Fuller).
19. Fuller, Letter to John Sutcliff, received 29 May 1811 (Letters of Andrew Fuller); Fuller, Letter to John Ryland, 31 May 1811 (Ryland, *Life and Death of the Rev. Andrew Fuller,* 1818 ed., p.348);Fuller, Letter to John Ryland, 5 June 1811 (*ibid.,* p.348).
20. Anderson, *Life and Letters of Christopher Anderson,* p.193.
21. *Periodical Accounts,* vol. IV, pp.315-17; 'Female Servants Society', *The Baptist Magazine,* 4 (1812), p.447.
22. Sutcliff and Ryland, 'To the Christian Females of Great Britain' in *Memoirs of Miss Susanna Anthony,* p.iv.
23. Fuller, Letter to William Ward, 7 October 1811 (Letters of Andrew Fuller); Fuller, Letter to John Saffery, 14 October 1811 (Letters of Andrew Fuller).
24. Anderson, *Life and Letters of Christopher Anderson,* p.193.
25. *The Baptist Magazine,* 4 (1812), p.40.
26. Thomas Torr, Letter to John Sutcliff, 12 March 1810 (Sutcliff Papers). Richards had written to Sutcliff in 1806 and made specific mention of the fact that he had heard Sutcliff was 'placed at the head of a little seminary which is likely to prove very useful in fitting pious young men for the ministry' (Letter to John Sutcliff, 28 September 1806, Sutcliff Papers). On Richards, see John A. Oddy, 'The Dissidence of William Richards', *The Baptist Quarterly,* 27 (1977-1978), pp.118-27.
27. *The Baptist Magazine,* 4 (1812), p.87.
28. Robert Aldrich Smith, *The Baptists in King's Lynn* (King's Lynn: Stepney Baptist Church, King's Lynn, 1939), p.15; Alexander..., Letter to John Sutcliff, 7 March 1813 (Sutcliff Papers); Fuller, Letter to John Sutcliff, 18 September 1812 (Letters of Andrew Fuller).

29. J. Drew, 'The Late Rev. Thomas Welsh', *The Baptist Magazine,* 54 (1862), pp.164-9; Ernest A. Payne, *The Baptists of Berkshire through Three Centuries* (London: The Carey Kingsgate Press Ltd, 1951), pp.97-8; W. J. Lewendon, *Notes on Newbury Baptists* (Newbury: G.W. Simpson & Son, 1940), pp.21-2.
30. See, for example, William Allen, Letter to John Sutcliff, 20 May 1811 (Sutcliff Papers), seeking a pastor for a Dublin congregation; Mr Lewis, Letter to John Sutcliff, 17 March 1812 (Sutcliff Papers), seeking a young man for Great Missenden Baptist Church in Buckinghamshire; Joseph Leese (?), Letter to John Sutcliff, 22 March 1814 (Sutcliff Papers), seeking a pastor for the Baptist work at Burton-on-Trent.
31. Joseph Kinghorn, Letter to John Sutcliff, 15 October 1811 (NLW Ms. 1207D); Maurice F. Hewett, 'Early Days at Worstead', *The Baptist Quarterly,* 11 (1942-1945), p.171.
32. *The Baptist Magazine,* 3 (1811), pp.234-7. Ivimey wrote his article under the pseudonym 'Iota'. For a discussion of this article, see Roberts, *Continuity and Change,* pp.213-14; Stanley, *History of the Baptist Missionary Society,* pp.28-9.
33. Stanley, *History of the Baptist Missionary Society,* pp.26-9.
34. Fuller, Letter to William Ward, 27 October 1804 (Letters of Andrew Fuller).
35. Stanley, *History of the Baptist Missionary Society,* p.27.
36. Andrew Gunton Fuller, 'Memoir' in Works, vol. I, p. 68; Fuller, Letter to William Carey, 6 August 1796 (Young, 'Andrew Fuller', p. 214); Fuller, Letter to William Ward, 5 March 1813 (BMS Archives).
37. Ivimey, *History of the English Baptists,* vol. IV, p.124.
38. John Ryland, Letter to John Sutcliff, 21 September 1805 (*Original Letters ... 1773-1813,* BMS Archives).
39. Ryland, 'Baptist Mission', *The Baptist Magazine,* 4 (1812), pp.351-3; 'The Zeal of the Lord of Hosts' in *Missionary sermons. A Selection from the Discourses delivered on behalf of the Baptist Missionary Society on various occasions* (London: Carey Press, 1924), pp.24-7.
40. Payne, *South-East from Serampore,* p.15.
41. 'General Association of Baptist Churches', *The Baptist Magazine,* 4 (1812), pp.356-9; Ernest A. Payne, *The Baptist Union. A Short History* (London: The Carey Kingsgate Press Ltd, 1959), pp.19-22.
42. D. W. Bebbington, 'Evangelical Christianity and the Enlightenment', *Crux,* 35, No.4 (December 1989), p.30.
43. Carey, *William Carey,* ed. Masters, pp.288-9; Fuller, Letter to John Sutcliff, 18 September 1812 (Letters of Andrew Fuller).
44. Olney Church Minute Book III, entry for 23 February 1809.
45. *Periodical Accounts,* vol. IV, pp. 519-50.
46. Fuller, Letter to William Ward, 7 January 1813 (Letters of Andrew Fuller).
47. For this section on the relations between the Baptist Missionary Society and the British government in India, I am indebted to Brian Stanley, *The*

*Bible and the Flag. Protestant missions and British imperialism in the nineteenth and twentieth centuries* (Leicester: Apollos, 1990), pp.98-9.
48. Fuller, Letter to William Ward, 7 January 1813 (Young, 'Andrew Fuller', p.225).
49. Fuller, Letter to John Sutcliff, 12 January 1813 (Letters of Andrew Fuller).
50. Fuller, Letter to John Ryland, 5 February 1813 (Ryland, *Life and Death of the Rev. Andrew Fuller,* 1818 ed., p.350).
51. Robin Furneaux, *William Wilberforce* (London: Hamish Hamilton, 1974), p.323; Fuller, Letter to William Ward, 5 March 1813 (Letters of Andrew Fuller).
52. Ivimey, *History of the English Baptists,* vol. IV, p.134.
53. Fuller, Letter to John Sutcliff, 29 March 1813 (Letters of Andrew Fuller).
54. Furneaux, *William Wilberforce,* pp.322-4.
55. Ivimey, *History of the English Baptists,* vol. IV, pp.137-48.
56. Fuller, Letter to Christopher Anderson, 14 June 1813 (Anderson, *Life and Letters of Christopher Anderson,* pp.219-20); Fuller, Letter to William Carey, Joshua Marshman and William Ward, 4 February 1813 (Young, 'Andrew Fuller', p.227).
57. Stanley, *Bible and the Flag,* p.99.
58. Furneaux, *William Wilberforce,* pp.326-9; William Wilberforce, Letter to John Ryland, 28 September 1819 (E. Daniel Potts, *British Baptist Missionaries in India 1793-1837. The History of Serampore and its Missions,* Cambridge: Cambridge University Press, 1967, p.17).
59. Stanley, *Bible and the Flag,* pp.99-100.
60. Fuller, Letter to D. Brown, 24 September 1800 (BMS Archives).
61. Sutcliff, 'Introductory Discourse', p.3.
62. Sutcliff, *On Reading the Word of God* (Kettering, J. G. Fuller, 1813).
63. Sutcliff, Letter to Christopher Anderson, 19 June 1813 (Anderson, *Life and Letters of Christopher Anderson,* pp.220-21).
64. 'Baptist Mission', *The Baptist Magazine,* 5 (1813), p.266; 'Missionary Meeting in London', *The Baptist Magazine,* 5 (1813), p.303.
65. Payne, *Baptist Union,* pp.17-18.
66. *Ibid.,* pp.44-5.
67. Ryland, Letter to John Sutcliff, 14 December 1811 (Sutcliff Papers); Hewett, 'Sutcliff: The Meeting and the Man', p.91.
68. Fuller, Letter to John Sutcliff, 15 November 1813 (Letters of Andrew Fuller).
69. Fuller, Letter to John Sutcliff, 30 December 1813 (Letters of Andrew Fuller).
70. 'Baptist Mission: Designation of Mr Eustace Carey', *The Baptist Magazine,* 6 (1814), p.125.
71. 'An Address to the Rev. Eustace Carey', *The Baptist Library,* eds. Charles G. Sommers, William R. Williams and Levi L. Hill (New York: Lewis Colby & Co., 1846), vol. II, p.87.

72. Hall, 'Character of the Rev. John Sutcliff', *Works of the Rev. Robert Hall, A. M.*, vol. II, p.389).
73. 'Address to the Rev. Eustace Carey', *The Baptist Library*, vol. II, p.96.

**Chapter 14: 'The fathers are dying'**

1. Wright, *Town of Cowper,* p.162.
2. Fuller, *Principles and Prospects of a Servant of Christ, Works,* vol. I, p.351.
3. David R. Bartlett, Letter to Michael Haykin, 27 October 1992.
4. Fuller, Letter to John Ryland, 24 March 1814 (cited by A. G. Fuller, 'Memoir' in *Works,* vol. I, p.97).
5. Bartlett, Letter to Michael Haykin, 27 October 1992.
6. Fuller, *Principles and Prospects of a Servant of Christ, Works,* vol. I, pp.351,352.
7. Fuller, Letter to John Sutcliff, 8 May 1814 (Letters of Andrew Fuller); Fuller, Letter to William Carey, 15 May 1814 (Letters of Andrew Fuller). That Fuller definitely did visit Sutcliff the following week is borne out by his letter to William Burls, 11 May 1814 (cited in 'A Memoir of the Rev. Andrew Fuller', *The Baptist Magazine,* 7 (1815), pp.272-3).
8. Fawcett, 'Memoir of Mr Daniel Sutcliff', pp.89-94.
9. 'Appendix' to John Ryland, Jr, *Christ, the great Source of the Believer's Consolation; and the grand Subject of the Gospel Ministry* (London: 1789), pp.59-60; 'The Address', *ibid.,* pp.38,39.
10. H. D. Rack, 'Evangelical Endings: Death-Beds in Evangelical Biography', *Bulletin of the John Rylands University Library of Manchester,* 74, (1992), pp.46-7.
11. Fuller, *Principles and Prospects of a Servant of Christ, Works,* vol. I, pp.352,354-5.
12. *Ibid.*, p.352.
13. 'Rev. J. Sutcliff's Account of the Baptist Mission to Rev. A. Fuller' (Sutcliff Baptist Church, Olney); J. Sutcliff, Letter to Andrew Fuller, 5 June 1814 (Sutcliff Baptist Church, Olney).
14. Fuller, Letter to John Ryland, 11 June 1814 (Ryland, *Life and Death of the Rev. Andrew Fuller,* 1818 ed., pp.350-51).
15. 'Obituary: Rev. John Sutcliff', *The Baptist Magazine,* 6 (1814), p.332.
16. Fuller, *Principles and Prospects of a Servant of Christ, Works,* vol. I, pp.351-2.
17. *Ibid.*, p.342.
18. Olney Church Book III, entries for 23 February 1804, 10 October 1813; Hewett, 'Sutcliff: The Meeting and the Man', pp.91-2.
19. Fuller, *Principles and Prospects of a Servant of Christ, Works,* vol. I, pp.355-6.
20. 'Obituary: Rev. John Sutcliff', p.332. His last words are recorded by Fuller in a slightly different form, see Fuller, *Principles and Prospects of a Servant of Christ, Works,* vol. I, p.353.
21. According to Thomas Wright (*Town of Cowper,* p.165), who probably

derived his information from an eyewitness who was present at the funeral (*ibid.*, p.166), 'The majority of the people [at the funeral] could not be accommodated in the Meeting-house.' Since the meeting-house could seat 700, this would mean that a good deal more than 1,400 people came to the funeral.

22. An indication of the respect that Sutcliff was generally accorded in the town of Olney may be seen in a story related by Thomas Wright (*ibid.*, pp.164-5). The long years of war between England and France had come to an end with the abdication of Napoleon on 11 April 1814, and the signing of the Treaty of Paris on 30 May (apart, that is, from his hundred days of power in 1815). The town of Olney, like other towns and villages in Britain, celebrated with 'hanging out flags, ringing bells, making feasts, and tapping barrels; a waggon too was hired, and the most celebrated musicians of the parish ... paraded through the town with fifes, triangles, fiddles, and best of all with a big drum, whilst the tag-rag, not being able to get a seat in the waggon, followed behind, each with the best instrument of music he could procure. But it was well known that Mr Sutcliff lay dying, and it is pleasing to be able to state that from so many yards before they came to his house to so many yards after they left it this joyous though somewhat unruly mob passed along with the quietness of a funeral.' According to Gravett (*Sutcliff Baptist Church*, pp.13-14), 'Straw had been laid across the road and on the pavement (in front of Sutcliff's home) to muffle horses' hooves and cartwheels and people's boots.'

23. Wright, *Town of Cowper*, p.165.

24. Fuller, *Principles and Prospects of a Servant of Christ, Works*, vol. I, pp.342-3.

25. John Bunyan, *Prayer* (London: The Banner of Truth Trust, 1965), p.32.

26. Fuller, *Principles and Prospects of a Servant of Christ, Works*, vol. I, p.343.

27. Joseph Ivimey, *The Perpetual Intercession of Christ for his Church; A Source of Consolation under the Loss of Useful Ministers* (London: T. Gardiner and Son/Button and Son, 1815), pp.25-6.

28. Fuller, *Principles and Prospects of a Servant of Christ, Works*, vol. I, p.344.

29. *Ibid.*, pp.344-5.

30. *Ibid.*, pp.345-6.

31. *Ibid.*, pp.346-9.

32. Memoirs of George Wallis, entry for 28 June 1814 (Fuller Church, Kettering).

33. Letter to William Carey, Joshua Marshman and William Ward, 4 August 1814 (Letters of Andrew Fuller).

34. Hall, Letter to Andrew Fuller, September 1814 (cited Olinthus Gregory, 'A Brief Memoir of the Rev. Robert Hall, A.M.' in *Works of the Rev. Robert Hall, A.M.*, vol. III, p.59).

35. 'Character of the Rev. John Sutcliff', *Works of the Rev. Robert Hall, A.M.*, vol. II, pp.388-9.

36. Fuller, Letter to William Carey, 29 September 1814 (BMS Archives); Fuller, Letter to a Young Lady, 20 October 1814 ('Memoir of the Rev. Andrew Fuller', p.273); Fuller, Letter to John Saffery, 26 October 1814 (Rev. B. Grey Griffith Collection, Angus Library, Regent's Park College).
37. Fuller, *Principles and Prospects of a Servant of Christ, Works,* vol. I, pp.353-4. See some similar remarks made by Fuller in his letter to William Ward, 7 January 1813 (BMS Archives).
38. Fuller, *Principles and Prospects of a Servant of Christ, Works,* vol. I, p.351; Fuller, Letter to a Young Lady, 20 October 1814 (Memoir of the Rev. Andrew Fuller', p.273).
39. William Hawkins, Letter to Joseph Kinghorn, 15 January 1815 (Ms. 4281, T143, Norfolk Record Office, Norwich); Charles B. Jewson, 'William Hawkins, 1790-1853', *The Baptist Quarterly,* 26 (1975-1976), p.276.
40. William Hawkins, Letter to Joseph Kinghorn, 15 January 1815 (Norfolk Record Office).
41. William Hawkins, Letter to Joseph Kinghorn, 4 April 1815 (Norfolk Record Office).
42. Joseph A. Conforti, 'Samuel Hopkins and the New Divinity: Theology, Ethics, and Social Reform in Eighteenth-Century New England', *The William and Mary Quarterly,* 34 (1977), pp.581-3.
43. *Ibid.,* p.582.
44. Fuller, *Principles and Prospects of a Servant of Christ, Works,* vol. I, p.344.
45. William Hawkins, Letter to Joseph Kinghorn, 17 April 1815 (Norfolk Record Office).
46. Fuller, *Principles and Prospects of a Servant of Christ, Works,* vol. I, pp.342-3.
47. Ryland, Letter to John Saffery, 22 May 1815 (Reeves Collection, Angus Library, Regent's Park College).
48. William Hawkins, Letter to Joseph Kinghorn, 17 April 1815 (Norfolk Record Office).
49. Fuller, Letter to John Ryland, 28 April 1815 in John Ryland, *The Indwelling and Righteousness of Christ no Security against Corporeal death, but the Source of Spiritual and Eternal Life* (London: W. Button & Son, 1815), p.34.
50. Ryland, *Indwelling and Righteousness of Christ,* p.47.
51. Hall, 'A Sermon occasioned by the death of the Rev. John Ryland, D.D.' *The Works of the Rev. Robert Hall, A. M.,* vol. I, pp.223,209.
52. William Carey and Joshua Marshman, Letter to the Committee of the Baptist Missionary Society, 15 November 1827 in *Letters from the Rev. Dr Carey* (3rd. ed.; London: Parbury, Allen, and Co., 1828), p. 52.
53. Christopher Anderson, Letter to Andrew Fuller, 7 July 1814 (Anderson, *Life and Letters of Christopher Anderson,* p.224).

## Appendix I: The published works of John Sutcliff

1. The earliest list of Sutcliff's published works can be found in Andrew Fuller's funeral sermon for Sutcliff (Fuller, *Principles and Prospects of a Servant of Christ, Works,* vol. I, p.351, note). Fuller erroneously attributed the circular letter of the Northamptonshire Association for 1805, *The manner of attending to divine ordinances,* to Sutcliff. This letter was written by John Webster Morris. More recently, Edward C. Starr, in *A Baptist Bibliography* (Rochester, New York: American Baptist Historical Society, 1976), 23, pp.108-110, has compiled a more comprehensive list. It has a number of items not found in Fuller's listing, which focused on Sutcliff's main works. Yet it also omits a few that Fuller had listed. Moreover, Starr wrongly includes *The mutual communion of saints* (Trowbridge: 1794) among the works of Sutcliff. This treatise was written by the Methodist minister, Joseph Sutcliffe (1762-1856).

2. Fuller states that this catechism was first published in 1783 (Fuller, *Principles and Prospects of a Servant of Christ, Works,* vol. I, p.350, note), which Joseph Belcher also maintains in 'Advertisement' in John Sutcliff, *The First Principles of the Oracles of God, represented in a Plain and Familiar Catechism, for the use of Children* (Whitchurch, Shropshire: R. B. Jones, 1820), p.2. However, on the final page of the 1784 Northamptonshire Association circular letter, *The Nature, Evidences, and Advantages, of Humility,* there is an advertisement for Sutcliff's catechism that states that it 'shortly will be published'. Has Fuller made a mistake with regard to the publication date of the catechism? I possess copies of two later editions of this work: the third edition, which was printed at Ewood Hall, near Halifax, around 1795; and an edition that was revised by Joseph Belcher and printed in 1820.

3. Sutcliff's 'Address' was given on 27 November 1788, but it was not printed till the following year. Though there is no date on the title-page of this work, advertisements on the final page regarding books lately published indicate that the 'Address', together with Ryland's sermon, was printed in 1789.

4. There is no indication of who wrote this 'Appendix' in the actual work. Joseph Ivimey identified Sutcliff as the author in his *The Life of John Bunyan* (3rd. ed.; Oxford: Bartlett and Hinton/ London: B. J. Holdsworth, 1823), p.37, note.

5. This article appeared under the pseudonym 'Swerdna,' which is 'Andrews' — the name of Sutcliff's landlady — spelt backwards. Confirmation that Sutcliff wrote it may be found in a letter from J. Webster Morris: Letter to John Sutcliff, 1 May 1801 (*Original Letters ... 1773-1813,* BMS Archives).

## Appendix II: Jealousy for the Lord of hosts illustrated

1. Sutcliff's use of the term 'negro' reflects the terminology of his day.

# Index


Act of Toleration (1689), 15, 126
Ampthill Baptist Church, Bedfordshire, 303
Anderson, Christopher, 12, 269, 274-9, 284, 308, 309, 315, 327, 329-30, 352
Anderson, Thomas, 122
Andrews, Mary, 87-90, 98, 115, 116, 238-41
Andrews, William, 115
Anthony, Susanna, 285, 293, 316
Antinomianism, 98, 102, 319
Arianism, 252, 289
Arnesby Baptist Church, Leicestershire, 27, 124-5, 223
Ash, John, 50
Ashburner, Sarah, 121
Ashburner, William, 121, 122
Ashworth, Caleb, 54, 252
Atonement, 300-302, 342-4
Ayer, John, 220, 221-2

Back Street Baptist Church, Trowbridge, 58
Baker, Frank, 35
*Baptist Magazine, The,* 308
Baptist Missionary Society, 13, 149, 198-235, 241-8, 251, 264-6, 279, 314, 315-16, 318-29, 345, 351
Baptist Union, 318, 321, 330-31
Baptists — see Calvinistic Baptists, General Baptists
Barker, John, 29
Barnoldswick Baptist Church, Lancashire, 41
Bartlett, David, 334
Baxter, Richard, 253
Bean, James, 218
Beck, James R., 182, 228
Beddome, Benjamin, 32, 50, 58, 70, 71-72, 75, 95-7, 120, 213, 225, 231
Beddome, John, 70
Bedfordshire Union of Christians, 305-8
Bell, George, 30
Bellamy, Joseph, 139, 209, 226, 253, 300, 348, 349, 351
Berkhof, Louis, 146
Berridge, John, 21, 292
Berril, Jonathan, 175
*Biblical Magazine, The,* 283, 285
Bibwell, Eleanor, 72
Birchcliffe Baptist Church, Yorkshire, 44
Biss, Hannah, 271
Biss, John, 271, 272-3
Biss, Mary, 271
Blackerby, Richard, 169

Blundel, Thomas (Sr), 168, 220, 222-3, 237, 248, 254, 284, 310-12
Blundell, Thomas (Jr), 310-11, 332
Boon, Martha, 276
Booth, Abraham, 75, 113, 169, 226, 231, 261, 296, 346
Bourton-on-the-Water Baptist Church, 69, 70
Brackney, William H., 305
Brainerd, David, 139, 154, 273, 351
Brewer, Samuel, 110
Brine, John, 17, 19, 31, 42, 70, 71, 77, 78, 79, 138, 146, 216, 319
Bristol Baptist Academy, 13, 47, 49-67, 204, 223, 227, 231, 257
Brittain, Mary, 121
Broadmead Baptist Church, Bristol, 49-50, 57, 227, 253, 256-7
Brown, John, 111, 113
Brown, William, 278
Brunsdon, Daniel, 252-4, 258-9, 267-8, 269
Buchanan, George, 53
Bull, Hannah, 115
Bull, William, 115, 241
Bunyan, John, 74, 75, 102, 124, 133, 138-9, 305, 341
Burditt, Elizabeth, 121-2
Burls, William, 325
Burr, Esther Edwards, 69
Burton, Joshua, 220, 221, 222
Butcher, James, 175
Butler, Joseph, 29-30
Button, William, 149, 213, 214, 261, 262, 266
Byrom Street Baptist Church, Liverpool, 22, 76

Calvin, John, 295-6
Calvinism,
evangelical, 41, 42, 55, 66, 117, 140-41, 149
High (or Hyper-Calvinism), 17-19, 22, 28, 41, 60, 61, 71, 72, 73, 77-81, 82, 97, 114, 117, 133, 134, 135, 136-52, 183, 190, 196, 197, 213, 276, 312, 319
Calvinistic Baptists,
and bankruptcy, 285-6
in Bristol, 49
and church polity, 26, 27
decline of, 24-26
and the Evangelical Revival, 26-32, 33
and evangelism, 21-2, 60
expansion of, 198
and High Calvinism, 17-19, 41, 60- 61
isolation of, 23-4
legal and social discrimination against, 20-21
and the Lord's Supper, 293-300
persecution of, 15
and preaching, 212
revival among, 198, 282, 300
and toleration, 15, 17
in Trowbridge, 57-9, 60-61
view of the Church of England, 27, 292
in the West Riding, Yorkshire, 35
Cannon Street Baptist Church, Birmingham, 28, 66, 92-3, 196, 203, 204-5, 224-5, 260, 290
Carey, Ann, 184-5
Carey, Dorothy (née Plackett), 182, 185, 189, 228, 230, 233, 234-5
Carey, Edmund, 178
Carey, Eustace, 193, 195, 197, 331-3
Carey, Felix, 189, 230, 233, 234
Carey, Elizabeth (née Wells), 178
Carey, Esther (née Fosbrook), 332
Carey, Jabez, 234, 321
Carey, Jonathan, 179
Carey, Mary, 179, 184-5

Carey, Peter (William Carey's son), 189
Carey, Peter (William Carey's uncle), 178-9, 184
Carey, S. Pearce, 186, 213-14, 220
Carey, William, 11-14, 33, 74, 155, 169, 173, 176-97, 198-9, 211, 212-20, 223-35, 236-7, 241-3, 245, 246, 247-8, 255, , 256, 257, 258, 269, 270, 273, 275, 277, 280, 294, 302, 314, 319, 320-23, 324, 328, 331, 335, 345, 351-2
Carey, William (William Carey's son), 189
Carlton Baptist Church, Bedfordshire, 119, 123
Carter Lane Baptist Church, London, 330
Chamberlain, Hannah (née Smith), 267-8, 269
Chamberlain, John, 252-4, 269-71
Chamberlain, John Sutcliff, 271
Charles II, King, 15, 20
Charnock, Stephen, 71
Chater, James, 278
Chater, Thomas, 181-2
Christology, 137-8
Church Missionary Society, 326-7
Cicero, 53
Clarendon Code, 15, 20
Clarke, E. D., 48
Clipsham, E. F., 226
Clipston Baptist Church, Northamptonshire, 280-84
Colchester Baptist Church, 32, 148-9
Coles, Elisha (Sr), 70-71
Coles, Thomas, 278
Coles, William, 272, 303, 305
Colet, John, 69
College Lane Baptist Church, Northampton, 64, 72, 87, 104-5, 224, 332
Collingham Baptist Church, Nottinghamshire, 304
Collins, Anthony, 130
Compere, Lee, 335
Concerts of prayer, 158-71, 172-3, 198, 203, 208, 209, 212, 216, 281, 292, 313, 331, 332
Conigre Baptist Church, Wiltshire, 57-8
Cook, James, 184
Cooper, John, 59-61
Corporation Act, 199-200
Cowper, William, 99-100, 113, 115, 123, 173, 174, 175, 176, 178, 181, 217, 219, 276
Cox, F. A., 141, 237, 271-2, 303, 321, 331
Crabtree, William, 35, 40, 41, 230
Cramp, J. M., 17, 19
Cripplegate Baptist Church, London, 70
Cromwell, Oliver, 17
Crosley, David, 21, 32, 35, 38

Davey, Sarah, 151-2
Davies, David, 278
Davis, Richard, 102, 104
Davisson, John, 57-8
Deacon, Moses, 104, 111, 113, 221
Defoe, Daniel, 34-35, 48, 49
Deism, 130-31, 257, 287-9
Derby Baptist Church, 255
Devonshire Square Baptist Church, London, 231
Dicey, Thomas, 148
Disinterested love, 209-10, 263-4, 342, 348
Diver, Joseph, 137
Dobney, George, 278
Doddridge, Philip, 29, 55, 72, 74, 252, 276, 286, 295
Dore, James, 231
Drake, John, 110

Drewery, Mary, 322
Drewry, John, 255
Dunscombe, Thomas, 54, 56, 97, 123
Dunstable Baptist Church, 284
Dutton, Anne, 295
Dwight, Timothy, 253

Eagle Street Baptist Church, London, 21, 169, 296, 318
Earls Barton Baptist Church, 182, 185, 186, 237
East India Company, 323-9, 331-2
Edwards, John, 138
Edwards, Jonathan, 13, 55, 78, 98, 138, 139-40, 145, 146, 153, 154-5, 158-169, 209-10, 226, 259, 273, 280, 300, 348, 350, 351
Edwards, Jonathan (Jr), 300-301
Enthusiasm, 28-32, 61, 194
*Epistle to Diognetus, The,* 54, 283
Erasmus, 69
Erskine, John, 158, 159, 265
Erskine, Ralph, 134
*Evangelical Magazine, The,* 282-3, 292, 308
Evangelical Revival, the, 26-32, 40, 60, 70, 72-3, 155, 158, 222, 293
  and enthusiasm, 28-32
Evans, Caleb, 50-51, 53, 54-7, 61, 62, 66, 94, 96-8, 114, 115, 119, 139, 140, 205, 206, 227
Evans, Hugh, 32-3, 50-51, 52-3, 56, 58, 60, 62, 64, 66, 94, 95-6, 140
Evans, John (of Foxton Baptist Church), 111, 118, 123
Evans, John (of Hand Alley Presbyterian Church), 25
Eve, John, 19, 133, 136-7, 138,147
Experimental Christianity, 97-8
Fawcett, John, 36, 40-47, 55, 58, 62-3, 65, 66, 91, 94, 95, 117-18, 119, 127-8,139, 140, 153, 203, 217, 221, 230, 233, 238-40,256, 296-7, 322
Fawcett, John (Jr), 36, 38, 41, 42, 44, 65,115
Feathers Tavern Petition, 125-6
Felts, Elizabeth, 309
Fenne, John, 102
*First London Confession of Faith,* 110-11
Flavel, John, 41
Fletcher, John, 204
Foskett, Bernard, 49-50
Fountain, John, 245-8
Fox, George, 49
Foxton Baptist Church, 221
Francis, Benjamin, 50, 95
Franklin, Francis, 260
French Revolution, 170-71, 199-200, 245, 246, 255, 287
Friar Lane Baptist Church, Nottingham, 182, 216, 304, 311
Fuller, Andrew, 12-14, 22, 23, 25, 33, 36, 42, 47, 52, 55, 64, 115, 127, 131, 132-52, 153, 157-8, 163, 164, 167-9, 171, 173, 180, 182-3, 188, 189, 193-4, 195, 196, 197, 198, 202, 205-6, 207, 210-12, 213, 214, 215, 217-20, 222, 224, 226-35, 237-8, 240, 241-8, 249, 251, 254, 257-8, 260, 261-6, 271-2, 275, 277, 279-80, 282-3, 284, 285, 286, 287-8, 290, 293, 294, 301, 302, 303-4, 309, 310-14,315, 317, 318-20, 322, 323, 324-9, 331-2, 334, 335, 337-8,339-42, 344-6, 348, 350-51
  *Gospel Worthy of All Acceptation, The,* 142-7, 149, 152
Fuller, Ann (née Coles), 272
Fuller, Bathoni, 219

Fuller, Philippa (née Gunton), 133
Fuller, Robert, 133
Fuller, Sarah, 219

Garrard, John, 251
Gauntlett, Henry, 339
Geard, John, 57, 59-60, 62, 95, 305, 346
General Baptists, 44, 64, 186-7, 188-9
George, David, 243-4
George, John (?), 278
George, Timothy, 155, 232
Gibbons, Thomas, 54
Gibbs, John, 100, 102, 103
Gifford, Andrew, 21-2, 32, 296
Gill, John, 17-19, 20, 24, 25-6, 27, 31, 42, 54, 55, 71, 74, 75, 77, 78, 79, 113, 138-9, 198, 216, 292, 319, 330
Gill, John (of St Albans, Hertford shire), 113
Gillies, John, 169
Glas, John, 264-5
Godwin, William, 247
Goodshaw Baptist Church, Yorkshire, 19
Grant, Charles, 225-6, 324
Grant, Edward, 57
Grant, William (missionary to India), 254, 256, 257-8, 261, 269
Grant, William (of Wellingborough Baptist Church), 110
Greatheed, Samuel, 241, 305-6
Greenwood, Abraham, 220, 221
Griffin-Allwood, Philip G. A., 290
Grigg, Jacob, 244-5
Grigg, Sally, 59
Griggs, Thomas, 121
Grimshaw, William, 38-41, 230
Grotius, Hugo, 53
Guilsborough Baptist Church, Northamptonshire, 200, 237-8
Gulliver, John, 281
Guy, William, 83-4, 123, 182-3

Hackleton, Congregationalists in, 180, 181-2, 185-6, 302
Haldane, James Alexander, 265-6, 275
Haldane, Robert, 265-6, 275
Hall, Robert (Jr), 52, 125, 175, 204, 206-7, 283, 321, 326, 332-3, 345, 351
Hall, Robert (Sr), 111, 113, 123, 124-7, 138, 140, 147-8, 168, 183, 193, 202, 205, 206, 221, 223, 252
Harris, Howel, 20-21, 22, 26-7, 28, 31, 72, 295
Hart, Honour, 133
Hartley, James, 40, 41
Harvey Lane Baptist Church, Leicester, 212, 228, 237
Haweis, Thomas, 222
Hawkins, Elizabeth, 309
Hawkins, William, 176, 346, 348-50
Hayden, Roger, 55
Haynes, Richard, 70
Heighton, William, 220, 222
Henry, Matthew, 41, 334
Herbert, William, 27
Hervey, James, 72, 73
Hewett, Maurice F., 104
Heywood, Oliver, 41
Hill, Rowland, 73, 81-3, 276
Hillyard, Thomas, 218, 305, 307-8, 339
Hinton, James, 200-201, 277, 325
Hobart, Robert, (Earl of Buckinghamshire), 325-6
Hobson, Jesse, 322
Hogg, Reynold, 220, 224, 232, 248, 258
Holy Spirit, his work in evangelism, 312-14
Home, Robert, 323
Hooker, Thomas, 157
Hopkins, Samuel, 285, 300, 348, 349

Hopkins, Thomas, 169
Hopper, Richard, 182
Horsey, John, 252
Howard, Kenneth W. H., 6, 248, 249, 346
Hull, Thomas, 119
Hussey, Joseph, 71, 81
Hutton, William, 92-3
Hyper-Calvinism, see Calvinism, High

Ingham, Benjamin, 39
Ivimey, Joseph, 58, 318, 320, 325, 331, 341

Jackson, Alvery, 41-2, 71
Jackson, Sarah, 121
Jarman, John, 311
Jay, William, 73, 203
Jenkinson, Robert Banks, (Earl of Liverpool), 325
Jenner, Edward, 63
Johns, William, 324
Johnson, John, 22, 41, 42, 76
Johnson, Samuel, 29
Johnsonianism, 22
Johnston, Francis (née Milley), 249
Johnston, James, 151-2, 249
Johnston, Mary (née Harrison), 249
Johnston, Ruth (née Herbert), 249
Johnston, Sarah, 249, 322, 337
Johnston, Simon, 249
Justification, 79-80

Keach, Benjamin, 17, 290
Kettering Baptist Church, Northamptonshire, 147
Kent, Joseph, 102
Kiffin, William, 22, 231
King, Thomas, 281-2
King's Lynn Baptist Church, Norfolk, 316-18
Kinghorn, Joseph, 209, 215, 231, 280, 317-18, 346, 348, 349
Knollys, Hanserd, 22, 106
Knowles, William, 150-51

Langdon, Thomas, 203
Langley, Arthur S., 221
Larden, Mary, 59
Laud, William, 157
Lawson, John, 324
Legge, William (Earl of Dartmouth), 77
Lindsay, James, 78
Lindsey, Theophilus, 126
Lister, James, 107-8, 275
Little Wild Street Baptist Church, London, 225
Llewellyn, Joshua, 121
Lloyd-Jones, D. Martyn, 13
Locke, John, 29
London Missionary Society, 326
Lord's Supper, 71-2, 151-2, 293-300
Lovegrove, Deryck W., 24
Luther, Martin, 210-11, 256
Luton Baptist Church, Bedfordshire, 223

Macaulay, Zachary, 244-5
McCulloch, William, 159
McLaurin, John, 159, 169
McLean, Archibald, 264-5, 315
Madan, Judith, 113
Madan, Martin, 113
Mann, Isaac, 302
Mardon, Richard, 271-3
Marriott, John, 151-2, 303
Marshman, John Clark, 195, 218, 246
Marshman, Joshua, 11, 12, 195, 196, 215, 218, 229, 254-8, 261, 270, 279, 314, 320, 322
Martin, John, 149-50

Mason, John, 240
Maurice, Matthias, 104
Maze Pond Baptist Church, London, 15, 24, 107, 231
Medley, Samuel, 127
Missions, 189-97, 208, 211-18
Mitchel, William, 21, 32, 35, 38
Moore, William, 271-3
Morgan, Thomas, 290, 291, 292
Morris, John Webster, 141, 193, 194-6, 206, 212, 214, 224, 240, 246, 247, 248, 263, 278, 279-86, 311, 314, 317-18
Mortification of indwelling sin, 45-6
Moulton Baptist Church, Northamptonshire, 185, 186-9
Murray, Iain H., 163, 217

Napoleon Bonaparte, 156, 322
Naylor, Peter, 18-19
Neill, Stephen, 270
Nettles, Thomas J., 18, 19
New Road Baptist Church, Oxford, 200, 277
Newbury Baptist Church, Berkshire, 317
Newton, John, 69, 73, 75-81, 85, 89, 100, 110, 113, 118, 119, 120,122-4, 125, 128, 140, 173-4, 175, 176, 180, 206, 241, 276, 292
Nichols, Clarke, 179, 180
Nichols, William, 304-5
Northamptonshire Baptist Association, 13, 23, 110-14, 122-7, 139, 142, 154, 163-8, 169, 182-3, 201-3, 206-7, 212, 214, 216, 248, 256, 262, 289, 311, 330
Nuttall, Geoffrey F., 104

Old Scots Independents, 274-5
Oliver, Robert W., 293
Olney Baptist Church, 87-90, 96-8, 99-100, 102, 104-9, 110, 113-22, 123, 124,167, 172-6, 178, 185-6, 267, 276, 344, 346-50
  the church covenant, 106-8
  High Calvinism in the congregation, 151-2
  the meeting-house, 108-9, 116, 258, 339, 347
Osborn, Thomas, 122, 152, 175-6, 322
Oulton, John, 76
Owen, John, 39, 71, 138, 145, 190

Page, Benjamin, 174
Paine, Thomas, 286-9
Pal, Krishna, 269-70
Palmer, John, 90
Parker, John, 40
Parsons, Thomas, 303
Payne, Ernest A., 186, 294, 299, 331
Payne, William, 305
Peace, William, 175-6
Pearce, Samuel, 12, 203-5, 214, 215, 220, 223, 224-5, 233, 236-8, 244, 246, 255, 256, 260-61, 263-4, 266
Pearce, Sarah, 266
Perry, John, 317
Phillips, Thomas, 65-6
Pilley, Thomas, 119
Pithay Baptist Church, Bristol, 49
Pius VI, Pope, 156
Plackett, Catherine (Kitty), 233, 235
Potts, Thomas, 196-197, 224
Prayer (see also Concerts of Prayer), 156-71, 191-2, 201, 203, 208-9, 212
Preaching, 56-7, 61, 211-12
Presbyterians (English) , 252
Prescott Street Baptist Church, London, 24, 75
Priestley, Joseph, 299

Providence, 127, 129-31
Pufendorf, Samuel, 53
Purdy, Thomas, 59, 61-2, 66, 85-7, 89-90, 95-6, 154, 205, 303
Puritans, 39, 71, 138, 256
Pyne, John, 64-5

Quakers, 49

Rack, Henry D., 336
Rawlins, Nathaniel, 58, 70
Razzell, Peter E., 63
Reformation, the, 210-11
Reynolds, John, 70
Richards, John, 278
Richards, William, 316
Rippon, John, 50, 54, 215, 231, 248, 261, 282, 321, 330
Roade Baptist Church, 222
Robe, James,159
Robinson, John (William Robinson's son), 175
Robinson, John (William Robinson's father), 273
Robinson, Robert, 21, 32
Robinson, William, 273-4, 277-8
Rodhill End Baptist Church, Yorkshire, 38
Rodway, James, 244
Rogers, Charles, 104-5
Rogers, Jacob, 104
Rogers, James, 102
Rogers, John (of Olney Baptist Church), 151-2, 175-6
Rogers, John (of Dedham), 169
Romaine, William, 94, 159
Roman Catholicism, 155-6, 199, 299
Rowe, Joshua, 271-3, 277
Rowland, Daniel, 27, 31
Rushden Baptist Church, Northamptonshire, 150-51
Rutherford, Samuel, 78
Ryland, David Brainerd, 273
Ryland, Freelove (née Collett), 69
Ryland, John (John Ryland, Jr's grandfather), 69
Ryland, John (Jr), 12, 17, 19, 33, 64, 67, 68-84, 85, 87, 88-90, 97, 131, 139-142, 147, 148151, 155, 157-8, 163, 168-9, 171, 173, 174-5, 183-4, 187, 188, 189, 195-6, 197, 203, 205-6, 209, 212, 213, 215, 216, 217, 218, 220, 224, 227, 228, 234, 235, 241, 244, 246, 248, 253, 256, 257, 259-60, 262, 263, 266-7, 271, 273, 276-7, 278, 283, 286, 293, 294, 301, 310, 314, 315-16, 317, 319, 320-21, 322, 327, 335, 337, 350-52
Ryland, John C., 25, 50, 64, 69-73, 74, 77, 81, 110, 113, 123, 183, 194-6, 221, 293, 294
Ryland, Joseph, 69

Saffery, John, 235, 267, 272, 280, 350
St Andrew's Street Baptist Church, Cambridge, 19, 21
St Mary's Baptist Church, Norwich, 32
Sandeman, Robert, 265
Sandemanianism, 265
Sandys, John, 65, 85-6, 90
Scotch Baptists, 264-5, 275
Scott, Thomas, 180
*Second London Confession of Faith*, 23, 79
Sellon, Walter, 93
Sharman, Edward, 220, 221
Shaw, William, 304
Shepshed Baptist Church, Leicestershire, 83-4
Shrewsbury Baptist Church, 64-7, 84, 85-6, 90-91
Sidmouth, Viscount, 324

Sierra Leone, 243-5
Simmonds, James, 346
Skinner, Thomas, 195
Skrymsher, Peggy, 90
Smalley, John, 78, 140, 300
Smallpox, 62-4
Smith, A. Christopher, 217, 255
Smith, John, 278
Smith, Richard, 38, 40, 41
Smith, Robert, 162-3
Socinianism (or Unitarianism), 58, 126, 202, 221, 252, 289
Soham Baptist Church, Cambridgeshire, 133, 136-7, 138, 139
Southwick Baptist Church, Wiltshire, 57-8
Spurgeon, Charles Haddon, 19, 127, 172, 236
Spyvee, Henry, 149
Stanger, John, 188-9
Stanger, Thomas, 186
Stanger, William, 186
Stanley, Brian, 264, 318, 319
Staughton, William, 223, 232
Staveley, Isaac, 296
Steadman, William, 214, 215, 312
Steevens, Thomas, 148, 230, 231, 232
Stennett, Samuel, 225, 226, 231-2, 262
Stephenson, Christopher, 277, 292, 322, 339
Stevenson, Philippa, 133
Strait Hey, Yorkshire, 36-7
Stuart, Charles Edward, 161
Stutterd, Thomas, 203
Supralapsarianism, 80-81
Sutcliff Baptist Church, Olney — see Olney Baptist Church
Sutcliff, Daniel, (John Sutcliff's father), 36, 62, 64, 241
Sutcliff, Daniel, (John Sutcliff's brother), 36, 335-6, 337
Sutcliff, Hannah, (John Sutcliff's mother), 36, 62, 64, 241
Sutcliff, Hannah (John Sutcliff's sister), 36
Sutcliff, Jane (née Johnston), 249-51, 271, 337, 343, 346
Sutcliff, John,
  on the atonement, 300-302
  baptism of, 42
  on baptism, 174, 291, 293, 308
  and the Baptist Missionary Society, 13, 178, 198-235, 241-8
  at the Bristol Baptist Academy, 48-67
  character, 151, 175, 271-2, 345, 346, 352
  circular letter on providence, 127-31, 157
  conversion, 42, 44
  criticized by High Calvinists, 151-2
  death, 338-9
  *Divinity of the Christian Religion, The,* 155-6, 287, 288-9
  early Christian experience, 44-7
  early years, 36-8
  ecclesiology, 289-93
  eschatology, 154-5
  evangelical Calvinism, 140-41, 151-2, 153-4
  on evangelism, 208-9, 213, 291, 336
  evangelistic preaching, 151, 306-8
  final days of, 334-9
  *First Principles of the Oracles of God, The,* 38, 153-4
  friendships, 12-14, 59-64, 94-8, 139-42, 178, 193, 205, 233, 236, 241, 262, 277, 279, 292, 309, 337-338, 346, 351-2
  fund-raising activities, 262, 264-6, 315-16

funeral, 339-44
influence of Jonathan Edwards on, 13, 55, 140, 153, 154-5, 158, 163-71, 209-10, 259, 348, 350-51
influence on Andrew Fuller, 140, 283, 303-4
*Jealousy for the Lord of Hosts illustrated,* 206-10, 355-65
kindness, 271-2
on the Lord's Supper, 261, 291, 293-300
marriage, 249-51
memoir of, 344-6
and the Olney Baptists, 87-90, 96-98, 115-22, 151-2, 173, 267-8, 309, 348, 349
*On obedience to Positive Institutions,* 297
*On Reading the Word of God,* 156, 329-30
ordination, 118-20
parsonage seminary, 251-254, 271, 273, 274, 278, 331
on politics, 245-8, 260, 328-9
portrait of, 173
on prayer, 13, 156-71, 208-9, 281, 292, 341-2
preaching, 57-9, 61, 96, 174-5, 188, 207-10, 267-8, 286-7, 321, 330, 348, 355-65
*Qualifications for Church Fellowship,* 289-93
respect for, 286-7
and the revival of the Calvinistic Baptists, 33
on the Scriptures, 207, 287-9, 329-30
and the Shrewsbury Baptists, 64-7, 84, 85-7, 90-91
on slavery, 244-5
spirituality, 264, 314
as a teacher, 189, 251-4
writings, 353-4
Sutcliff, William, 58, 66, 87, 93, 118
Symonds, Joshua, 75, 118-19, 123, 336

Tapp, John, 151-2
Taylor, Dan, 44, 204
Taylor, Henry, 204, 223
Teare, Joan, 102
Teedon, Samuel, 233, 294
Terrill, Edward, 49
Terry, Henry, 32
Test Act, 199-200
Thelwall, John, 255
Theological education, 46-47, 49-67, 251-4
Thomas, John, 225-9, 232-5, 236, 242
Thomas, Micah, 285
Thomas, Richard, 38
Thomas, Thomas, 261
Thomas, Timothy, 231, 261
Thomas, William, 45, 62-4
Thrapston Baptist Church, Northamptonshire, 220
Timms, Joseph, 223
Timms, Lucy, 302
Tindal, Matthew, 130
Tiverton Baptist Church, Devon, 32
Toland, John, 130
Toplady, Augustus M., 72-3, 75, 93, 94
Torr, Thomas, 316-17
Trinity, doctrine of, 124-7
Trivett, Edward, 279
Tully, George, 49
Turner, Daniel, 293
Turner, James, 28, 66, 86-7, 92-4, 117, 120, 127-9, 141-2, 196, 204

Unitarianism — see Socinianism
Universalism, 202

Vidler, William, 202
Virgil, 53
Voltaire, 257

Wainsgate Baptist Church, Yorkshire, 22, 38, 41-3, 44, 45, 47, 117-18
Walgrave Baptist Church, Northamptonshire, 104
Walker, Francis, 104
Walker, Michael J., 212, 295, 298, 299
Walker, William (pastor of Olney Baptist Church), 105-6, 110-11, 113, 114, 115
Walker, William (member of Olney Baptist Church) 151-2
Wallin, Benjamin, 15, 25-6, 75, 231, 292
Wallis, Beeby, 167, 219-20, 344
Wallis, George, 344
Wallis, Martha, 218-220, 223, 224, 232, 246, 322, 344
Wallis, Thomas, 220
Wallis, William, 219
Walls, Andrew F., 192
Ward, William, 11, 47, 254-62, 270, 279, 280, 314
Warr, John, 179-80, 181
Warwick Baptist Church, 71-2
Watts, Isaac, 54, 55
Welsh, John Sutcliff, 317
Welsh, Mary (née Weldone), 338
Welsh, Thomas, 316-17, 338
Wesley, Charles, 27, 28, 70-71, 72, 83
Wesley, John, 27, 28, 30-31, 49, 72, 83, 93, 94, 295
West, Stephen, 300-301
Westbury Leigh Baptist Church, Wiltshire, 256
Western Association, 23-4
White, Capt., 234
Whitefield, George, 21-2, 26-32, 33, 40, 49, 72, 73, 74, 75, 76, 82, 104, 110, 115, 128, 295
Whitley, W. T., 25
Wilberforce, William, 152, 322, 325, 327-8
Wilkins, William, 95
William III, King, 15, 17, 23
Williams, John, 84
Williams, Joseph, 40
Williams, William (of Cardigan, S. Wales), 31-2
Williams, William (Pantycelyn), 27
Wilson, Samuel, 24, 124
Wilson, William, 173-6, 201, 276, 322, 336
Witsius, Herman, 71
Wolfe, James, 178
Woodman, Isaac, 111
Worstead Baptist Church, Norfolk, 279-80, 317-18
Wright, Thomas, 108
Wright, Mrs, 150-51

Xenophon, 53

Yates, William, 346
Yorkshire and Lancashire Association, 24
Young, Solomon, 346